Hitler's War Machine

War

a Salamander book

published by

Hamlyn

London. New York. Sydney. Toronto

Hitler's Machine

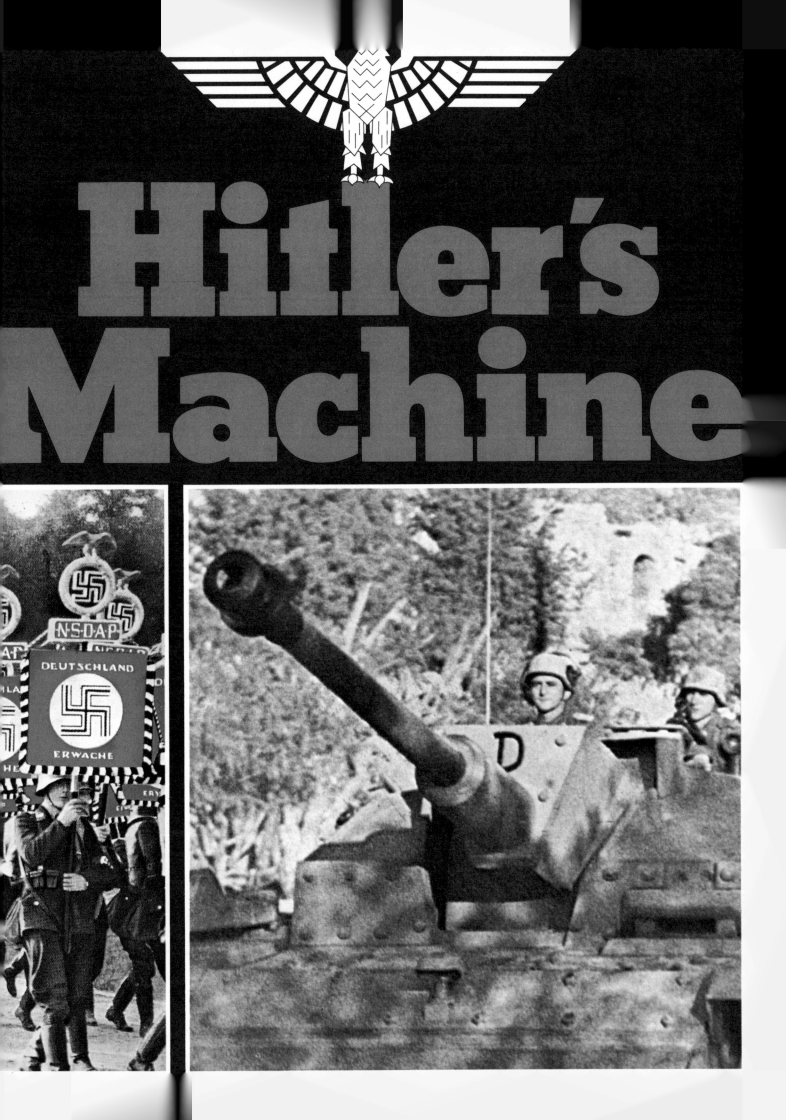

A Salamander Book

This edition published 1976 by
The Hamlyn Publishing Group Ltd
London · New York · Sydney · Toronto
Astronaut House, Feltham
Middlesex, England

ISBN 0 600 34500 9

© Salamander Books Ltd 1975
Hammer House
113 Wardour Street
London W1
United Kingdom

This book may not be sold in the
United States of America, Canada
or Australasia

Filmset by
Ramsay Typesetting (Crawley) Ltd
through Reynolds Clark Associates
Ltd, London, England

Reproduced by
Paramount Litho Company
Basildon, Essex, England
and Essex Colour Services
Rochford, Essex, England

Printed in Belgium by
Henri Proost, Turnhout,
Belgium

All correspondence concerning the
content of this volume should be
addressed to Salamander Books
Limited.

CREDITS

Robert Cecil CMG: Editorial
consultant
Simon Goodenough: Editor
Chris Steer: Design
**Jonathan Moore and Matthew
Cooper:** Picture research
Richard Natkiel: Maps
John W. Wood: Weapon drawings
pages 70/71, 74/75, 78/79, 82/83,
86/87, 90/91
Pilot Press: Aircraft drawings pages
132-153, © Pilot Press
Profile Publications: 178/179, 182/
183, 186/187, 190/191, © Profile
Publications
A&A Plans: Ship drawings pages
180/181, 184/185, 188/189

THE AUTHORS

Dr William Carr
*Dr W. Carr is Reader in Modern History in
the University of Sheffield and specializes
in Modern Germany. His main publications
include:* Schleswig-Holstein 1815–1848.
A study in national conflict *(1963);* A
History of Germany 1815–1945 *(1969);*
Arms, Autarky and Aggression. German
foreign policy 1933–1939 *(1972). He is at
present working on a study of Hitler.*

Robert Cecil CMG

Robert Cecil, who is Reader in Contemporary German History at the University of Reading, was born in 1913, first visited Germany in the summer of 1933 – the year in which Hitler came to power – and joined the British Foreign Service in 1936. He returned to Germany in 1955 as Consul-General in Hanover and later became Cultural Counsellor at H.M. Embassy in Bonn.

Mr Cecil was made a Companion of the Order of St Michael and St George in 1959 and in that year became Director-General of British Information Services, New York. After nearly six years as Head of the Cultural Relations Department of the Foreign Office, he retired in 1967 to take up his present post at Reading University.

Matthew Cooper

Matthew Cooper was born in 1952 and was educated at St Dunstan's College and King's College, London, where he took an Honours degree in History, specializing in war studies. Having worked in the Imperial War Museum and the Tower of London, he is now an Officer of the House of Commons.

Richard Humble

A former editor and managing editor of two extensive series publications on the history of World War II and the author of several books on World War II, a subject of which he has made a special study.

Dr Paul Kennedy

Dr Paul Kennedy was born in 1945 and is now married with two children. He took a BA at Newcastle-upon-Tyne and a D.Phil. at Oxford; he is a Fellow of the Royal Historical Society and a Fellow of the Alexander von Humboldt Foundation. He has published Pacific Onslaught 1941–43 *(London/New York 1972),* Pacific Victory 1943–45 *(London/New York 1973),* The Samoan Tangle: A Study in Anglo-German-American Relations 1878–1914 *(Dublin/New York/Brisbane 1974),* The Rise and Fall of British Naval Mastery *(London/New York – forthcoming) and about 30 articles on modern history, international relations and strategic studies. At present he is Lecturer in History at The University of East Anglia.*

Professor Donald Watt

Professor Donald Cameron Watt was educated at Rugby School and Oriel College, Oxford after his year's national service in Austria. From 1951–54 he worked for the Foreign Office Research Department on the publication of the German diplomatic documents captured in 1944–45. In 1954 he joined the staff of the London School of Economics and Political Science where he now holds the position of Professor of International History. His published works include Personalities and Policies *(Longman 1965),* A History of the World in the Twentieth Century *(Hodder and Pan Books 1967), an edition of Hitler's* Mein Kampf *(Hutchinson 1969) and* Too Serious a Business – European Armies and the Approach of the Second World War *(Temple Smith 1975).*

Dr Z. A. B. Zeman

Dr Z.A.B. Zeman was born in Prague and educated there and in England. He graduated in History in London and Oxford and has taught at both these universities as well as at the University of St Andrews. His books have been translated into several European and Asian languages and include two editions (1964 and 1973) of Nazi Propaganda *and* The Break-up of the Habsburg Empire*. Dr Zeman is currently working in the field of East-West relations and has recently co-edited and partly written* East-West Trade: The International Year Book, 1975.

Thirty-five years after the death of Hitler the interest in him continues to grow. In every age there has been keen interest in world conquerors —from Alexander to Napoleon; we marvel that one man could have accomplished so much. The wonder persists, even if the conqueror's evil career, as in the cases of Tamerlane and Hitler, was devoted to destruction. 'To ride in triumph through Persepolis . . .' For Hitler, as for Tamerlane, it was the heat of battle and the victory parade that excited him, not the laborious work of reconstruction that should have followed.

It was this destructive power that transformed our world and still exercises our minds. Hitler's regime, which lasted barely 12 years, destroyed the unity of Germany, which had been one of the major political achievements of the nineteenth century. His wars finally destroyed the European balance of power, which had precariously survived World War I, and thus opened the way for the current reign of the Russian and American super-powers. By destroying Europe, Hitler ended, too, the long hegemony of the European powers over Asia and Africa; against every intention of his racialist policies he terminated an imperial era that had begun some four centuries earlier.

It is right, therefore, that we should study not only the morbid aspects of the Third *Reich*—the euthanasia and the genocide—but also the massive deployment of power, which enabled the initial conquests to be achieved, and the defects of political and strategic planning, which led to the final disaster. This book by a distinguished group of contemporary historians looks at the German war effort from all sides.

Dr Carr deals with Hitler's war leadership and the reconstruction of the *Wehrmacht* after the shackles of Versailles had been discarded. Mr Humble, Dr Kennedy and Mr Cooper depict for us the fighting forces, whilst Dr Zeman discusses the control exercised by Hitler's henchmen, Goebbels and Himmler, over the civilian population, which had greeted the outbreak of war without enthusiasm. Two further chapters examine aspects of the war effort that have been less often studied: Professor Watt shows how Hitler applied in practice the maxims of psychological warfare, of which he had given a foretaste in '*Mein Kampf*'; Matthew Cooper writes of the science and technology that in 1939 underpinned the relatively short-lived superiority of German arms.

Many reasons, both practical and pathological, motivated Hitler's precipitate plunge into war in 1939; but his chief military reason was his determination to profit by the superiority of the German war machine, which could hardly be

expected to last for long with British and Russian
rearmament building up and even that recumbent
giant, the USA, turning uneasily in its sleep. This
superiority was symbolised by the Panzer Divisions,
operating under dashing leadership and close air
support, and in the early summer of 1940 they
pulverised the Anglo-French armies almost as
completely as they had the Polish. The menace of
the *Luftwaffe*, especially its dive-bombers, impressed
itself equally deeply upon the minds of its victims.
It was only in the autumn of 1940 that expert
observers began to realise that Goering had no
grasp either of the requirements of strategic
bombing or of the capabilities of British air defence.

When Hitler invaded Russia in the summer of
1941, he seemed to be at the height of his power;
but in fact the relative superiority of the
Wehrmacht had already declined. In any case it
could have been maintained only on two
assumptions, both of which Hitler ignored. The
first was that he could avoid confrontation with a
coalition of major powers including the USA; the
second that he allowed time, as some of his
military advisers wished, to prepare for the
possibility of a long war. But Hitler's concept of
Blitzkrieg was of a series of short, sudden wars,
each fuelled by the spoils of the previous one,
which would obviate the need to impose undue
burdens on the Aryan master-race, in whose name
his conquests were ostensibly undertaken.

The widespread contemporary belief that
Germany was from the start engaged in 'total war'
was a myth created by German propaganda. In
terms of total mobilisation of human and material
resources, the climax of the German war effort was
reached in the summer of 1944 after the war had
been irretrievably lost. For by then Hitler was
involved, as Ludendorff had been, in a war of
attrition in which he could only fail.

In both World Wars the magnificent German
military machine was seriously deficient only at the
place where it mattered most, that is, at the top,
where the vital politico-military decisions were
made. In the spring of 1938 Hitler dismissed
Blomberg as Minister of War and took over his
functions with Keitel as Chief of the *Wehrmacht*
High Command (OKW); but Keitel had no
authority over the three Commanders-in-Chief,
who came together, with their Chiefs-of-Staff, only
at Hitler's behest and to receive his instructions.
No institution with regular meetings was set up,
comparable to the British Chiefs-of-Staff
Committee. At one period in the late summer of
1940, when Germany had been at war for nearly a
year, Hitler was at Berchtesgaden in Bavaria, where
Keitel also spent most of his time; the rest of the

staff of OKW, together with the staff of the *Luftwaffe* High Command, were near Potsdam; the Army High Command (OKH) was at Zossen, south of Berlin, and the Navy High Command was in Berlin itself. The physical separation expressed a lack of coordination that could only have been deliberate on Hitler's part; he did not want his military advisers, most of whom he mistrusted, to 'gang up on him'.

Much the same was true in the equally important field of politico-economic and military coordination; there was nothing equivalent to the British War Cabinet. Hitler's Cabinet never met after 1938. It is true that a *Reich* Defence Council (*Reichsverteidigungsrat*) was then set up with Hitler as nominal chairman and Goering as his deputy; but this, too, soon ceased to meet and was never revived, although this was vainly suggested to Goering by Goebbels and Speer in the crisis after Stalingrad. Hitler would tolerate no institutional brake upon his instant and arbitrary decision-making. Flanked by his three 'Yes-men', Bormann, Keitel and Lammers, in the 'Wolf's Lair' in East Prussia, he remained insulated from any mechanism through which collective pressure could have been brought to bear on him to modify his intentions.

In view of the monopoly of responsibility to which the *Fuehrer* laid claim, nothing could have been less rational or just than the way in which at the end of the war, when he was confined to the bunker under the besieged Chancellery in Berlin, he disavowed all blame for defeat. Chiefly, of course, he blamed his Field-Marshals, Generals and hated General Staff officers; those of them who survived have repaid him in the same coin and shown themselves well able to take care of their reputations, if not always of the truth.

More unjust was Hitler's attempt to saddle the German people with the blame. The fact is that ordinary Germans, and especially the soldiers themselves, fought on to the bitter end with astonishing obduracy. It is a fact that perhaps deserves more attention than it has received from historians with sociological leanings. It will not do to describe this tenacity as a typical German characteristic, since the Second *Reich* had met its end in 1918 in conditions of disorder and defeatism, although the enemy was nowhere on German soil

nd bombardment from the air was in its infancy.

The contrast at the end of World War II was complete; many German cities had literally been levelled and the invading armies had pinched the ruined Third *Reich* into the shape of an hour-glass. Yet the people, young and old, fought on. A few years after the war I found in a remote wooded area of Schleswig-Holstein a rudimentary cemetery containing the graves of men who had made a last stand in that neighbourhood. They had not belonged to any one organised formation, but were the miscellaneous survivors of many broken army and navy units, supplemented by the 'Were-wolves' of the Hitler Youth, the last combings of Goebbels' pitiful *levée en masse*. They did not fight because they were exposed to terror and coercion; the power of the SS was broken; they could have given themselves up, singly or collectively, without fear of reprisal. They were not even opposing, as would have been the case on the Russian front, an enemy whom their inhumanities had outraged. It is impossible to avoid the conclusion that they fought because the *Fuehrer* had imbued them with the will to fight, and his evil magic was not yet exhausted.

The same supernatural belief in Hitler's capacity to extricate himself from a hopeless situation could be observed at the end of the war among German prisoners in camps in this country, who were exposed daily to convincing evidence that their leader was doomed. Such men were not simply victims of propaganda in the familiar sense; they had been indoctrinated and brain-washed in a more profound and sinister way.

As long as Hitler could command human material of this order and find weapons for them, the once mighty war machine continued to function, even if only as a faint tintinnabulation in comparison with the great hammer beat of earlier years. By May 1945 the German army had been fighting continuously for five years and eight months and was encircled by foes so numerous that they called themselves 'the United Nations'. This massive German effort was exerted in the worst cause known to history; but its scale and duration must elicit our astonished attention, even though not our commendation. The chapters which follow have the primary aim of making this phenomenon better understood.

ROBERT CECIL CMG

Germany in the Thirties—
a decade of regeneration

Hitler reviews his guard on parade.

Dr William Carr

The capitulation of Imperial Germany in November 1918 brought to an end an era in international affairs dominated by the sabre-rattling figure of the Kaiser. After World War I, *Weimar* Germany was reduced to the status of a weak, second-rate power, weighed down by intractable economic problems, ringed around by enemies and militarily incapable of defending herself against attack. Twenty years later, Germany was once again a power to be feared and respected. The shackles of Versailles had been broken; German troops had reoccupied the Rhineland; Austria had been annexed and the Sudeten Germans brought into the Third *Reich* after an international crisis which had carried Europe to the brink of war. Instead of the puny army of 1920, Hitler's Germany had a formidable striking force of over 50 divisions trained in *Blitzkrieg* tactics and ready for the conquest of Europe. Was this transformation the work of Hitler alone? Or did he simply continue the policies of the *Weimar* republic? There are no easy answers to these questions for the threads of continuity and discontinuity are woven inextricably into the pattern of German history from 1871 onwards. The seeds of World War II were planted deep in the past of the German nation.

Above: Hitler, the master orator.
Below: Hitler with Hermann Goering, his appointed successor and man of influence in the creation of Germany's war machine.

Left: Dr Josef Goebbels, Minister of Propaganda and Public Enlightenment, who had invaluable powers of persuasion.

Right: Standard-bearing political leaders parading at the 1934 Nuremberg Rally. Such men helped prepare the German people for war.

Germany in the Thirties—
a decade of regeneration

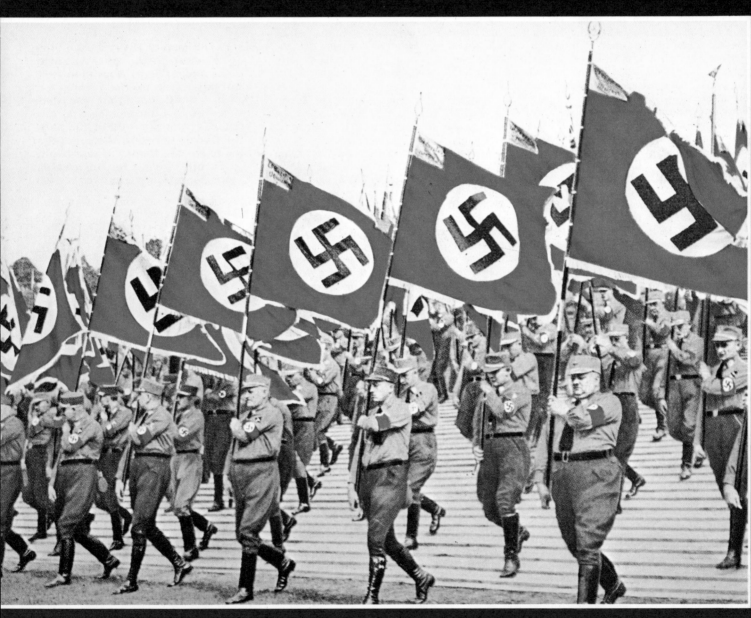

> *A people must gain territory in order to survive. Nothing less will do for Greater Germany, for without living space it will stagnate, wither and die. But first, and this must remain the basis for our actions over the next few years, we must prepare the German people for this expansion, both politically and militarily. We must at the same time unite the German world, and when this is done we shall be able to begin our move outwards – a move which will undoubtedly be achieved only through force of arms.*
>
> **Adolf Hitler 1932**

The Treaty of Versailles, signed in the Hall of Mirrors in the palace of the French Sun King on June 28, 1919, the anniversary of the Sarajevo murders, would, it was fervently hoped by Mankind, banish for ever the spectre of German aggression. Under the Treaty Germany lost 25,000 square miles of territory, six-and-a-half million subjects, over half of them German-speaking, and much valuable industrial potential, particularly in Upper Silesia. In the west Alsace-Lorraine, annexed by victorious Prussia in 1871, was restored to France. As partial compensation for the ravages of war, the industrial Saarland was placed under French administration for 15 years. In the north a plebiscite returned Danish-speaking North Schleswig to Denmark. In the east the triumph of nationalism—a dynamic historical force, largely outside the control of Woodrow Wilson, Lloyd George and Clemenceau, which had already destroyed three giant empires in a matter of weeks before the Peace Conference met—cost Germany much land in Posen, West Prussia and Pomerania.

It was here that the peace settlement was most bitterly resented; the separation of East Prussia from the rest of the Reich by the so-called Polish Corridor and the creation of the anomalous Free State of Danzig

The Diktat restrictions

under League of Nations control (to guarantee Polish access to port facilities) were in German eyes intolerable impositions to be endured just so long as Germany was weak and despised. Resentment—though less acute —was aroused by the allied powers' refusal to permit the union of Austria and Germany so that when Hitler annexed Austria in 1938 his action could be represented, plausibly enough, as a rectification of a blatant injustice in the application of the self-determination principle. Germany lost all her former colonial possessions, which were taken over by the League of Nations and administered by the victorious powers as mandated territories.

As 'Prussian militarism' was widely regarded as a major cause of the war, Germany was severely restricted in respect of armaments. She was forbidden to have military aircraft, heavy weapons and tanks; the general staff was abolished; conscription was forbidden; and she was allowed a professional army of no more than 100,000 men and

4000 officers. In addition, the Rhineland and a 50-kilometre strip on the right bank was permanently demilitarised and an allied army of occupation stationed there for 15 years. Severe restrictions were imposed on the navy which was limited to 15,000 men, forbidden to have submarines, and allowed a total of 12 cruisers and 24 destroyers. The Kiel Canal was internationalised and coastal defences restricted. Finally, Germany was forced to acknowledge her sole war guilt and was saddled with an unknown burden of reparations. The fact that the German delegation was allowed only 48 hours in which to register objections strengthened the widespread conviction in Germany that the treaty was a '*Diktat*' deriving its validity exclusively from the armed might of the victors.

No major power takes kindly to defeat, especially a country as accustomed to the ostentatious display of power as Imperial Germany. The shock of defeat, revolution and economic dislocation failed to bring about any radical re-appraisal of Germany's foreign policy objectives. The permanent officials who staffed the foreign office in the Wilhelmstrasse and the military establishment in the ministry of defence in the nearby Bendlerstrasse lived on happily in the power-conscious world of 1914 believing as steadfastly as ever in Germany's natural right to dominate Europe. Left to their own devices by successive chancellors and presidents, they set about the uphill task of reversing the verdict of the battlefield as quickly as possible.

Geography made Germany the country of the middle destined to live in constant fear of being 'encircled' and trapped into disastrous two-front wars by envious and powerful neighbours to east and west of her. Subjugation or conquest were the stark strategic alternatives facing her in the twentieth century. No middle way was open to her —or so it seemed to Germany's political and military rulers between 1871 and 1945. The same reasoning was applied to her future as a highly industrialised power. Unless she wished to remain dangerously

Right: Hitler at the beginning of the road that led to his supreme power. Here he reviews his stormtroopers at Nuremberg in 1927, the National Socialist para military organisation which proved indispensable to his political rise.

Above: Conscription swelling the ranks of Germany's revitalised armed forces. Here, a propaganda parade of conscripts in an Infantry Regiment barracks in 1936. Men such as these were to increase the size of Germany's army from 100,000 in 1933 to over three million in 1939. Hitler described the training these men were to receive as 'creative of a new German, a breed that will be invincible in any war'. It was a training that led them, at first, to outstanding victories.

Right: The map of Hitler's expanding 'Grossdeutschland' as it was after the aquisition of Austria in 1938. Contemporaries likened its shape to that of a wolf's head that was ready to bite off Czechoslovakia. Also shown, at the top right of the head, is the Danzig corridor, the spark that was to set the flames of war alight. Europe was set for the greatest conflagration it had ever known.

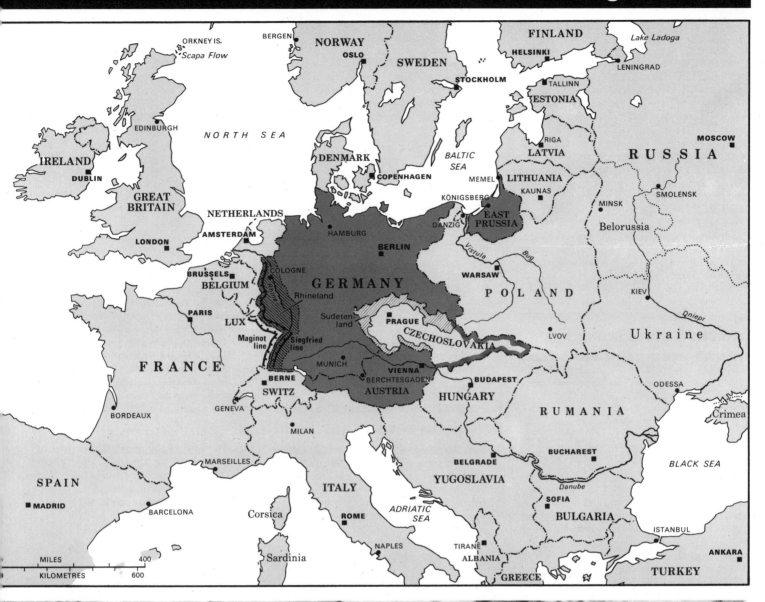

dependent on foreign countries for the ever-increasing quantities of food and raw materials essential for survival, then the only alternative compatible with 'national independence' was the creation of a *Grossraumwirtschaft* in Central and Eastern Europe, an economically self-sufficient area dominated by Germany and responsive to her economic needs. And in a sense the preoccupation with *Weltpolitik* at the beginning of the twentieth century was an attempt to correct the precarious balance of diplomatic and economic power in Europe in Germany's favour by transforming her into a broadly-based world power with colonial possessions and a large navy.

Paradoxically enough, the general strategic situation in 1919 was potentially much more favourable for the realisation of these ambitions than ever before in German history. The collapse of Imperial Russia and its replacement by a weak and ostracised

Blitzkrieg beginnings

Bolshevik regime removed at a stroke the 'Slav nightmare' that so oppressed Germany's leaders in 1914. Where the mighty Romanov and Habsburg empires once stood, was a mosaic of medium-sized and small states, economically weak, divided by deep suspicions and unlikely in the long run to represent a serious obstacle to German ambitions notwithstanding strenuous French efforts in the 1920s to create a *cordon sanitaire* in the Little Entente and to cultivate the Polish connection. In the west victorious Britain and France were manifestly weakened by the economic price of war and by the withdrawal of America into isolation. French power might be irresistible in the short term as the traumatic experience of the occupation of the Ruhr by French forces in 1923 and the subsequent capitulation of the German government amply demonstrated. But the essential unity of the Bismarckian *Reich* had survived peace treaty and Ruhr invasion; so that once Germany had a sizeable army at her disposal she stood every chance of being able to re-establish her political and economic hegemony in Europe in the long run in the absence of countervailing Russian and American pressure.

Within the narrow constraints of the treaty the foundations of a first-class army were already being laid in the 1920s largely through the efforts of General Hans von Seeckt, the talented and imaginative chief of army command. What the new *Reichswehr* lacked in numbers was more than compensated for by a high level of efficiency and intensive training in the tactics of mobile warfare. The *Blitzkrieg* tactics of 1939–41 with their emphasis on armour and air power were forged twenty years before in the manoeuvres and war games Seeckt made an integral part of officer training. With government connivance, the army successfully evaded many of the disarmament provisions of the treaty. The general staff survived thinly disguised as a *Truppenamt*; through short-term enlistment, cadres for a much larger army were illegally trained; prototypes of heavy weapons forbidden under

the treaty were manufactured abroad in Holland and Spain with the help of German industry; and from 1921 onwards, in return for German financial and technical assistance to help build a Russian armaments industry, German pilots and tank crews were trained in Russia. By 1926 when Seeckt resigned, Germany already possessed a great army in miniature which could be transformed into a mass army when the political situation was ripe.

The rehabilitation of German military power was accompanied by corresponding steps in the diplomatic field. At first co-operation between army and foreign office was strictly limited; Seeckt, ever suspicious of the 'frocks', tended to plough his own furrow. But after his resignation the army ceased to pursue an independent line in foreign affairs and accepted the general line laid down by the foreign office largely because senior officers came to realise that Seeckt's hopes of a Russian alliance were exaggerated and that more could be gained out of good relations with the western powers.

For the next few years Germany benefited considerably from the growing feeling in Britain, France and America that Europe needed a stable and prosperous Germany.

European reconciliation

France, too, was forced to try the policy of reconciliation with the old enemy if only because the Ruhr episode had shown the futility of trying to extract reparations at bayonet point. With the Dawes Plan of 1924

for a final reparations settlement, allied troops left the Rhineland five years ahead of schedule. Yet the success, though real enough, was strictly limited; it cannot be denied that the major provisions of the treaty were all intact at the time of Stresemann's death in October 1929. That did not surprise him. For, though widely regarded as an apostle of European reconciliation—he was awarded the Nobel Prize for Peace—Stresemann remained what he had always been: an old fashioned *Machtpolitiker* from the Wilhelminian era with no illusions about the role of force in the international jungle. Only countries with large armies were likely to be respected by other powers and until Germany was again in that enviable position the correct policy in respect of

Right: Reichswehr soldiers during manoeuvres in 1929. It was in these early years that the strategy and tactics of *Blitzkrieg* were evolved, a concept of war that was to shatter Germany's enemies from 1939 to 1942. Mechanisation and mobility, as exemplified by these recce troops, were the key aims of many *Reichswehr* officers, and Hitler was to take them up with rich enthusiasm.

Below: The results of defeat and of the Treaty of Versailles – the barrels of one of Germany's powerful coastal guns of World War I being cut up for scrap in 1919. From such defeat the new *Wehrmacht* arose.

a more realistic attitude was at last adopted on that question. In 1925 Gustav Stresemann, who bore responsibility for foreign policy between 1924 and 1929, was able to play a significant role in the negotiation of the Locarno Pacts which made Germany a member of a western security agreement. In 1926 the War Guilt clause was conveniently forgotten when she was allowed to join the League of Nations with a permanent seat on the Council. Finally, in 1929, in return

Right: 'The spectacle of the Nuremberg Rallies was at once both overwhelming and immensely invigorating', wrote Goebbels. 'What impressed me so much was that the arena was a mass of humanity all worshipping their *Fuehrer*.' Here, Hitler and his entourage are halted to talk to members of the crowd as they moved up to the rostrum.

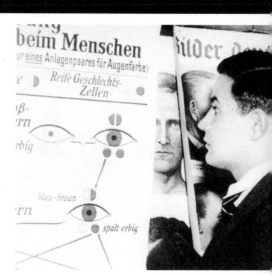

Left: Men of the *Reichsarbeitdienst* – the National Labour Service – a Nazi organisation designed to promote health and education through youth work.

Right: Racial propaganda. The National Socialists mounted many exhibitions to 'educate' the German people as to the differences between the Aryan *'Herrenvolk'* and the Jewish *'Untermensch'*. This one, in 1933, shows the difference in colour of eyes and shape of face.

Below: Hitler surrounded by some of the men who helped him to power. Ley, Leader of the German Workers Front; Streichen, the fanatical anti-semite; and Himmler, head of the SS and the police.

the recovery of Danzig, the Polish Corridor and Upper Silesia and the Anschluss with Austria was 'to finesse and avoid major decisions'.

Three years later the Republic was in its death throes and Hitler's accession to power was a matter of weeks away. The rise of the Nazis is too complex a phenomenon to be investigated here. In general one can say that the great economic crisis which swept through Europe in the early 1930s exposed

Growing nationalism

grave structural weaknesses in the social and political fabric of *Weimar* Germany and favoured the growth of what in good times had been nothing more than a fringe movement destined to permanent opposition. What is of interest in this context is that even before Hitler became chancellor in January 1933 German foreign policy was entering a new and more aggressive phase.

A recrudescence of xenophobic nationalism accompanied the economic crisis in most European countries in the early 1930s as a kind of group reaction to the stimulus of external peril. In Germany mounting nationalist resentment of the Government's record obliged successive chancellors to pursue a bolder policy if only to maintain their quasi-authoritarian regimes. Bruening's abortive attempt to arrange a customs union with Austria in 1931 as the first step towards political Anschluss, and Papen's refusal to return to the Disarmament Conference in 1932 until the German demand for equality of armaments was met reveal a greater readiness than in Stresemann's day to challenge the status quo of 1919. This was also reflected in the growing confidence of the military. At this stage the army was still thinking exclusively in terms of defence against possible Polish aggression. Nevertheless, in April 1930 Wilhelm Groener, the Minister of Defence, issued a directive ordering the army to plan for rapid expansion from ten to twenty-one divisions in a future emergency—in effect a mobilisation plan and as such forbidden by the treaty. So that in one sense Chancellor Hitler, heading an orthodox right-wing cabinet with two other Nazis in it, simply continued and radicalised this new trend in German policy.

The Nazi movement itself expressed in a more extreme form ideas commonplace in

Politics of Living Space

right-wing political circles for generations. The Nazis glorified physical violence, accepting the crude Social Darwinian proposition that life is struggle, i.e. they popularised what 'respectable' foreign office officials had believed since the days of Bismarck. Nations, like individuals, struggled for existence and survived only at the expense of the weak; that was Hitler's constant theme from *Mein Kampf* to the last days in the Berlin bunker. War was a natural instrument of policy and within certain limits had a therapeutic value as a purgative of weak elements in a people.

Hitler's rabid anti-semitism and his fanatical belief that Germany had a mission to save the Aryan race from the infamous schemes of 'World Jewry' infused a sense of cosmic urgency into traditional nationalist demands for the union of all Germans in one *Reich* and for eastward expansion to obtain 'living space' for the German people. Possibly, too, as many German historians now believe, Hitler envisaged a second phase of expansion in the distant future when a German dominated continent would wrestle with America (and possibly Britain) for Western Mastery. To realise the immediate objectives in Europe, whether by war or intimidation, Germany needed a large army.

The form rearmament took under Hitler was determined by internal and external constraints. For the first 18 months relatively little was done partly because of the overriding need to get Germany back to work again and partly because the form military expansion should take was in dispute. Ernst Roèhm, leader of the restless and powerful Brownshirts, pressed for the creation of a peoples' militia under Brownshirt control. Only in February 1934 did Hitler finally decide in favour of a mass army trained and led by professional soldiers. And not until after the Blood Purge of June, which decimated the Brownshirt leadership, did rearmament get under way in earnest.

Rearmament posed serious economic problems for Germany because of her heavy

Strategy of rearmament

dependence on food and raw material imports. Once the slack in the economy had been taken up by 1935, continued emphasis on rearmament lead inevitably to balance of payments difficulties. What is significant is Hitler's refusal to tolerate any substantial depression of living standards as the price of rearmament, for the very good reason that dictatorships are in practice more sensitive than democracies to the mood of the public or what their secret police suppose is the public mood. Gestapo reports revealed much dissatisfaction just below the surface which Nazi leaders feared (probably quite erroneously) would assume serious proportions should economic conditions worsen appreciably. Another consideration that weighed heavily with Hitler was an instinctive feeling that long-term investment in the armaments industry and the general disruption of the peace-time economy consequent upon in-depth rearmament of the 1914-18 variety would endanger his personal rule by placing too much power in the hands of economic overlords.

The alternative strategy of rearmament in breadth fitted the bill exactly. For by restricting war production to a limited sector of the economy it proved possible to combine the production of large quantities of tanks and guns with minimum dislocation of the economy. No undue strain was placed on the people and in addition Hitler was able to build up an impossibly large army in the shortest possible time. The existence of a considerable army would of itself tend to demoralise Germany's small neighbours.

Above: This was Hitler's study in the new *Reich* Chancery, a room in which decisions were taken that were to change the world and affect the lives of almost every living person. Many of those people who saw it found the decor to be stultifying, lacking any kind of taste, but Hitler saw in it a 'strength' which, he thought, characterised the 'New Germany' that he was building.

Right: Even more weightily impressive than Hitler's study was the entrance to the *Reich*'s centre of power. These are the portals to the new Berlin Chancery, guarded by men of Hitler's elite, the *Leibstandarte* SS 'Adolf Hitler' — fit bodyguard for a dictator.

Top right: The last of the old order — *Reich* President Paul von Hindenberg, who was to die in 1934, reviewing a guard of honour in Berlin. His weakness and inability as a politician helped greatly Hitler's rise to power as *Reich* Chancellor in 1933.

Far right: Hitler speaking at the *Reichstag,* Germany's nearest equivalent of a parliament. After his assumption of supreme power, the *Reichstag* became an impotent body. Its members, who were all National Socialists, merely existed in order to rubber-stamp government policies. All the same, with customary cleverness, Hitler made full use of the propaganda possibilities of the *Reichstag,* making many of his most important speeches there.

Hitler regarded the youth of Germany as the most vital element in the nation's future and did all he could to train them politically and militarily.

And to this end the propaganda machine deliberately exaggerated the extent of rearmament so effectively in practice that only after the war did it become apparent how far Germany had been from total mobilisation in 1939. The fact was that, despite Goering's defiant boast of a choice between 'guns and butter', the Germans continued to have reasonable quantities of both up to 1942.

Finally, rearmament in breadth made military sense in the opinion of at least some of Hitler's generals. If it came to war, a small army with a core of powerful armoured units supported by motorised infantry and trained

The Wehrmacht grows

in *Blitzkrieg* tactics could strike quickly and win decisive battles in a matter of days, always provided of course that the Führer could isolate the victim and guarantee that Germany would not be plunged into a long war which she could not possibly win.

Externally, the progress of rearmament was dependent upon the attitude of the Great Powers towards the Nazi regime. As Hitler expected vigorous reactions from the French he moved cautiously at first, seeking to reassure the powers of his peaceful intentions though not with any great success. What proved decisive was not Hitler's manoeuvres but the feeling in British, Italian and American government circles that it was intolerable for Germany to remain disarmed while other powers—especially France—refused to reduce their arms levels. With the tacit consent of the powers Hitler was able to take Germany out of the Disarmament Conference and the League of Nations in October 1933, a defiant gesture calculated to show the German people that, like preceding chancellors, he intended to pursue an active foreign policy. By the spring of 1934, when France precipitately broke off further disarmament negotiations, it was clear that Hitler's fears of France had been grossly exaggerated and that rearmament could proceed without hindrance from that quarter.

It was the gathering pace of German rearmament that dictated the next move. By the beginning of 1935 the *Reichswehr* had

Above: Hitler at his birthday parade in 1937, with the heads of his armed forces: Goering, chief of the *Luftwaffe;* von Blomberg, the war minister; Raeder, naval chief; and von Fritsch, the commander of the army.

Right: Hitler at the memorial service for General von Seeckt, in Berlin, 1934. The *Fuehrer* is being greeted by Hindenberg and being saluted by the heads of the military and the police.

increased in size from 100,000 to 240,000 men (not counting another 200,000 police-men trained outside the army as infantrymen), and military command was already planning a peace-time army of twenty-one divisions. But without conscription it was impossible to produce the reserves that army would need in wartime. The opportunity to put this right presented itself in March 1935 when France increased the period of compulsory service and lowered the age of enlistment to offset the effects of a falling birthrate. On March 9 Goering had already

The Rhineland rearmed

announced the existence of a German air force, which amounted to some 2000 machines, few of them fit for front line service. As the news met with little adverse reaction in the west, on March 16 Hitler announced the re-introduction of conscription and the creation of a peace-time army of 36 divisions (the army's revised target). The western powers, as expected, confined themselves to verbal protests at this clear breach of treaty.

In March 1936 Hitler re-militarised the Rhineland, his most daring diplomatic move so far. The disunity of the western powers over the Abyssinian affair was too good an opportunity to miss and three battalions were sent into the demilitarised zone as a

Left: The early *Luftwaffe* in 1936. Two aircraftmen stand alongside the machines it is their responsibility to maintain. They belong to the fighter squadron *'Horst Wessel'*, named after the Nazi 'hero', who was killed in a brawl in the early days of the Party. This illustrates the close links which the *Luftwaffe* had with the National Socialists from the very beginning. Its leader, Hermann Goering was also Hitler's successor and, until the middle of the war, was one of the most influential men in the *Reich*. The *Luftwaffe* owed its existence to the Nazis, for it was they who helped develop the force in secret, who confirmed its existence in 1936 and who gave it priority in expansion from that date. Hitler announced later: 'Never let it be forgotten that it was we who created the German *Luftwaffe* out of nothing. This is yet another illustration of our energy, of our determination to make the German people strong again.'

token of the restoration of complete sovereignty. The re-occupation marked a new and more aggressive phase in German foreign policy. For had France ordered immediate counter measures—as common prudence suggested she ought to have—it would have been quite beyond the military capacity of Germany to have resisted at this stage; in that event the battalions were under orders

Mobilisation for war

to stage a fighting withdrawal. Hitler's intuitive judgment—supported by the experience of the last three years—that France would remain passive proved right. Germany derived considerable strategic advantage from the re-occupation. Her exposed western flank could now be protected and work commenced on the famous West Wall. But it was the psychological significance of the French failure to resist that encouraged Hitler most, revealing as it did a deep malaise at the heart of Germany's old foe.

In September 1936 Hitler began to mobilise the German economy for war. The

Four Year Plan announced by Hitler at the Party Congress was intended to make Germany as self-sufficient as possible in respect of certain raw materials with particular emphasis on petrol and rubber, both essential ingredients of a modern war machine. Of course complete self-sufficiency was not possible within Germany's existing frontiers as Hitler knew full well. Only by expanding eastwards to the Ural mountains could Germany achieve a degree of autarky corresponding to her political ambitions. Meanwhile, the measures adopted in 1936 were more in the nature of a crash programme to prepare the German army for war by 1940. In the summer of 1938, under the pressure

Continuing expansion

of the Czech crisis, the wider aspects of the plan were abandoned in favour of intensified efforts to attain maximum production of gunpowder, high explosives and vital chemicals by—significantly enough—the end of 1939.

Towards the end of 1937 Hitler was growing restless and inclined to accelerate the pace of German expansion. There were good reasons for this. In recent months the strategic situation had changed dramatically in Germany's favour. Italy was now the friend of Germany. The Abyssinian War strained Italy's relations with Britain and France, and close upon its heels came the Italian involvement in the Spanish Civil War. Italy moved closer to the German camp and in November the so-called Berlin-Rome Axis came into being. Hitler could now feel reasonably confident that Italy would be too pre-occupied with Mediterranean problems to intervene—as she had done over Austria in 1934—should Germany move eastwards.

In the west France was gravely weakened by the collapse of the Locarno system. Belgium had lapsed into neutrality. Britain, though prepared to aid France in the event of German aggression, made it clear that this promise did not extend to France's allies in Eastern Europe; Poland and the Little Entente were, in effect, left to their own devices whilst the weakness of Russia, ally of France since 1935, was dramatically illustrated by the purges in the summer of 1937 which decimated the top echelons in the Red Army.

Hitler was aware, too, that any military advantage Germany might possess over her opponents would certainly disappear by the mid-1940s when those powers would themselves have rearmed. Possibly he sensed that his regime, rigidly committed to rearmament, could not satisfy the growing social aspirations of a people now back at work; only by intensifying the pace of his foreign policy could he preserve his own dictatorial power, escape the inflationary effects of rearmament and maintain the dynamic of the Nazi state. Therefore, in the autumn of 1937 he decided, as he informed his closest associates at the Hossbach meeting on November 5, that Germany must secure her 'living space' by 1943-5 at the latest, and might seize Austria and Czechoslovakia before that date if favourable circumstances

arose.

As a preliminary to a more aggressive policy, Hitler extended his control over the army. So far he had left the army to get on with the task of rearmament without interference. But he had grown increasingly impatient of conservative-minded von Fritsch, commander-in-chief of the army since 1934 and a constant opponent of Hitler's pressure for accelerated rearmament. Early in 1938 a scandal concerning the wife of von Blomberg, the Minister of War, and false charges against Fritsch were pounced upon by Hitler as a pretext to be rid of them both. The pliable von Brauchitsch replaced Fritsch. Blomberg was not replaced; instead Hitler assumed the post of commander-in-chief of the Wehrmacht and appointed the subservient Wilhelm Keitel head of a new planning staff—the *OKW* or armed forces command—immediately responsible to himself. The balance of power in the high command shifted decisively in his favour and a process commenced which ended logically with Hitler's assumption of personal command of the army in 1941.

For some years after Hitler's accession to power army strategy remained defensive in nature. Plan Red, a deployment plan to deal with a possible French attack, was drawn up in 1935. Although Blomberg had been interested in studying at that time the feasability of attacking Czechoslovakia, not until 1937 was work begun upon Plan Green for a pre-emptive strike at Czechoslovakia and only then in the event of a two-front war. However, by the summer of that year the army was beginning to adopt a more aggressive posture largely because Blomberg, an ardent Nazi, was under Hitler's influence. Already the army was instructed to be ready for the exploitation of favourable circumstances as and when they arose. After the

The rape of Austria

Hossbach meeting pride of place was given by Germany's military leaders to Plan Green. Army and air force leaders were now prepared to launch an attack on Czechoslovakia in peace-time if conditions were favourable, i.e. the army was no longer pursuing a defensive strategy but consciously underwriting Hitler's imperialist plans for living space.

Even so, when Hitler seized Austria in March 1938 it was by accident rather than design. Since July 1934 when an abortive Austrian Nazi coup resulted in the death of the then Chancellor Dollfuss and aroused world opinion against Germany, Hitler handled Austria with kid gloves. By the winter of 1937/8 the Austrian Nazis, like the Sudeten Germans, were growing restless. When Chancellor Schuschnigg visited Hitler in February 1938 to discuss Austria's future, the latter succeeded in driving a hard bargain with the Austrians which went a long way

The occupation of Czechoslovakia by German troops in March 1939. Here, Panzers parade through the streets of Prague in a demonstration of strength to impress the locals.

Juni 1938

toward the peaceful absorption of Austria in Germany. Hitler was perfectly satisfied, and there the matter would probably have rested had not Schuschnigg tried to upset the arrangement by announcing a plebiscite to allow the Austrians to decide their own future. An angry Hitler, under pressure from the more aggressive Goering, intervened and when he had 'arranged' an invitation from a pro-Nazi chancellor ordered German troops into Austria.

Next day, March 13, Austria became part of the *Reich*. The Great Powers acquiesced in the Anschluss. Neither Britain, France nor Italy was prepared to help Schuschnigg as Hitler knew before his troops marched. Overnight the strategic situation in Central Europe was transformed. Control of historic Vienna gave the Germans a dominant posi-

War draws even closer

tion in the Balkans. In the south Germany now had a common frontier with her friend Italy while in the north Czechoslovakia's strategic position suddenly worsened.

The ease of his victory undoubtedly encouraged Hitler not to wait any longer—as he might have done despite the Hossbach 'timetable'—but to turn his attentions to Czechoslovakia without delay. The 'neutralisation' of this democratic state, king-pin of the anti-German Little Entente and a spearhead in the German flank, was a strategic necessity to give Germany freedom of manoeuvre for eastward expansion. To achieve this end, Hitler relied on a mixture of political and military pressure. The grievances of three-and-a-half million Sudeten Germans against the Prague government were ruthlessly exploited by the local Nazis under strict orders from Berlin to keep the

Left: **National Socialist propaganda was often visually extremely attractive. This poster advertises a Gau meeting at Stettin before the war. This was one of many such meetings to promote unity.**

tension at boiling point throughout the summer and so demoralise the Czechs that military intervention in the autumn—a course to which Hitler committed himself in May— would deliver the *coup de grâce*. All the indications were that Britain and France would remain passive spectators while Italy was still too pre-occupied with Mediterranean problems to be concerned about a German attack on Czechoslovakia.

Though one cannot entirely discount the possibility that Hitler was bluffing from start to finish and never intended war over Czechoslovakia, the balance of probability strongly supports the view that the military threat to Czechoslovakia was a very real one and that the Germans could have defeated her. Thirty-seven divisions, including three armoured and four motorised, were concentrated around Czechoslovakia in a menacing semi-circle from Austria to Silesia when Chamberlain's unexpected intervention in mid-September upset Hitler's plans. To maximise the surprise element (so vital for the success of Blitzkrieg tactics) the Germans adopted the cunning stratagem of calling up reservists not for war—formal mobilisation would have been a provocative step likely to stretch French and Czech patience to breaking point—but ostensibly for routine autumn manoeuvres. In this way Germany 'mobilised' so effectively that an attack on Czechoslovakia could have been launched without waiting for formal mobilisation orders. Significantly, too, assault divisions were moved into advanced positions at night and heavily camouflaged. An element of bluff entered the picture only in respect of Germany's military preparations in the west where five divisions were stationed to defend the half-completed West Wall which could not, in fact, have been held for more than two to three weeks in the face of a French offensive as Hitler must have realised.

It was precisely this fear of French intervention and the corollary of a two-front war which Germany could not possibly win that explains the mounting opposition in high military circles to Hitler's plans. In so far as Hitler could not guarantee absolutely that war with Czechoslovakia would be strictly localised, his entire policy in the autumn of 1938 amounted to a piece of reckless brinkmanship based on intuitive judgment about

Move against the Czechs

western reactions and not on the logistical reality of German military capabilities. On the other hand, Hitler did not allow his primitive desire to smash the Czechs by force to blind him to changes in the tactical situation. Thus, when the Czechs mobilised on September 23 and reports came in of partial mobilisation in France, Hitler was quick to appreciate that the vital surprise element was virtually eliminated from the picture leaving him with no viable alternative but to settle, reluctantly, for the surrender of the Sudetenland at the Munich Conference.

Six months later German troops drove through the snow-covered streets of Prague and completed the destruction of the Czech state. Once again Hitler relied upon a

judicious blend of political and military pressure. In the spring of 1939 the Slovaks acted as his Trojan horse; their demands for independence were fostered by the Germans and precipitated a crisis which gave Hitler his chance to intervene—as always—at the 'invitation' of the victim. The army had been alerted to Hitler's intentions as early as October 1938 whilst, significantly, no-one anticipated serious opposition from the western powers. The balance of military power in Central Europe shifted decisively in favour of Germany. The Little Entente was smashed to pieces and Romania and Yugoslavia hastened to make their peace with Hitler. German influence became predominant in the Danubian Basin and exploitation of the economic resources of the area entered a new and more aggressive phase. In the mid-1930s Schacht, Hitler's minister of economics, negotiated barter agreements with the coun-

The outbreak of war

tries of South-eastern Europe in order to acquire the essential raw materials for rearmament. In the late 1930s Goering, the new 'economic overlord of Germany, was attempting to create a *Grossraumwirtschaft* in the area, reducing Yugoslavia, Romania and Bulgaria to quasi-colonial territories; Germany not only took their grain and ores but was pumping in capital sums to ensure that they produced the raw materials Germany needed.

In June 1939, exactly 20 years since the peace of Versailles had been forced on a resentful people, Germany's position had changed out of all recognition. She was again a power to be reckoned with and every utterance of her leader was studied in minute detail in every European chancellery. For example, pressure from her foreign minister von Ribbentrop was sufficient to make little Lithuania decide hurriedly in March 1939 to hand over the Memelland taken from Germany in 1919. Internally, though political opposition was ruthlessly repressed and the Jews were being systematically persecuted from 1933 onwards, the German people was back at work. Instead of the mass unemployment conditions which plagued western lands material conditions were tolerable and a shortage of labour actually existed in Germany on the eve of war.

Three months later Germany was at war with Poland, Britain and France and Hitler was set on a course which led in the end to the total and utter collapse of Nazi Germany in 1945. How did this come about?

Wars do not have trivial causes. Several factors must combine to produce an inflammatory situation where only a spark is needed to cause the final explosion. Such was the case in August 1939. A crisis existed in German-Polish relations ever since the breakdown of negotiations over the Corridor in March, a failure which signified the end of genuine German attempts to win Poland over as a junior partner for adventures in the east. In this tense situation the British guarantee to Poland on March 31 and the formal alliance in August—suggesting that Britain had reversed the traditional policy of

disengagement in Eastern Europe and would now resist Hitler's designs in the east—strengthened his resolve to teach the Poles a lesson. Whether economic pressures played a significant role in the decision to strike at Poland it is difficult to say. Undoubtedly stresses and strains were mounting in Nazi Germany because of the unwise acceleration of rearmament in an already overheated economy, and may well have confirmed Hitler in his decision. That is very far from saying that economic pressures were so intense that Hitler was obliged on that account to go to war. But there were sound military reasons for striking soon. In two or three years, as Hitler often remarked in the winter of 1938/9, Germany's opponents would have a military advantage over her. If war was unavoidable to achieve his aims in the east then better war in 1939 than 1943. In that sense it can certainly be said that Hitler was driven to war ahead of the Hossbach 'timetable'. The parallel with Imperial Germany springs to mind. In the summer of 1914 a not dissimilar 'either-or' situation faced her (or so her leaders supposed); either Germany waited passively until the balance of military power moved inexorably against her and 'encirclement' turned into subjugation; or else she exploited her waning military power to break the ring of 'encirclement' closing round her and re-eastablish her hegemony in Europe.

Without doubt Germany's armed forces were ready for war with Poland. Instead of the ten divisions of 1920 Germany possessed a peace-time army of 52 divisions to call on, her total mobilised strength was 103 divisions; of these 70 were fit for active service. By 1942 it was estimated that Germany would have sufficient reserves for 150 divisions and would then reach the maximum capacity of her arms-producing industry.

German air power

Morale was high in the armed forces on the eve of war. In the west the defences had been greatly strengthened and Hitler's generals were much more confident of holding the line (with ten divisions) than at the time of the Czech crisis.

Though air power was primarily a support weapon for the ground forces, Germany's progress was impressive here also. In 1920 she had no military aircraft; in 1939 she possessed about 3000 aircraft including 1180 medium bombers, 771 single-seater fighters and 336 dive bombers. Most of the craft were types first produced in 1936 whereas French and British aircraft were of an older vintage. But once the western powers started to rearm in earnest from 1938 onwards, their aircraft were inevitably equipped with machines of slightly better design and performance than the Germans. From about mid-1939, all things being equal, the balance of air power would begin to move against Germany slowly but surely, another good reason for exploiting the temporary advantage quickly.

Economically, Germany was in a position to wage a short successful war in 1939. It is true that her dependence on foreign supplies

of copper, zinc, lead and iron ore was greater in 1939 than ever before. On the other hand, Germany was producing sufficient synthetic rubber (22,000 tons in 1939) to meet current needs; aluminium output was in excess of demand; and though synthetic oil production at 2.8 million tons (all types of fuel) was disappointing and left Germany dependent on Romanian and Yugoslavian supplies she had considerable stocks of diesel oil and petrol. Thanks to Nazi agricultural policy,

Poland is defeated

she was practically self-sufficient in bread, potatoes, milk, sugar and meat. Bearing in mind that Hitler intended to plunder occupied territory and to depress the living standard of the inhabitants to recoup his material losses, it can certainly be maintained that Germany was ready for war.

Not, of course, for a major war. Nor did Hitler intend to wage such a war. He assumed that Britain and France would abandon Poland in the final resort as they had abandoned Czechoslovakia. If there were any lingering doubts in the west these would surely be removed, so he supposed, by the Non-Aggression Pact Ribbentrop signed with Russia on August 23. The western powers were stunned by the news. Their hopes of an alliance with Russia to contain Nazi Germany were dashed; Poland was completely isolated and an attack on her virtually certain unless she capitulated, of which there was no sign. In the short term Hitler was surely right. Britain and France made no serious effort to aid Poland when Germany attacked her on September 1 and she was defeated within a month in the first *Blitzkrieg* of the war. Probably Hitler did not suppose the British and French declarations of war represented more than a fleeting mood, a face-saving device by elderly politicians who would soon see reason once Germany had defeated Poland. The attack on Poland was not an irredeemable error. The fatal mistakes came later between the summer of 1940 and the summer of 1941; it was the failure to drive Britain out of the war in 1940 and the attack on Russia in 1941 which trapped Germany once more in a two-front war which it was beyond her military and economic capacity to win.

Suggested reading
A. Bullock: **Hitler a Study in Tyranny** (Pelican books, 1962)
W. Carr: **Arms, Autarky and Aggression. A Study in German Foreign Policy 1933–1939** (London, 1972)
K. Hildebrand: **The Foreign Policy of the Third Reich** (trans. London, 1973)
G. Scheele: **The Weimar Republic. Overture to the Third Reich** (London, 1946)
R. M. Watt: **The Kings Depart. The German Revolution and the Treaty of Versailles 1918–19** (Pelican books, 1973)
G. L. Weinberg: **The Foreign Policy of Hitler's Germany. Diplomatic Revolution in Europe 1933–36** (Chicago and London, 1970)

The Home Front—
the carrot and the stick

Josef Goebbels — master of propaganda.

World War II inevitably made a strong impact on the German people as well as on their enemies. The propaganda machine utilised this impact. The place of propaganda in the Nazi scheme of things changed on the outbreak of war and control of it passed, partly, into different hands. It had a marked effect on the morale of the nation and the ways in which the people reacted to the fortunes and, later, misfortunes of the war at several stages: at the outbreak of the war with France and Britain; at the time of the attack on the Soviet Union; on the declaration of total war by Goebbels; and during the final disintegration of the German war effort.

In the minds of the Nazi leaders, propaganda and violence, and propaganda and coercion, were always closely linked. The war opened up new opportunities for them and for the various services. The violence at the front line in a way legitimised the violence at home and especially in the occupied territories. The extermination of the Jews and other 'impure' races was made possible by the war. This chapter shows how the Nazi leaders, in a comparatively short time, made their obscene best of the opportunities provided by that war, to the horror of Europe and the World

Above: Ernst Kaltenbrunner, successor to Heydrich as controller of secret police. *Below:* Reinhard Heydrich, who was known as 'the killer'.

Left: Heinrich Himmler, head of the SS and police, one of the most powerful men on the home front.

Right: Himmler's SS parading its standards at Nuremberg, 1936. It was to become the single most powerful and sinister organisation in the *Reich*

The Home Front—
the carrot
and the stick

The German people want to be led – this is shown by our history – but our experience in the Party has made us realise that a bit of a push from behind does no harm. Indeed we National Socialists would not have been in power today had we not been willing and able to use our considerable force of persuasion, by word and by fist, in the streets throughout Germany during our period of struggle. It is because part of our creed as National Socialists demands that we mobilise the population towards an ideological goal that we are so eminently successful in this.

Josef Goebbels 1941

On April 21, 1945, the last conference at the Ministry of Propaganda took place. Dr Joseph Goebbels, the Minister, limped into the shuttered, candle-lit room, slightly late; as always, his appearance was dapper, his hair oiled and carefully brushed. German defences on every front had disintegrated; the Russians were closing in on Berlin. Goebbels developed the theme of treason by the old officers' clique at length: Hitler's Germany had been destroyed from the inside. Perhaps the Minister remembered 1918, and the 'stab in the back' excuse for Germany's failure in the war. The Social Democrats, rather than the officers, had then allegedly committed the act of treason. In 1945, there existed no organisation of consequence in Germany, apart from the Nazi party and the army, which could be blamed for the disaster.

The differences between 1918 and 1945 went further. In 1918, Germany itself had escaped comparatively unharmed; the destruction of the war had stopped short of the country's frontiers. In 1945, however, Hitler had issued, on March 19, his destruction order. The German people had failed him; there was no other alternative before Germany than Bolshevism; the Allies were therefore to find a desert in the place of the Third *Reich*. Hitler ordered that:

'1. All military, transport, communications, industrial and supply installations as well as equipment with the *Reich* which the enemy might use for the continuation of his

A desert of destruction

struggle now or in the future must be destroyed.

2. The destruction of all military objects, including transport and communication installations, is the responsibility of the military commando posts; that of all industrial and supply installations as well as other materials is the responsibility of the *Gauleiters* and *Reich* Defence Commissioners. The troops must give the *Gauleiters* and *Reich* Defence Commissioners the necessary assistance for the execution of their work.

3. This order must be made known to all commanders as quickly as possible.'

Even without Hitler's destruction orders, Germany lay in ruins in the spring of 1945; Hitler and Goebbels, who had won control of Berlin from the Communists in the street battles of the early 1930s, were now defending

the capital in a last-ditch effort against the Red Army. In the last months of the Third *Reich*, the fortunes of Joseph Goebbels—the Minister for Enlightenment and Propaganda, to give him his full title—and of the skills he represented, stood high. In the second part of his political testament of April 29, 1945, Hitler rewarded Goebbels by appointing him the *Reich* Chancellor—while at the same time, expelling Hermann Goering, and the *Reichsfuehrer SS* and Minister of Interior, Heinrich Himmler, from the party and all other offices.

The National Socialist state was founded and run by the means of a blend of persuasion and coercion—of the carrot and the stick—in a starker and more visible form than other one-party states. Joseph Goebbels and Heinrich Himmler were the leading exponents of

Creation of a myth

the two arts: Goebbels was the persuader; Himmler wielded the stick. Like their chosen instruments of power, their personalities sharply differed. Goebbels was the intellectual: flamboyant in his youth, he toned down his manner and appearance when he assumed Ministerial responsibilities. But there remained something of a showman about him; everything he did was calculated to impress. He had written a novel in his youth; but his main strength lay in the manipulation of words for political purposes. He was good at coining phrases and constructing images. For instance, in terms of Nazi predilections, Goebbels and his propagandists described the Italians as ideologically sound but racially questionable; the English the other way round; of the Austrians Goebbels said that they were not a nation, but a 'hallucination'.

But it was the construction of the Hitler myth that was Goebbels' masterpiece. The Minister of Propaganda, who usually took a very detached view of his art as well as of his performance, perhaps came closest to believing his own propaganda when it concerned Hitler. Goebbels depicted him at first as a

Right: **Goebbels' importance grew immensely in the middle war years. Then his skill as a persuader was needed to convince the people that all was well. Here, he is on his way to make his famous 1943 'total war' speech.**

Above: Success was the greatest aid in controlling the German people. Here, Hitler receives a crowd's greeting after the occupation of Austria.
Left: Hitler's personality cult — children formed a large part in this and propaganda carefully played on it.

representative of a hard-pressed generation—the symbol of the Nazi view of post-war Germany; then as both a super-man and a man of the people. Goebbels used quasi-religious imagery; miracle, mission, Messiah were words which occurred frequently. Hitler was the far-sighted planner of Germany's recovery: he was tolerant of other people's foibles; he was, basically, an artist. By the outbreak of the war, the image of Hitler had so many facets to it that it appeared to the great majority of Germans to shine; Hitler as the great military expert emerged in the course of 1939. With one exception, the imagery was purely masculine. On only one occasion, Goebbels wrote of Hitler that 'The whole nation loves him because it feels safe in his hands like a child in the arms of his mother'.

The personality cult of Hitler was the kingpin of Nazi propaganda and, during the

Unfit to wage war

war, doubtless made a great contribution to the maintenance of the morale of the nation. One of the last photographs of Hitler shows him, on a bleak early spring day in 1945, reviewing a ragged row of young boys, members of the *Hitlerjugend*. They, together with pensioners and veterans unfit to wage

Overpage: A poster appealing for help in providing money for youth hostels and homes. The Germanic-looking girl is a member of the BDM – Union of German Girls – a part of the Hitler Youth, an organisation that cultivated discipline, physical education and 'political awareness' in order to create a youth movement loyal to, and capable of fulfilling, National Socialist ideals. Very many fine youth hostels were built during the Nazi era, since great emphasis was placed upon outdoor activities. This poster well illustrates the type of young person Germany's leaders were hoping to produce.

HAMBURG

Baut

Jugendherbergen und Heime

another war, made up the *Volkssturm*—the people's last reserve. Their loyalty to the synthetic image of Hitler, rather than to the Germany lying in ruins around them, probably made it possible for them to wage the unequal struggle.

Goebbels himself, however, hardly ever believed his propaganda. He was too much of an intellectual for that: but he was a very tough kind of intellectual. He remained with Hitler to the last moment; he, as well as his large family, died with their Fuehrer. He had never wavered in his determination to win the war for Germany; he never even winced, in public, when the war was lost. His judgment, especially when he was

Unwavering determination

flushed with fight as a young man, was questionable. On April 13, 1926, for instance, Goebbels wrote in his diary '. . . with Himmler in Landshut; Himmler a good fellow and very intelligent, I like him.'

Himmler was then 26 years old; Goebbels was some three years older. He is the only person on record who described Himmler as 'very intelligent'. Himmler's strength lay elsewhere: in 1926, this may not yet have been apparent. Himmler was the second son of a schoolmaster, who was born, and spent his youth in Bavaria, the stronghold of National Socialism. He married in 1928, a woman seven years older than himself, of Polish origin. She then owned a small nursing home in Berlin: she sold it after her marriage and bought a smallholding outside Munich. Himmler had a diploma in agriculture: his wife reared chickens, while he gave a lot of his time to the Nazi party in Munich. In January 1929, his devotion to the cause was rewarded. He was appointed, by Hitler, the *Reichsfuehrer SS*: in spite of the grand title, he had only some 300 men under his command, and a salary of 200 marks a month. The SS, or *Schutzstaffel*, was originally intended to protect Nazi speakers: but Himmler had other plans for it. He wanted to make the SS into an utterly reliable body of carefully chosen men. He succeeded in doing this, and thereby laid the basis for his future fortune.

Himmler was a dedicated perfectionist: his drab personality and appearance, as well as his hidden conviction, made him a person who was easily underestimated. Those of his colleagues and enemies who made the mistake paid for it dearly. He was far from detached: he was totally committed. He was totally committed to Hitler, though he betrayed the *Fuehrer* in the end, and ran away from Berlin; he was totally committed to his vision of the kind of people the Germans should be. But Himmler was neither an intellectual nor was he very intelligent. He had only his early training in agriculture to fall back on, and his practical experience of breeding chickens: he had to rely heavily on the wisdom, and advice, of others. It was not his habit to exercise discrimination in the choice of his mentors.

In 1929, Walter Darré, who became the Minister of Agriculture in 1933, published the book *Um Blut und Boden*. It expatiated on the essential nobility of the Nordic peasant, his blood and the soil he tilled, which Darré thought was especially rich and fruitful. He contrasted the Nordic Aryan peasant with the Jews and the Slavs, who according to the author preferred to lurk in the decaying, decadent city streets. Darré was neither saying anything new nor did he say it in a new way. The mood against towns, against all the complexities of modern industrial civilization, was a part and parcel of German populist philosophy. In the nineteenth century, it had spread especially among schoolmasters; it struck a cord among the Nazi thinkers: Darré, together with Alfred Rosenberg, gave it currency within their party. They stressed the reasons why the German nation was so particularly privileged, and they succeeded in convincing the party that true Nordic Germans had a special claim to racial superiority.

The drab, pedantic person who, together with his wife, believed in efficiency, thrift and herbal cures, really thought that Rosenberg and Darré made an important and valid point, that it amplified the teachings of Hitler, and that he should dedicate his life to its realization. Goebbels, on the other hand, could not take the low quality intellectual outpourings of Rosenberg and Darré, and mocked them whenever the opportunity arose. The image of the blue-eyed, blond giant of the Nordic myth was too much for the black-haired, dark eyed Rhinelander with a club foot.

Nevertheless, by the outbreak of the war, Himmler had all the means of coercion under his control just as Goebbels controlled the instruments of persuasion. They were complementary, though neither the relative positions of their instruments nor of their masters remained static at any given time. In the *Kampfzeit*—the period of struggle after

Nazi Security Service

World War I until the *Machtergriefung* when Hitler became the Chancellor in January 1933—the importance of propaganda was paramount. It helped Hitler to capture power: in the process, the services of Goebbels were indispensable. While Goebbels was helping Hitler to win Berlin and then Germany for the Nazi cause, Himmler was still busy constructing the SS and, with the aid of Reinhardt Heydrich, the SD, the *Sicherheitsdienst*. The best the SS could do was to create incidents of violence which were then exploited by Nazi propaganda.

It was in 1931—a year of great importance for Himmler—that the foundations of his later empire were laid. Walter Darré then joined Himmler's staff to organize the *Rasse und Siedlungshauptamt*, an office which was set up to establish the racial standards required of good German stock; it was to enquire into extant ethnic groups in Europe

Right: **Boys of the Hitler Youth at a parade. Their leader, Baldur von Schirach, once stated that 'trumpets echo the spirit of the Germanic warrior throughout the centuries of his struggle'.**

which could be claimed for Germany; it was to settle doubts as to the racial status of individuals. In the summer of the same year, Reinhardt Heydrich joined Himmler: his work was to develop the *Sicherheitsdienst*, the Nazi security service. The year ended with the publication of the famous SS marriage code, which legislated for the racial purity of a fast-growing organization. Thousands of young men were joining the SS in 1931, the darkest year of the world economic crisis.

After January 1933 Goebbels still used propaganda to secure maximum popular support for the Nazi party and then for the Nazi state; but from then on it could be reinforced by the coercive machinery of the state. Propaganda therefore had to find its place as one of the instruments for the maintenance

Night of the Long Knives

of political power, rather than being the main means of achieving it. Broadcasting, the film industry, publishing of every kind passed under Goebbels' control, and their administration, as well as the excitement they offered, somewhat distracted him.

After Hitler came to power, Goebbels was free to address himself to propaganda abroad: but here he ran into all kinds of difficulties. Among these were the diplomats, who did not want to relinquish any of their responsibilities; the poverty of Nazi ideology and its restricted, nationalist appeal; the lack of international experience of the Nazi leaders themselves. Nazi propaganda abroad, unless it was directed at German minorities, was mostly ineffective. On the whole, Goebbels and the art of propaganda entered the war relatively weakened. There had also been a

Left: Hitler and Himmler, the two most powerful men in wartime Germany. Throughout the war the latter's prestige and influence grew, so that Hitler could describe him as 'the pillar upon which my house stands'.

crisis in Goebbels' personal life: he had asked Hitler, in the summer of 1938, to be relieved of his duties. The Minister of Propaganda wanted to divorce his wife, one of the leading Nazi ladies, to marry a young Czech actress, Lida Baarova.

Himmler's rise, on the other hand was less spectacular. It was steady, slow and somewhat stealthy. In 1933, Himmler became the Chief of Munich police; in that year, he set up the first concentration camp in Dachau. The SS was still nominally a part of the SA, and Ernst Roehm was still the chief of staff of the stormtroopers. On June 30, 1934, during the Night of the Long Knives, Himmler and the SS smashed the power of the SA, on Hitler's orders. The SS then came directly under Hitler's command: Himmler thus gained direct access to the *Fuehrer*. In 1934 he also gained control of the Secret Police of the State of Prussia, the dreaded Gestapo. By 1936, Heinrich Himmler had control of all the police forces in Germany.

The war, we shall have on occasion to see, vastly added to Himmler's empire; though Goebbels' powers increased as well during the war, he had to fight hard to find his way back into Hitler's favour. By skilfully using the German minorities in central and eastern Europe, Nazi propaganda, linked with the party organisation, was able to shatter the established order in that area. But after it had achieved its most impressive victories—in the Rhineland, in Austria and in Czechoslovakia—a certain exhaustion appeared in the Nazi propaganda effort. It was also, in the summer of 1939, pursuing too many objectives: it was becoming diffuse, from having once been ruthlessly concentrated.

Hitler always grasped for any instruments which could underpin and extend his power. For some time before the beginning of the war, he had fixed his attention on the army: in the months before the war, Goebbels and his Ministry had to give much of their time and resources to publicity on behalf of the army. After the outbreak of the war the Ministry of Propaganda had to hand over some of its functions to the *Abteilung Wehrmachtpropaganda* of the OKW, the High Command. Central direction of the press disappeared after the outbreak of the war and the Propaganda Ministry became largely responsible for disseminating the material fed to it by the army. Though

Propaganda for Europe

propaganda had to move into a subordinate place in the summer of 1939, the territory in which it operated vastly increased. As one country after another fell, Goebbels gradually became responsible for information media in the whole of occupied Europe.

Propaganda, after all, could not win the

Overpage: German propaganda in French, illustrating the agricultural and industrial riches to be found and won in the Soviet Union. The poster also states that the surface area conquered by the German forces was six times that of Britain.

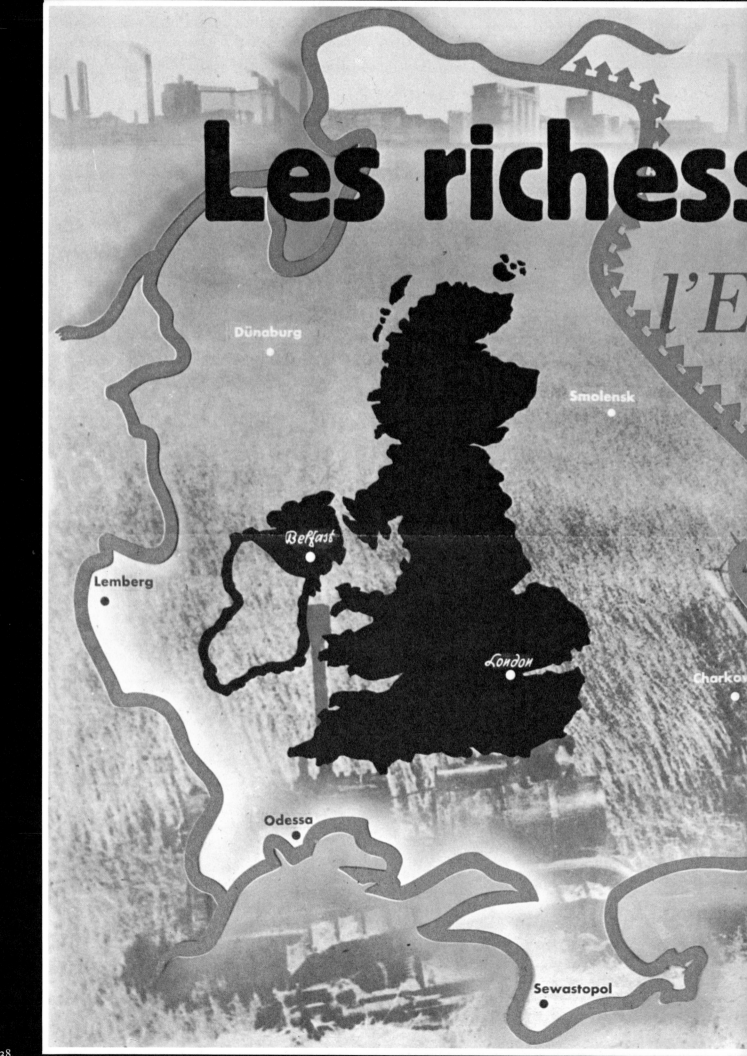

Les richess
l'E

Dünaburg

Smolensk

Lemberg

Belfast

London

Charkow

Odessa

Sewastopol

es de l'est

rope les a gagnées!

La superficie
conquise représente
six fois celle de l'Angleterre

war for Hitler; nor could it do much to save Germany from defeat. (The peoples of occupied Europe came into direct contact with the realities of German control: their attitudes were formed by this contact rather than by the outpourings of Nazi-controlled propagandists.) But propaganda could try to keep up the morale of the Germans and in this area it scored some notable points. Indeed it may have helped to make the war last longer. It is difficult precisely to assess the morale of a nation, even using the instruments available at the present: opinion polls, audience research and all the other innovations of social science. But the war took place well before the sampling of public opinion was established in Europe as either a game or a science: though samples were taken, they were either primitive and limited, or totally misleading. On the whole, more and probably better information on the attitudes of the Germans in the war has survived in the files of Himmler's *Sicherheitsdienst* (SD) than anywhere else: the papers of the Propaganda Ministry were severely depleted towards the end of the war. Nevertheless, both Goebbels and Hitler had very sensitive

Two moonlight nights

antennae with regard to popular mood; their actions at any given time—often reactions to the mood of the people—are an extremely good indicator of the movements of the German mass psyche during the war.

It had started badly: on the day of the invasion of Poland, or two days later, when Britain and France came into the war, there were no wild scenes of enthusiasm in Berlin, comparable to August 1914. On September 3, 1939, William Shirer, an American correspondent in Berlin, wrote in his diary: 'It has been a lovely September day, the sun shining, the air balmy, the sort of day the Berliner loves to spend in the woods or on the lake nearby. I walked in the streets. On the faces of the people astonishment, depression. Until today they have been going about their business pretty much as usual. There were food cards and soap cards and you could not get any petrol and at night it was difficult stumbling around in the blackout. But the war in the east has seemed a bit far away to them —two moonlight nights and not a single Polish plane over Berlin to bring destruction —and the papers saying that German troops have been advancing all along the line, that the Polish airforce has been destroyed. Last night, I heard Germans talking of the 'Polish thing' lasting but a few weeks, or months at the most. Few believed that Britain and France would move.'

On the same day, a decree was issued which made listening to foreign broadcasts illegal; and Heydrich instructed the *Gestapo* on matters of internal security of the state in wartime. Any attempt, Heydrich wrote, to undermine the unity of the people would be severely punished: anyone who was in doubt as to the final outcome of the war was to be arrested. Imprisonment and fear were meant to maintain the morale of the people: arrests were to be followed immediately by interrogation. Defeatism was to be eradicated

Above: The *Reichsfuehrer* SS, Heinrich Himmler, talking to German settlers on their way to farm in the occupied Russian territories. Resettlement played an important part in National Socialist policies toward victors and vanquished.

by admonition, or worse. Here again, other agencies—in this case the *Gestapo*—were poaching on Goebbels' preserves. Goebbels himself was unhappy about the war: he said that Hitler would 'soon listen to his Generals only and it will be very difficult for me.'

Key reports on the war situation were published in the form of communiqués of the Army High Command: in this process the Ministry of Propaganda played only a small part. And as long as victory followed victory, there was no need for a special propaganda effort: the morale of the nation floated on the waves of military success. A security service report of June 24, 1940, confidently asserted that 'Under the impression of the great political events and under the spell of military success, the whole German nation is displaying an inner unity and a close bond between the front and the homeland which is unprecedented. The soil is no longer fertile for opposition groups. Everyone looks up to the *Fuehrer* in trust and gratitude, and to his armed forces pressing forward from victory to victory.'

Poland had fallen with the greatest of ease; France was defeated; many of the smaller countries of western Europe were occupied. Plans had been made for the invasion of Britain: but here, the general mood of

euphoria was broken. On September 4, 1940 —a year after the outbreak of the war— Hitler, in another of his *Sportpalast* performances, issued a stern warning to the British. 'If people in England are at the moment highly inquisitive,' Hitler shrieked at one point, 'and ask "Well, why doesn't he come?" I say to them: "Don't worry, he's coming!"' One shouldn't go on being so inquisitive.' But in the first year of the war, the Germans had been spoilt: they had come to expect too much of their leader. Early in October 1940, another security report suggested that large sections of the population did not much appreciate what they read in the press and the radio (was that a thrust of the *Sicherheitsdienst* aimed at Goebbels?) and that they were impatient about the coming of the 'big blow' against Britain.

But the blow against Britain never came, and soon Hitler's thoughts started turning elsewhere. By December 18, 1940, his directions for the invasion of Russia had been issued; after postponements, the campaign was finally launched on June 22, 1941. Demands of military secrecy had of course ruled out a preparatory campaign; the Nazi-

Right: A historic occasion – Goebbels proclaiming to the German people on June 22, 1941, that the invasion of the Soviet Union had begun. The National Socialists regarded radio as an important method of propaganda; as a result, they took considerable trouble in perfecting their techniques.

Soviet Pact of 1939 was still in force when the German army crossed the border into the Soviet Union; the operation against Russia was not expected to last long. The propagandists themselves seemed, at first, to have been taken by surprise: they simply repeated Hitler's arguments on the necessity for action against the Soviet Union, and on the British-Bolshevik conspiracy against Germany.

The first instructions to newspaper editors from the Ministry of Propaganda, on June 22, were therefore hesitant: 'Unfortunately we had been unable to prepare the German nation, as on previous occasions for the forthcoming decisions: this must now be done by the press. It must provide intelligible reasons, because it is politically educated, and the nation is not. We must make it clear that this (the attack on Russia) does not represent a change. Reporting on Russia was

Hate for England

banned for months, so that the press would be spared difficulties during the necessary switch (of policy). Now at last we can speak fairly of hypocrisy, by which the Soviets tried to deceive us for many years. The true feelings, which the German nation instinctively entertains towards Bolshevism, must be freed again. Bolshevism has waited for its hour. We have proof that it would have stabbed us in the back at a suitable moment.'

Four days later, on June 26, 1941, the *Sicherheitsdienst* reported that the initial state of shock, noticeable especially among the women, which followed the invasion of Russia, lasted only a few hours. After that, 'as a result of the comprehensive campaign of enlightenment, an attitude of calm and confidence generally spread'. References to Napoleon and the fate of his armies in Russia had been, the SD agents reported, very rare. Nevertheless, 'The events in the east have injected into the population a new degree of bitterness and hate towards England. They are now again longing for the day on which the attack on the island will at last begin.' The theory of British-Bolshevik conspiracy did, after all, prove popular.

Whereas popular reaction to the attack on the Soviet Union was swift and strong, the entry of the United States into the war against Germany failed to make a similar impact. The leaders of the Third *Reich* had learned nothing from the mistakes of their predecessors in World War I: the strategic thinking of the Germans was firmly fixed on Europe, and on the continental landmass; in both wars, the global connections had not much meaning for them. On the occasion of the second entry of America into a European war, an SD report of December 15, 1941, indicated that no-one was very surprised by

Roland Freisler, President of the People's Court, opening the hearing against those accused of taking part in the July bomb plot. The backlash against all opposition which occurred after the abortive attempt on Hitler's life showed the strength of the forces of coercion.

Germany's declaration of war on America, and that it simply officially confirmed the *status quo*. 'Only among the peasantry were there a very few who reacted with surprise and with a certain anxiety about the addition of another opponent.'

The actions of Hitler did indeed have a certain perversity about them; when attack against one country was frustrated, he turned round and attacked another. The advance on Moscow had run into difficulties and, with it, faith in swift victory through *Blitzkrieg*; war on America was then declared. Until then Goebbels had been marking time, and busied himself with various projects as best he could. He toured armament factories in the Ruhr; received Japanese youth leaders; founded a prestige magazine for intellectuals; interested himself in the sexual needs of foreign workers in Germany. But then, early in 1942, the interests of the Minister of Propaganda acquired a new sense of direction. Hitler apparently asked him to write a report on the subject of defeatism in high places.

There were signs some time before the Stalingrad defeat that the war was turning sour for the Germans. On April 26, 1942, Hitler spoke to the *Reichstag*; after the speech, Goering introduced a new bill giving Hitler full executive legislative and judiciary powers. Reports on the reactions of the public to the event which reached the Ministry of Propaganda were not all favourable. The people were asking why Hitler was given plenary powers, and why he had criticised conditions at home so sharply. There was

Cry of a drowning man

some concern about the military situation; Hitler had spoken of another winter campaign. As far as the mood of the people was concerned, early in the spring of 1942, there was a touch of chill in the air.

On April 28, 1942, Goebbels wrote in his diary that 'the *Fuehrer*'s speech represents, as it were, the cry of a drowning man.' In his public speaking, Goebbels chose a different technique from that of Hitler; from the end of 1942, Goebbels began to conduct a propaganda of deep pessimism. It was modelled on Churchill's 1940 approach, and was designed to mobilise the total resources of the country. On January 4, 1943, he told the departmental heads of his Ministry: 'I myself want to see disappear from my mind and the mind of the Ministry the idea that we cannot lose the war. Of course we can lose the war. The war can be lost by people who will not exert themselves; it will be won by those who try hardest. We must not believe fatalistically in certain victory; we must take a positive view.'

Goebbels appealed to the deepest instincts of the nation: to hate and fear, to the need for self-preservation. On November 12, 1942, for instance, he disclosed that, 'We want our nation to be filled not only with deep love for its community, but also with an infernal hate of all the men and all the forces who attack this community, and who want to destroy it. When somebody objects that this is un-German, then I have to say: an exaggerated objectivity is a fault of the German character.'

An important victory on the eastern front was needed: Stalingrad did not provide it. The defeat was a devastating blow for the morale of the nation. A *Sicherheitsdienst* report of January 28, 1943, suggested that 'At the moment the whole nation is deeply shaken by the impression that the fate of the Sixth Army is already sealed and by concern about the further development of the war situation. Among the many questions arising from the changed situation, people ask above all why Stalingrad was not evacuated or relieved and how it was possible, only a few months ago, to describe the military situation as secure . . . Fearing that an unfavourable end of the war is now possible, many compatriots are seriously thinking about the consequences of defeat.'

Goebbels' second rise to prominence in fact coincided with the fall of the Third *Reich*. He delivered the 'total war' speech in the Berlin *Sportpalast* on February 18, 1943. He said that the situation reminded him of that of the *Kampfzeit*, before the Nazis came into power. As before 1933, the Germans were again hard pressed: again there were wounded men in the halls where Goebbels was speaking. 'Before me sit rows of German wounded from the eastern front who had their arms and legs amputated, men with shattered limbs, men blinded in the war, who had been brought here by their Red Cross nurses, men in the best years of their lives . . .'

A Spartan way of life and a total war effort was Goebbels' offer to the Germans in the first months of 1943. They were to do the fighting, and the whole of occupied Europe

An increase in brutality

would work for them. Goebbels fully committed himself to postponing Germany's defeat, and he may well have succeeded in doing so, against many odds. The debits included a desolate, uncaring Hitler; a population which itself was going the same way; defeat after defeat. Goebbels knew that he had been beaten at his own game; that the Nazi monopoly of information, not only in occupied Europe, but in Germany itself, had been broken. On May 25, 1943, he recorded in his diary that 'There are reports . . . that many people are again listening to foreign radio stations. The reason for this, of course, is our completely obscure news policy which no longer gives people any insight into the war situation. Also, our reticence regarding Stalingrad and the fate there of our missing soldiers naturally leads the families to listen to Bolshevik radio stations, as these always broadcast the names of German soldiers reported as prisoners.'

Though the means of persuasion may have failed Hitler towards the end of the war,

The final solution in action – Polish Jews being shot by members of the *Einsatzgruppe*. These mobile units began in 1939 and accounted for many hundreds of thousands of lives by shooting, gassing and beating.

Goebbels, the last remaining pillar of the crumbling Nazi order, never did. The means of coercion went on being used until the bitter end, with increasing brutality. Heinrich Himmler, however, made an attempt to sue for peace, before he escaped out of the beleaguered capital. In Hitler's last testament, we have seen, Himmler was

Himmler's armed force

struck out of the list of the heirs of the *Fuehrer's* diminishing powers.

Coercion was used, in the Nazi state, both to punish political opposition and to intimidate the people; it had a number of other uses such as, for instance, the provision of a foreign labour force for Germany's industries. Though Goebbels pursued a more or less unitary information policy in Germany and in the occupied territories, Himmler, on the other hand, offered a number of different security policies. The hand holding the whip was given more freedom of action in eastern than in western Europe. In the East Himmler was not only responsible for the security of the Nazi system; his task was to produce a better and more dominant

German race.

He became, in October 1939, 'Commissioner for Strengthening Germandom', with responsibility for resettlement in conquered Poland; in 1943, he was appointed the Minister of the Interior. The last desperate *levée en masse* which Hitler ordered in October 1944, was to be carried out under Himmler's command. Himmler's only failure was his bid to extend, early in 1941, the *Gestapo's* power over the German courts of justice. Otherwise, Himmler's control over both criminal and political police had been established already on the outbreak of the war; he was the master of the *Schutzstaffel* as well of the *Reichssicherheitshauptamt*, the central Security organisation. Himmler's SS came to supplement provincial administration: for every *Gauleiter* in every *Gau*, there was a high SS leader. Himmler even challenged the monopoly of the army to fight for Germany and of industry to supply Germany's economy. The *Waffen*-SS—the armed force of the SS—was formally established in 1940, when it comprised three divisions. By the end of the war, there were 35 *Waffen*-SS divisions. The concentration camps, for which Himmler was also responsible, developed into a great industrial

empire during the war.

On the whole, Hitler allowed or encouraged the expansion of Himmler's power. The *Waffen*-SS spiked the army's guns; but, most important, the SS ran the kind of state Hitler needed. Though the legal system was subservient to the Nazi regime, Hitler needed an organisation which would be free of bureaucratic and other restraints. The SS became such an organisation. Though it was independent of the state, it controlled an important organ of the state: the police, including the *Gestapo*. The struggle between Himmler and the Minister of the Interior, Frick, which had taken place in the years 1935 and 1936, ended in Himmler's victory.

The *Reichsfuehrer-SS* therefore controlled the concentration camps as well as the sources of supply for the camps—the

Heydrich's growing power

police—and a considerable intelligence network. In 1944, his only rival in the intelligence field, Admiral Canaris, was forced to disband his *Abwehr*, thus leaving Himmler the sole master of all security and intelligence operations of the Third *Reich*. At one point,

however, Himmler came near to being pushed out of his commanding position. Reinhard Heydrich was made the head of the *Reichssicherheitshauptamt*. It meant that Heydrich came to control the *Gestapo*, the *Kripo* (the criminal police) and the SD, which soon became a state rather than a party organisation. This gave Heydrich direct access to Hitler, and considerable freedom of action. Himmler depended on Heydrich's judgement and intelligence; he was apparently unable to stand his own ground in Heydrich's presence.

In September 1941 Heydrich added another office to those he already held: he became the Acting *Reich* Protector of Bohemia and Moravia. He commuted between Prague and Berlin: the register of telephone calls between Himmler and Heydrich's offices show the degree of dependence of Himmler on Heydrich. But fate was slowly moving towards Heydrich's destruction. It was ironical that Himmler himself had given a reference of good character to Paul Thuemmel, a friend of his youth, and a senior officer in the *Abwehr* based in Prague. Thuemmel was born in Landshut, where Himmler had spent his youth; Himmler knew his parents well and knew Thuemmel

as a good Nazi party member. Himmler said so when the *Gestapo* in Prague started making enquiries about Thuemmel. In fact, Thuemmel had been one of the main contacts for the Czechoslovak intelligence services since before the war; he remained in

The Final Solution

constant touch with them when they moved to London after the outbreak of the war. It was in London that the decision was made by the Czechoslovak government in exile to assassinate Reinhard Heydrich. On May 27, 1942, two British-trained parachutists fatally injured Heydrich on his way to the airport.

Though Himmler cried when he heard the news of Heydrich's death, his only serious rival was in fact eliminated. Himmler could go on administering his empire undisturbed, assisted by subservient men. A few months before his death, Heydrich had attended the Wannsee conference on January 20, 1942, which was to make arrangements for the 'final solution' of the Jewish problem. There, he had staked his own claims. According to the minutes of the conference, 'the Chief of the Security Police and the SD, SS *Obergruppenfuehrer* Heydrich, began by announcing his appointment by the Reichs-Marschall Goering as the agent responsible for the preparation of the final solution of the European Jewish question . . .'

The 'final solution' meant the deportation of the Jews to territories in the east and the destruction of those who were unable to contribute to Germany's war effort. When the war started going badly for the Germans, the Nazi régime asked for far-reaching provisions for tightening their security and for the exploitation of all the resources available to them. Under Adolf Eichmann's command, Oswald Pohl was in charge of the economic administration of the concentration camps. He was a parsimonious man, and a former paymaster captain in the navy. Photographs of the by-products of mass extermination, including mountains of toothbrushes, shaving brushes, spectacles and dentures, which used to belong to the inmates of the camps, bear witness to the neatness and thrift of Pohl's administration, where nothing was ever wasted. He was given the impossible task of making starving and weak men and women work efficiently and operate the whole system of expendable labour.

Early in the spring of 1942 concentration

The concentration camps

camps—apart from the Jews, they contained members of the anti-Nazi opposition from all over Europe—became forced labour camps. The prisoners were either on hire to war production factories, or were employed by the SS in their own industries. Special extermination camps were built, at the same time: Auschwitz, Birkenau, Belsen, Treblinka. Before the war, the number of detainees—they were members of the German opposition to Hitler—were not above 10,000; in 1939, 25,000 prisoners were being held in the concentration camps and some 100,000

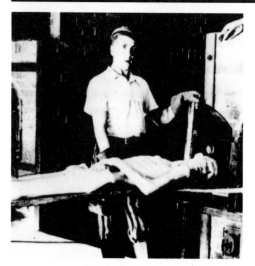

Left: The stark realities of anti-semitism. An emaciated body for burning in the ovens of Auschwitz concentration camp.

Right: These were the men behind the system of control of the Home Front in 1939. Arthur Nebe, Director of Criminal Police, on the left, sitting at a conference with Himmler, centre, and Heydrich. Nebe was later to be implicated in the bomb plot against Hitler of July, 1944.

Below: Planning the extermination. Himmler and Kaltenbrunner, on the right, inspecting the concentration camp of Mauthausen, and being shown the quarry.

in 1940. On April 30, 1942 the Chief of the SS Office, Economics and Administration, reported that:

'1' At the outbreak of the war there existed the following concentration camps:

(a) Dachau	1939	4000 prisoners, today 8000
(b) Sachsenhausen	1939	6500 prisoners, today 10,000
(c) Buchenwald	1939	5300 prisoners, today 9000
(d) Mauthausen	1939	1500 prisoners, today 5500
(e) Flossemburg	1939	1600 prisoners, today 4700
(f) Ravensbrück	1939	2500 prisoners, today 7500

'2. In the years 1940 to 1942, nine further camps were erected: (a) Auschwitz, (b) Neuengamme, (c) Güsen, (d) Natzweiler, (e) Gross Rosen (f) Lublin, (g) Niederhagen, (h) Shutthof, (i) Arbeitsdorf.'

Though the formal acceptance of genocide by the Nazi party did not take place before 1941, when it was very closely linked in the mind of Heinrich Himmler with the invasion of Russia, the SS had started gaining its experience with mass murder in 1939. In October that year, Himmler was requested by Hitler to assist in a euthanasia programme for the mentally sick. Two years later, some 60,000 patients in mental asylums throughout Germany had been killed. In August 1941 the experiment was stopped after protests, especially from the churches. In any case, another similar programme was then beginning, this time in the occupied territories in Russia.

Himmler and the SS were to look after 'political' and security administration of the occupied territories in the east and they did so with the assistance of special units, the *Einsatzgruppen*. Otto Ohlendorf, who was in charge of such a group, made the following sworn statement: 'In June 1941, I was appointed by Heinrich Himmler to lead one of the special action groups which were then being formed to accompany the German armies in the Russian campaign... Himmler stated that an important part of our task consisted in the extermination of Jews—women, men and children—and of communist functionaries... When the German army invaded Russia I was leader of Action Group D in the Southern Sector . . . it liquidated approximately 90,000 men, women and children.'

In November 1945, at the trial of the Nazi

5,700,000 Jewish victims

war criminals at Nuremburg, the indictment gave the figure of 5,700,000 Jewish victims. Though the figure has been subsequently questioned, it is certain that at least five million Jews were murdered by the SS in the course of the 'final solution'. Again, at Nuremburg, the French prosecution gave the figure of the number of hostages taken from the civilian population and shot by the Germans in revenge for attacks on the occupation forces: the figure was 26,660. In the Soviet Union, at least seven million civilians were killed during the war. It has

been impossible to estimate the exact figure of the losses suffered by the civilian population of Europe at the hands of Himmler and his assistants in murder.

Nevertheless, in the mind of Himmler, administration of death and the preservation of life, in the manipulative way of the livestock breeder, went hand in hand. When the Jews started being evicted from Poland, and Himmler's SS doctors embarked on the euthanasia programme, Himmler issued the *Lebensborn* decree on October 28, 1939, in the belief that 'every war is a drain on the best blood . . . Beyond the bounds of bourgeois laws and customs it will now become the general task, even outside the marriage bond, for German women and girls of good blood, not in frivolity but in deep moral earnestness, to become mothers of children of soldiers going to war . . .' On the one hand, Himmler pledged himself and the SS to look after all children of pure blood, legitimate or bastards, whose fathers died fighting; on the other hand, he ordered the hanging of a Polish farm labourer who had had sexual relations with a German woman.

The *Lebensborn* decree had, however, to be supplemented. On January 30, 1940, Himmler had to correct misunderstandings which the decree had given rise to: 'The worst misunderstanding concerns the paragraph which reads: "Beyond the limits of bourgeois laws and conventions . . ."

Breeding the pure race

According to this, as some people misunderstand it, SS men are encouraged to approach the wives of serving soldiers. However incomprehensible such ideas may be to us, we must discuss it. What do those who spread or repeat such opinions think of German women? Even if in a nation of 82 million people some man should approach a married woman from dishonourable motives or human weakness, two parties are needed for seduction . . .'

Finally, on August 15, 1942, the 'SS Order to Last Sons' was issued:

'1. As last sons you have been withdrawn from the frontline by the *Fuehrer*'s orders. This step has been taken because nation and state have an interest in your families not dying out.

'2. It has never been the way of SS men to accept fate and not to contribute anything to change it. It is your duty to ensure as quickly as possible by producing children of good blood that you are no longer last sons.

'3. Endeavour to guarantee in one year the survival of your ancestors and your families so that you may be available once again to fight in the frontline.'

The *Lebensborn* and subsequent orders did not unfortunately make Himmler the laughing-stock of the Third *Reich*. He continued to be obeyed and feared; breeding, race, and associated subjects continued to add ideological zeal to his actions. The ideology of pure race justified the breeding as well as the killing.

When in October 1939 Hitler appointed Himmler *Reich* Commissioner for Strengthening Germandom his first function was to replace Jews and Poles in the eastern provinces, annexed by Germany, by German settlers. Himmler was able to establish his own administration in the occupied territories, and put his theories into practice. On February 6, 1940, General Blaskowitz, commander of the *Ober-Ost* region in former Poland, and by no means a hard opponent of Hitler's regime, wrote that: 'It is misguided to slaughter tens of thousands of Jews and Poles as is happening at present; because, in view of the huge population, neither the concept of the Polish state nor the Jews will be eliminated by doing so. On the contrary, the way in which this slaughter is carried out is causing great damage; it is complicating the problems and making them more dangerous . . .'

The war in eastern Europe opened up new vistas before Himmler and the SS: in an

A war of extermination

address to SS leaders, Himmler laid down the guidelines for their behaviour in Slav Europe: 'One basic principle must be the absolute rule for the SS man: we must be honest, decent, loyal, comradely to members of our own blood and to nobody else. What happens to a Russian or to a Czech does not interest me in the slightest. What the nations can offer in the way of good blood of our type we will take, if necessary by kidnapping their children and raising them here with us . . . Whether 10,000 Russian females fall down from exhaustion while digging an anti-tank ditch interests me only insofar as the anti-tank ditch for Germany is finished . . . We Germans, who are the only people in the world who have a decent attitude towards animals, will also assume a decent attitude towards the human animals . . .'

Himmler echoed the sentiment, which was expressed in Hitler's 'order of the day' of October 2, 1941: 'this enemy does not consist of soldiers but to a large degree only of beasts'. Hitler had been making a sharp distinction between the war in the west and in the east: when he talked, for instance, to the Commanders-in-Chief of the Armed Forces on ideological warfare a few months before the launching of the campaign against Russia, he described the forthcoming invasion as 'a struggle between two *Weltanschaungen*'. Hitler described Bolshevism as the equivalent of social delinquency; the war as a 'war of extermination'. Bolshevik Commissars and the Communist intelligentsia had to be destroyed: 'In the east toughness now means mildness for the future', Hitler explained to his senior Commanders.

Acute antisemitism and weird racial theories had been Hitler's gift to the Nazi movement from the early days of their association; now, when enormous tracts of territories in the east were under German occupation, eccentric theories were being translated into an appalling practice. Himmler, we have seen, had come to his disastrous conclusions in the domain of racial theory before Hitler and the Nazi movement came to power; during the war, Himmler was responsible for administering the practice of terror.

The directive on the administration of the 'final solution' of the Jewish problem, or on the activities of the *Einsatzgruppen* in Russia, of course remained largely hidden from public view during the war; the criminality of the regime was known chiefly to those who were taking a part in the crime. It was however reflected in the ideological propaganda during the war. Though Goebbels tended to mock Rosenberg and other theorists of race, the theme concerning the subhumanity of the enemy in the east—of the Slav *Untermensch* —was pushed hard by the Nazi propagandists. Photographs of Red Army prisoners of war were constantly appearing in German newspapers, on posters, in newsreels. They usually contrasted with clean-cut, cleanshaven defenders of western civilisation: the threat from the east was there, for everyone to see.

There were, however, indications that Goebbels was trying to revise the intellectual standards of Nazism. It had long been an anti-intellectual movement: the capture of the masses, the lowest common denominator, and how to appeal to it, were its main concerns. On May 26, 1940, the first number of *Das Reich* appeared in Berlin, under Goebbels' sponsorship. It was intended to appeal to the *denkende* Nazis—to the thought-

Military supremacy

ful, if not intellectual, members of the movement. In terms of quality journalism, this was as far as Goebbels and the Nazi journalists ever got: it presents a record of their ideas and of their ambitions. The ideas expressed in *Das Reich* were firmly based in the belief in Germany's military supremacy. In the early days of the newspaper, the

The ultimate control – a German soldier hanged by the SS in Berlin, 1945, for desertion.

Germanic Empire was seen as holding sway in the north of Europe, while in the south scope was allowed for the Roman Empire of Mussolini. Europe—the Nazis found it rather difficult to fit France into their scheme—was to be a self-contained economic unit, run on national-socialist lines, capable of resisting blockade and breaking the supremacy of Great Britain.

Until the summer of 1941, however, the Europe of Nazi propaganda had been an

Ideological crusade

elusive image with most of its outlines rather blurred. The campaign against Russia brought the image of *Festung Europa* into a sharper focus: the German press was instructed, for instance, a week after the invasion, that 'Reports from the whole world make it apparent that a rising of the whole of Europe against Bolshevism can be noted . . . Europe marches against the common enemy in a unique solidarity, and it rises, as it were, against the oppressors of all human culture and civilisation. This hour of birth of the new Europe is being accomplished without any demand or pressure from the German side . . .'

Almost all European peoples in fact took some military part in the Russian campaign —Finnish, Hungarian, Slovak and Romanian units were later joined by volunteers from Spain, Belgium, France, Holland and Norway. However insignificant the participation of these groups in Germany's war effort was, the whole of Europe was represented, by Nazi propagandists, as defending itself against the threat of *Judeo-Bolshevismus*. The Jews, who supposedly manipulated the Soviet states, were also described as the 'cement of the alliance between Soviet Russia and the Western Powers.' Somehow, all the ideological lunacies which the Nazis had been, for a long time, gathering from various corners of the European mind, started clicking into place for them in the summer of 1941.

Soon, there was to be an empire in the east; soon, the Germans were to be racially pure and therefore unbeatable; the *apartheid* lines between the Germans on the one hand and the Jews and the Slavs on the other, could now be firmly drawn. The master race was about to prevail: in Europe first, and then in the world. It is impossible to tell how many people really believed in the ideals which were held before them by their Nazi rulers. Military success and then military disaster were the hard currency of propaganda. In the end, it mattered little who believed in Nazi ideology. The master race came to fail Hitler, and he was no longer interested in its fate.

Suggested reading
E. K. Bramsted: **Goebbels and National Socialist Propaganda** (London, 1965)
The Goebbels Diaries: Translated and edited by Louis P. Lochner (London, 1948)
R. Mannell and H. Fraenkel: **Joseph Goebbels** (London, 1960)
Dr Zbynek Zeman: **Nazi Propaganda** (London, 1973)

The Economy— guns and butter

Hitler together with Germany's workers.

Robert Cecil CMG

Hitler was not interested in economics as such; for him there were no economic laws which statesmen could break only at their peril. Economics was simply the means by which certain objectives were achieved in the shortest possible time, such as hewing more stone to beautify Berlin and Linz, or driving more labour into factories to increase production of shells and aircraft. When economic problems intruded, as they soon did in the Third *Reich*, Hitler's reaction was not to modify his programme but to appoint an overseer to drive it forward: Goering headed the Four-year plan; Fritz Todt was made Minister for Armaments and Munitions and was succeeded after his death by Albert Speer.

The striking achievements of *Blitzkrieg* in 1939–41 fortified Hitler in the belief that the fighting power of the German soldier could overcome any strategic economic defects. In this rash spirit he embarked on the invasion of Russia, which led to his downfall.

Despite a total war effort, once the impetus of *Blitzkrieg* had died out, Germany was again faced, as she had been in World War I, with a long drawn-out war of attrition against a coalition of powers with superior resources at their disposal for her destruction.

Above: The production of heavy artillery in the summer of 1942. It was after this time that the war economy began its prodigious increase in output.

Left: Speer, driving force of the economy. *Above:* Hitler with Saur, Speer's indispensable aid.

Right: A steel works – The capacity of Germany's war economy was significantly stunted through lack of raw materials, including iron ore.

The Economy— guns and butter

The Economy

Who would have thought that in seven years we should have come so far from being an economically weak, even corrupt European country to the greatest military and industrial power in the world. As a result I have nothing but the greatest faith in our economic future. It is only if we fail to achieve what is so essential – living space – that I foresee difficulties. But this, gentlemen, is unthinkable, for there is no other nation on this earth who can rival our present economic miracle – and it is from economic miracles that all else derives.

Hermann Goering 1940

From the day that Hitler came to power at the end of January 1933 there was never a time when the economy of the Third *Reich* was not being directed towards war. Rearmament, by reflating the economy, helped in the solution of some of the immediate problems, such as unemployment; but from the start it was pursued for its own sake. It was to provide the solid base for Hitler's foreign policy, which, to paraphrase a favourite Nazi slogan, was to restore the unity and honour of the *Reich*.

This fundamental aim took precedence even over important elements of Nazi ideology, which before 1933 had proclaimed the intention of the NSDAP to promote the business interests of the small man and the growth of a rural population of peasants and small farmers. Instead, as rearmament got under way, big business flourished, the cities grew and the flight from the land continued. Rearmament, indeed, provided the cement for the uneasy alliance between the NSDAP, big business and the army, which marked the first three or four years of Hitler's reign. Big business made high profits and held down wages; the army expanded and officers enjoyed opportunities for advancement that had not existed since 1919. In 1934 Hitler conciliated their convergent interests by cutting down Roehm, Strasser and others who might have promoted 'the second revolution' at the expense of the traditional elitist elements.

Hitler was only biding his time. By 1935

Raw material shortage

the unstable triumvirate was beginning to give way under the economic pressures set up by the furious tempo of rearmament, upon which Hitler insisted, and his indifference to the sound economic arguments advanced by Schacht, who in 1934 became Minister of Economics, and Goerdler, who shortly afterwards took over the unenviable function of controlling prices. The core of the problem, which even Schacht's ingenuity could not overcome, lay, as in World War I, in Germany's lack of the raw materials necessary for carrying on war. In 1939 the *Reich* was dependent upon external suppliers for 45 percent or more of its vital requirements of iron ore and scrap, oil, rubber, lead, copper, chrome, tin, nickel and bauxite; imported supplies of the four last-mentioned accounted for over 90 percent of German needs. Imports of these and other commodi-

ties, even though Hitler set his face against stock-piling on the scale requested by the army, imposed an intolerable strain on foreign exchange reserves. The balance of payments could have been eased if Hitler had slowed the pace of rearmament and (as in West Germany after World War II) orientated the economy towards exports; but except during the period of profitable trading relations with the USSR from 1939 to 1941 Hitler's mind always rejected strength through production and exchange in favour of strength through conquest, which in the end destroyed his co-existence with Stalin.

The first major domestic crisis was precipitated in 1935 by a poor harvest, which necessitated use of scarce foreign currency in

A stab in the back

order to buy grain abroad. The army proposed food rationing, but Hitler refused and in this was strongly supported by his *Gauleiters* (regional leaders); the Nazi dictatorship was designed, so far as possible, to be a popular dictatorship. Even after the outbreak of war, when the coercive power of the regime had been immensely increased, Hitler never forgot that in 1918 it had been the home front that had succumbed in the face of growing privation and (according to the legend of the 'stab in the back', in which the NSDAP passionately believed) had betrayed the front-line soldiers. Hitler rejected not only the army's proposal, but also Schacht's recommendation in favour of diverting a greater proportion of resources into exports; insisting on the absolute priority of rearmament, he appointed Goering in 1936 as Plenipotentiary for the Four Year Plan, instructing him that within four years the army and the national economy must be ready for war. In the event a bare three years elapsed before the invasion of Poland. Goering's magic formula was autarky; discarding the industrialists' traditional preference for buying in the cheapest market,

Right: Hitler speaking to assembled workers in the Siemens factory in Berlin, November 1933. The National Socialists spent much effort in winning over the workers and satisfying their needs, regarding them as, in Goering's words, the 'central cog in the economic machine'.

Above: Hermann Goering opening the Four Year Plan in the *Sportspalast* in Berlin, 1936, together with other German economic leaders.

Left: Goering with miners in the Ruhr, in his capacity as Special Representative for the Four Year Plan.

whether foreign or domestic, he accepted the arguments advanced by I. G. Farben in favour of heavy investment in home production of synthetic oil, aviation spirit and rubber (*Buna*). Ignoring the opposition of Ruhr magnates, who declined to cooperate, he also set up a state-owned corporation to extract low-grade domestic ores. In each case the overriding argument was that the Reich would achieve a greater degree of independence from foreign suppliers, as well as saving foreign exchange. By this time the NSDAP was flexing its muscles and the Corporation Law of 1937 was a clear indication that big business was expected to toe the line. Cartels and price-fixing had largely eliminated free competition; the state had become the principal investor and virtually controlled the capital market. Before war broke out, the Third *Reich* had ceased to be capitalist, in the accepted sense, but had not

The army is decapitated

yet achieved a planned economy; the war forced it to move further in that direction.

Whilst the NSDAP, which now dominated the state, was acquiring a measure of control over big business, Hitler moved to decapitate the third element in the original partnership, namely the army. Late in 1937 he had allowed Blomberg, his War Minister, and Fritsch, the Commander-in-Chief of the army, to catch a glimpse of the full scope of his restless ambition. Neither General displayed any liking for what he saw and early in the

Overpage: A German poster attempting to recruit Frenchmen to work in German industry, so that they would be 'an ambassador of French quality'. During the war, foreign workers came to make up an important part of the workforce. Without them, it is almost certain that the economic miracle that was created in the later war years could not have come about. Germany's strength required the strength of the peoples that she conquered.

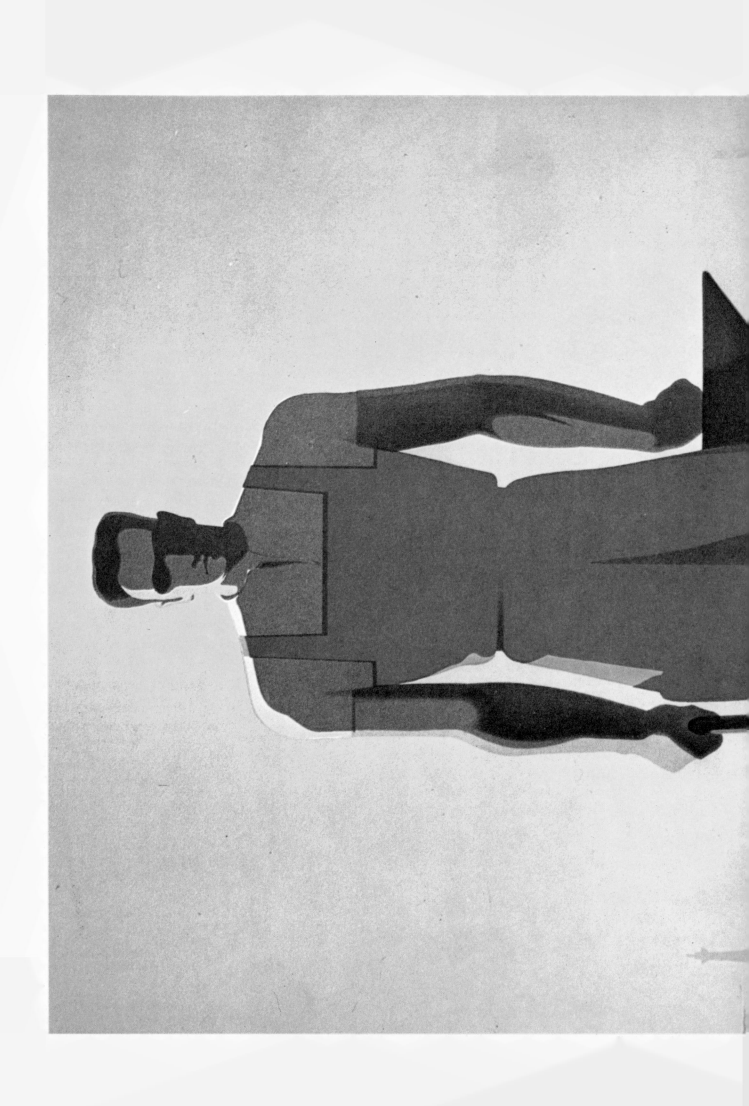

Left: Launching of the *Scharnhorst* at Wilhelmshaven, in 1936 – a visible triumph of the expanding German economy, a glorious moment.

Right: Hitler at the unveiling of the Volkswagen, the car designed for the people, which, he hoped, would 'provide the people with cheap and easy transport and the economy with necessary prestige' – one success that was to survive Hitler.

Below: A tank production line in 1939 – preview of the mechanised might to come. Production of armoured fighting vehicles increased from 224 in January 1941 to 1817 in November 1944.

following year both were removed as a result of sordid manoeuvres involving Goering and the SS. In the autumn of 1938 General Beck, the army Chief of Staff, appalled by Hitler's aggressive designs against Czechoslovakia, also tendered his resignation. With the concurrent expansion of the military units of the SS (*Waffen*-SS) it became apparent that the *chasse gardée* of military privilege was no longer secure. In due course the army was to lose its cherished right over

A lack of any system

procuring raw materials and allocating armament contracts.

The Prussian tradition had been that the General Staff was responsible for procurement and production for the Armed Forces. So little foresight had been shown at the beginning of World War I, that the Generals had had to avail themselves of the services of Jewish industrialist, Walther Rathenau, in order to remedy their shortcomings. Nonetheless, the system had the merit of imposing a single channel and eliminating competitive bidding for scarce resources and skilled labour. In 1933, however, Goering asserted his independence, insisting that the speedy expansion of the *Luftwaffe* could only be assured if it entered the market directly to supply its needs. The Navy then followed suit, as did, in due course, the *Waffen*-SS. This system—or rather lack of one—was recognised in 1935 by the *Reich* Defence Law, which provided that the *Wehrmacht* (Armed Forces) should remain in time of war responsible for their own equipment.

Some degree of coordination could still have been imposed, if the Services had been subjected to civilian financial control, as would have been normal in a constitutional state. But the Third *Reich* reversed normal practice; each branch of the Forces, after appealing, if it thought it necessary, to Hitler for special treatment, presented its requests entire to the Ministry of Finance, which then had to adjust taxation and credit policy, as far as possible, in order to cover the aggregate demand on national resources. Such chaotic procedures could not have continued indefinitely without leading to disaster; but disaster was progressively deferred by Hitler's conquests, which replenished the barrel before the danger level was reached. When war broke out, there was still no systematic allocation of raw materials to meet

An unresolved conflict

competing demands, though Hitler from time to time decreed priority for certain sectors of the armaments industry.

The lack of coordination was exacerbated by the fact that by 1938 the *Reich* Cabinet had ceased to meet. A Defence Council had been set up, of which Hitler was nominal Chairman with Goering as his deputy; but this, too, soon ceased to meet and in any case never attempted to exercise control over arms production and distribution. Nor did a Combined Chiefs of Staff Committee come into existence. The defects of this vacuum at

the heart of the military machine were aggravated by an unresolved conflict between the *Fuehrer* and his military planners about the strategic aims of the resurgent *Reich* and the means of achieving them. It was Hitler's belief that hegemony in Europe, as a first step to world power, could be won by successively isolating his opponents and defeating them singly in a series of short, sharp wars. Since each of those wars would make significantly different demands upon the *Wehrmacht* as a whole, it followed that the armaments industry had to be flexible, so that manpower and resources could be switched from one sector of production to another to meet changing strategic requirements. This concept, to which the designation *Blitzkrieg* was given (though not by Hitler), was predicated upon armament in breadth; in Hitler's eyes it had the added merit of imposing less strain on the consumer sector of production; the army were to have their guns and the people their butter.

This seemed altogether too optimistic to most of the military planners and especially to General Georg Thomas, who was their principal economic expert from 1934 to 1942, when Hitler silenced his Cassandra-like voice by removing him from his post. Thomas did not believe that Hitler could avoid a confrontation with a coalition of major powers, nor that in a long war of

Hitler shuts his eyes

attrition, as World War I had proved to be, the *Reich* could be defended without the full mobilisation of its human and economic potential. This meant austerity on the home front and armament in depth with adequate stock-piling and investment in the railways and other parts of the military infrastructure. Thomas lamented that 'Hitler shut his eyes to the need for fixed, long-range planning...' It seemed to him (as it has since seemed to some historians) that Hitler's moves were opportunistic and lacked any inner cohesion. This was to underestimate Hitler's discernment; he had seen from the outset that, as he put it, there was no solidarity in Europe, so that he could divide his opponents. He had also sufficient grasp of modern military technology to know that, whilst the *Wehrmacht's* equipment was one jump ahead of that of its enemies, they could be eliminated in quick, mobile wars, before they could apply the lessons of defeat. At first his judgment was brilliantly vindicated; Austria and Czechoslovakia fell to him without a struggle and he was able to add their un-

Overpage: **Germany's economic strength, as her leaders liked to present it to the people. This was an erroneous impression of an overwhelming agricultural and industrial might knocking at the door of Soviet Russia. Reality, however, was somewhat different, and by the time the poster was published, Germany's *Blitzkrieg* had already failed. The mailed fist was less confident.**

Europas Sieg
dein Wohlstand
der

damaged resources to those of the *Reich*. In the autumn of 1939 he added Poland to the list, whilst the Anglo-French forces remained inactive behind their fortifications. Early in 1940 Denmark, Norway, the Low Countries and France were also subdued and became available for economic exploitation.

The machine had been creaking even whilst Hitler was achieving these great successes. The invasion of Poland, brief as it was, led to a munitions crisis; instead of taking steps to rationalise production, Hitler adopted his usual expedient of appointing a Party man to get things done. His choice fell upon Fritz Todt, who had made his name building the strategic roads of the Third *Reich* and in 1938 had been put in charge of construction of the West Wall, taking over from the army which, in Hitler's opinion, lacked a proper sense of urgency. For this

Scramble for resources

purpose Todt set up on para-military lines the Organisation Todt, which Albert Speer inherited. Todt's powers were circumscribed by the fact that Goering, being in charge of the Four Year Plan, was his superior, as well as being the worst offender in the scramble for scarce resources. Although the *Wehrmacht* was not obliged to place orders with industry through Todt, he managed to impose some economies on them and in March 1940 Hitler made him Minister for Armaments and Munitions. This was the first step towards taking away from the soldiers the right to control their equipment. Todt began the process, which was later greatly extended by Speer, of giving industry and its technical experts a greater share of responsibility for weapon design and development. A Munitions Committee was set up and underpinned by special committees in the various sectors of the armaments industry; this not only tightened links with factory managements, but forced the Services to place their orders with the most efficient firms. Although the latter continued to make substantial profits, their voracity was restrained by 'fixed price' contracts. The state was at last beginning to dominate both big business and the economic operations of the *Wehrmacht*.

In July 1940, when Hitler's power was at its height, he was turning over in his mind the alternatives of invading England or invading the USSR. The very fact that he was able to contemplate these alternatives appeared to vindicate the concept of *Blitzkrieg* and armament in breadth; but by September it was clear to him that deficiencies in Navy and *Luftwaffe* denied sea-borne invasion an even chance of success and his intention to embark on 'Barbarossa' against the USSR became fixed. Hitler and many of his Generals

Top: **Fritz Todt, the Minister of Armaments, at the ceremony on the completion of submarine pens.**

Right: **The men behind the German economy in 1942. From left to right, Speer, Ley, Funck, Heinkel and Porsche.**

had grown so over-confident that the military problems of following Napoleon's footsteps in the snow did not greatly worry them; but Thomas and others had serious misgivings about the economic implications, since German industry was heavily dependent on the supply of Russian raw materials and on the transit trade, which was also assured by the Russo-German economic agreements of September 1939 and January 1941. In 1940, for example, over 600,000 tons of the total mineral oil imported by the *Reich* came from the USSR, as compared with one million tons from Romania, Germany's other main supplier. In the long term, therefore, the success of Hitler's new venture would turn on his securing the oil wells of the distant Caucasus before these could be destroyed. The immense expanse to be covered by the advancing *Wehrmacht* would also impose great strain on transport, especially as the gauge of the Russian railways differed from the German.

Against these economic counter-arguments, Hitler could point to the vast war booty won by his campaigns and the productive resources of the conquered countries. It is easy to understimate these, if only because, after the defeat of Nazi Germany, those who collaborated were either silenced, or chose to remain silent; historians and writers of memoirs have therefore tended to concentrate on the resistance to Hitler in occupied Europe. It must in all candour be said that, until 1942 at earliest, apart from scattered and gallant acts of defiance, resistance in Europe did not amount to much. It

Economic collaboration

is true that in occupied France, for example, there was a marked decline in production between 1940 and 1941; but this was mainly because Germany was exploiting the territory by deporting labour, fixing a fictitious exchange rate and imposing massive occupation costs, as well as keeping France short of iron, coal and oil. Later, the French aircraft industry was brought into the *Luftwaffe's* production programme and, after the Anglo-American bombing offensive on the *Reich* had begun to bite, the Germans attempted to increase textile production in France, in order to enable factories in Germany to concentrate on arms and munitions.

The only countries in which virtually no economic collaboration took place were Poland and Yugoslavia (apart from Croatia, where a puppet dictatorship was set up). In Poland the Nazis sought no collaboration, though they impressed slave labour. In Yugoslavia the case was different; Hitler had not at first intended to invade the country, which provided German industry with significant proportions of its intake of tin, lead, copper, aluminium, bauxite and antimony. He reversed this prudent policy after the coup of March 27, 1941, removed the Germanophile Regent and his Government. By April 13 Belgrade was in his hands; but the Bor copper mines were sabotaged and partisan movements, though often in conflict with one another, soon began to interfere with the production that the *Reich* required. In most other countries serious sabotage only started after Hitler's invasion of Russia, when Communists in occupied Europe, most of whom had observed the Comintern's instructions to promote the aims of Stalin's pact with Hitler, at last turned against the latter and became the hard core of resistance in industry. Resistance movements were a sensitive barometer of fluctuating German fortunes and, after the Soviet recapture of Stalingrad in January 1943, the ranks of the various movements were swelled by the prospect of the ultimate triumph of the anti-Hitler coalition.

Hitler, if indeed he foresaw how 'Barbarossa' would aggravate the problem of European security, would have discounted it, because the invasion, which began on June 22, 1941, and incomprehensibly took Stalin by surprise, was confidently expected to end victoriously within a few months. Instead, the bitter Russian winter found the *Wehrmacht* in December still outside the defences of Moscow and Leningrad. Failure to arm in depth worsened their plight; too little warm clothing was available; even if it had been, the railways could not have moved

The armament miracle

it to the front. Transport deficiencies deprived some factories of coke and coal; others were short of electricity. *Blitzkrieg* had failed and Hitler, with a war of attrition on his hands, was at last forced to take the measures he had so long deferred; the first decrees were issued restricting production of consumer goods and rationalising arms production. The chief beneficiary was not Thomas, whose earlier warnings were resented, nor Todt, who was killed in an air crash early in February 1942, but Speer, who succeeded him.

The achievements of Speer, though he shared in Germany's defeat, deserve comparison with those of Carnot, *l'organisateur de la victoire*. Speer, who was only 36 when he was called upon to fill one of the most vital posts in the *Reich*, had been Hitler's architect and his personal link with the *Fuehrer* remained the foundation of his power until 1944, when it began to weaken. He was more fortunate than his predecessor in that by 1942 Goering was a spent force; but he had to contend with the growing hostility of Himmler, Bormann and most of the *Gauleiters*, who, as *Reich* Defence Commissioners, were well placed to set regional and Party interests against the national need for efficiency and austerity. Nevertheless, there was still so much slack in the economy after nearly two-and-a-half years of war that striking increases in war production were recorded. Taking production for January-February 1942 as 100, a rise of 53 percent had been achieved by July of that year; 229 percent by July 1943 and 322 percent by July 1944. It was what Speer designated in a speech in the last-mentioned month as 'This armaments miracle'.

Speer soon absorbed Thomas' department of the *Wehrmacht* High Command (OKW) and was then in a stronger position to co-ordinate the demands of all three Services.

Partly through his good relations with Field-Marshal Milch of the *Luftwaffe* and Admiral Doenitz, who in 1943 replaced Raeder as Commander-in-Chief of the Navy, Speer restricted the independence of these two Services. He chaired a Committee of Three, including Milch and Paul Koerner, representing the Four Year Plan, which allocated raw materials. As pressure on manpower grew, he also used his authority to prevent the Services from calling up skilled men from vital industries.

Speer never achieved the same control over manpower that he had over industry; in March 1942 Hitler appointed a senior *Gauleiter*, Fritz Sauckel, to be Plenipotentiary for Labour. This division of authority, however inefficient, almost certainly saved Speer

Above: U-boats under construction in 1942. Only then did they receive top priority in output.

Right: Putting the finishing touches to powerful naval guns for one of Germany's new battleships.

at Nuremberg from the death sentence meted out to Sauckel. Sauckel press-ganged labour all over occupied Europe and doled it out at exiguous wages to such firms as Krupp and I. G. Farben. Workers from Poland and Russia were the worst treated; a German witness, giving evidence at Nuremberg about Krupp's camps, observed, 'The food for Eastern workers was completely inadequate.

They received 1,000 calories less per day than the minimum for Germans . . .' Whilst imported labour was being exploited in this way, it was not until 1943 that any serious attempt was made to use German female labour; indeed between 1939 and 1941 the number of women in employment actually fell.

The worst exploitation of labour occurred within the economic enclave operated by the SS. The idea of using the labour in concentration camps to enrich the SS and enable it to achieve financial independence from the state originated with Theodor Eicke, who in 1934 became Inspector-General of Camps, as well as Chief of the Death's Head units, which guarded them. It was a major factor in ensuring an ever-growing camp population at a time when political dissidence, except within the army, had ceased to represent a threat to the regime. In 1939 the various

Total War commences

camps had about 25,000 inmates, but the war greatly increased the number, on account of Himmler's assumption of control over subject populations in the East. In 1940 the numerous SS firms employing slave labour were organised in a trust under Oswald Pohl, Chief of the Main Office of SS Economic Administration. The largest of the component firms, the German Earth and Stone Works (DEST), branched out into arms production and by 1944 was even producing aircraft. DEST, like other SS operations, entirely escaped Speer's attempts at coordination. Their use of labour was notoriously inefficient, as well as offending against every canon of humanity.

Hitler's belated recognition of the implications of a war of attrition faltered in the summer of 1942; but the disaster of Stalingrad fortified his resolve. Speer found an ally in Joseph Goebbels and in mid-January 1943 Hitler signed a decree for the direction of women into war work and the combing out of able-bodied males, many of them holding posts in the massive bureaucracy of the NSDAP. In mid-February 1943 Goebbels hurled at his carefully selected audience. in the Sports palace in Berlin his famous rhetorical question: 'Is it total war you want?' There came back the answering roar of well rehearsed assent; but it came too late. By May 1944 nearly 3.3 million men were dead, missing or maimed; sullen foreign labour could not replace them, whatever means of coercion were used. In July 1944 Goebbels was made Plenipotentiary for Total War and at once clashed with Speer: were men to be withdrawn from the *Wehrmacht* to produce arms, as Speer wished, or withdrawn from industry to fight, as Goebbels insisted? The dilemma underlined the fact that the war was lost. Goebbels got his way and in October 1944 the Home Guard (*Volkssturm*) was created; but by then it did not matter.

If lack of manpower played an important part in Germany's defeat, so too did the strategic bombing of the British and American Air Forces, which were able to exploit three fatal defects in the defence of the *Reich*. First, too much vital production was located in the Ruhr and the attempt to disperse it, or bury it underground, was left too late. Secondly, Hitler and Goering, in their savage determination to trade atrocity for atrocity, insisted until early in 1944 on maintaining bomber production, long after Speer and Milch had been pleading on military and economic grounds for concentration on fighters. Thirdly, Hitler's misplaced hopes of a short war led to neglect of research, which was not reversed until February 1941; crucial innovations, such as jet-propelled fighters and rocket-projection (V2), came just too late.

In spite of these errors and a tonnage of Anglo-American bombs rising from 200,000 in 1942 to five times that weight in 1943, war production in Germany continued to rise steeply until mid-1944. Moreover, the belief of Marshal of the RAF Sir Arthur Harris that persistent bombing of German cities would destroy morale proved unfounded; the Germans, in contrast to 1918, fought to the end. The increase in production in 1944 was partly due to a switch to mass production of standardised weapons, instead of an attempt to maintain the qualitative superiority, on which Hitler had earlier insisted; but on any terms it was an astonishing achievement. An authoritative view, expressed after post-war research, was that, 'until the last six months of war the (German) army was never critically short of weapons or shells'. On the other hand, when the U.S. Eighth Air Force concentrated after May 1944 on German oil production, it soon reduced the mobility of the *Wehrmacht*; indeed shortage of aviation spirit in July 1944 came close to grounding the *Luftwaffe* and inhibited training of pilots. By that date the diminishing area of Europe over which the *Reich* exercised control was in any case fatally restricting Hitler's capacity to wage war.

As far as the war effort within the *Reich* itself is concerned, Speer has expressed the view that by 1944 armaments production had reached the maximum level that could be expected of a nation of 70 million people; that this proved inadequate to stave off defeat was due, in his opinion, to the fact that Germany confronted a hostile coalition of far greater economic potential. To this fact was attributable Anglo-American domination of the skies over the dying *Reich*, bringing with it the constant interruption of production, which we have already discussed. To this fact was attributable also the defeats and withdrawals before the Red Army on the Eastern front with the loss of weapons, munitions and vehicles on a scale that could no longer be made good by replacement. Speer concludes, however, that there was another factor determining the German collapse, which could only be ascribed to mistaken policies: 'In the years 1940 and 1941 the chance was lost to develop more efficient weapons; the precipitate introduction after 1942 of new systems of production necessarily caused technical set-backs.'

Therefore, as another captive Nazi leader wrote at Nuremberg, all questions from every side always lead back to Hitler. It was he who at the end of 1939, when the first munitions crisis lead to an investigation, remarked that, 'he had no interest in what could be produced after October 1941'. It was he who in the autumn of 1940 decided to invade the USSR before Britain had been defeated. It was he who believed that the USSR could be crushed during the summer and early autumn of 1941 before the latent threat of United States intervention could materialise. It was these misjudgments that proved fatal to the German war effort; they could not be rectified by the organising ability of Speer, nor by the pertinacity and endurance of the

Scorched earth policy

German soldier and worker.

These circumstances give a special poignancy to the struggle that developed in the latter part of 1944 between Speer and his *Fuehrer* over the latter's 'scorched earth' policy. Speer, who was prepared privately to admit, at least by August 1944, that the war was lost, wished to preserve enough plant and equipment to permit the survival of the German people. In this endeavour he was backed by the industrialists themselves and even by certain *Gauleiters*, such as Karl Kaufmann of Hamburg. But Hitler, who was, of course, seconded by Bormann, had lost faith in his people even before they lost faith in him; he was no longer interested in their survival once his own power was broken and his evil career at an end. For nearly six months Speer devised ways of circumventing Hitler's vicious orders. When in mid-March 1945 the confrontation finally occurred between the two former friends, Hitler bitterly informed his Minister: 'If the war is to be lost, the nation also will perish. This fate is inevitable. There is no need to consider the basis even of a most primitive existence any longer. On the contrary it is better to destroy even that and to destroy it ourselves. The nation has proved itself weak, and the future belongs to the stronger Eastern nation.'

Hitler's Viking funeral, which followed his suicide on April 30, 1945, was consummated with 180 litres of scarce petrol, which had with difficulty been collected in the area of the besieged Chancellery in Berlin. Three days later a message recorded by Speer was broadcast, appealing to the German people in their own interests to produce food, repair communications and keep famine at bay. It was a message of hope, marking the end of Nazi nihilism. It opened the way for a new era, in which the creative and productive capacities of the German people could again be employed in the cause of prosperity and peace.

Suggested reading
W. Carr: **Arms, Autarky and Aggression** (London, 1972)
B. Carroll: **Design for Total War** (The Hague, 1968)
A. S. Milward: **The German Economy at War** (London, 1965)
A. Schweitzer: **Big Business in the Third Reich** (London, 1964)
A. Speer: **Inside the Third Reich** (London, 1970)
C. Webster and N. Frankland: **The Strategic Air Offensive against Germany** (London, 1961)

Das Heer—
an army of strengths and weaknesses

Blitzkrieg in Russia, 1941.

Richard Humble

Long before Hitler became Chancellor of Germany, the German army had begun the work of recovery from the humiliation of 1918. The very restrictions imposed on it by the Treaty of Versailles helped it to become more efficient and enabled it to develop new strength. In the early 1930s, there was some balance of power between the army leaders and Hitler: they both had need of each other. But in the five years after the death of Hindenburg, in 1934, the relationship tipped heavily in favour of Hitler. Perhaps it was as well that it did so: again and again, events proved Hitler right and the army leaders wrong.

Meanwhile, Hitler kept his promise to give Germany powerful armed forces, building up the army to strengths undreamed of by its own experts. Events were to show that the German army was not always the well-oiled war machine that it is usually thought to have been but its mistakes were dwarfed by those of Germany's enemies between 1939 and 1941. Soviet Russia, however, proved too tough and the German army found itself committed to a front from which there was no escape.

Above: The ignominy of defeat. Infantry during the hard winter fighting that took place in Russia in 1941.

Above: The scent of victory. A parade in Berlin during the happier days of *Blitzkrieg* success.

Left: Advancing under heavy fire.

Right: Infantry street fighting during the *Blitzkrieg* campaign in Norway, 1940. Such fighting was often the most bitter undertaken by the army.

Das Heer —
an army of strengths
and weaknesses

> *The army must fight on. Waver, and Germany is lost ......*
> *Throughout the centuries it has been shown that German*
> *power rests upon her military might, upon her ability to move*
> *qualitatively, but not necessarily numerically, superior armies*
> *around the Continent of Europe. We shall*
> *not be the ones to fail in that tradition.*
>
> ### Adolf Hitler 1941

> *The time has come to admit that the army has betrayed not*
> *only myself but also Germany. I have had*
> *too great a reliance upon its Generals.*
>
> ### attr. Adolf Hitler 1945

When the terms of the Treaty of Versailles were presented for Germany's acceptance in 1919, the victorious powers intended that never again must Germany have an army capable of waging an aggressive war. The maximum strength of the postwar German Army—the *Reichswehr*—was not to exceed 100,000 men: ten divisions, three of them cavalry and seven infantry. It could not recruit or, much more important, train, by conscription. It must have no heavy guns or tanks. Nor must it import any weapons at all.

But the Treaty could not prevent the wide acceptance of the legend that the defeat of 1918 had not been the fault of the German Army, nor dispel pride in the achievements of that Army between 1914 and 1918. Such anger that did flare out against the Army after the Armistice of 1918—soldiers and officers being insulted or beaten up for the uniform they wore—belonged to the immediate period of angry disillusionment between 1918 and 1920. The General Staff of the Army survived; and under the direction of Colonel-General Hans von Seeckt the *Reichswehr* began a period of consolidation and training.

The officers and men of the 'hundred thousand army' were taught to regard themselves as *professionals*—a hardcore force of experts, a functioning nucleus working for the future. Almost right from the signing of the Treaty the restrictions of Versailles were quietly and successfully broken. Shooting clubs trained the young civilians in marks-

An army of leaders

manship. Demobilisation and welfare departments kept the organs of mobilisation alive. And officers were sent on official visits to other countries to keep abreast with the latest military techniques. Perhaps the most important of the latter were the visits made by German 'tank enthusiast' officers such as Heinz Guderian to the Soviet tank training centre at Kazan in Russia.

A typical example of how Germany infringed the weapons restrictions may be given. In the 1920s, a team of designers from Krupp were attached to the Bofors gun company in Sweden. They came back in 1931 with the working design for one of the most famous German weapons of 1939-45: the 88mm anti-aircraft gun, renowned for its devastating punch in the anti-tank rôle.

But the most influential long-term result

of the *Reichswehr* period was the training of an 'army of leaders'. This marked a growing swing away from the old rigidity of *Junker* discipline in the Imperial German Army. It was generally agreed that a new type of fighting man was needed: a soldier who could think for himself. An Army Psychology Research Institute was set up in 1920 with a staff of seven professional psychologists. They had an uphill task in convincing 'old guard' soldiers that their newfangled doctrines were worthy of respect. But the atmosphere remained one of experimentation; and German Army Training Directions for 1931 announced that 'the individual soldier must be educated so that he is able to accomplish his tasks in battle even if left to himself. He must know that he alone is responsible for his acts and failures'. Leadership training moved up to rank with the foremost priorities and psychological criteria were applied to Army Selection Committees. Candidates for Army service before the reintroduction of conscription in 1935 were given rigorous testing in groups of four or five, scrutinised by three psychologists, a medical officer and an Army colonel. The average yearly number of candidates examined on the eve of Hitler's accession to power was in the region of 2500.

Yet there was plenty of resistance to the new ideas. An obvious one was traditional 'class prejudice' against excessive promotion from the ranks. Worst of all was the 'cavalry mentality', which is perhaps the least of the criticisms normally levelled at the German Army. Whether or not massed tanks would be accepted as a revolutionary new battlefield arm was touch and go. After 1945, Panzer virtuoso Heinz Guderian recalled his difficulties in obtaining facilities and materials for tank experiments. In 1931 he was told by the Army Inspector of Transport: 'Believe me, neither of us will ever see German tanks in operation in our lifetime', and General Beck, hailed as one of the best military brains Germany could boast, told him: 'No, no, I don't want anything to do with you people. You go too fast for me.'

The *Reichswehr* period, then, was a blend of old and new with the new predominating. It was a constructive, forward-looking period. And Brigadier Desmond Young has summed it all up by calling the German Army of the period 1920-1933 as 'the reinforcement, the steel frame, on to which the concrete of conscripts could quickly be poured, if and when it became possible to reintroduce conscription'. Ingeniously cutting their coat ac-

cording to the cloth permitted by the hated limitations of Versailles, the leaders of the German Army worked consciously on the shape of things to come.

The German Army, which prided itself on its obsession with keeping out of politics, was in fact deeply involved with the accession to power of Hitler in January 1933. The President who made Hitler *Reich* Chancellor was the living embodiment of the Army's

Top left: Manoeuvres in 1932. The *Reichswehr* was extremely interested in the tactical and strategic possibilities of mobility and of armour. The Versailles Treaty prohibited Germany from possessing tanks, so that dummy tanks made of thin sheet plate or of canvas, which were either pushed or fitted over motor cars, were used for training and experimentation. These *Reichswehr* days were significant for the development of the *Blitzkrieg* concept.

Top right: Hitler, at the 1936 Nuremberg Rally, parading with General von Blomberg, the *Reich* War Minister.

Right: Upon the death of President Hindenberg in 1934, the armed forces swore an oath of loyalty to Hitler. The oath read: 'I swear by God this holy oath, to obey unquestionably Adolf Hitler, the supreme military leader, *Fuehrer* of the German *Reich* and its people, and to serve as a brave soldier even unto death.' The oath itself is shown in German.

Ich schwöre bei GOTT diesen heiligen Eid, daß ich dem Führer des Deutschen Reiches und Volkes ADOLF HITLER, dem Obersten Befehlshaber der Wehrmacht, unbedingten Gehorsam leisten und als tapferer Soldat bereit sein will, jederzeit für diesen Eid mein Leben einzusetzen.

Panzerkampfwagen II (Ausführung F)

Engine: Maybach six-cylinder petrol, 140-hp.
Dimensions: length 15 ft 10 ins (4·8 m); width 7 ft 4 ins (2·2 m); height 6 ft 6 ins (2 m).
Weight: 9·5 tons.
Performance: speed 25 mph (40 kph); range 125 miles (200 km).
Armament: one 2-cm KwK 30 or 38, one 7·92-mm mg.
Armour: (max.) 35-mm.
Crew: three.

History: the Panzerkampfwagen II was the type of tank used in the greatest numbers in the German attack in the West in 1940: 955 were in service out of the total tank strength of 2500. The second of a family of four types designed before World War II, the PzKpfw II, like the smaller and earlier PzKpfw I, was intended for a reconnaissance role rather than as a battle tank although its design enabled it to be developed so that improved models gave useful service until the end of the war.

A three-man vehicle, the PzKpfw II was armed with a 2-cm gun and a coaxial 7·92-mm machine gun mounted in the turret. The Ausfuehrung F (model F) illustrated, which appeared in 1941 in time to be used in the North African campaign, was similar to earlier models but was slightly better armoured, with maximum frontal protection of 35-mm.

Panzerkampfwagen III (Ausführung J)

Engine: Maybach 12-cylinder petrol, 300-hp.
Dimensions: length 18 ft 1 in (5·5 m), 21 ft (6·4 m) including gun; width 9 ft 8 ins (2·9 m); height 8 ft 3 ins (2·5 m).
Weight: 22 tons.
Performance: speed 25 mph (40 kph); range 110 miles (176 km).
Armament: one 5-cm KwK 39 L/60, two 7·92-mm mg.
Armour: (max.) 50-mm.
Crew: five.

History: intended as the principal battle tank of the German armoured formations, the Panzerkampfwagen III, which first appeared in 1936, was the mainstay of the Panzer divisions until well into 1942. Various prototypes and early production vehicles were tested. A Daimler-Benz design, the Ausfuehrung E, was the first model built in quantity and this had the now familiar suspension consisting of six smallish road wheels each side, sprung on transverse torsion bars. Although the chassis remained basically the same, the main armament and armour of PzKpfw III were considerably increased from the short barrel 3·7-cm gun and 14·5-mm protection of the earliest models to the 5-cm KwK.39 L/60 (60 calibres long) and 50-mm frontal armour of the Ausf.J of 1941, illustrated here. The PzKpfw III took part in all the major German campaigns up to 1943 and many remained in service until the end of the war.

tradition: Field-Marshal von Hindenburg. The President's son, an Army colonel, was won over by Hitler and backed the upstart's case. An Army general, Werner von Blomberg, was specially appointed Defence Minister to see to it that the Army would back Hitler. Even the man whom Hitler replaced, Schleicher, was an Army general. Basically, however, the German Army backed Hitler because its leaders could find little comfort elsewhere. Nobody else looked capable of suiting their book.

What the Army commanders wanted from Hitler above all was *reassurance*, and this they got in full measure. They were flattered again and again with Hitler's assurances that they were indeed the official arms-bearers of the *Reich*, and that no 'private army' would be allowed to usurp that rôle. Both Army and Navy looked the other way when Hitler smashed their biggest worry—Ernst Roehm's brown-shirted SA—having already suspended the constitutional liberties of the German Republic in the name of 'National Security'. Nor were either of them kept long in waiting for the reward for this connivance. Hitler became Chancellor on January 30,

A treaty is torn up

1933. The seven guarantees of individual and civil liberties were suspended on February 28. The Nazi Party was proclaimed the only political party of Germany on July 14. The SA purge—'the Night of the Long Knives'—occurred on June 30, 1934. Hindenburg died on August 2, 1934, and Hitler proclaimed himself 'Fuehrer'—President and *Reich* Chancellor—of Germany on the same day. The traditional oath of allegiance to the Head of State was transformed in an oath of allegiance to the *person* of Adolf Hitler and immediately administered. On March 16, 1935, Hitler 'tore up' Versailles, announced conscription and the new German air force—and Blomberg, effective head of the Army, practically went down on his knees to thank the *Fuehrer*.

The Army was staggered by Hitler's announcement of a new conscript Army of 36 divisions—the Army professionals, in their wildest dreams, had never hoped for more than 21. And on May 2, 1935, Army staff planners began work on Hitler's first international move: the military occupation of the Rhineland, demilitarised since the ignominy of 1918.

By the time of the denunciation of Versailles in March 1935, experiments with dummy tanks had come up with impressive results, upon which Hitler seized. With the *Fuehrer* backing the new ideas for mechanised warfare, the expansion of Germany's *Panzer* (armoured) forces began with the creation of the first three Panzer divisions in the same year. A point was made of selecting famous cavalry regiments to form the backbone of the new formations, a cunning retention of the best of the Army's old traditions. Rapid though the Army's growth was after the re-introduction of conscription, it was still dwarfed by the forces of Germany's neighbours when Hitler took the gamble of re-occupying the German Rhineland in March 1936.

Above: Hitler reviews his new tank troops on the occasion of his 50th birthday, April 20, 1939. The creation of the armoured force owed a great deal to Hitler's interest and energy in this field.

This was the move that would set the seal on Germany's repudiation of Versailles and the Army leaders were convinced that Germany's neighbours would not let Hitler get away with it. Hitler believed otherwise, but he was not taking a complete gamble: he had already seen Mussolini get away with the invasion of Abyssinia in the face of the feeble protests of the League of Nations, while France was obsessed with making the decision to sign a mutual-assistance pact with Stalin. The move into the Rhineland was made at dawn on March 7, 1936. The German forces involved were tiny: one division. The generals were worn to the point of breakdown, particularly Blomberg; the troops were under orders to pull back at once if the French moved against them. After 48 nerve-

The miracle coups

racking hours it was clear that nothing was going to happen. Hitler had pulled off the first of his 'miracle' coups and his generals had been proved utterly wrong.

Army, Navy and Air Force expansion—all three branches of the *Wehrmacht*, or 'Armed Forces', as the old *Reichswehr* was now termed—continued throughout 1937. At the close of the year an incident occurred which

Above: Hitler and the Army Commander-in-Chief, General von Fritsche, visiting manoeuvres, 1937. The experimentations that went on during these large-scale exercises were of the utmost importance in the evolving of the new aggressive *Blitzkrieg* tactics. Here, a machine gun detachment covers an attack.

Right: The confrontation of the armies, May 1940. While the Germans were outnumbered in men and equipment, the quality of their leadership, organisation, geographical concentration and tactics was to give them an easy victory.

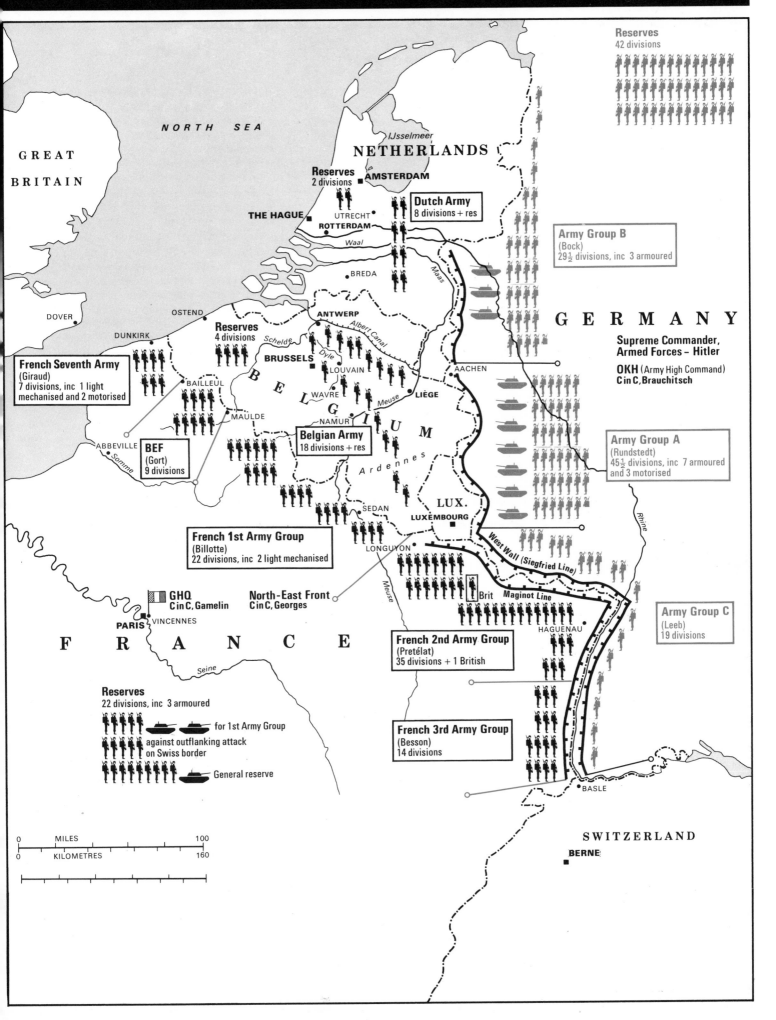

Reserves
42 divisions

NORTH SEA

IJsselmeer

NETHERLANDS

GREAT
BRITAIN

Reserves
2 divisions   AMSTERDAM

THE HAGUE   UTRECHT
ROTTERDAM

Dutch Army
8 divisions + res

Waal

BREDA

Maas

Army Group B
(Bock)
29½ divisions, inc 3 armoured

DOVER   OSTEND

DUNKIRK

Reserves
4 divisions

ANTWERP

Albert Canal

GERMANY

Schelde

French Seventh Army
(Giraud)
7 divisions, inc 1 light
mechanised and 2 motorised

BAILLEUL

BRUSSELS

Dyle

LOUVAIN

WAVRE

B
E
L
G
I
U
M

AACHEN

**Supreme Commander,
Armed Forces – Hitler**

OKH (Army High Command)
C in C, Brauchitsch

MAULDE

Meuse

LIÈGE

ABBEVILLE

Somme

BEF
(Gort)
9 divisions

NAMUR

Belgian Army
18 divisions + res

Ardennes

Army Group A
(Rundstedt)
45½ divisions, inc 7 armoured
and 3 motorised

SEDAN

LUX.
LUXEMBOURG

French 1st Army Group
(Billotte)
22 divisions, inc 2 light mechanised

LONGUYON

West Wall
(Siegfried Line)

Rhine

GHQ
C in C, Gamelin

PARIS   VINCENNES

North-East Front
C in C, Georges

Meuse

Brit   Maginot Line

Army Group C
(Leeb)
19 divisions

FRANCE

Seine

French 2nd Army Group
(Pretélat)
35 divisions + 1 British

HAGUENAU

Reserves
22 divisions, inc 3 armoured

for 1st Army Group

against outflanking attack
on Swiss border

General reserve

French 3rd Army Group
(Besson)
14 divisions

BASLE

MILES   100
0
KILOMETRES   160
0

SWITZERLAND

BERNE

73

Panzerkampfwagen IV (Ausführung H)

Engine: Maybach 12-cylinder petrol, 300-hp.
Dimensions: length 19 ft 4 ins (5·9 m), 23 ft 0 in (7 m) including gun; width 10 ft 10 ins (3·3 m); height 8 ft 10 ins (2·7 m).
Weight: 25 tons.
Performance: speed 24 mph (38 kph); range 125 miles (200 km).
Armament: one 7·5-cm KwK 40 L/48, two 7·92-mm mg.
Armour: (max.) 80-mm.
Crew: five.

History: although originally planned as a 7·5-cm gun support vehicle for the PzKpfw III to complete the quartet of basic pre-war tank models, the PzKpfw IV became the standard German battle tank of World War II. The sound principles used in the design of the chassis allowed it to be progressively up-gunned and up-armoured so that it was expedient to continue production up to the end of the war, when some 8500 had been built.

The low-velocity 7·5-cm KwK L/24 of early models of PzKpfw IV was replaced in Ausf.F onwards by longer-barrel weapons, much more effective against enemy armour. The Ausf.H illustrated here had the 7·5-cm KwK L/48, with nearly twice the muzzle velocity of the L/24 gun. Armour was increased to a total thickness of 80-mm and this was supplemented by spaced skirting plates on the turret and hull sides as a protection against rocket projectors and other hollow-charge weapons.

Panzerkampfwagen Panther (Ausführung A)

Engine: Maybach 12-cylinder petrol, 700-hp.
Dimensions: length 22 ft 7 ins (6·9 m), 29 ft 1 in (8·8 m) including gun; width 11 ft 3 ins (3·4 m); height 10 ft 2 ins (3·1 m).
Weight: 44·8 tons.
Performance: speed 28 mph (45 kph); range 110 miles (176 km).
Armament: one 7·5-cm KwK 42 L/70, two 7·92-mm mg.
Armour: (max.) 80-mm.
Crew: five.

History: the Panther's origin can be attributed more-or-less directly to the influence of the Russian T-34 medium tank, which was encountered for the first time in Russia in July 1941. A proposal to copy the Russian tank, which was far better than any comparable German tank then in service, had to be rejected as impracticable, but features of the T 34, notably the sloping front glacis plate of the hull, were used in the German design which went into production in November 1942. The early production Panthers (Ausf.D) were beset by mechanical troubles but these were largely overcome in the second model (designated Ausf.A) illustrated here. This had the same long 7·5-cm gun and coaxial machine gun but there were improvements to the hull machine gun mounting and protection for the fuel tanks. A total of 5805 Panthers of three models was built in World War II. One of the best medium tanks of its period, features of the Panther's design were reflected in many post war tanks.

gave Hitler the chance to strengthen his hold over the *Wehrmacht*. On November 5 he informed the armed forces commanders-in-chief that his expansionist policies were aimed at both Austria and Czechoslovakia and that war must be regarded as inevitable. Blomberg and Army C-in-C Fritsch protested—not on moral grounds, but at the prospect of a premature war before the *Wehrmacht* was strong enough. Hitler reacted by sacking them on trumped-up charges. (Blomberg had dug his own professional grave by marrying an ex-prostitute.) The charge of homosexual acts levelled against Fritsch caused an uproar in the German officer corps; they demanded and got a military hearing to clear the name of their former chief. This was done, but Fritsch was not reinstated. Instead Hitler set up the 'Armed Forces High Command' with himself as chief and Keitel as chief-of-staff and, later, Jodl as operations head. And the whole furore was eclipsed by Hitler's opportunist decision to annex Austria.

A snap order went out for the Army to enter Austria on March 12. The Army was totally unprepared and frantic improvisation was needed—particularly in the Panzer divisions, where the main problem was fuel supply. Fortunately for the German Army there was no resistance. Austria was incorporated into the 'Greater German Reich' on the pretext that she had been saved from Communist-inspired internal anarchy. And the German Army absorbed the lessons of the crisis: the need for more balanced deployment and adequate, faster supply.

Hitler's next objective was Czechoslovakia, now surrounded on three sides by German territory. The biggest military worry was the

Bloodless victory march

formidable defences in the *Sudetenland*, the frontier territories inhabited by a high percentage of racial Germans. Hitler's initial pretext was that Czechoslovakia must cede these territories to the *Reich*. Czechoslovakia stood firm, and the result was the crisis of September 1938, which France and Britain resolved by abandoning the Czechoslovak cause at Munich. Once again the German Army got a bloodless victory march.

Germany was not the only neighbour of Czechoslovakia with territorial ambitions against that country: Poland and Hungary also helped themselves. For a while war had seemed imminent. General Beck, Army chief-of-staff under Fritsch's successor, Brauchitsch, had tried to trigger off mass resistance by the Army. He had resigned in protest when no action was forthcoming, but the prevailing mood was one of relief—not only that the *Fuehrer* had got away with it again, but that the German Army would never again have to worry about the military defences in the Sudetenland.

The rump of Czechoslovakia was swal-

The armour battle. Both sides began with obsolete tanks but the demands of war necessitated the development of heavier, more powerful vehicles. Here is the German Tiger, armed with the dreaded 88mm gun.

lowed in March 1939. The Slovaks were persuaded to set up an 'independent' Slovakia under German patronage; and the German Army marched into Prague on March 15, again on the fake pretext that its victims had asked for German protection. Now the situation was transformed. Germany's eastern frontier was eminently defensible—the diges-

The Siegfried Line

tion of Czechoslovakia had shortened the frontier of the *Reich* by some 700 miles. The excellent weapons of the Czech army were placed at Germany's disposal, together with the arms factories—the *Wehrmacht* received so many Czech tanks that it was able to set about the formation of three new Panzer divisions.

One equally important but less dramatic result of Hitler's aggressive designs on Czechoslovakia was the resignation of Beck as Army Chief-of-Staff. Although hailed as one of the best brains in the Army, he was a vacillator and a reactionary who had never understood the new doctrines of mobile, armoured warfare and had sought to block their development. General Halder, Beck's

successor, became respected for his practical approach to the new ideas and the technique of putting them into practice.

Fears in Army circles that a premature war might still explode over Poland were largely dispelled by Hitler's surprise pact with Soviet Russia in August 1939, which effectively sealed off Poland from any practical military aid. There were still worries about the viability of the western defences—Hitler's much-vaunted *Westwall* or 'Siegfried Line'—but discussion on this subject was discouraged by the *Fuehrer's* habit of exploding in rage whenever the subject was raised.

In general, the German Army went to war on September 1, 1939, with the feeling that the *Fuehrer* would pull it off again. Even if the French and British did come to Poland's help, they could do nothing before Poland had been battered into defeat. It was widely believed (as events in fact proved) that the Western Allies would in fact do nothing.

In terms of *materiel* the German Army was still in the process of evolution from the old days of the *Reichswehr* when war came in 1939. Horse-drawn transport and guns predominated; nor had the Army yet said farewell to its last horsed cavalry units. The

Panzer formations included the ill-fated 'Light Divisions' and their hitting-power was still in dispute. (The early campaigns of the war proved this inadequate, and the light divisions were used as foundations for new Panzer divisions, of which Germany had six in September 1939.) But the German Army's best card was *mobility*: not only from the six Panzer and four light divisions, but from the four motorised divisions as well. The basic infantry and artillery weapons were sound and the supply machine had been vastly improved.

Another vital advantage possessed by the German Army in September 1939 was the speed of mobilisation. This, when coupled to the strategic advantage of commencing hostilities, proved decisive in the early days of the Polish campaign.

In more general terms, suffice it to say that since Hitler's arrival in January 1933, the German Army had been built up from the ten divisions permitted by Versailles to 53, shielded and assisted by the best air force in Europe.

The immense victories won by the German Army from the invasion of Poland in September 1939 to the Battle of Moscow in December 1941 are deceptive. They give the impression of having been won by an impeccably-functioning machine, unleashed on its enemies according to a series of detailed plans. This is not so. The Army owed its triumphs as much to the disunity, timidity, and material inadequacy of its enemies as it did to the German High Command.

Technical advantages, admittedly, reaped full dividends in Poland, where deep armoured thrusts could not be threatened by strong armoured countermoves. It was found that the idea of using the *Luftwaffe*'s dive-bombers as 'flying artillery' for the advancing ground troops worked well. But there was constant bickering between the German infantry and Panzer generals about the true role of the Panzers: should the latter cut loose on their own, or stay and help the infantry grind down the surrounded pockets of enemy troops? It is also easy to forget that Poland was conquered by the Red Army (which invaded on September 17) as well as by the *Wehrmacht*, which limited German Army operations to the western two-thirds of the country.

Yet there was adequate proof that the German Army owned impressive reserves of flexibility, as when the unexpected Polish counter-attack across the Bzura river was brilliantly handled by General von Rundstedt's southern army group.

Despite Hitler's initial enthusiasm for the idea, there could be no question of an immediate assault in the West in 1939. Deployment would take too long, and ammunition

Invasion of Norway

stocks had to be built up. In addition the Army staff plan for the attack ('Plan Yellow') was little more than an unimaginative rehash of the notorious 'Schlieffen Plan' of 1914. Hitler was not happy about it. Nor was Rundstedt's staff officer Manstein, whose repeated suggestions for a central break-through at Sedan on the Meuse and a thrust to the Channel were sat on by Brauchitsch and Halder. Not until January 1940 did Hitler hear of the idea and accept it at once. But before Manstein's plan of attack in the West could be tried, Hitler had made the snap decision to reduce Denmark and Norway.

This was ideal from the Navy's point of view: it was a maddening distraction for Brauchitsch and Halder, who were kept in the dark until the last minute. The entire plan ('Exercise Weser') depended on the Navy landing a division at the key ports of Norway simultaneously; they would then push inland and link up. Again, there were snags. The landings at Oslo were initially repulsed; British and French landings threatened the German beach-head at Trondheim; General Dietl's mountain troops were flung out of Narvik by another Allied landing. The day was saved by the *Luftwaffe*, which made it impossible for the British and French warships to supply the Allied troops ashore; and by the speed with which the German troops landed in the south pushed north.

Before the Allies pulled out of Norway in the first week of June—but not before the German hold on southern and central Norway was secured—the bulk of the German Army, 136 divisions strong, attacked in the West. Once again, results were spectacular. The youngest arm of the *Wehrmacht*, the airborne and parachute troops, took a mere 24 hours to capture 'the strongest fort in the world', Belgium's Fort Eben-Emael on the Albert Canal. The Panzer divisions—seven concentrated in one *Panzergruppe* under General von Kleist—tore through the centre of the Allied line at Sedan and plunged west to the Channel, sealing off the French and

Rotterdam is razed

British troops which had advanced into Belgium, all according to plan. Once again, there were near-fatal mistakes. At Rotterdam, a crass breakdown in air-ground communications resulted in the razing of the city centre while surrender talks were under way. At The Hague, the airborne attacking forces were totally beaten, badly mauled, and flung off their objectives. The scorching pace of the *Panzergruppe*'s advance across the Meuse panicked senior commanders through Kleist, Halder and Brauchitsch, right up to Hitler himself. The advance only went as fast as it

Panzerkampfwagen Tiger I

Engine: Maybach 12-cylinder petrol, 700-hp.
Dimensions: length 20 ft 4 ins (6·2 m), 27 ft (8·2 m) including gun; width 12 ft 3 ins (3·7 m); height 9 ft 5 ins (2·9 m).
Weight: 55 tons.
Performance: speed 24 mph (38 kph); range 62 miles (99 km).
Armament: one 8·8-cm KwK 36 L/56, two 7·92-mm mg.
Armour: (max.) 110-mm.
Crew: five.

History: of all the enemy tanks encountered by the British Army in World War II, the Tiger I probably created the deepest and longest-lasting impression, its powerful 8·8-cm gun and heavy armour making it almost invulnerable to all Allied tanks in North Africa in 1943. First used in action on the Russian front in September 1942, the Tiger was the outcome of a design by the Henschel firm originated the year before, although elements of earlier, unsuccessful, designs were incorporated. Built around the 8·8-cm KwK 36 L/56 and having maximum armour protection of 110-mm on the turret and 100-mm on the hull, the Tiger weighed well over 50 tons and was relatively under-powered. A total of 1350 Tiger Is was built and they exerted a strong influence in most of the major German campaigns in which the tank took part, from late 1942 onwards.

Panzerkampfwagen Tiger II

Engine: Mayback 12-cylinder petrol, 700-hp.
Dimensions: length 23 ft 10 ins (7·2 m), 33 ft 8 ins (10·2 m) including gun; width 12 ft 4 ins (3·7 m); height 10 ft 2 ins (3·1 m).
Weight: 68·6 tons.
Performance: speed 24 mph (38 kph); range 68 miles (108 km).
Armament: one 8·8-cm KwK 43 L/71, two 7·92-mm mg.
Armour: (max.) 185-mm.
Crew: five.

History: anticipated improvements in Russian armour led the Germans to develop during 1942–1943 a more powerful version of the Tiger. Another Henschel design, Tiger II was similar in mechanical layout to Tiger I but had a sloping glacis plate like the Panther and, with a view to improving standardisation between medium and heavy tanks, also had engine layout features in common with the Panther. It was proposed later also to standardise elements of the torsion bar spring suspension system with overlapping road wheels. Mechanically unreliable due to the relatively short time allowed for development, nevertheless, the Tiger II, with an 8·8-cm gun 71 calibres long and hull armour up to 150-mm thick, was arguably the most formidable tank to see service in numbers (485 were built) in World War II.

Above: German infantry in the attack. Their role in battle was secondary to that of the armoured divisions during the first half of the war, but as Germany went on the defensive their burden became a lot harder.

Right: The panzers in action, 1940. Their role was decisive from the very beginning and, along with the *Luftwaffe,* they were the prime weapon of the notable *Blitzkrieg* victories.

did because of the brilliant insubordination of Guderian with his Panzer corps. He interpreted the cautious orders he received in the light of the situation at the front, and as a result got to the Channel in five days. As in Poland, an unexpected Allied move required prompt and unorthodox handling: at Arras on May 21, a British tank attack was halted by General Rommel's 7th Panzer Division (the first time that the 88mm AA gun was used against tanks).

The decision of Hitler and Rundstedt not to charge on to Dunkirk has been fiercely

The front is ripped open

criticised. Rundstedt argued that the battle of France had still to be fought, and that it would be folly to send Panzer divisions into a head-on clash on unsuitable ground. Thus the British forces were allowed to escape— but the Panzer divisions, now regrouped into three new *Panzergruppen,* were largely intact when the final assault on France began on June 10. The French fought superbly on the line of the Somme and the Aisne, but there was nothing behind their front once the *Panzergruppen* had ripped it open. By June 22 the French had sued for, and signed, an armistice, by which time German spearheads were not only on the Swiss frontier but as far south as Lyons and the approaches to Bordeaux. Hostilities finally ended on

Above: One of the five assault guns used in the invasion of France. Inferior as attacking machines, their importance grew during the years of defeat.

Left: Heavy machine gunners taking cover during an artillery barrage in the attack on Holland, 1940. Shown here is the MG34, the standard machine gun until 1943.

June 25.

Between May 10 and June 25, 1940, the German Army had utterly destroyed the Anglo-French military line-up in the West and had occupied Holland, Belgium, Luxembourg, and northern France. But it had cost the Army 27,074 killed, 111,034 wounded, and 18,234 missing—and as the Dutch, Belgian, and French armistices re-

Savage losses suffered

sulted in the immediate release of German prisoners, most of those 'missing' were dead. With Britain resolved to fight on under Churchill, the hollowness of this great victory became apparent, for Britain could not be invaded. The German Navy had taken savage losses during the Norwegian campaign; the German airborne forces had suffered equally badly in the West. And when the *Luftwaffe* failed to win the certainty of an unopposed crossing in the skies over Britain, the war went on.

Thwarted in the West, Hitler turned to the gigantic gamble of ending the war by

Sturmgeschütz G. III

Engine: Maybach 12-cylinder petrol, 300-hp.
Dimensions: length 17 ft 9 ins (5·4 m), 22 ft 3 ins (6·8 m) including gun; width 11 ft 2 ins (3·4 m); height 7 ft 1 in (2·1 m).
Weight: 23 tons.
Performance: speed 25 mph (40 kph); range 90 miles (144 km).
Armament: one 7·5-cm StuK 40 L/48.
Armour: (max.) 50-mm.
Crew: four.

History: the assault gun — a heavily armoured self-propelled weapon for the support of the infantry — was essentially a German invention, earlier self-propelled guns of other nations having been partially armoured or lightly armoured only. With a short 7·5-cm gun (L/24) set low in the front of the hull, the first model of the Stu.G. built on a PzKpfw III chassis was produced in 1940, a small number taking part in the campaign in France. Although successful, the need for a gun also able to tackle tanks led by stages to the intro-duction of the much more powerful 7·5-cm Stu.K.40 L/48 used in the Stu.G.III, Ausf.F/8, shown· here. The frontal armour was increased in this model to 50-mm from the original 30-mm. In later models it went up to 80-mm.
Some 10,000 of these vehicles were built in World War II.

7.62-cm Pabe (r) on Panzerkampfwagen 38 (t)

Engine: Praga six-cylinder petrol, 125-hp.
Dimensions: length 15 ft (4·6 m) excluding gun; width 7 ft (2·1m); height 8 ft 1 in (2·4 m).
Weight: 10·8 tons.
Performance: speed 26 mph (41 kph); range 110 miles (176 km).
Armament: one 7·62-cm Pak 36(r), one 7·92-mm mg.
Armour: (max.) 25-mm.
Crew: four.

History: German experience on the Russian front showed the need to get the maximum possible number of anti-tank weapons on to self-propelled carriages in the shortest possible time. A programme of using the chassis of obsolescent German tanks, Czech and other foreign tank chassis for mounting German and captured foreign anti-tank guns was instituted, so that con-siderable numbers of serviceable 'tank hunters' became available from early 1942 onwards.
The mounting illustrated, of which 344 were built in early 1942, was one of the earliest and crudest. It used the Czech LT-38 tank chassis, (numbers of which were taken over in 1938 and was subsequently produced under German occupation) mounting a captured Russian 7·62-cm gun, rechambered to take German 7·5-cm Pak ammunition. Later designs using Czech chassis were lower and better protected, the Jagdpanzer 38(t) Hetzer being one of the best self-propelled guns of its type of World War II.

Above: German infantry during the early days of 'Operation Barbarossa', 1941. Here, left behind by the panzer divisions, they set about the capture of the fortifications at Ivangorod. Throughout the campaign, it was left to the infantry to mop up the isolated centres of resistance that were often bypassed by the hastening armour.

Right: Infantry breaking down a door in the search for Soviet soldiers hiding from their potential captors.

Above: The German panzers took the leading role in the Russian campaigns of 1941 and 1942. In this photograph, a PzKw IV enters a town in the Orel, greeted by an empty street.

Right: The drive for the Caucasus. Soldiers against a background of burning oil refineries. Hitler's gamble for the economic resources of this area was a strategic failure.

Above: Infantry in the attack. An N.C.O. beckons on his men during the battle around Kiev, a battle that ended in the capture of half a million Russian soldiers by the Germans.

smashing Soviet Russia. The great invasion —'Operation Barbarossa'—was scheduled for the early summer of 1941, but in April Hitler had to send large numbers of German troops into the Balkans. Mussolini's ill-advised war with Greece had proved a disaster; Yugoslavia had repudiated the Axis. Yugoslavia and Greece were reduced with little trouble and Crete was taken by German airborne troops—but the latter suffered so heavily that never again in the war was the German airborne arm able to mount such a powerful operation.

With the German invasion of Russia on

The fight for life

June 22, 1941, it was seen how much had been learned from previous campaigns. *Luftwaffe* support was superb. Panzer advances were unprecedented. Such huge 'bags' of prisoners were taken that two-thirds of the pre-war Red Army strength had been wiped out by December. But the Red Army fought on. It got reinforcements from the Far East, from Siberia—crack troops, well-equipped for the Russian winter. On December 6 the Russians counter-attacked and drove the German forces back from the gates of Moscow. For the first time, the German Army of the Third *Reich* was forced to fight for its life.

What had gone wrong? The basic viewpoint of the German generals was the plaint that nothing kept them out of Moscow except for Hitler and the cloying mud of the Russian autumn. But this argument does not seem good enough.

Nor, basically, was the 'Barbarossa' plan itself adequate: three army groups, North, Centre, and South, were to advance along the respective axes of Leningrad, Moscow, and Kiev and destroy the Red Army as far west as possible. But two elementary flaws eroded 'Barbarossa'. The first was the *size* of Russia, which enlarged the battle-tried *Blitzkrieg* format until it went out of focus. It was impossible for the *Luftwaffe* to wipe out, or break up, the Soviet armies to the East—not to mention in Siberia—and prevent them from entering the battle. The huge

85

15-cm F.H. 18/1 on Geschützwagen IV (Hummel)

Engine: Maybach 12-cylinder petrol, 300-hp.
Dimensions: length 19 ft (5·8 m), 21 ft 10 ins (6·6 m) including gun; width 9 ft 8 ins (2·9 m); height 9 ft 3 ins (2·8 m).
Weight: 23·5 tons.
Performance: speed 25 mph (40 kph); range 125 miles (200 km).
Armament: one 15-cm sFH 18/1.
Armour: (max.) 30-mm.
Crew: six.

History: the Hummel (Bumble Bee) is representative of German self-propelled field artillery of World War II. A modified PzKpfw IV chassis was used for this medium howitzer self-propelled carriage. It was intended to rationalise production of the PzKpfw III and IV by producing a common chassis. The resulting design, which embodied transmission and suspension elements of both tanks was used only as Geschuetzwagen ('gun vehicle'), however, and principally for the 15-cm sFH 18/1 (Hummel) and a companion anti-tank vehicle (Nashorn) for the 8·8-cm Pak 43/1.

The Hummel had only a lightly armoured superstructure but the chassis was reliable and the gun, with a range of 14,550 yards, was a successful weapon. A total of 666 of these vehicles was produced between 1942 and 1944.

8.8-cm Panzerjager (Jagdpanther)

Engine: Maybach 12-cylinder petrol, 700-hp.
Dimensions: length 22 ft 7 ins (6·9 m), 32 ft 4 ins (9·8 m) including gun; width 10 ft 9 ins (3·3 m); height 8 ft 11 ins (2·7 m).
Weight: 44·8 tons.
Performance: speed 28 mph (45 kph); range 130 miles (208 km).
Armament: one 8·8-cm Pak 43/3 L/71, one 7·92-mm mg.
Armour: (max.) 80-mm.
Crew: five.

History: a very formidable weapon for its size, the Jagdpanther was an adaptation of the Panther tank mounting an 8·8-cm gun, with limited traverse, in the front sloping glacis plate. The gun was the Pak 43/3 L/71, the same as that used on the Tiger II. Although the Jagdpanther was at first thought to be a very undesirable diversion of Panther tank production, these vehicles proved to be ideal defensive weapons, being protected and easily concealed. A total of 230 was built in 1943–1944 and they were much in demand in the closing stages of the war.

An even more powerful vehicle than the Jagdpanther, although built under the same philosophy, was the 70-ton Jagdtiger, based on the Tiger II chassis and armed with a 12·8-cm Pak 44 L/55 gun.

distances covered exhausted the men and sent the vital Panzers to the repair workshops by the hundred from wear and tear alone. Apart from the solitary Minsk/Smolensk/Moscow 'motorway' metalled roads were non-existent and dissolved in mud when rained on; and the Russian railways had to be painfully converted to the German gauge. These factors alone made it inevitable that the German advance must run out of steam sooner or later. The further East the Army went the wider it was dispersed, the harder it became for it to concentrate in emergency, and the more easy it became for the Red Army to gain local superiority in repeated spoiling attacks. Above all, where was the German advance to *stop*? The much-vaunted 'A-A' (Archangel-Astrakhan) Line was no answer, for it had no naturally-defensible features. And there were certainly none along a front connecting Leningrad, Moscow, and the Black Sea.

The advance was to be on a broad front, and this raised the delicate question of co-operation between the army groups. There could be no irrevocable objectives for each army group commander, for it would be impossible to forecast precisely where the biggest enemy masses would polarise once the front line had been driven deep into Russia. Thus, if events made it advisable for Army Group Centre to help Army Group North, swift orders from the top and whole-hearted co-operation on the part of the army group commanders must be the order of the day. Neither materialised once the campaign had been launched.

Five key generals stood out as recalcitrants of one kind or another, each pulling in

Rommel's empty victories

different directions. Bock, commanding Army Group Centre, secretly longed to be hailed by German posterity as the Captor of Moscow and the Arch-Hammer of the Bolshevik Horde—but during the crucial months of 'Barbarossa' his conscience was nagged by officers on his staff who belonged to the anti-Hitler underground movement and wanted a field-marshal to take the lead in a *putsch*. Subordinate to Bock were two arch-rivals: the petulant Kluge and the impetuous Guderian. Kluge always complained that Guderian's Panzers, dashing on into the blue, left Kluge's infantry without adequate support; Guderian, subordinate to Kluge, chafed at all restrictions. Then came the impotent duo, Halder and Brauchitsch, at the head of OKH—impotent because, by June 22, 1941, it was crystal clear that the reins would not be left in the hands of OKH. And all five knew that Hitler's unpredictable 'intuition' would get its own way in any case.

It has long been commonplace to heap all the blame on Hitler for ordering the Ukraine to be cleaned up before the decisive drive on Moscow, which meant that the latter was launched too late. It would be more just to blame him for not bringing his generals sharply to heel—for allowing them, in effect, to waste two and a half vital weeks. This period of vacillation was caused by the uncertainties thrown up by conferences at Novy

Borisov (July 27) and Lotzen (August 23). The Lotzen conference was the decisive one —Moscow or the Ukraine? Halder and Bock had 'passed the buck' to Guderian, who had the job of persuading Hitler to push for Moscow at once; Brauchitsch, by now almost totally unnerved, forbade Guderian even to mention Moscow to Hitler; Guderian dis-

Passing the buck

obeyed, but found himself isolated, watching the other officers nodding sycophantically while Hitler announced that his generals knew nothing about the economic aspects of war—the Ukraine must come first.

As events moved to their crisis before Moscow and the first terrible winter frosts set in, the omens were already clear to see. On paper, the German Army had achieved its original brief: it had destroyed the estimated strength of the Red Army, but more and more Russian divisions were encountered. The Russian T-34 had been a hideous surprise to German tank crews and anti-tank gunners; one of the best tanks of the war, it, too, was threatening to achieve dominance of the battlefield. And fatuous over-confidence at OKW meant that when the first frosts came to wither the German Army on the Eastern Front, its winter equipment was still stuck in Warsaw station. The cold, not the Red Army, was the main foe of the Germans during the Battle of Moscow.

But they stood, and the man responsible was Hitler. He sacked every general who counselled strategic retreat. He did more— he took over command of the Army from Brauchitsch and kept it until the end in Berlin. He ordered that every inch of ground must be held, that the men must die where they stood. Digging-in was impossible in the intense cold and the men died by the thousand—but their comrades were still holding an intact front when Stalin's ill-co-ordinated offensive petered out in March 1942.

Since September 1939 the German Army had won the greatest victories in its history. They were all meaningless, in that they had all been pursued to end the war—and they had failed to do so. Now Britain had an ally which the German Army could never escape. Two-thirds of Hitler's *Wehrmacht* had fallen on Soviet Russia and seized it by the throat. But after Moscow it could never dare let go—or flee.

When the diminutive *Afrika Korps* under General Erwin Rommel was originally sent to Libya in February 1941, the sole idea was to preserve Tripoli for Mussolini after a disastrous series of Italian defeats in the Western Desert. The build-up for 'Barbarossa' was the obsession of the German High Command; and the original forces scraped together for the *Afrika Korps*—5th Light Division and 15th Panzer Division—would not be up to full strength until May 1941. Then, it was hoped, Rommel might try a limited attack to recover western Cyrenaica.

Rommel's lightning string of victories two months before he was even supposed to start appalled OKW and OKH. It was im-

possible to reinforce him—even to supply him properly. The shaken British later put it about that the *Afrika Korps* were an élite of supermen trained in hot-houses for the desert. This was not so. The German soldier did not take to the desert as did the British. The *Afrika Korps*—the German hard core of what became Rommel's German-Italian *Panzerarmee Afrika*—ate badly compared to the British 8th Army (British Army bully-beef was a prized German spoil of battle, which gives one some idea of how bad German rations were). Health was a major problem, chief villain being amoebic dysentery. Rommel himself was invalided out, chronically ill, as the crisis in North Africa approached in early autumn 1942.

The German psychological and material advantages over the 8th Army were, however, vital. First was Rommel himself, who became a bogeyman to the British desert soldier. His three major bungles—the first attack and siege of Tobruk, his throwing-away of victory at Sidi Rezegh in November-December 1941, and his attack at El Alamein in July 1942—went almost unnoticed at the time. He was flexible, unpredictable and a born leader of men. His retreat from Alamein to Tunisia was a masterpiece.

Next came weapons: the battle-tried Panzers were more than a match for the Allies until the 8th Army received American Grants and Shermans in 1942. Mechanically reliable, their tracks did not fall off at the least excuse. Rommel's enthusiastic use of the 88mm AA gun as a tank-killer was another brainwave. A more lowly German advantage was the 'jerry-can'—the ultra-practical metal liquid container which never

Fatuous over-confidence

leaked and from which every drop could be poured. This was vital because of the chronic Axis supply problem in North Africa, with Malta lying squarely across the supply-lines from Sicily and Italy. Fuel was Rommel's bugbear: the further away he got from his base in Tripolitania after winning a victory, the harder it was to supply him.

Twice, however, Rommel was helped in that the British had to pull out desert-wise troops to send elsewhere. This aided Rommel in his first offensive (March-April 1941, when Wavell was obsessed with reinforcing Greece) and his second (January 1942, when the Japanese offensive in the Far East again drew off British troops from the desert theatre).

By mid-April 1941 Rommel had overrun Cyrenaica and was besieging Tobruk. 'Barbarossa' still lay two months in the future and Halder at OKH thought Rommel had gone mad. Tobruk was still holding out in May and June, when Rommel beat off two clumsy British attacks on his frontier positions. In November 1941, after initial successes against the 8th Army's first serious attempt to relieve Tobruk, Rommel mishandled the battle and had to retreat into Tripolitania to avert the destruction of his forces. He recoiled brilliantly in January-February 1942, reaching Gazala. In May-June 1942 he broke the 8th Army at Gazala and took Tobruk at last. There he was supposed to stop while Malta was taken—but in a brainstorm of opportunism Hitler and Mussolini backed Rommel's pleas for an immediate invasion of Egypt, which was halted at Alamein in early July.

At last, Hitler was willing to take Africa seriously. It was too late. Anglo-American landings in Algeria coincided with Rommel's defeat by the vastly superior 8th Army at Alamein. German troops were poured into Tunisia to keep a bridge-head open for Rommel's retreating *Panzerarmee*. By February 1943 the vice had closed. After a last throw—a counter-attack against the Americans at Kasserine, which met with initial success—the Axis forces in Tunisia were thrown on the defensive. Rommel, sick again, was withdrawn from Africa before the final débâcle on May 12, 13, 1943—but a quarter of a million German troops had been ripped from the strength of the German Army.

The Army lost in North Africa largely because Rommel's victories raised the theatre to high-priority status at a time when little or nothing could be done to reinforce the Axis forces there. Thus Rommel's victories in Africa proved as empty as the earlier victories in France and western Russia. Worse—the more victories Rommel won, the further his troops advanced, the weaker their position became. The German Army troops under Rommel created the legend of the *Afrika Korps* and fought superbly. But that legend was all they had to show for their magnificent efforts.

In the first days of February 1943 the German summer offensive of 1942 reached its disastrous end with the annihilation of the 6th Army, trapped at Stalingrad on the Volga since November 23, 1942. Russia's retaliatory second winter offensive snatched back all the territorial gains won by the German Army since June 28 and pushed it back behind its start-line. Brilliant manoeuvres by General Manstein stabilised the front, leaving a

The map shows the disposition of the belligerents in 'Operation Barbarossa', June 22, 1941. Hitler's master plan was to prove a failure largely through its own weaknesses and not so much through the unexpected strength of the Russians. The main striking force was positioned in the centre, opposite Moscow, but it was to be dissipated during the campaign when the two panzer groups were sent to aid Army Groups North and South before resuming their advance on the Russian capital. This delay proved fatal to the German chances of success. Initial victories turned to defeat as the German armies came to a standstill against the Soviet determination. What had seemed certain victory, as German troops made their way with astonishing speed across Russian territory, was turned sour by mistakes and painful by the cold.

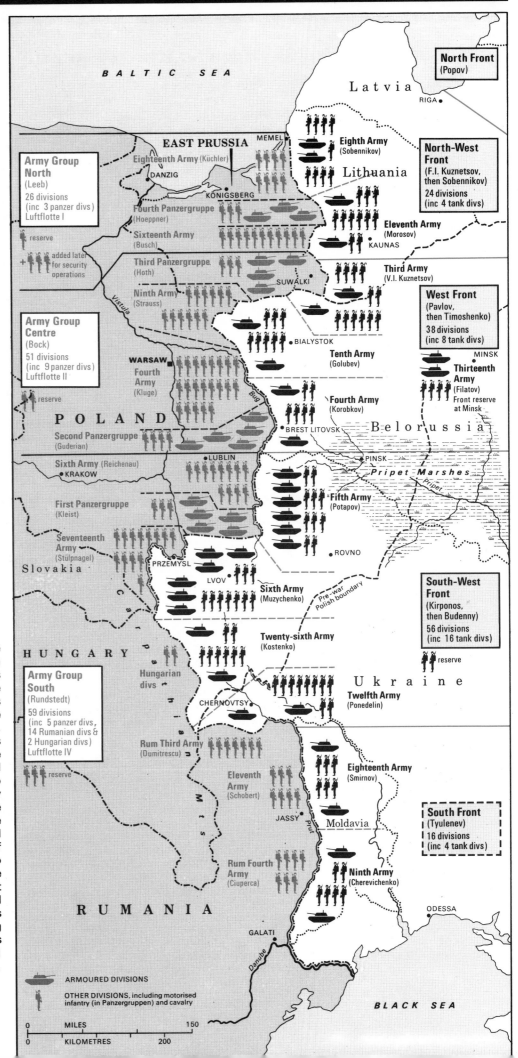

Schwerer Panzerspähwagen Sd.Kfz 231 (8 rad)

Schwerer Panzerspähwagen Sd.Kfz 231 (8 rad)

Engine: Buessing–NAG eight-cylinder petrol, 155-hp.
Dimensions: length 19 ft 1 in (5·8 m) without spaced armour; width 7 ft 3 ins (2·2 m); height 7 ft 10 ins (2·4 m).
Weight: 8·15 tons.
Performance: speed 53 mph (85 kph); range 186 miles (297 km).
Armament: one 2-cm KwK 30 or 38, one 7·92-mm mg.
Armour: (max.) 14·5-mm.
Crew: four.

History: built to replace a six-wheeled heavy armoured car with the same Sonderkraftfahrzeug (SdKfz – 'special motor vehicle') ordnance number, this eight-wheeled Buessing–N.A.G. vehicle first entered service in 1938. Powered by an eight-cylinder engine located at the rear, with transmission to all wheels, the SdKfz 231 (eight rad) also had all-wheel steering and a complete set of duplicate driving controls at the back for use in emergency. Although having a very good cross-country performance (comparable to that of a tracked vehicle) it was only lightly armed for such a heavy vehicle. The armour, too, was light, at a maximum of 14·5-mm, although this was sometimes supplemented at the front by spaced armour in the form of a box-like structure. Other vehicles in the SdKfz 231 (eight rad) series were built as wireless, command or close support cars.

Mittlerer Sd.Kfz 251/1 Schutzenpanzerwagen

Engine: Maybach six-cylinder petrol, 100-hp.
Dimensions: length 19 ft 7 ins (5·9 m); width 6 ft 11 ins (2·1 m); height 5 ft 9 ins (1·7 m) to top of hull.
Weight: 8·4 tons.
Performance: speed 31 mph (49 kph); range 186 miles (297 km).
Armament: one or two 7·92-mm mg.
Armour: (max.) 14·5-mm.
Crew: twelve.

History: one of the most characteristic German military vehicles of World War II was the half-track, and the medium armoured personnel carrier SdKfz 252/1 was one of the most important vehicles of this type.

Derived from earlier unarmoured three-ton half-tracks used chiefly for towing artillery, the SdKfz 251/1 was designed to carry infantry accompanying armour. The prototypes were tested in 1938 and the first vehicles were issued to the Army in time for the campaign in Poland. As World War II progressed, variants of the basic vehicle for a variety of different functions, such as wireless and command, S.P. mountings and ambulances were brought out. The mechanical layout of a front-mounted engine driving the tracks at the rear (the front wheels were not driven) remained basically unchanged although the hull shape was simplified slightly during the war, an Ausf.D vehicle, built from 1943 onwards, being shown here.

westward-bulging salient around Kursk; but the loss of the 6th Army deprived the Army in Russia of its strongest single field force. Then came the second disaster of Tunis. Together, the two defeats lowered the German Army's fighting strength by around half a million men.

Nevertheless, strenuous efforts by Guderian and Speer had started the re-equipment of the Panzer divisions with Panther and Tiger tanks, and Hitler was determined to launch a third summer offensive. Thus there were no reserves at all to spare when the Allies launched their assault on southern Europe by invading Sicily on July 10. At this time Mussolini was still in the saddle and Italy still in the war; the defence of the island was predominantly left to the Italian Army. Field-Marshal Kesselring, C-in-C southern Europe, reinforced the shaky Italian garrison with two German divisions, whose tenacious fighting did much to delay the Allied advance. Both were evacuated to the Italian mainland to join the German garrison already assembling there under Kesselring's direction. His dispositions were aided by Hitler's determination to secure Italy with German

Battle of Monte Cassino

troops, which had been effected in the nick of time by the moment when Mussolini's successor, Badoglio, took Italy out of the war and Eisenhower's forces invaded on

Kesselring's second piece of luck was that the Allies decided not to 'go for broke' and strike direct for Rome.

Instead their follow-up force landed at Salerno on September 3, hours after the 16th Panzer Division had moved into the area to disarm the local Italian troops. The narrowness of the Salerno battle (September 9-17) was an immense shot in the arm for the German defenders of central Italy. As the shaken Allies joined up and prepared to continue their advance, they were faced not only by a determined enemy and the foulest Italian autumn known for years, but by every natural feature of the Italian peninsula (mountain ranges, foothills, and watercourses), all of which favoured the German troops.

These features were exploited to the maximum by the Germans in the brilliant defensive battle at Monte Cassino (December 1943-May 1944). Once again the endurance and flexibility of the German troops was constantly underestimated by the Allied commanders. The German successes were won by small units of paratroops and Panzer Grenadiers (as the old motorised divisions had been styled since 1942) working in close co-operation even when temporarily isolated.

Kesselring's men held firm even when the Allies made a surprise landing behind their front at Anzio-Nettuno in January 1944. With another brilliant piece of improvisation, Kesselring held the Anzio front with a scattering of cooks, clerks, and other rear-echelon forces scraped together and thrown into the sector. The Cassino line was eventually breached by French colonial mountain troops, and the confused German defenders

Above: Defensive fighting on the Eastern front in 1944. Here, Panzer Grenadiers pass a burnt-out Soviet tank during a local counter attack which had temporarily halted the slow but very sure Russian advance.

were faced with engulfment. Again, Kesselring's determination not to give up averted total disaster and a fighting retreat was made to the more northerly 'Gothic Line'—a chain of positions most of which had not been completed. Again, the German forces were helped by the drawing-off of Allied forces to be sent to other theatres. As the winter of 1944 approached, Kesselring was still holding a firm front in northern Italy south of the River Po; his opponent, General Alexander, was forced to sit down and plan another set-piece assault.

This was launched on April 9, by which time Kesselring had been called to take command on the crumbling Western Front; his continued presence in Italy would have made little difference. The energy and inge-

Undercover surrender

nuity of the Allied attack—particularly the amphibious assault across Lake Commachio —unseamed the German front, and the withdrawal across the Po was a shambles. Undercover surrender negotiations between the SS chief in Italy and the American Office of Strategic Services brought forward the inevitable surrender of the German troops on the 'southern front'—Austria and Italy,

Above: German infantry dug in defensive positions on the Italian front, during the winter of 1944. They wear camouflage helmet covers and the rifle has a grenade-throwing attachment. The conditions in Italy were ideal for defensive fighting and, with enough forces, the Germans could have held on.

Right: Street fighting on the Eastern front. Here, infantry, snapped by a fearless war correspondent, rush through the main street of Rostov. In such fighting, the infantry units would regularly lose half their strength, while for panzer divisions it proved fatal to get bogged down in the streets.

about a million men all told—on May 2, 1945.

If any single campaign justified the aims of the German Army training of the *Reichswehr* period—the production of the 'thinking fighting man' who could operate effectively in small units—it was the Italian campaign. Time and again the Allies were stopped, not only by their own mistakes and miscalculations, but by the resilience and endurance of the German soldier. A propaganda myth was fostered by the Allies that the German troops in Italy were fanatical Nazis. This was not so—they were the proverbial collection of 'odds and sods', but one held together by a common professionalism.

The Stalingrad disaster was due to three

Death at Stalingrad

main factors. First, the Russians were learning fast not to throw away vast numbers of men by ordering them to risk encirclement. Second, the German strategy ordered by Hitler was a mess—neither one thing nor another, a fatal halving of the German Army's available resources. When it resulted in the unexpected encirclement of the 6th Army at Stalingrad, Hitler's obstinate insistence that the latter must hold its ground sealed its death sentence.

Stalingrad could have been 'snatched' in August by a powerful drive, but the power, in the form of the 4th Panzer Army, was not to hand: it was wasting its time pulling back from the Don crossings in the south, where it was not needed and should never have been sent. Stalingrad could have fallen to a sophisticated series of concentric attacks in September, but the heads-down 'sledgehammer' attacks of the German commander Paulus (in his first independent command) were immensely wasteful and resulted in a grinding battle of attrition in which the Russians were able to hold their own. Meanwhile, the down-at-heel Italian and Romanian divisions on the 6th Army's flanks were marked down as the targets for the counter-offensive which Zhukov was preparing.

Nor had Hitler's obsession—the oilfields of the Kuban and the Caucasus—been attained. Kleist's 1st Panzer Army found that the further it got the tougher it had to fight, over increasingly bad going. By the end of October 1942 the Germans had been halted in the High Caucasus and along the line of the Terek river.

The resultant disaster at Stalingrad was partly due to previous defensive battles brilliantly won by the German Army—at Demyansk and at Kholm during the Moscow counter-offensive. There, large bodies of surrounded German forces had successfully beaten off the Russians until relieved. But Stalingrad was a different matter: the 6th Army was the biggest single unit fielded by the Germans on the south-east front—about 300,000. The men trapped in Stalingrad died or went into captivity because of the appalling weaknesses in the High Command which Hitler had created. Paulus and his staff said they could hold if adequately supplied by air; Goering said they could be; Hitler chose to believe both; the supply and combat officers who knew the real position were sat

on when they protested.

The 6th Army achieved one thing in their hopeless struggle: they pinned down *seven* Russian armies which would otherwise have been thrown into the gap in the German front. This gap was brilliantly sealed by Manstein's series of armoured counter-attacks in February-March 1943, which recovered Kharkov but left a westward-pointing salient in the front around Orel and Kursk.

Manstein's successes had the same fateful effect as the earlier airlifts at Demyansk and Kursk: they produced over-confidence. Hitler was convinced that a fresh offensive, this time with the new tanks which were being rushed to the Panzer forces, would finally reap success. He played down the hideous truth of the Russian tank strength, the knowledge that the Kursk salient was the strongest sector of the Russian line, and awareness that the new German armour was not fully battle-worthy. These three factors resulted in the titanic armoured battles on the northern and southern flanks of the Kursk salient (July 4-13), which ended any chance of forming a strong German reserve on the Eastern Front and placed the German armies there on the defensive for the rest of the war.

'Barbarossa' had ducked realities from the beginning. No final strategic objective made sense—the only one mentioned had been the meaningless 'A-A' Line. Also underestimated was the supply problem: the further the German armies marched, the wider their front became, and the logistic problem of an orthodox campaign was first squared, then cubed. On the other hand, the first three years of the campaign in Russia showed how the magnificent fighting qualities of the German Army could restore an apparently hopeless position. Kursk wasted all that; it was little more than a desperate

Make peace you fools

squandering of the last handful of chips in a single throw.

In attack and defence, the burden fell on the German infantry—inevitably. This had been the case ever since Moscow. Conversely, the German Army had learned much about the Red Army's cardinal weaknesses— wooden adherence to the letter of orders, a comfortable tendency to panic when surprised. But the weight and pace of the Russian pursuit in the summer and autumn of 1943 prevented the Germans from conducting that military dream, 'an ordered tactical retreat' to the hoped-for bastion of the Dniepr river. And it was on the Dniepr that the German Army learned another lesson—the virtual impossibility of eliminating Russian river bridgeheads once established and reinforced. The long retreat to the very ruins of Berlin had begun.

'What can you do? Make peace, you fools! What else can you do?' That was Rundstedt's

A German field gun that has been camouflaged from aerial detection on the Eastern front in 1943. The Soviets were by then gaining air superiority over the German forces.

A powerful assault gun moves up to the front. This is in Italy, toward the end of 1944. By this time in the war, production of assault guns had outnumbered that of tanks.

testy response to a panicky Keitel on July 1, 1944. That, too, was the situation plain and simple, and it did not take a seasoned professional like Rundstedt to see it. But, six months before, that was not the case. Germany could have struggled on with a fair chance of fighting the Allies to a standstill, if only a temporary one.

The crucial conundrum was the problem of what would happen when the Allies launched their invasion in the West—the inevitable recipe for Germany's defeat. It was Jodl, of all people, who had already

The plot of the generals

come up with the daring plan to pull right back to the eastern frontier of the *Reich*, thus halving the breadth of the Eastern Front, and sending the troops thus released to buttress the garrisons along the Channel coast. With Rommel just beginning his bid to make the invasion coast impregnable—and given a couple more months he would probably have done it—this could, on paper, have taken the impossibility out of the situation and given the *Reich* a fighting chance.

Hitler, inevitably would have none of this. He held to his obsession of holding every inch of ground, however useless. Thus the German Army in the East was doomed to the terrible battles in White Russia of June-July 1944, which carried the Red Army on to the Vistula and had destroyed the Eastern Army Group Centre by the time the British and Americans finally ground down the threadbare forces in Normandy and broke out, eastwards to the Seine. The jaws of the Allied vice had begun their inexorable closing which was to end in May 1945 with Germany squeezed in half.

The 'Generals' Plot' of July 1944, which all but killed Hitler, was in fact the work of a tiny body of determined activists motivated by the mistaken belief that the Allies would be happy to negotiate with them once Hitler was removed from the scene. And the reaction of the Army majority—officers and men—was one of outraged betrayal of their efforts in the field. Even Guderian consented to sit in judgment on his fellow officers after the failure of the plot. This was an individual decision significant in itself.

For the German Army, the tragedy was that, by the time of the Normandy landings, it had never been better equipped. Its infantry had anti-tank rocket missiles (*Panzerfaust* and *Panzerschreck*) and heavy tanks which only the Anglo-American hybrid Sherman 'Firefly' with its 17-pounder gun, and the Russian JS-2 and JS-3, could tackle with confidence. Production of weapons had never been higher—but it was too late. The Allied air offensive, at last turned against Germany's bifold Achilles' heel—oil and the transport system—was beginning to bite.

Nevertheless, the Allied landslide advances in both East and West during the high

summer of 1944 did peter out from sheer exhaustion and make an autumn and winter campaign inevitable. By now it was a question of nothing more or less than the defence of the *Reich*, which again could have been protracted. But the armoured striking force which Hitler managed to assemble during autumn 1944 was squandered in the Ardennes sideshow in the West, removing the last high-quality reserves which could have intervened in the terrible Russian offensive of January-February 1945. This carried the Red Army forward to the Oder, while the British and Americans were still grinding away at the Siegfried Line in the West.

Two additional factors attenuated the German Army still further during the defence of the *Reich*: the need to detail forces in the south-east to buttress the flagging morale of Hungary, and Hitler's new obsession: 'Fortress' defence. This boiled down to declaring every large town a 'fortress' and throwing away troop concentrations in futile defence. There were also 18 useless divisions trapped in Courland, which Hitler refused to evacuate.

The Western floodgate collapsed first, when the British and Americans cracked the Rhine barrier in March and surrounded the Ruhr, complete with German C-in-C West, Model. The Ruhr pocket was the biggest 'bag' ever made: 317,000 POWs were eventually taken, by which time Zhukov and Koniev had launched the final drive on Berlin from the Oder. Even then, outnumbered by well over two to one in men and aircraft, and four to one in tanks and guns, General Gotthard Heinrici stopped Zhukov in his tracks for over 48 hours before being surrounded from north and south. With forces that in the 'glory days' of 1940

The impossible demanded

and 1941 would have been considered a pitiful rabble, the German Army made the Russians pay dearly for their final victory. Between April 16 and May 8, 1945, the Russians lost about 300,000 men killed, wounded, or missing.

For having achieved so much, endured so much, and held for so long against such odds, the German Army of the Hitler era stands unique in military history. It lost because it was asked to do the impossible. It should never have been set to tackle the tasks it did. It is the job of strategists to see that their armies are not asked to do the impossible.

Hitler's armies started the war with one mighty advantage over those of their enemies. Unlike the latter, whose armed services had been eroded to the verge of impotence by cheese-paring peacetime governments in the 1920s and 1930s, the German Army was very well equipped for war in 1939.

It was not, however, a picture of modern warfare incarnate. Horsed transport (especially as gun tractors) was still vital, and even as late as the invasion of Russia the German Army still boasted an entire cavalry division. Nor was it a picture of impeccable organisation—like every army, the German Army of World War II had plenty of brainchildren which died in infancy, taking an unnecessary

amount of good soldiers' lives with them. But all in all the 'guns or butter' motivation of Hitler's Germany had done an excellent job for the German armed forces.

To start at grass roots, with infantry weapons, provides a good example. Standard infantry rifle in 1939 was the time-tested Mauser '98k, a worthy opponent to the British Lee Enfield .303. The '98k with its lower rate of fire was not, *per se*, an inferior weapon: it existed because the German Army had very definite ideas on the correct rate of fire to achieve accuracy. (German recruits were taught to fire their five deliberate rounds and take a deep breath, rather than work up to the British standby of 'fifteen rounds rapid'.) But this did not mean that high fire-power was discounted. The German Army had some of the best automatic weapons of the war. These included the famous (but often wrongly-named) 'Schmeisser'—*Maschinenpistole* MP38, and its immediate successor, the MP40. This was the standard German submachine-gun of the war and over a million were produced. Later came the

The race for armour

Sturmgewehr StG44, a short automatic rifle.

As far as machine-guns were concerned, a totally new format emerged with the light-weight MG34 and MG42, two more classic weapons with amazing rates of fire—the MG42's cyclic rate of fire was 20 rounds per second, and the gun when firing was said to sound like tearing calico.

In artillery, too, the German soldier was well served with conservative models. Massive siege guns appeared—*Moerser Karl* (60cm) and *Kanone Dora* were among the most famous. They did score successes, such as the cracking of the Soviet armoured turrets at Sebastopol; but they were given a crazed over-importance by Hitler, who once flabbergasted Guderian by wanting to use them against tanks!

Armoured warfare in World War II triggered off the inevitable escalation-race between armour-cracking guns and shell-resistant armour, and until the *Panzerjaeger* ('tank-hunting') crews ran into the Russian T-34 the 35mm Pak gun with which the German Army went to war was adequate. The armour race then produced the Pak 50 and the Pak 75, but long before these two made their battlefield debuts the Luftwaffe's 88mm AA gun had been pressed into service as the ultimate tank-killer. Despite its tall scaffold-like silhouette (unless dug in, in a static position), the '88' was found to be a match for any Allied tank.

The two-year 'glory days' period of the Panzer division had the Pzkw Mks III and IV as the twin mainstays. Both were comparatively small machines, mechanically reliable (they had not been designed with the appalling distances of Russia in mind). The Allies had nothing to beat them, although the British 'Matilda' with its massive shell could survive them, lumbering along at a valiant but totally inadequate eight miles an hour on its London bus engine. The best advantage the Germans had was that the Panzer virtuosos never bothered with pro-

ducing 'infantry' tanks intended to co-operate with the foot-sloggers. But Russia changed all previous Panzer specifications—or to be precise, the T-34 tank did. Now more speed was needed, more armour, sloped as much as possible, and a bigger gun. The result was the superb Panther (Pzkw V) with its 75mm gun; and the two classic German 'heavies', the Tiger I and Tiger II with 88mm guns.

One of the biggest surprises about the German war machine is the time it took to get it organised, which explains why Panther and Tiger were not really ready for the massive tank collision at Kursk in July 1943. Hitler's influence, however, was a baneful one, and in some ways epitomises his whole record as German supreme warlord. He had been right in wanting the 50mm 'long' gun for the Mk III; the Army Ordnance office had flouted him and given him the 'short' 50, with its lower hitting-power. Hitler never forgave this. What made matters worse was his gradual departure from reality. He insisted that a tank be developed for street fighting. The 88mm *Elefant* was a useless concept because this turretless assault-gun was an infantry support weapon and needed machine-guns for infantry fighting. *Elefant* had none. Hitler's obsession with size produced the design for *Maus*, 188 tons of sluggish juggernaut which was to be armed with a 128mm turret gun with a co-axial 75! (It never got past mock-up stage, but far too much time was wasted on it.) Then there was *Stuermtiger*, a Tiger hull packing a 15 inch rocket mortar—a battle-field White Elephant if ever there was one.

One field in which the German Army blazed a trail was in that of rocket missiles. In Russia the German soldier learned of the horrifying effects of mass bombardment by rocket missiles—the dreaded *Katyusha* or

Nerve-shaking rocketry

'Stalin's organ', as the Germans sardonically called it. By early 1943 the German Army had its own six-barrelled rocket mortar—*Nebelwerfer* or 'smoke-thrower', a nerve-shaker in its own right although it was too top-heavy to permit a simultaneous discharge of all six rockets. By 1944 and 1945 experiments were being made to emulate the mobile Katyushas by mounting racks of rocket missiles on half-tracks. By this time, too, the first infantry bazookas had appeared with the recoilless *Panzerfaust* and *Panzerschreck* missile projectors. These prompted un-orthodox counter-measures—Russian tanks smashing into Berlin in April 1945 mounted bed-springs on their frontal armour to detonate the hollow-charge missiles away from the armour.

In the field, the German soldier was basically well served, with disastrous exceptions. The most famous of these occurred during the first campaign in Russia, when over-confidence at the top failed to get the Army's winter uniforms up to the front in time for the battle of Moscow. There was plenty of bureaucratic insubordination in the German Army, but it never seemed to work on the side of the German soldier. The story

of the frozen *Gluehwein* solemnly dropped into the Stalingrad pocket was an absurdity, but a justified one. (Soldiers freezing to death before Moscow while the good citizens of the Reich donated their spare fur coats to be sent to the front were ready to believe stories like that.)

The German Army was a *European* army, and in the one theatre outside Europe in which it performed—North Africa—its essential services did not do well. The original

Too little and too late

tropical kit issued to the *Afrika Korps* included a massive solar topee. Much more serious was the failure of the Germans to *adapt* to the desert. They were never really happy there and both food and medical services left much to be desired. Rommel himself had to go on sick leave on the eve of Alamein with amoebic dysentery. Food was monotonous and deficient in vitamins: British Army field-baked bread and tinned 'bully' were prized spoils of battle. Field medicine, however, was certainly up to standard, although no army of World War II ever reached the sophistication of the American system. (Patton's 3rd Army set the record, with 90 per cent hospital admissions and only 2 percent mortality of that total.) The German medical services even functioned during the Stalingrad tragedy—as long as the aircraft kept coming.

To sum up, we must return to the blunt fact that Germany was not fully 'geared up' to total war until 1944 and it was inevitable that the Army should suffer from this. What the men had to work with was good. But the experts back in the Reich, let alone factory production, could never match the ruthless speed with which the Russians or Americans latched on to a good idea, ironed out the essential teething troubles, and rushed the product into action. It was, in a way, inevitable that as far as material was concerned the Allied story between 1941 and mid-1942 was 'too little, too late'. From then onwards the boot was on the other foot. It is easy to put the whole blame on Hitler, and to say that if he wanted to wage total war he should have prepared for it. He had his experts and they let him down far more often than is frequently admitted. None of this detracts from the achievements of the fighting men who had to suffer in consequence.

Suggested reading
Peter Bathy: **The House of Krupp** (London, 1966)
Alan Clark: **Barbarossa** (London, 1965)
Heinz Guderian: **Panzer Leader** (London, 1952)
Richard Humble: **Hitler's Generals** (London, 1973)
W. L. Shirer: **The Rise and Fall of the Third Reich** (London, 1960)
Albert Speer: **Inside The Third Reich** (London, 1970)
Sir J. W. Wheeler-Bennett: **Nemesis of Power** (London, 1953)

Die Waffen-SS— a European crusade?

The *Waffen* SS on the march.

Richard Humble

Starting as Hitler's own 'Praetorian Guard', the armed units of the SS were trained to standards of perfection. Not only did they look impressive on ceremonial occasions and on guard duty but they were soon built up into full-sized divisions capable of taking the field alongside regular German army forces. There, given time and experience, as well as top priority for new weapons and equipment, several *Waffen*-SS divisions earned fighting reputations second to none.

German propaganda attempts to expand the *Waffen*-SS into a multi-national army crusading against bolshevism were less successful. When the purely German concept of recruitment was abandoned in order to expand the number of divisions, the activities of 'foreign legions' proved a ludicrous failure. But the propagandists did not fail completely. The reputation of the hard-core *Waffen*-SS divisions has always been darkened by their atrocities but they are still regarded as an elite of elites. Was it just the uniform? Was it military achievement? Or was it genuine, if perverted, idealism that was responsible for this?

Above: Waffen SS armour on the move through the streets of Rome, 1944.

Above: The *Waffen* SS included many creeds, including these Croatian Muslims.

Left: Waffen SS artillerymen manning a heavy howitzer on the Eastern front, in the northern sector, 1942.

Right: Victorious *Waffen* SS men, probably of Hitler's bodyguard, holding a captured Soviet flag.

Die Waffen-SS— a European crusade?

Die Waffen-SS

▌*The Waffen SS embodies the highest ideals of National Socialism. It is the successor to the famous bands of Nordic warriors of old. It is the unity of sword and creed, of military power and political belief, which makes the Waffen SS so invincible, so feared upon the battlefields of Europe . . . . . . Never has an elite military force been raised to such perfection in so short a time.* ▌

Heinrich Himmler 1943

▌*The Waffen SS is now not just a German force – it is a European ideal which has as its aim the total eradication of Bolshevism.* ▌

Heinrich Himmler 1943

The SS (*Schuetzstaffeln*) followed the SA (*Sturmabteilung*) as the second—and, to start with, emphatically smaller—of the 'private armies' of the Nazi movement. The SS leader Heinrich Himmler had been a *protégé* of Gregor Strasser, Hitler's greatest rival for the leadership of the Party; and until 1934 Himmler remained, at least in theory, subordinate to Ernst Roehm, boss of the SA.

The SS, which Himmler took over in 1929, had as its immediate aim the provision of a bodyguard to Hitler, who soon saw the advantages of having to hand a more tightly-knit force than the SA. Finally, in June 1934, Hitler used the SS to eliminate Roehm and the other SA leaders in the 'Night of the Long Knives'. Himmler then began to expand the SS to fill the power vacuum—and to provide Hitler with an executive arm beyond the control either of the law or of the state. At the same time, strenuous efforts were made to invest the SS with spurious honours as the visible expression of the Nazi ideal.

The *Waffen*-SS or 'armed SS') was as old as the Nazi state. It came into being as the 'SS *Leibstandarte* Adolf Hitler' (Adolf Hitler's lifeguards) in 1933, an outfit destined to become the first field unit of the *Waffen*-SS. It is not hard to see why Hitler encouraged the formation of SS military units—he profoundly distrusted the 'old boy' mentality of the traditional German Army officer caste and knew very well that it was the only institution in Germany which could turn against him. He wanted his own Praetorian guard;

Death's Head units

and if it made the regular German army look slack and inferior by comparison, so much the better.

After the hard-core *Leibstandarte* came the formation of *Verfuegungstruppen* or 'armed reserve troops' throughout the *Reich*. These were described as 'exclusively at the service of the *Fuehrer*, for special tasks in peace and war'. Selection standards were high—originally candidates were failed if they had fillings in their teeth. Standards of drill, training, and turnout were perfectionist—one in three SS men applying for a walking-out pass would be turned down because of some minute fault in his dress or bearing.

There were applicants in plenty, for any new élite unit attracts recruits with a multitude of motives. Many regular Army officers transferred to the *Waffen*-SS (it should be

remembered that the official term did not begin to be used until the 1940 campaign) because promotion was faster.

In addition to the SS-VT units there were the *Totenkopfverbaende* or 'Death's Head units', originally raised as concentration camp guards, for use against any civil strife in the event of Germany going to war.

By 1940 four regiments had been raised: *Leibstandarte, Deutschland, Germania,* and *Der Fuehrer,* most of which had taken part in the occupations of Austria, the Sudetenland, and Prague, and were gradually becoming accepted as part of the military machine. There were also four *Totenkopf* units, the regiments being given provincial names: *Oberbayern, Brandenburg, Thuringen,* and the Austrian *Ostmark.* Typical of the regional formation of *Waffen*-SS units in the year 1939 was

The Asphalt Soldiers

Heimwehr Danzig, raised in that city as the Nazi programme of threats and demands against Poland increased in tempo. As its name suggests, it was a hardcore Nazi vigilante outfit, used to police the city and beat up recalcitrant Poles.

The army's situation was intricate. Its leaders had backed Hitler's accession to power because Hitler had promised them that the brown-shirted SA would not be permitted to challenge the army for the title of official arms-bearers of the Reich. These new SS regiments were doing just that, but as every officer and man in the Army had sworn personal allegiance to Adolf Hitler it was not good for the conscience to worry about them. It was easier to regard the SS regiments as 'Asphalt soldiers', very pretty on the parade-ground, but basically amateurs who could not shape up if ever they were to be exposed to combat.

The *Waffen*-SS units which received their baptism of fire in Poland were the *Leibstandarte* and *Verfuegungstruppe* regiments, well corseted by regular Army units to which they were subordinate. For all their much-vaunted training with live ammunition and balancing

Right: Hitler reviews his Guard. After their success in Poland, in 1939, Hitler inspects a motorcycle reconnaissance unit of the *Leibstandarte* SS 'Adolf Hitler'. This unit was to develop to panzer divisional size.

Above: The 'European Army'. Danes recruited for the *Waffen* SS parade before their compatriots.

Left: Men of an SS *Verfuegungstruppe* machine gun detachment supporting an attack in Holland, 1940.

of live grenades on helmets, the *Waffen*-SS troops put up a generally mediocre performance and suffered proportionately heavy loss. Had the German High Command possessed any sane structure, the decision must certainly have been made to break up the *Waffen*-SS formations and post the men to Army units. Instead a highly complicated series of orders up-graded and re-formed the battered regiments to divisional status—and even more of them were planned.

Leibstandarte, surprisingly enough, was merely retained as a strengthened motorised infantry regiment; but a new division was

A breach in perfection

formed from the *Totenkopfverbaende* and was christened *Totenkopf*. Another division was raised from the police forces of the Reich: *Polizei*. The latter SS unit was the first noticeable breach in the original perfectionist standards of recruiting—but more soon followed.

Inevitably, the members of the imitation movements which were to be found among Germany's neighbours—and imminent victims—were soon regarded as suitable recruiting material. These included the followers of future collaborationists Quisling (Norway), Degrelle (Belgium) and Mussert (Holland), who formed the first non-German *Waffen*-SS unit. This was the *Nordland* regiment, formed in 1940 and soon followed by *Westland*.

Two further modifications of the *Waffen*-SS 'order of battle' in 1940 improved upon these beginnings. *Nordland* and *Westland* were merged with the *Germania* regiment to form the *Germania* Division. This was subsequently re-christened *Wiking*, while the *Verfuegungsdivision* was re-christened *Das Reich*.

The campaign in the West did two things for the *Waffen*-SS: it confirmed its title and established a reputation for efficiency, but at the same time put an enduring black mark on its reputation for atrocity. The culprits were the men of *Totenkopf* who massacred surrendered British POWs at Le Paradis, triggering off a ripple of uneasy protest from regular Army commanders that was never translated into punitive action. And more expansion was promised. Addressing *Leibstandarte* officers in September 1940, Himmler announced: 'We must attract all the Nordic blood in the world to us so that never again will it fight against us.'

It remained to be seen what definitions would be drawn for 'Nordic blood', and just how much of it would in fact be attracted.

A mixture of opportunism and desperation helped make an utter nonsense of the original Nazi definitions of what made a worthwhile citizen—and potential soldier—of the *Reich*. Germany never lacked for direct allies down to the end of the war—Italians, Hungarians, Romanians. But the racial creed of the *Waffen*-SS had originally stood above foreign integration. As Hitler's Germany strengthened its grip on Europe, the categories of German citizens (*Reichsdeutsch*) and ethnic Germans (*Volksdeutsch*)

Muslims among recruits

were increased by the addition of 'honorary Germans'—and for this latter category the sky was the limit.

A total of about 6000 Norwegians and Danes served in the *Waffen*-SS under a bewildering kaleidoscope of titles. *Freikorps* —foreign legions—were raised in addition to the *Wiking* Division. In early 1943 the Scandinavian troops were merged in a reborn *Nordland* Division which was finally immolated in the battle of Berlin. These, at least, were recognisable 'Nordics', and so were the volunteers from Holland, which was granted the status of being closest by blood to Germany herself. The Dutch produced a record crop of SS volunteers—the figure has been set as high as 50,000. What was finally described as the *Nederland* Division ended up trapped in Courland, and only a few survivors were evacuated. The Belgians, led by Léon Degrelle, produced two paper divisions: *Langemarck* and *Wallonie*, both of which were ground to pieces on the Eastern Front.

The campaign in the East produced the most promising crop of foreign recruits, starting with the Baltic States, in particular Latvia and Estonia. By the spring of 1943, 22,000 had volunteered and were formed into three divisions—two Latvian and one Estonian. Their survivors, too, ended up in the Courland pocket. Down in the occupied Balkans Himmler made strenuous efforts to recruit Balkan Muslims disenchanted by the Yugoslav state, officially dismembered by the conquest of April 1941. Three divisions reached paper strength: the Muslim *Handschar*, the Albanian *Skanderbeg*, and the Croat *Kama*. After blotting their copybook by mutinying under training, the Muslims were set to deal with Tito's partisans. Their

Rifle practice for one of Hitler's guardsmen. Much emphasis was placed upon efficiency in the martial arts, although before 1939 men of the *Leibstandarte* were often jeered at for their low standard in everything but drill.

successes in this field were negligible and their main achievement was the massacre of Yugoslav civilians.

In Russia proper the Ukraine and the Cossack lands of the Don and Kuban were also fruitful recruiting-grounds until the true nature of German occupation made its mark. Some 100,000 anti-Communist Ukrainians volunteered, were formed into the 14th Galician Division, and virtually wiped out in their first (and last) battle: the Tarnov-Brody pocket in June 1944. Several Cossack units were raised, but none of them achieved any military successes, although they were encountered by the Allies as far afield as France and northern Italy.

Perhaps least effective of all were the attempts made to recruit from Allied POWs. The Indian independence leader Subhas Chandra Bose tried to raise an Indian

Elite striking force

nationalist army from POWs taken in North Africa, but never attracted more than 2000. Recruitment among the French produced the volunteer *Sturmbrigade 'Charlemagne'*, subsequently elevated to divisional status but never up to actual brigade strength. *Charlemagne*, too, was wiped out in the Berlin battle. And most ignominious of all was the failure to form a British SS unit, the *Britisches Freikorps* or 'Legion of St George'. These military drop-outs never made up more than two platoons, and caused their German patrons constant headaches by their insatiable demands for loose women and drink. Here indeed was a case of pure propaganda winning out over military practicability.

For their failure to make more out of the available recruits (particularly in the East) the Germans could blame lack of time and their own atrocious behaviour to conquered populations. Both were key ingredients in the destruction of Germany and her SS.

By the middle of 1941 the overall strength of the *Waffen*-SS was six divisions, of which the majority were manned by native Germans. A year later, in the fearful battles of the Eastern Front, they had more than won their spurs. All six had suffered heavily and *Leibstandarte*, *Das Reich*, *Totenkopf* and *Wiking* were withdrawn to be re-equipped with the newest weapons and restored to strength. Nos 1, 2, 3, 5, 9, 10 and 12 were to be raised to the status of full Panzer divisions. They formed the élite striking force with which Manstein restored the Eastern Front during the Stalingrad crisis. But by this time Hitler had come to the decision that more must be raised.

Hohenstaufen and *Frundsberg* were the next German SS divisions raised, followed by *Hitler Jugend*, one of the most frightening combat units of the war: recruited from the 1926 class of dedicated young Nazis.

The first time that *Waffen*-SS Panzer divisions were used as a unified bloc was during the superb Manstein counter-offensive of February-March 1943, which recovered Kharkov. From then on Hitler used his SS divisions as a mobile 'fire-brigade' and rushed them mercilessly about the map

Above: Tanks and grenadiers of an SS Panzer Division during the 1943 winter counter-attack against Kharkov. Shown here, is the PzKw III with the short 50mm gun, which was then being phased out of service with the troops.

Right: SS Panzer Grenadiers of 6SS Panzer Army at the opening of the Ardennes offensive, December 1944, by a wrecked US half-track.

of Europe. They were sent to France. They were rushed back to Russia. They served in northern Italy. The record was put up by the most renowned of them all, *Leibstandarte*, which oscillated between East and West seven times, each time being required to throw in a major attack immediately upon arrival. Between Kursk and the Normandy landings *Waffen*-SS divisions were constantly in action, carrying out this emergency rôle. And during this time Hitler, thanks to his growing distrust of the regular Army generals, came to develop an exag-

The fire-brigade units

gerated respect for the indifferent military skills of the SS generals—Dietrich, Steiner, Meyer.

Perhaps the most crucial of these 'fire-brigade' battles was the containment of the British and Canadians at Caen in June-July 1944, where the seven *Waffen*-SS divisions employed fought themselves to virtual destruction. Here, too, the *Waffen*-SS added to its atrocity dossier with the Oradour massacre (*Das Reich*) and the slaughter of 64 Allied POWs (*Hitler Jugend*). The latter atrocity could not be cancelled out by the superhuman efforts made by *Hitler Jugend* in keeping open the Falaise Gap for the escape of their defeated comrades.

The last major event in the *Waffen*-SS

story was the Ardennes offensive of December 1944, which saw the first attack by a full-blooded SS Panzer Army (the 6th) spearheaded by *Leibstandarte*. Superbly equipped with the 'King Tiger' heavy tanks, *Leibstandarte* nevertheless got itself bogged down on the northern flank of the 'Bulge' which was hammered into the Allied front. The furthest advance was made in the centre by

Hitler's lost confidence

regular Army troops—and *Leibstandarte* was the culprit for the infamous murder of 86 American POWs at Malmedy.

It should be remembered that by the last months of the war Hitler had lost all confidence in every single fighting arm of the *Wehrmacht*—including the *Waffen*-SS. When he ordered *Leibstandarte* to remove their armbands as a punishment for failing to bring off an impossible attack, the reaction was one of bewilderment, resentment and fury. It was to this that the original concept of the *Waffen*-SS as the Nazi Praetorian Guard had come.

Above: Men of the SS *Polizei* division in their winter camouflage. *Left:* Tigers of an SS Panzer division covering withdrawal of assault guns.

Below: Officers of *Leibstandarte* SS Panzer Division planning a counter attack in Hungary, 1945. By then, this elite unit was so weak that it ended the war with only 12 tanks.

The men of these superb divisions had an *esprit de corps* second to none, however reluctantly this must be granted. Their achievements were frequently remarkable. The most dedicated men in their ranks fought as super-patriots, members of a unique comradeship. But their survivors today owe their Jekyll-and-Hyde reputation to the fact that the evil that they did lived after them.

Fight against Bolshevism

One of the most frightening aspects of the *Waffen*-SS is the fascination which it still has for military collectors and modellers. The glamour which that service undoubtedly had for the Germans of Hitler's day has by no means been dissipated by the passage of time. Nor can it be claimed that the survival of this interest stems purely from the detached academic motives of the military historian. There is something else. But what?

Muddled thinking is one of the clearest guidelines to the Nazi mentality, and we have seen how this came to affect the composition of the *Waffen*-SS. The propaganda slogan 'Join us in the Crusade Against Bolshevism' came late in the day, and this is hard for many to accept. Indeed, many *Waffen*-SS veterans go so far as to insist that they were the prototype of the United Nations and NATO multi-national armies. One fact that is obvious is that the origins of the force lay in the desire of Hitler to have at his disposal an iron guard which owed allegiance to nothing and nobody but himself, and that the deliberate efforts to build up this hard core into a Nazi field army woefully dissipated the resources of Nazi Germany's war effort. It is impossible to create a *corps d'élite* overnight: time is needed for that, and once Hitler had made his decision to bring on a war in Europe in 1939, time was the one thing he did not have. Nevertheless, by 1943 the German divisions of the *Waffen*-SS *did* regard themselves as a *corps d'élite* and by the end of the war could claim, with justification, that their efforts in the field had made them one.

Certainly the story of the *Waffen*-SS reflects the dehumanising effect of World War II. It was *impossible* for Nazi Germany to produce a combat arm that could claim to emerge from the whole mess with an unspotted record. To coin a phrase, it might be said that the entire Nazi system was 'self-soiling'. The 12 years of Hitler's Reich offered scope for, and fulfilment to, Germans motivated by genuine ideals of patriotism,

The *Waffen* SS withdraws. Here, a Tiger tank of an SS Panzer Division moves back over the Rhine into the *Reich*, carrying with it a number of paratroopers. The SS divisions were now among the strongest of the armed forces, having received priority in new, improved equipment. Their armoured units were usually at least one-third above the strength of their army counterparts. They were used as Hitler's 'fire-brigade', and there can be little doubt that their activities in many a place helped to delay Germany's final defeat.

public service, and self respect. But the institutions of brute force which upheld Hitler's *Reich*—of which the *Waffen*-SS was clearly one—offered not only scope and fulfilment but rapid promotion to the thugs and brutes who alone could do the dirty work without going mad. Hence regular Army combat units fighting at the front could voice their contempt for, and disgust with, the murderous thugs of the *Einsatzkommados* in their rear. *Waffen*-SS commanders, too, could and did pride themselves on their military honour—while belonging to a force which was capable of Oradour, Malmedy, Le Paradis, and other atrocities. The comic-opera characteristics of the worst of the foreign SS units might be the object of general mirth among 'real German soldiers' but it all stemmed from the same source.

The *Waffen*-SS can claim one justification for its mottled reputation: the dehumanising influence of war. By 1944 those soldiers which had survived Moscow, Stalingrad, Kursk, and a score of other murderous battles were not as other men. But in the case of the *Waffen*-SS, with its self-imposed standards of ruthless efficiency, of being the best soldiers in the world bar none, this dehumanisation was all too often carried beyond all acceptance. And none of the military glamour with which the *Waffen*-SS is still invested today can change the fundamental misdirection of so much dedication and sacrifice.

Top left: **Sepp Dietrich, commander of Hitler's bodyguard, the elite** *Leibstandarte* **SS 'Adolf Hitler', and later commander of the 6SS Panzer Army. For many, Dietrich personified the** *Waffen* **SS spirit – bold in action, he was of a swash-buckling disposition, enjoying fighting for fighting's sake. Considerate to his men, he could be ruthless when required, brooking no obstacle. He was a special favourite of Hitler, and German propaganda made much of his exploits. He was not so convinced a Nazi as not to be able to demur at Hitler's decisions and even to support those decisions that were made against the** *Fuehrer*.

Left: **Waffen SS men at the ready, waiting for the order to advance. The military efficiency of these forces was at least the equal of the German army and their successes in battle were to become legendary. Whatever their reputations for cruelty – reputations that became notorious and with which they were justly connected – they nonetheless bore the brunt of much of the fighting and gained reputations also for courage and tenacity.**

Suggested reading
R. J. Bender and Hugh Page Taylor: **Uniforms, Organisation and History of the Waffen-SS** (Bender Publishing, Calif., U.S.A.)
John Keegan: **Waffen-SS** (London, 1969)
Gerald Reitlinger: **The SS—Alibi of a Nation** (London, 1956)
Martin Windrow: **Waffen-SS** (London, 1971)

Die Luftwaffe—
strategically a failure

Destination England, ready for take-off.

Matthew Cooper

The *Luftwaffe* was a failure. Despite its early victories the German air force proved unable to retain control of the air over Europe and after five years of war it lay broken. The importance of this failure is too often overlooked. It was, however, immense. Air power in World War II was a precondition of success in both tactical and strategic terms. Tactically, its use could significantly affect the course of land warfare, as exemplified by the Germans in their *Blitzkrieg* campaigns. Strategically, the air force could be used as an instrument of war in its own right, capable of the destruction of the enemy's capacity to continue the conflict, by means of the bombing of vital industries, communications and, more questionably, of civilians. Defensively, too, air

Above: The Heinkel 111, which was the standard bomber with which Germany entered the war and made her initial conquests in Europe.

power was indispensible, denying to the enemy the above advantages. All this the RAF and USAAF mastered to varying degrees. But not so the *Luftwaffe*, which was regarded primarily as an offensive, tactical weapon. This was the fatal error. Strategic bombing and fighter defence were developed too little, too late and with too much muddle. More than any other single military factor, the failure of the *Luftwaffe* contributed to the eventual defeat of the Third *Reich*.

Above: The navigator and bomb-aimer in the He111, as it flies toward its target somewhere in the south of England.

The twin-engined Me110 had many uses, two of which are illustrated here: *Left:* as a fighter. *Right:* as a photo reconnaissance plane.

Die Luftwaffe—
strategically
a failure

Die Luftwaffe

My Luftwaffe is invincible. Just look at its achievements in Poland and in France – can one conceive of a war machine in history which has contributed so much towards such total victories as these. As a fighting force surely the Luftwaffe is a living monument to National Socialism . . . . . . And so now we turn to England. How long will this one last – two, three weeks? Our bomber fleets will make short work of the little islanders.

Hermann Goering 1940

What has gone wrong? . . . . . The Luftwaffe lies a broken wreck, unable to halt the Allied advance for one hour, let alone one day.

Adolf Hitler 1945

The men of the High Command must be held responsible for the development of the *Luftwaffe*'s limiting, and ultimately fatal, tactical rôle. The influence of three in particular, Hitler, Goering and Udet, was of prime importance, and gave to the Luftwaffe its particular mentality, concentrating on numbers and ground attack to the detriment of all else.

Hitler's dedication to a land-based *Blitzkrieg* strategy, coupled with his measuring of air power in numerative rather than qualitative terms, can be seen throughout the *Luftwaffe*'s history. He shared with his subordinate, Hermann Goering, the *Luftwaffe* Commander-in-Chief and *Reich* Air Minister, an inability to grasp the strategic importance of the air-force. They were also unable to comprehend the technical problems of aircraft and air-warfare. Goering's over-optimism proved disasterous in his decision making and, although his abilities should not be underestimated, his character ensured that *Luftwaffe* policy would be determined more by impulse and emotion rather than by logic and reality.

Ernst Udet was responsible for the vital design and procurement of aircraft but his inadequate policies ensured that the *Luftwaffe* was to face a crisis in late 1941, thereby prompting his suicide. Goering was to an extent right when he announced in 1943, 'If he were alive today I should have no alterna-

Failure and suicide

tive but to tell him that he had been responsible for destroying the *Luftwaffe*.'

Udet's successor and Goering's deputy, Erhard Milch was an excellent administrator and a man who saw more clearly than most the needs of the *Luftwaffe*, especially from 1942 on. Although his personal influence had waned before the beginning of the war, he came to be the key man in the development of the aircraft industry and in the continuance of the *Luftwaffe*.

Two other men deserve mention, Walther Wever the first *Luftwaffe* Chief of Staff, and one of his successors, Hans Jeschonnek. The former's influence upon the *Luftwaffe* in its formative years was great, but his death in 1936 proved unfortunate for the development of any wider rôle for the air force. Jeschonnek was a dedicated exponent of

tactical air power, his term of office from 1939 to 1943—the vital years—ensured that no 'deviation' was possible. Only too late did he realise his error, and his suicide was largely the result.

The senior field commanders of the *Luftwaffe* reflect similar weaknesses in outlook. Having held high positions in the army they gave to the *Luftwaffe* their ability and their belief in the tactical support rôle of air forces. There was a touch of amateurism in these men which did not compare well with the true professionalism of the junior commanders such as Galland and Kammhuber, and the officer cadets of 1933-35. The failures of these 'founders' of the *Luftwaffe* will be dealt with in more detail later.

Ideologically unsound

The organisation of the German Air Force reflects the dominance of its tactical rôle. The support of large and mobile armies demanded a corresponding mobility and flexibility in the *Luftwaffe*, this leading to a unique system based upon the traditional military pattern. The *Luftflotte*, then, was the equivalent of an army group, its composition varying according to the requirements of the campaign and its territorial area of command being moveable and extendable. Of these, the highest field command, there were four, but by 1944 three more had been added to cope with the expansion of *Luftwaffe* operations. A *Luftflotten* was composed of several *Fliegerkorps*—again units of extremely elastic composition (a *Jagdkorps* was purely a fighter unit). The Geschwader (squadron) was the largest homogenous units of the *Luftwaffe*, consisting of 100-120 aircraft (numbers varying considerably). This was divided into three *Gruppen*, which were in turn composed of three *Staffeln*, the basic aerial units. Administrative services were dealt with by the territorially-based *Luftgaue* which came under the control of the *Luftflotten*. Goering would have done better to place them under army command. He refused to do so partly out of pride and partly because of his belief that most of the army leaders were ideo-

Right: Goering with his deputy, Milch, who more clearly than most understood the *Luftwaffe*'s true needs.

Above: Hermann Goering, Commander-in-Chief of the Air Force, in 1938. The history of the *Luftwaffe* reflects his strengths and weaknesses as a leader.

Left: Luftwaffe recruits swearing allegiance to their *Fuehrer,* in 1936.

logically unsound.

This structure was an obvious asset in *Blitzkrieg* warfare, but it had many disadvantages. The worst was that the *Luftwaffe* had no bomber or fighter command, and this had the effect of allowing these aircraft to be dispersed at a time when strategic considerations demanded their concentration—as shown by the Battle of Britain, Russia and the defence of the *Reich*. No 'bomber' or 'fighter' policy could be properly formulated or adequately executed without such an organisation.

The Luftwaffe was composed of other units apart from the flying ones—Flak and ground troops being the most important. By mid-1943 there were over one million people engaged in anti-aircraft units, and while the heaviest concentration was in the *Reich*, their most valuable contribution was, arguably, in the field. By October 1941 Flak had shot down no less than 5381 aeroplanes, but

Crowning glory at Crete

of these the greater majority had been scored in the *Blitzkrieg* campaigns in support of ground units rather than home defence. It was organised upon military lines— from Division to platoons—and used some excellent and versatile guns—the 88mm being the most notable.

The paratroops were a part of the overall tactical role of the *Luftwaffe*. As such they were successful in Norway and Denmark, Holland and Crete, but this latter action, their 'crowning glory', so crippled them that their airborne role was over for the rest of the war. However, they continued to serve in a ground combat role, their numbers expanding to just under a quarter of a million and organised into ten divisions. The other ground troops of the airforce were the *Luftwaffe* Field Divisions (22 had been raised by the end) and the élite Hermann Goering Regiment, which was expanded to a panzer and parachute corps. Their organisation was strictly military.

The armaments of a force necessarily reflect the rôle of that force. Therefore, since the

Luftwaffe was thought of fundamentally in tactical terms, it followed that its aeroplanes would be designed primarily to fit this task. As such they were successful. But their failure became only too apparent when they were required to perform other rôles from mid-1940 on. At this point the offensive tactical doctrine and its existing equipment was found to be totally inadequate for the *Luftwaffe*'s activities in two vital areas—strategic bombing and fighter defence. Even worse, it was to inhibit the future development of the necessary rôles and aircraft. As Milch was to assert in early 1944—'Luftwaffe armament has just not been given the proper treatment and support—that's why things look so black today.'

Bomb-carrying aircraft are first and foremost aggressive weapons. As such they served as the *Luftwaffe*'s main strength until the middle of the war. Hitler, even at the end, continuing to insist upon the offensive advantages of the bomber in support of ground operations. The *Luftwaffe* bomb-carriers were of two types—medium bombers and ground attack aircraft—both designed to meet the requirements of a *Blitzkrieg* war.

The medium bombers were well suited to a tactical rôle, designed as relatively small but highly powered and manoeuvrable aircraft, capable of delivering medium-sized bomb loads while at the same time having a fair chance of eluding fighter interceptors. Their specifications would take them either to targets just beyond the front line or to those such as airfields and lines of communications well within the territories of Germany's continental neighbours. Their range and payload, however, would not allow them to assume a worthwhile strategic rôle.

The Dornier 17 was the first of the Luftwaffe's bombers which exemplified this stress upon tactical operations, specialising as it did in low-level contour flying. With a bomb load of 2205 lbs the Do17Z-2 had a maximum speed of 255 mph at 13,120 ft and a tactical radius of 205 miles. Its high manoeuvrability, coupled with its shallow diving

Early obsolescence

ability made it the most successful bomber at eluding fighters during the Battle of Britain, but it was extremely vulnerable to attack, especially from the rear. It was never widely used, and by mid-1941 its rôle as a bomber was largely over. The Do215 was a further development upon this design, its greater power allowing it to outpace the early Spitfires. The Do217, similar in appearance to the above, nevertheless differed considerably. Capable of dive-bombing, the Do217E-2 had a maximum bomb load of 8818 lbs, a maximum speed of 320 mph at 17,060 ft and a tactical radius of well over 600 miles. As with the Do215, few were operational, being used mainly against shipping.

Of more importance was the Heinkel 111 which opened the war as the *Luftwaffe*'s standard bomber, the H-16 version of which carried 4410 lbs of bombs at a maximum speed of 270 mph at 19,685 ft over a tactical radius of some 550 miles. While being extremely versatile and easy to handle, the

Above: Two of the most important creators of the *Luftwaffe*, Ernst Udet and Erhard Milch. Udet's failure to equip the force properly brought about his suicide, and Milch proved unable to improve the lamentable situation.

He111 was reaching obsolescence by mid-1940. However, it continued in operational bombing service on the Eastern front until mid-1943, by which time its lack of effective defensive armament was not compensated for by a weak opposition.

The Junkers 88, some 15,000 of which were produced by the end of the war, was in many ways the backbone of the *Luftwaffe*, its rôles extending outside the bombing field into night fighting, ground attack and reconnaissance. As a bomber, the Ju88A had a maximum speed of 292 mph at 17,390 ft, and could carry a bomb load of 4420 lbs over a tactical radius of well over 700 miles. As always, the *Luftwaffe* planners had overestimated the defensive power of one or two rear-firing guns and although the Ju88's high diving speed had enabled it to evade

Luftwaffe planning faults

even the Spitfire during the Battle of Britain, its armament needed improvement. This was done, but it was not enough. In 1944 an improved version was produced, with a maximum speed of 340 mph, in an attempt to give the bomber a chance of eluding fighters.

However, while the Ju88 was up to a point a successful plane, it nevertheless revealed many of the weaknesses in *Luftwaffe* plan-

Above: Heinkel 111s, nicknamed 'spades' by their crews, crossing the English Channel during the Battle of Britain. Their bombs were carried tail-down in vertical cells in the fuselage and, later in the war, external racks were fitted for large bombs and torpedoes, to increase their firepower.

Right: The Ju87, or Stuka, the prime tactical ground support aircraft of the *Luftwaffe*, whose contribution to the *Blitzkrieg* campaigns of Poland, France and Russia was considerable. Its employment continued until the end of the war, despite its poor showing during the Battle of Britain.

ning. Heralded as a 'super-bomber', the Ju88 was to have flown with over two tons of bombs at speeds over 300 mph over a tactical radius of 1000 miles. But the obsession with tactical support had caused Udet to stipulate a further fatal requirement—a dive-bombing capacity, thus allowing pinpoint accuracy. Due to the heavy air-brakes and structural strengthening needed, the Ju88's loaded weight doubled to 12 tons from 1936 to 1939. Its performance was therefore reduced. Milch called it a 'flying barn door'. Udet, in his concern to save time, had even ordered mass production before its test flying was completed. This resulted in repeated breakdowns and stoppages, so that only by 1943 was the aircraft fully satisfactory. Up until the summer of 1940 it had undergone no less than 50,000 design changes. The pilots were uneasy about the Ju88 at first, prompting one medical officer to delcare that 'It's not the enemy the squadrons' frightened of, it's the Ju88'. Goering, upon realising that the plane was not to live up to its promise, called it 'the product of a pigsty!'.

Worse than this was the absolute reliance that the German planners placed upon this medium bomber for the *Luftwaffe*'s offensive capacity. At a conference in 1938 it was decided to adopt the Ju88 as the future standard bomber. Only in 1939 was it decided to launch a 'Bomber B' programme which would create an entirely new type of bomber to replace it from 1942 on. This new bomber was to have been able to undertake strategic missions. But not only would it have come rather late, it also failed to arrive at all. The plane decided upon, the Ju288

Dive-bombing obsession

was another that suffered from Udets' obsession with dive-bombing. At the end of 1941 Milch, realising the inadequacies of the Ju288 and the fact that it could not be produced until 1944 at the earliest, decided to concentrate upon continued production of the Ju88 and its improved version, the Ju188. This latter aircraft entered service in May 1943. By the end of the war 1036 had been produced. As a medium bomber it was a sensible plane, the E-1 version being capable of a maximum speed of 310 mph at 19,685 ft, a tactical radius of some 600 miles and a bomb load of 6614 lbs. In June 1943 'Bomber B', already a dead-duck, was finally cancelled.

It is ironic that despite the emphasis laid upon the bomber before 1942, the *Luftwaffe* failed to develop any practicable heavy bombers. Wever had seen more clearly than most the strategic possibilities of airpower, but his death in June 1936 ensured that the protagonists of the tactical ideal would dominate. In April 1937 Goering signed the order which effectively set the seal upon the

Top left: The Ju188 bomber.
Top right: The ill-fated He177.
Bottom left: The Me210, which was a ground attack aircraft.
Bottom right: The Hs129, one of Germany's close-support planes.

development of two four-engined strategic bombers (known as the 'Ural' bombers in reference to one of their possible destinations), the Ju89 and Do19. Despite the very definite possibilities of the former, the arguments against the building of a strategic bomber force were persuasive. It was said that at a time of shortage it would involve

The flying firework

far too high a proportion of raw material, fuel and manpower supplies; that, at the time, Germany needed a tactical force for a continental war since no conflict with Britain was envisaged; and that two or three double-engined bombers could be produced for every four-engined machine. As Goering said, 'The Fuehrer will never ask me how big our bombers are, but how many we have.'

So a purely strategic bomber was ruled out at a time when the Flying Fortress was just beginning to be developed. The idea of a heavy bomber, however, was not ruled out but its technical specifications were so dominated by a dive-bombing requirement that its failure was ensured. The 'Bomber A' project envisaged strategic possibilities, but

they came to nothing. The He177 was the plane decided upon, but its design faults were such that only a very few ever became operational and their results were poor. Due to a disturbing propensity to catch fire, it was dubbed 'the flying firework'. Goering summed up the fault, 'It is straightforward idiocy to ask of a four-engined bomber that it should dive.' Idiocy it was, and it ensured that the *Luftwaffe* was never to have an effective heavy bomber and be equipped for a strategic rôle.

In its heyday, the Ju87, 'Stuka' was the ground attack aircraft without rival—a vital component of *Blitzkrieg* war, second only to the tank. As a dive-bomber it may be said to epitomise the *Luftwaffe*'s stress upon an offensive tactical rôle. Its intended use was against targets such as gun emplacements, entrenched positions and, later, armoured vehicles; it was able to drop its bomb load with an accuracy of less than 30 yards. Although some thought it obsolescent even before the outbreak of war, the Ju87 nevertheless proved itself extremely valuable not just in Poland and France but in the Balkans, Russia and Africa. Despite popular belief, the Stuka was not phased out after its disastrous commitment in the Battle of

Britain; its initial success and continuing usefulness, plus the fact that there was no plane to replace it (the one intended, the Me210, never overcame its design faults), ensured that production continued until the summer of 1944. By this time more than 5700 Ju87's had been manufactured, no less than 1844 of them in 1943. Udet was the Stuka's champion and Goering, in one of his more generous moments, said of him: 'It will always be recognised as his greatest contribution that he created the weapon with which we achieved such magnificent victories.'

The Ju87B-1 (the details of its successor, the 'D' which began to emerge in mid-1941, will be given in brackets) carried one 1102 lb bomb or one 551 lb and four 110 lb bombs (maximum of 3,968 lbs) over a maximum

The tank destroyers

range of 370 miles (510 miles) at a maximum speed of 238 mph (255 mph with 1102 bomb load). It was fitted with a cannon for its tank-destroying rôle. However, due to its slow speed and light defensive armament, the Stuka was particularly vulnerable to

fighter opposition, and therefore relied upon the Luftwaffe's complete control of the air. When this was not available the Ju87 was a failure. Its final demise came from the increasing activity of the Soviet airforce; by October 1943 most Stuka units were night attack formations only.

Other ground support aircraft included the Ju88, the Fw190 and the successor to the Me210, the Me410. This aircraft came into service in Mid-1943 and fitted many rôles—heavy fighter, light bomber, reconnaissance, and so on. Of good performance, the Me410A had a maximum speed of 388 mph, a bomb load of 2205 lbs and a maximum range of 1050 miles. More important was the Henschel 129 which came into service in early 1942. Pilots were not overwhelmed by its performance: it was only 20 mph faster and less manoeuvrable than the Ju87D and had poor engine reliability. However, its serviceability improved and flyers were grateful for the Hs129's sturdier fuselage and wide range of weapons. The Hs129B-2 had a maximum range of 428 miles and a maximum load of 771 lbs and a variety of cannon—the largest being the BK 37mm. While it was well suited to a close support and anti-tank rôle, only 841 Hs129's were produced. The

Luftwaffe planners simply failed to fully appreciate its importance and therefore did not place sufficient stress upon its development. This was a pity, for the Russians had learnt to respect its tank-destroying capacity.

The bombers and ground attack aircraft, then, were the Luftwaffe's prime offensive weapons and while the Wehrmacht was everywhere victorious they would inevitably remain so. Fighters, on the other hand, were regarded as secondary until the middle of the war; until, that is, the Luftwaffe began

The greatest error

to go over to the defensive. In the first years, the fighters, as weapons designed to ensure control of the air for the uninhibited use of the bombers, were somewhat neglected. In 1940, therefore, out of a total of 10,247 aeroplanes produced, 3455 were bombers and ground attack and only 2746 fighters, and in 1942 it was 5586 to 5518. Only in 1943 was the relationship reversed. The failure to stress the fighter until too late will be dealt with later; suffice it to say here that Milch regarded the greatest error of the Luftwaffe to be the 'one hundred and forty thousand unbuilt fighter aircraft'.

The Luftwaffe opened the war with the Messerschmidt Bf109 as its standard fighter. There is still controversy as to its relative performance but its advocates assert that when handled properly the later versions of the Me109 were certainly a match for any other conventional fighter. When the 'F' series was introduced in late 1940 many said it had the edge over the contemporary Spitfire, and the 'G' and 'K' versions, once teething troubles had been dealt with, went on to become among the best high-altitude fighters in the world. By the end of the war not less than 30,480 Me109's had been produced.

The Me109F had a maximum speed of 388 mph at 21,325 ft, was able to cover 528 miles at 298 mph at sea level with a drop tank, could climb to 16,400 ft in 2.6 minutes and had a service ceiling of 39,370 ft. With two 13mm machine guns and two 20mm

An inspired design

cannon, the weight of fire from a three-second burst from a Me109G was some 35 lbs—as good as any Allied fighter. While it could be adapted for bomb carrying missions (up to 1000 lbs), its speed and manoeuvrability suffered greatly.

If its fighter-bomber rôle left much to be desired, so did its bomber-support rôle. It simply did not have the mileage for strategic missions; the official cruising range of 412 miles for the Me109E (used in the Battle of Britain) was misleading. Its real radius of action was only just over 100 miles, having a total flight duration of some 95 minutes, of which 75-80 minutes was tactical flying time. This was wholly inadequate.

The Me109 was, however, an inspired design for the times, the essence of which was the coupling of the smallest possible airframe with the most powerful engine.

Above: The FW190, one of the best fighters of the war. Goering called it a 'deadly horsefly' but its pilots were more complimentary. The general consensus of opinion was that the plane was versatile, fast and well-armed.

Right: The Me110, designed as the *Luftwaffe's* main long-range fighter, was a flop. Instead of its intended use, it had to evolve night-fighter and reconnaissance roles.

Although it was far from perfect (for example, it had a fragile landing carriage) the Me109 was an excellent fighter of good handling characteristics; especially noteworthy was its exceptional climbing speed and angle.

The Focke-Wolf 190 was the other main fighter of the *Luftwaffe*, and was without doubt one of the most outstanding aeroplanes of the war. The first FW190s began to arrive in the West in July 1941, when they gained immediate ascendency over the Spitfire V, maintaining it over the Mark IV. But

A formidable opponent

its introduction was slow (due in part to the initial unreliability of its engine) and it was September 1942 before it appeared on the Eastern Front. However, by the end of the war, 20,000 FW190s had come off the production lines, and by July 1944 the *Luftwaffe* was accepting over 1000 of them monthly (approaching acceptance of the Me109).

The FW190-A8 had a maximum speed of 408 mph at 20,670 ft, reached 32,800 ft in 17.2 minutes, had a service ceiling of 37,400 ft, and a maximum range of 497 miles (942 miles with two drop tanks). Its weight of fire with two 7.9mm machine guns and four 20mm cannon was 37 lbs. It had well-balanced controls and a good speed, proving

itself a formidable opponent at its best altitudes of between 16,400 and 24,600 ft. It was also an extremely versatile aircraft, serving in heavy fighter, fighter bomber, ground attack, torpedo carrier and reconnaissance rôles.

The Me262 is often described as one of the great 'might-have-beens' of the war. It has been claimed that this, the first operation jet

Lunatic specification

aircraft in the world, could have restored to Germany the control of her skies, had it not been for disastrous planning. Certainly the necessary impetus for development of the jet was not evident until the middle of the war, and certainly such a lunatic specification as Hitler's, that the Me262 be fitted out as a fighter-bomber, did not help matters. However, the consensus of opinion of those who actually worked on the project, is that the Me262 was in fact introduced at the earliest possible time. The problems posed by the turbo-jets, for example, were only resolved in mid-1944, thereby ensuring that deliver-

Above: The Stuka, as it turns to dive. Its whine, as it dived, was designed to strike fear into the enemy on the ground and in this it was successful.

Left: The Me262, one of the great might-have-beens of the war. With sufficient numbers, the *Luftwaffe* might well have regained air superiority over the Allies.

Left: Hans Rudel, the *Luftwaffe*'s ace tank killer, the only man to win Germany's highest military award.

Far right: Major Barkmann, who was the second top scorer in Germany's *Luftwaffe* during World War II.

Right: Erich Hartmann, who was known as the Black Devil of the Ukraine. Hartmann was the *Luftwaffe*'s top scoring pilot.

Below: Adolf Galland, considered by many to have been Germany's best fighter pilot, resting during the Battle of Britain.

Below right: Hans Joachim Marseille, the *Luftwaffe*'s most legendary *Expert*.

ies could not begin in any numbers until September–October of that year.

In May 1943 Galland, after having flown a Me262 prototype, wrote to Goering, 'This model is a tremendous stroke of fortune for us . . . This aircraft opens up entirely new possibilities in so far as tactics are concerned.' Indeed, the Me262A-1a had a maximum speed of 540 mph at 19,685 ft, a maximum range of 652 miles, and a weight of fire of no less than 96 lbs in a three second

Inferior manoeuvrability

burst from four 30mm cannon. These were all significant improvements. However, its manoeuvrability was in some ways inferior to that of conventional fighters, as was its rate of climb, taking 13.1 minutes to reach 29,530 ft. However, by avoiding fighters (no difficult task) and concentrating upon the bombers, the Me262 was of great potential value to the Luftwaffe. In one month, at a time when the Allies had gained complete air ascendency, one Me262 unit with a nominal strength of 25 planes, scored 50 kills. By the end of the war 1294 Me262s had been produced, but too late to alter the course of the air war.

The Me110 was designed as a long-range multi-purpose heavy fighter (a 'destroyer') to support bomber operations deep into enemy territory, and as such it may be described as the Luftwaffe's only fully operational strategic aeroplane. The Battle of Britain, however, proved that they were totally unsuited to the task, their weight due to the necessary fuel, fire power and double engines, meant that they had to suffer a consequent lack of speed and manoeuvrability. In the end, the Me110 itself was provided with escorts. The Me110C-1 had only a maximum speed of 336 mph at 19,685 ft, but a range of 680 miles at 13,780 ft. Subsequent versions improved upon this, reaching a maximum range of 1305 miles with two drop tanks.

Failure in the skies over Britain, however, did not result in the Me110 being phased out; production was continued until March 1945, by which time 6050 had rolled off the assembly lines. As a successor was not immediately forthcoming, the Me110 was used in Russia at first and, equipped with intercept radar, as a night-fighter. Although it was not ideal in this rôle, it did have the necessary range and endurance; it was fairly

The Luftwaffe Experts

successful until well into 1943.

Other night-fighters were variants of the Do217 and the Ju88, the latter being one of the most widely used, as it was able to carry an upward firing cannon mounted in the central fuselage. The most promising was the He219 'Owl', which had a maximum speed of 416 mph at 22,965 ft, a range of 1243 miles, and effective armament. Introduced in 1942, and although an excellent plane, it was never produced in large numbers; only 268 were built. This was due to the not unfamiliar saga of the Luftwaffe's

style of planning.

The Luftwaffe did, of course, have a multitude of other planes—the Arado 234 jet bomber, the Me163 jet fighter, the Fi156 communication plane, the FW200 reconnaissance aircraft, the Ju52 transport and so on. But either too few of these were produced, or they did not affect the Luftwaffe's fighting ability to any extent significant enough to be considered here.

The Luftwaffe, then began the war equipped solely for an offensive tactical rôle. Due to the inadequate planning and development of new aircraft, the Luftwaffe's planes, in the main, declined in comparative performance with those of their enemies. But worse than this was the Luftwaffe's failure to have any form of strategic force or to stress the fighter rôle until too late. It is from this that its defeat stems.

By Allied standards, the Luftwaffe had some 2500 'aces' (with 5 'kills' or more). In the harder Western Theatre of operations, the top Allied flyer was accredited with 38 kills, while eight German pilots scored over 100. Such was their superiority, a fact which cannot be disregarded merely by stating that the Germans had the advantage of flying over their own territory for much of the time (false, anyway) or that conditions forced them to fly a far higher number of missions than their rivals. The figures for the Battle of Britain go a long way to disprove this argument. The top RAF scorer in the battle

The Black Devil

achieved only half the victories scored by the three top Luftwaffe airmen—Wick, Moelders and Galland—even though he had all the advantages of defence and a considerable number of bombers to attack.

Perhaps the most legendary and skilful of the Luftwaffe Experten was Hans Joachim Marseille. Born in 1919, his amazing success was achieved in the desert against the RAF. In his last month of combat in September 1942 he scored no less than 57 kills, 17 of which occurred in one day. His total, before his unfortunate death due to engine failure, was 158 in 482 sorties. His outstanding achievement was due to particularly good aerial gunnery and flying skill. Unorthodox in character, he was unorthodox in tactics, his individuality sometimes being taken to extremes—as when he strafed the area near the tent of an officer who had refused him combat assignments.

Erich Hartmann, the 'Black Devil of the Ukraine,' was the highest scoring Luftwaffe Experte, whose 352 kills on the Eastern Front puts him above all other fighter pilots in history. His achievement is all the more considerable when it is remembered that he only began his career in October 1942 and had less than 30 victories by the summer of 1943. Hartmann's Jagdgeschwader 52 was the highest scoring of the Luftwaffe, having some 11,000 kills to its credit. Shot down many times, Hartmann was even captured by the Russians, but managed to escape.

Other Experten were Gerhard Barkhorn with 301 kills in 1104 operational sorties (300 less than Hartmann), Guenther Rall with 275, Otto Kittel with 267 victories in 583 flights, and Walther Nowotny who scored 250, 167 of them in four months. The highest ratio of victories to flights was achieved by Wilhelm Batz with 237 kills in 455 missions. Adolf Galland deserves special note, for, of his total of 104, 96 were scored in the West, and this was achieved before his appointment in December 1941 as General of Fighters. Heinz-Wolfgang Schnarfer was a night-fighter pilot with a score of 121 against the RAF. Some consider the most impressive achievement to be that of Heinrich Baer, the top scorer against the RAF and USAAF with 124 kills, plus another 96 in the East. Another type of record belongs to Kurt Weller. He 'killed' 33 in 40 flights, scoring 14 and being shot down no less than nine times in his first 11 sorties! The highest decoration for a serving officer in the war went to Hans-Ulrich Ruedel who, in his beloved Ju87, armed with two 37mm cannon, accounted for no less than 519 Soviet tanks in the last two-and-a-half years of the war. In recognition for this he was awarded the Golden Oak Leaves to the Knights Cross in January 1945—the only one of its kind. Such were the *Luftwaffe Experten*.

Magnificent victories

The *Luftwaffe* opened the war seemingly well equipped for a *Blitzkrieg* campaign against her militarily inferior continental neighbours. The magnificent victories won by the German Air Force, should not, however blind anyone to the fact that the *Luftwaffe* was substantially weaker than it appeared. Although it was the largest contemporary air force, of some 4093 front-line aircraft, only just over one quarter of these were prime offensive planes—1176 bomb-carriers and 1179 fighters (only 771 single-engined). Its reserves were inadequate; Germany lacked proper stock piles of such vital building materials as aluminium and rubber; the air industry's capacity was then only a quarter of what it was later to become under considerably more difficult conditions; and there were no viable plans for future armament development. In short, the *Luftwaffe*

The He115 was a *Luftwaffe* seaplane that was obsolete by the time it was phased into service at the beginning of the war. This general purpose seaplane was primarily a torpedo carrier and, although the aerial-borne torpedo was to be an important weapon, the suitability of a slow and vulnerable float plane was to diminish considerably during the course of the war. This was recognised and accepted, and little efforts were made to produce such planes in any numbers. At sea, the prime torpedo carriers were the lethal submarines, the U-boats that carried the war across the Atlantic and into the Pacific. U-boats could strike without warning and remain unseen, whereas the seaplane could make a far less surreptitious attack.

Above: A squadron of Me 109s during the Battle of Britain, 1940. This, the standard *Luftwaffe* fighter until the end of the war, was to perform excellent service in the skies over England, despite disabilities such as range, inflicting severe casualties on the RAF Fighter Command. Had they continued, the RAF would have lost.

Right: Hitler with the *Luftwaffe* Field Marshals, in September, 1940. From left to right, Milch, Sperrle, Hitler, Goering and Kesselring.

Above: Defence against aircraft was a vitally important part of the *Luftwaffe* activity, especially from 1942 onwards. Here, a heavy anti-aircraft gun crew prepares for action early in 1940.

Right: Stukas in action. The *Blitzkrieg* that was practised by the *Luftwaffe* was a revolutionary kind of warfare in both practice and theory. It combined ground and air forces.

Above: A Stuka preparing for action. Its most important function was to provide support for the ground forces that, with mechanised impetus, were breaking through the enemy lines.

was only equipped for a quick *Blitzkrieg* war, preferably on one front.

The air-war against Poland in September 1939 was an unqualified success, and the *Luftwaffe* lost only 285 of its 1939 aircraft there. The initial task was to gain control of the air so that the support of the army could continue unhindered. Contrary to belief the Polish air force was not destroyed on the ground, the Poles having withdrawn their front line aircraft from the aerodromes in the days of tension preceding the war. Their bomber brigade in particular continued to make determined attacks against the Wehr-

The bombing of Warsaw

macht until mid-September. However, the Poles were finally defeated in the air by the considerably superior *Luftwaffe*. Polish air activity did not prevent the *Luftwaffe* from supporting ground operations, and in this the *Luftwaffe* must take a large share of the credit for the German victory. Their 'flying artillery' not only battered the strong points but, even more important, disrupted totally the Polish communications, causing havoc with troop movements. The most important single event of the campaign was the *Luftwaffe*'s bombing of Warsaw, when after repeated attacks and demands for surrender a single heavy air raid on the 26th ensured its capitulation.

In the invasion of Norway in April 1940, the *Luftwaffe* (with some 800 operational aircraft) took a leading rôle, overawing resistance and paralysing Allied counter-measures, causing the British commander to protest, 'I see little chance of carrying out decisive, or indeed any, operations, unless enemy air activity is considerably restricted.' Air transport figured prominently in this campaign—for the first time in history.

The *Blitzkrieg* in France and Flanders still furthered the *Luftwaffe*'s reputation. Some 3500 aircraft were amassed for the invasion, which began on May 10, 1940, of which 1482 were bomb-carriers and 1264 fighters. The usual pattern of operations was followed. The first attacks were aimed at the enemy air forces; over 70 airfields were bombed on the first day and by the evening of the 11th it was reported that the enemy had lost 1000 aircraft. This was an exaggeration; again the enemy, although mauled, were still able to pose some sort of a threat in the air. It was not until May 14 that the Allied bomber force ceased to be any menace. The British lost 60 percent of the bombers sent on missions that day. Although enemy opposition continued the *Luftwaffe* was able from the start to carry out a highly effective co-operation between plane and tank. The *Luftwaffe* was used to gain control of the vital Eben Emael fortification and the Albert Canal bridges as well as occupy Rotterdam by means of airborne troops. Bombers and Stukas hammered a way through the Franco-Belgian fortifications and repulsed counter attacks upon the Panzers' undefended flanks. However, success eluded the *Luftwaffe* at Dunkirk. It proved impossible for it to destroy the British army due to bad weather, a

The peak of success

lack of forward airfields and the effectiveness of British fighters. Despite this, the Luftwaffe ended the French campaign well, having averaged some 1500 sorties per day.

At this point the *Luftwaffe* had reached the peak of their success, having significantly shaped *Blitzkrieg* war. But the defeat of France had not brought about the end of the conflict with Britain. The *Luftwaffe* now had to evolve a new strategic rôle, one which it was woefully ill-equipped to tackle. The air offensive against Britain was to be the first failure. There are two aspects to this. The first is that the total lack of a strategic bomber force ensured that the attack, whatever form it would take, would be limited in range and bomb load and therefore in effect. There could be no strategic bombing of the type undertaken later by the RAF and USAAF with such devastating results. (This was due in no small way to the fact that Hitler and the High Command had never envisaged a war with Britain and therefore had not prepared the necessary equipment or plans for it.) Secondly the form of offensive undertaken was ruined by faulty command decisions.

The aim of the *Luftwaffe* was two-fold. It was to destroy the RAF defensive ability so that it would pose no threat to any further action, and then it was to undertake terror raids and blockade Britain to break the will to resist of the British People. This was somewhat different from supporting Panzers and bombing railways. Much has been written about the Battle of Britain and no attempt to describe its many facets can be undertaken here. Suffice to say that, despite the

The view of the He111 as it manoeuvres to attack enemy shipping in the North Sea. The perspex clearly offered no protection to the machine gunner and bomb-aimer. Casualties among these members of the crew were very high during the war.

Luftwaffe's losses from July onwards, the inadequacy of the Me109 in a support rôle, the total failure of the Ju87 and Me110, the strain on the crews and the strengths of the British defence system, the German Air Force came to within an ace of victory. The important facts lie not so much with the total losses of the *Luftwaffe* (percentage bomb-carrier losses were lower than in the French campaign) but with the loss to the RAF of their fighters and, far more important, their pilots. In August the RAF lost 338 Hurricanes and Spitfires in combat, with 104 badly damaged, while the Germans only lost 177 Me109s with 28 badly damaged. On August 31 the *Luftwaffe* shot down 39 fighters for a loss of 41 of all types of their aircraft. Between August 11 and September 7 the total wastage of the RAF's fighters exceeded production, and reserves were running low. By the end of August, too, most of the vital airfields in the South-East of England were rendered either unusable or nearly so. But far more critical were pilot casualities: during August and September nearly one quarter of Fighter Command's flyers were either killed or wounded. The training schools were turning out less pilots than were lost; few of these were really battle-worthy and most of the experienced flyers, by the end of August, were battle weary. At the beginning of September the German pilots were reporting a definite slacking off in RAF opposition. The *Luftwaffe* was winning the first round of its new strategic rôle.

But the *Luftwaffe* command failed to see this. For a number of reasons the effort was switched away from Fighter Command onto aircraft factories and, from September 7, to

Still a powerful force

London. This was the fundamental error. The Me109s were now entirely relegated to a support rôle and the bombers simply did not have the capacity to undertake daylight raids in the face of the now resurgent British fighters, or to inflict significant damage. The *Luftwaffe* was forced into the night-bombing of cities, industrial centres and ports in November, but although the bombers could now fly slower and lower and therefore carry heavier loads, the *Luftwaffe* was still far away from having a proper strategic force. In that month 6205 tons of high explosive and 305 tons of incendiaries were dropped (compared to the average monthly bomb load of the Allies in 1944 of 49,072 tons). The offensive finally finished in May 1941. By that time only four bomber Gruppen were still operational (there had been 44); the rest had been transferred to the East.

The *Luftwaffe* was still a powerful force, the following campaigns showed that it continued to be a vital element in Germany's *Blitzkriegs*. Over 1100 aircraft took part in the Balkan campaign, opening on April 6 with a heavy attack upon the Jugoslav capital and airfields. Within hours of war breaking out, Belgrade was paralysed and 17,000 people dead. By the 21st Greece was defeated, the *Luftwaffe*'s prime rôle through-

Above: A Stuka coming out of its dive, just missing the tree tops, during a ground support mission in the campaign of France, 1940. Such near misses were common for the Stuka pilots, when low dives were essential for pin-point accuracy. Owing to the high standard of training, however, accidents were rare.

Right: Bomber pilots equipped for high altitude flying. Theirs was a job little envied by the fighter men, who regarded it as too dangerous.

Above: The FW200 Condor reconnaissance bomber. Although it had been designed primarily for commercial purposes, it was described by Churchill as the scourge of the Atlantic.

Right: An Me110 long range fighter effecting an emergency landing in the middle of the English Channel, 1940. The Germans evolved an excellent air-sea rescue service for their pilots.

Above: A pilot decorated with the Knights Cross by Field Marshall Milch on the Eastern front. Aggressive pilots were said to be 'medal chasing' by their more cautious colleagues.

out having been the support of ground troops and tactical bombing. On May 20 the final episode was begun with the invasion of Crete from the air. The ferrying in of troops by transport planes ensured ultimate success and, with the defeat of the British fleet by the *Luftwaffe*, the fate of that part of the Mediterranean was sealed.

From the Balkans to Russia: for 'Barbarossa' on June 22 the *Luftwaffe* had amassed 2770 aircraft. Their priorities were the usual ones: within 24 hours some 2000 Soviet aircraft had been destroyed and the army was being supported with considerable success. However, in these few opening weeks the *Luftwaffe* was experiencing its second major failure—one directly attributable to its lack of a strategic bomber force. For while its aircraft could knock out scores of Russian planes and tanks, it did not touch the factories from which they came in such prodigious quantities. Few attempts were made to knock out the centres of production and, as one historian has summed it up 'the result was that in a week of operations against tanks, at great cost to themselves, the bombers would succeed in destroying perhaps one day's output of T34's by the Goski factory.' Its attempt to disrupt the rail communications also met with little success, the scale of the task ensuring that the *Luftwaffe*'s efforts were mere pin pricks. The attacks against Moscow likewise proved fruitless. A few strategic missions were undertaken with appreciable effect in 1943. But the *Luftwaffe* continued to remain split up into tactical units deployed directly upon the front for the whole war; the enemy grew stronger, year by year. The last major event for the *Luftwaffe* in the East was its participation in 'Operation Citadel' in July 1943, when 1700 aircraft assisted the army attack. From then on, however, it was more and more reduced to a defensive rôle, fuel shortage and increasing Soviet air strength causing losses to mount and effectiveness to drop. By the autumn of 1944, for example, only one Stuka unit could operate in daylight. But the air effort against the Russians continued to occupy a huge part of the *Luftwaffe*'s resources till the end, and home defence suffered as a consequence.

Other tactical deployment for the *Luftwaffe* was in North Africa, where its fortunes rose and sank with those of Rommel and the Western Front from June 1944 on. The weakness of the *Luftwaffe* here is underlined by the fact that on D-Day it only flew 319 sorties over France, the majority of which were ineffectual. By the end of June, out of a total day-fighter strength on all fronts of 1523, one third was in France—wholly inadequate against the Allies. In the middle of July more than half the fighters sent to the Western Front were destroyed and the supply was drying up. Control of the air was completely unattainable and the *Luftwaffe*'s impact upon events in the West

Nothing but pin pricks

was minimal. The last concentrated effort by the *Luftwaffe* in the whole war—operation 'Bodenplatte', being a mass attack of 700–800 fighters on Allied airfields as part of the Ardennes Offensive on January 1, 1945—gives emphasis to this. While it caused the destruction of some 300 Allied planes (the losses were soon made good) it exhausted the force taking part, which lost 150 pilots and used valuable fuel. This marked the end of the *Luftwaffe*'s tactical rôle.

The *Luftwaffe*, as a *Blitzkrieg* force, was not designed for a long campaign or war on two fronts. Thus in late 1941 there came about a crisis of numbers. The *Luftwaffe* was now operating on three fronts, one of them 1000 miles wide, and was therefore not only thin on the ground but found that losses had begun to outpace production. Unit strengths began to decline and by July strength in the East was down to 1888 fighters and bombers. The average monthly production in 1939 was 133 fighters and 217 bombers, this having been raised only to 244 and 336 in 1941. A belief that the war was to end, a low priority in procurement priorities, shortages of materials, the failure of the Me210 and He177s to fill the gaps as was expected, and bad planning—all this caused a situation

The ground crews were indispensible to the efficiency of the *Luftwaffe*, just as they were to the airforces of the Allied nations. Goering recognised their importance and stated that, 'Without their service nothing can be achieved'. He added in acknowledgement of what they contributed to success, 'I must say that their endurance, their skill, their patience, although different, is in every way the equal of that of the aircrews'. When the pressure was on Germany to follow up her advances or to beat back those of the Allies, it was the ground crews who were responsible for making sure that Germany had enough airplanes ready for action. Here, a ground crew is loading up a Ju88 with bombs, preparatory to another sortie.

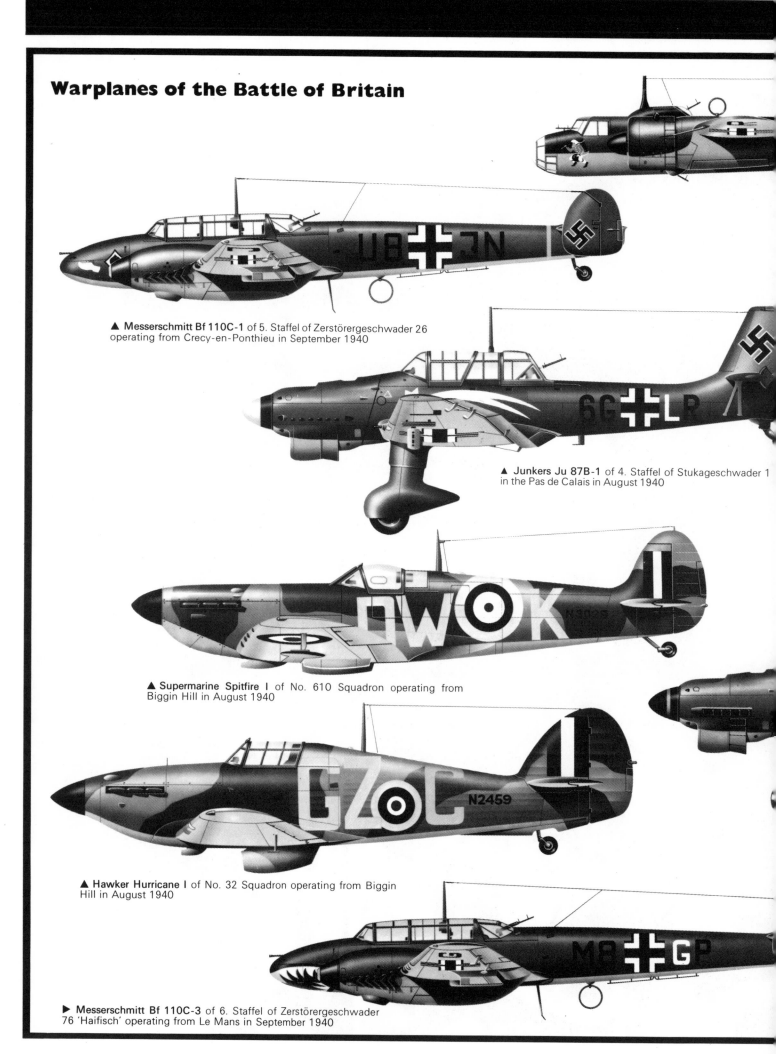

Warplanes of the Battle of Britain

▲ **Messerschmitt Bf 110C-1** of 5. Staffel of Zerstörergeschwader 26 operating from Crecy-en-Ponthieu in September 1940

▲ **Junkers Ju 87B-1** of 4. Staffel of Stukageschwader 1 in the Pas de Calais in August 1940

▲ **Supermarine Spitfire I** of No. 610 Squadron operating from Biggin Hill in August 1940

▲ **Hawker Hurricane I** of No. 32 Squadron operating from Biggin Hill in August 1940

▶ **Messerschmitt Bf 110C-3** of 6. Staffel of Zerstörergeschwader 76 'Haifisch' operating from Le Mans in September 1940

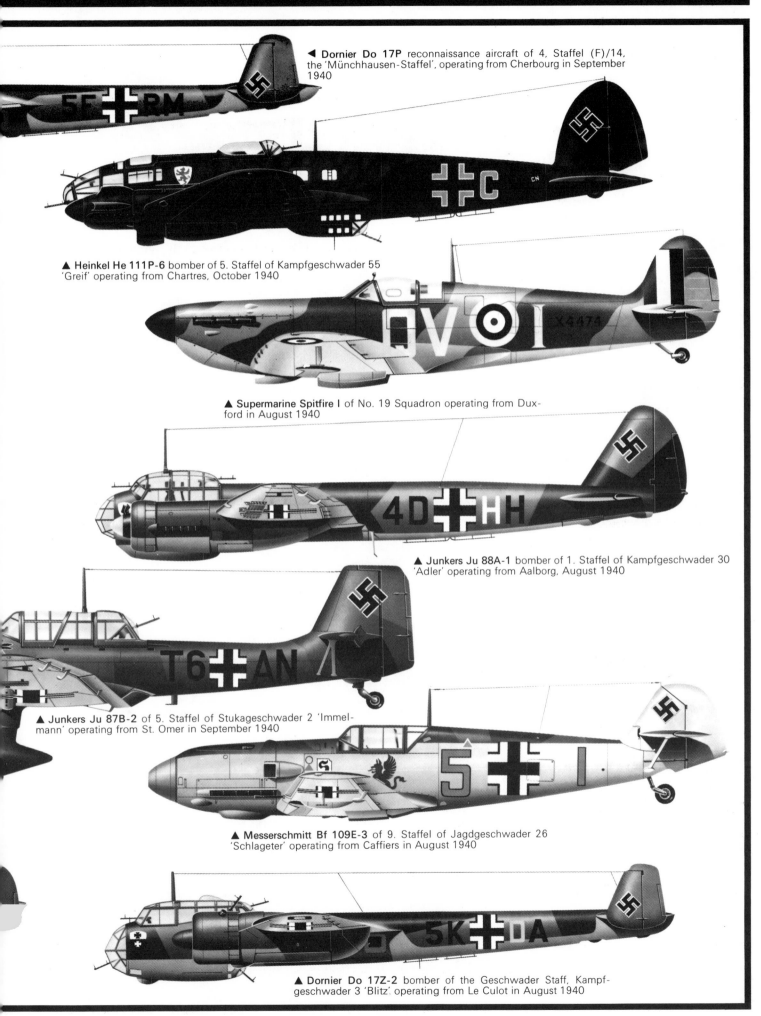

◄ **Dornier Do 17P** reconnaissance aircraft of 4. Staffel (F)/14, the 'Münchhausen-Staffel', operating from Cherbourg in September 1940

▲ **Heinkel He 111P-6** bomber of 5. Staffel of Kampfgeschwader 55 'Greif' operating from Chartres, October 1940

▲ **Supermarine Spitfire I** of No. 19 Squadron operating from Duxford in August 1940

▲ **Junkers Ju 88A-1** bomber of 1. Staffel of Kampfgeschwader 30 'Adler' operating from Aalborg, August 1940

▲ **Junkers Ju 87B-2** of 5. Staffel of Stukageschwader 2 'Immelmann' operating from St. Omer in September 1940

▲ **Messerschmitt Bf 109E-3** of 9. Staffel of Jagdgeschwader 26 'Schlageter' operating from Caffiers in August 1940

▲ **Dornier Do 17Z-2** bomber of the Geschwader Staff, Kampfgeschwader 3 'Blitz' operating from Le Culot in August 1940

Messerschmitt Bf 109

▲ **Messerschmitt Bf 109E-3**

Messerschmitt Bf 109E-3

(see pages 152/153 for cutaway drawing of Bf 109G-14/U4)

Type: single-seat fighter (later fighter bomber).
Engine: 1175 hp Daimler-Benz DB 601A 12-cylinder inverted-vee liquid-cooled.
Dimensions: span 32 ft 4½ in (9·87 m); length 28 ft 4½ in (8·64 m); height 8 ft 2½ in (2·5 m).
Weights: empty 4189 lb (1900 kg); loaded 58/5 lb (2665 kg).
Performance: maximum speed 348 mph (560 kph) at 14,560 ft (4440 m); initial climb 3280 ft (1000 m)/min; service ceiling 34,450 ft (10,500 m); range 410 miles (660 km).
Armament: two 20 mm Oerlikon MG FF cannon in wings, each with 60-round drum, and two 7·92 mm Rheinmetall-Borsig MG 17 machine guns above engine, each with 1000 rounds (in some aircraft, only 500 rounds, to provide room for 200-round magazine for extra MG FF cannon firing through propeller hub). From mid-1940 an increasing number of Bf 109s, including E sub-types, were equipped to carry one 551 lb (250 kg) bomb on external centreline rack, or alternatively four 110 lb (50 kg).

History: first flight (first Bf 109) early September 1935 (date is unrecorded); (first Bf 109E) January 1939; operational service February 1939; replacement in production by later Bf 109F, May 1941.

During World War II the general public in the Allied nations at first regarded the Messerschmitt as an inferior weapon compared with the Spitfire and other Allied fighters. Only in the fullness of time was it possible to appreciate that the Bf 109 was one of the greatest combat aircraft in all history. First flown in 1935, it was a major participant in the Spanish Civil War and a thoroughly proven combat aircraft by the time of Munich (September 1938). Early versions were the Bf 109B, C and D, all of lower power than the definitive 109E. The E was in service in great quantity by the end of August 1939 when the invasion of Poland began. From then until 1941 it was by far the most important fighter in the *Luftwaffe,* and it was also supplied in quantity to Bulgaria, Hungary, Romania, Slovakia, Yugoslavia, Switzerland, Japan and the Soviet Union. During the first year of World War II the 'Emil', as the various E sub-types were called, made mincemeat of the many and varied types of fighter against which it was opposed, with the single exception of the Spitfire (which it greatly outnumbered). Its good points were small size, fast and cheap production, high acceleration, fast climb and dive, and good power of manoeuvre. Nearly all 109Es were also fitted with two or three 20mm cannon, with range and striking power greater even than a battery of eight rifle-calibre guns. Drawbacks were the narrow landing gear, extremely poor lateral control at high speeds, and the fact that in combat the slats on the wings often opened in tight turns; while this prevented a stall, it snatched at the ailerons and threw the pilot off his aim. Later in the war the dominant version was the 109G ('Gustav') which made up the bulk of the 35,000-odd constructed of all versions.

Messerschmitt Bf 110

▲ **Messerschmitt Bf 110C-4/B**

Messerschmitt Bf 110C-4/B

Type: two-seat day and night fighter (also used on occasion for ground attack and reconnaissance).
Engines: two 1100 hp Daimler-Benz DB 601A (later C-4s, 1200 hp DB 601N) 12-cylinder inverted-vee liquid-cooled.
Dimensions: span 53 ft 4¾ in (16·25 m); length 39 ft 8½ in (12·1 m); height 11 ft 6 in (3·5 m).
Weights: empty 9920 lb (4500 kg); loaded 15,430 lb (7000 kg).
Performance: maximum speed 349 mph (562 kph) at 22,966 ft (7000 m); climb to 18,045 ft (5500 m), 8 minutes; service ceiling 32,800 ft (10,000 m); range 528 miles (850 km) at 304 mph (490 kph) at 16,400 ft (5000 m).
Armament: two 20 mm Oerlikon MG FF cannon and four Rheinmetall 7·92 mm MG 17 machine guns fixed firing forward in nose, one 7·92 mm MG 15 manually aimed machine gun in rear cockpit; C-4/B also fitted with racks under centre section for four 551 lb (250 kg) bombs.

History: first flight (Bf 110V1 prototype) May 12, 1936; (pre-production Bf 110C-0) February 1939; operational service with Bf 110C-1, April 1939; final run-down of production (Bf 110H-2 and H-4) February 1945.

As in five other countries at about the same time, the *Reichsluftfahrtministerium* decided in 1934 to issue a requirement for a new kind of fighter having two engines and exceptional range. Called a *Zerstoerer* (destroyer), it was to be capable of fighting other aircraft as well as small single-seaters, possibly making up in firepower for any lack in manoeuvrability. Its dominant quality was to be range, to escort bombers on raids penetrating deep into enemy heartlands. Powered by two of the new DB 600 engines, the prototype reached 316 mph, considered an excellent speed, but it was heavy on the controls and unimpressive in power of manoeuvre. Too late to be tested in the Spanish Civil War, the production Bf 110B-1, which was the first to carry the two cannon, was itself supplanted by the C-series with the later DB 601 engine with direct fuel injection and greater power at all heights. By the start of World War II the *Luftwaffe* had 195 Bf 110C fighters, and in the Polish campaign these were impressive, operating mainly in the close-support role but demolishing any aerial opposition they encountered. It was the same story in the *Blitzkrieg* war through the Low Countries and France, when 350 of the big twins were used. Only when faced with RAF Fighter Command in the Battle of Britain did the Bf 110 suddenly prove a disaster. It was simply no match for the Spitfire or even the Hurricane (which was no faster), and soon the Bf 109 was having to 'escort' the escort fighters! But production of later versions continued until the final collapse, the later versions being packed with radar and night-fighting equipment and playing a major part in the night battles over the *Reich* in 1943–45.

Dornier Do 17Z and 215

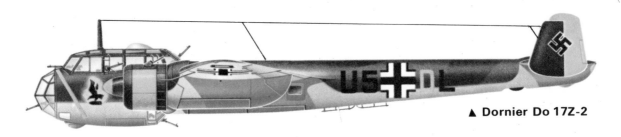

▲ Dornier Do 17Z-2

Dornier Do 17Z-2 and Do 215A-1

Type: four-seat medium bomber and reconnaissance aircraft.

Engines: (Do 17Z-2) two 1000 hp Bramo Fafnir 323P nine-cylinder radials; (Do 215B-1) two 1075 hp Daimler-Benz DB 601A 12-cylinder inverted-vee liquid-cooled.

Dimensions: (both) span 59 ft 0½ in (18 m); length 51 ft 9½ in (15·79 m); height 14 ft 11½ in (4.56 m).

Weights: empty (Do 17Z-2) 11,484 lb (5210 kg), (Do 215B-1) 12,730 lb (5775 kg); loaded (both) 19,841 lb (9000 kg).

Performance: maximum speed (Do 17Z-2) 263 mph (425 kph), (Do 215B-1) 280 mph (450 kph); service ceiling (Do 17Z-2) 26,740 ft (8150 m), (Do 215B-1) 31,170 ft (9500 m); range with half bomb load (Do 17Z-2) 721 miles (1160 km), (Do 215B-1) 932 miles (1500 km).

Armament: normally six 7·92 mm Rheinmetall MG 15 machine guns, one fixed in nose, remainder on manually aimed mounts in front windscreen, two beam windows, and above and below at rear; internal bomb load up to 2205 lb (1000 kg).

History: first flight (Do 17S prototype) early 1938; (Do 17Z-2) early 1939; (Do 215V1 prototype) late 1938; first delivery (Do 17Z-1) January 1939, (Do 215A-1) December 1939; termination of production (Do 17Z series) July 1940, (Do 215 series) January 1941.

Whereas the slenderness of the first families of Do 17 bombers had earned them the nickname of 'Flying Pencil', the Do 17S introduced a completely new front end with much deeper cabin and extensive window area all round. Such a change had been evident from the inadequate defensive armament of the earlier models, revealed in the Spanish Civil War, and the penalty of increased weight and drag was to some degree countered by a search for more powerful engines. The S prototype had DB 600 liquid-cooled engines, as did the Do 17U five-seat pathfinder, of which 12 were delivered to the nine Bomber Groups already using earlier Do 17s. The Do 17Z, powered by the Bramo radial engine, was at first underpowered, and full bomb load had to await the more powerful Fafnir 323P of the 17Z-2. Between late 1939 and the summer of 1940 about 535 Do 17Z series bomber and reconnaissance machines were delivered, and though they suffered high attrition over Britain they did much effective work and were the most popular and reliable of all *Luftwaffe* bombers of the early *Blitzkrieg* period. The Do 215 was the Do 17Z renumbered as an export version, with the more powerful DB 601 engine. The Do 215A-1 for Sweden became the Do 215B-0 and B-1 for the *Luftwaffe*, and altogether 101 were put into service for bomber and reconnaissance roles; 12 were converted as Do 215B-5 night intruders with a 'solid' nose carrying two cannon and four machine guns and operated by night over Britain before transfer to Sicily in October 1941.

Heinkel He 111

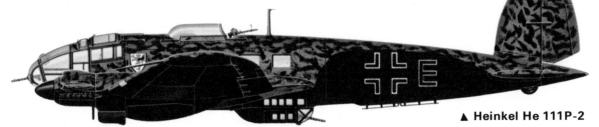

▲ Heinkel He 111P-2

Heinkel He 111P-2 and H-3

(see pages 136/7 for cutaway drawing)

Type: four-seat (P-2) or five-seat medium bomber (later, torpedo bomber, glider tug and missile launcher).

Engines: (He 111H-3) two 1200 hp Junkers Jumo 211D-2 12-cylinder inverted-vee liquid-cooled, (He 111P-2) two 1100 hp Daimler-Benz DB 601A-1 12-cylinder inverted-vee liquid-cooled.

Dimensions: span 74 ft 1¾ in (22·6 m); length 53 ft 9½ in (16·4 m); height 13 ft 1½ in (4 m).

Weights: empty (H-3) 17,000 lb (7720 kg), (P-2) 17,640 lb (8000 kg); maximum loaded (H-3) 30,865 lb (14,000 kg), (P-2) 29,762 lb (13,500 kg).

Performance: maximum speed (H-3) 258 mph (415 kph), (P-2) 242 mph (390 kph) at 16,400 ft (5000 m) (at maximum weight, neither version could exceed 205 mph (330 kph); climb to 14,765 ft (4500 m) 30–35 min at normal gross weight, 50 min at maximum; service ceiling (both) around 25,590 ft (7800 m) at normal gross weight, under 16,400 ft (5000 m) at maximum; range with maximum bomb load (both) about 745 miles (1200 km).

Armament: (P-2) 7·92 mm Rheinmetall MG 15 machine gun on manual mountings in nosecap, open dorsal position and ventral gondola, (H-3) same, plus fixed forward-firing MG 15 or 17, two MG 15s in waist windows and (usually) 20 mm MG FF cannon in front of ventral gondola and (sometimes) fixed rear-firing MG 17 in extreme tail; internal bomb load up to 4410 lb (2000 kg) in vertical cells, stored nose-up; external bomb load (at expense of internal) one 4410 lb (2000 kg) on H-3, one or two 1102 lb (500 kg) on others; later marks carried one or two 1686 lb (765 kg) torpedoes, Bv 246 glide missiles, Hs 293 rocket missiles, Fritz X radio-controlled glide bombs or one FZG-76 ('V-1') cruise missile.

History: first flight (He 111V1 prototype) February 24, 1935; (pre-production He 111B-0) August 1936; (production He 111B-1) October 30, 1936; (first He 111E series) January 1938; (first production He 111P-1) December 1938; (He 111H-1) January or February 1939; final delivery (He 111H-23) October 1944; (Spanish C-2111) late 1956.

To a considerable degree the success of the early elliptical-winged He 111 bombers in Spain misled the *Luftwaffe* into considering that nothing could withstand the onslaught of their huge fleets of medium bombers. These aircraft – the trim Do 17, the broad-winged He 111 and the high-performance Ju 88 – were all extremely advanced by the standards of the mid-1930s when they were designed. They were faster than the single-seat fighters of that era, and (so the argument went) therefore did not need much defensive armament. So the three machine guns carried by the first He 111 bombers in 1936 stayed unchanged until, in the Battle of Britain, the He 111 was hacked down with ease, its only defence being its toughness and ability to come back after being shot to pieces. The inevitable result was that more and more defensive guns were added, needing a fifth or even a sixth crew-member. Coupled with incessant growth in equipment and armour the result was deteriorating performance, so that the record-breaker 1936–38 became the lumbering sitting duck of 1942–45. Yet the repeated failure of the RLM and German industry to find a replacement meant that the 111 had to soldier on right to the end of the war, still being built until the end of 1944 (by which time the total built in Germany and Romania was more than 6086 and possibly more than 7000).

Heinkel He 111H-3

1. Starboard navigation light
2. Starboard aileron
3. Wing ribs
4. Forward spar
5. Rear spar
6. Aileron tab
7. Starboard flap
8. Fuel tank access panel
9. Wing centre section/outer panel break line
10. Inboard fuel tank (154 Imp. gal./700 l capacity) position between nacelle and fuselage
11. Oil tank cooling louvres
12. Oil cooler air intake
13. Supercharger air intake
14. Three-blade VDM airscrew
15. Airscrew pitch-change mechanism
16. Junkers Jumo 211D-1 12-cylinder inverted-vee liquid-cooled engine
17. Exhaust manifold
18. Nose-mounted 7·9-mm MG 15 machine gun

19. Ikaria ball-and-socket gun mounting (offset to starboard)
20. Bomb sight housing (offset to starboard)
21. Starboard mainwheel
22. Rudder pedals
23. Bomb aimer's horizontal pad
24. Additional 7·9-mm MG 15 machine gun (fitted by forward maintenance units)
25. Repeater compass
26. Bomb aimer's folding seat
27. Control column
28. Throttles
29. Pilot's seat
30. Retractable auxiliary windscreen (for use when pilot's seat in elevated position)
31. Sliding entry panel
32. Forward fuselage bulkhead
33. Double-frame station
34. Port ESAC bomb bay (vertical stowage)

35. Fuselage windows (blanked)
36. Central gangway between bomb bays
37. Double-frame station
38. Direction Finder
39. Dorsal gunner's (forward) sliding canopy
40. Dorsal 7·9-mm MG 15 machine gun
41. Dorsal gunner's cradle seat
42. FuG 10 radio equipment
43. Fuselage window
44. Armoured bulkhead (8-mm)
45. Aerial mast
46. Bomb flares
47. Unarmoured bulkhead
48. Rear fuselage access cut-out
49. Port 7·9-mm beam MG 15 machine gun
50. Dinghy stowage
51. Fuselage frames
52. Stringers
53. Starboard tailplane
54. Aerial

55. Starboard elevator
56. Tailfin forward spar
57. Tailfin structure
58. Rudder balance
59. Tailfin rear spar/rudder post
60. Rudder construction
61. Rudder tab
62. Tab actuator (starboard surface)
63. Remotely-controlled 7·9-mm MG 17 machine gun in tail cone (fitted to some aircraft only)
64. Rear navigation light
65. Elevator tab
66. Elevator structure
67. Elevator hinge line
68. Tailplane front spar
69. Semi-retractable tailwheel
70. Tailwheel shock-absorber
71. Tailsurface control linkage
72. Fuselage/tailfin frame
73. Control pulley
74. Push-pull control rods
75. Master compass
76. Observation window fairing

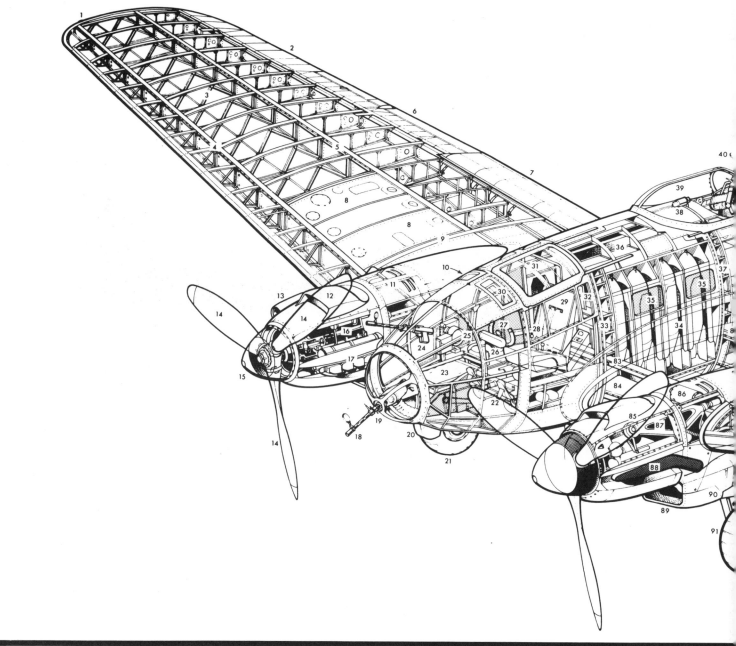

77 Glazed observation window in floor
78 Ventral aft-firing 7·9-mm MG 15 machine gun in tail of 'Sterbebett' ('Death-bed') bath
79 Ventral bath entry hatch
80 Ventral gunner's horizontal pad
81 **Forward firing 20-mm (Oerlikon) MG FF cannon (for anti-shipping operations)**
82 Rear spar carry-through
83 Forward spar carry-through
84 Oil cooler
85 Anti-vibration engine mount
86 Oil tank
87 Engine bearer
88 Exhaust flame-damper shroud
89 Radiator air intake
90 Radiator bath
91 Port mainwheel
92 Mainwheel leg

93 Retraction mechanism
94 Mainwheel door (outer)
95 Multi-screw wing attachment
96 Trailing-aerial tube (to starboard of ventral bath)
97 Rear spar attachment
98 Port outboard fuel tank (220 Imp. gal./1,000 l capacity)
99 Flap control rod
100 Landing light
101 Pitot head
102 Pitot head heater/wing leading-edge de-icer
103 Flap and aileron coupling
104 Flap structure
105 Aileron tab

106 Tab actuator
107 Rear spar
108 Forward spar
109 Port aileron
110 Port navigation light

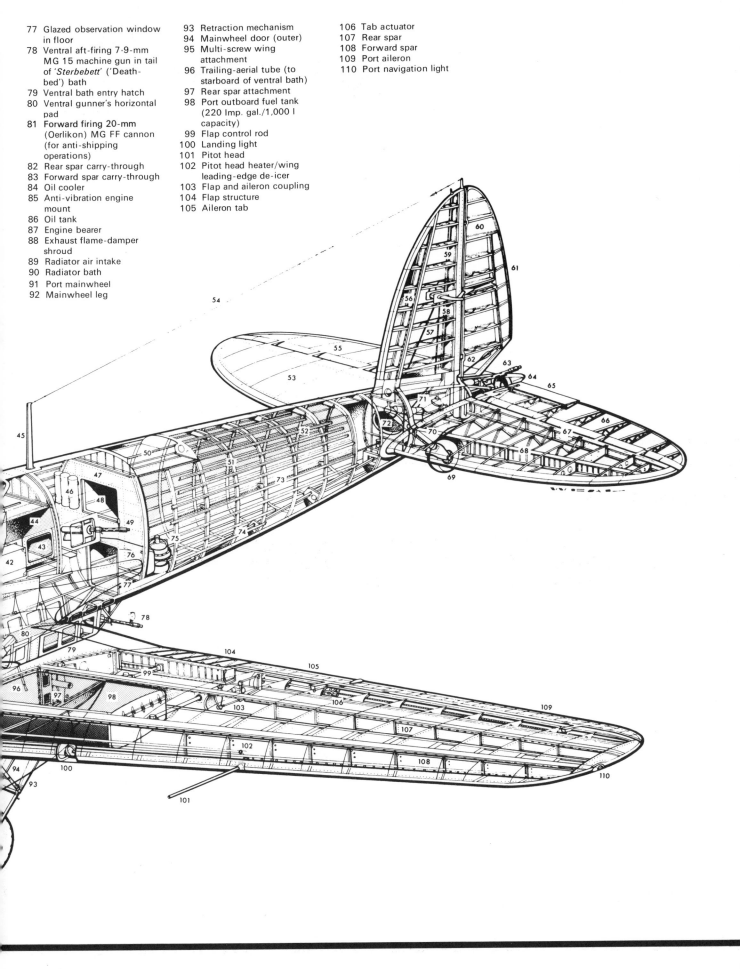

Junkers Ju 88

▲ Junkers Ju 88A-4

Junkers Ju 88A-4, C-6, G-7, S-1

(see pages 148/149 for cutaway drawing of Ju 88G-1)

Type: military aircraft designed as dive bomber but developed for level bombing, close support, night fighting, reconnaissance and as pilotless missile. Crew: two to six.

Engines: (A-4) two 1340 hp Junkers Jumo 211J 12-cylinder inverted-vee liquid-cooled; (C-6) same as A-4; (G-7) two 1880 hp Junkers Jumo 213E 12-cylinder inverted-vee liquid-cooled; (S-1) two 1700 hp BMW 801G 18-cylinder two-row radials.

Dimensions: span 65 ft 7½ in (20 m); length 47 ft 2½ in (14·4 m); (G-7, 54 ft 1½ in); height 15 ft 11 in (4·85 m), (C-6) 16 ft 7½ in (5 m).

Weights: empty (A-4) 17,637 lb (8000 kg), (C-6b) 19,090 lb (8660 kg), (G-7b) 20,062 lb (9100 kg), (S-1) 18,300 lb (8300 kg); maximum loaded (A-4) 30,865 lb (14,000 kg), (C-6b) 27,500 lb (12,485 kg), (G-7b) 32,350 lb (14,690 kg), (S-1) 23,100 lb (10,490 kg).

Performance: maximum speed (A-4) 269 mph (433 kph), (C-6b) 300 mph (480 kph), (G-7b) (no drop tank or flame-dampers) 402 mph (643 kph), (S-1) 373 mph (600 kph); initial climb (A-4) 1312 ft (400 m)/min, (C-6b) about 985 ft (300 m)/min, (G-7b) 1640 ft (500 m)/min, (S-1) 1804 ft (550 m)/min; service ceiling (A-4) 26,900 ft (8200 m), (C-6b) 32,480 ft (9900 m), (G-7b) 28,870 ft (8800 m), (S-1) 36,090 ft (11,000 m); range (A-4) 1112 miles (1790 km), (C-6b) 1243 miles (2000 km), (G-7b) 1430 miles (2300 km), (S-1) 1243 miles (2000 km).

Armament: (A-4) two 7·92 mm MG 81 (or one MG 81 and one 13 mm MG 131) firing forward, twin MG 81 or one MG 131 upper rear, one or two MG 81 at front of gondola; (C-6b) three 20 mm MG FF and three MG 17 in nose and two 20 mm MG 151/20 firing obliquely upward in Schrage Musik installation; (G-7b) four MG 151/20 (200 rounds each) firing forward from ventral fairing, two MG 151/20 in Schrage Musik installation (200 rounds each) and defensive MG 131 (500 rounds) swivelling in rear roof; (S-1) one MG 131 (500 rounds) swivelling in rear roof; bomb loads (A-4) 1100 lb (500 kg) internal and four external racks rated at 2200 lb (1000 kg) (inners) and 1100 lb (500 kg) (outers) to maximum total bomb load of 6614 lb (3000 kg); (C-6b and G-7b, nil); (S-1) up to 4410 lb (2000 kg) on external racks.

History: first flight (Ju 88V1) December 21, 1936; (first Ju 88A-1) September 7, 1939; (first fighter, Ju 88C-0) July 1939; (Ju 88C-6) mid 1942; (first G-series) early 1944; (S series) late 1943; final deliveries, only as factories were overrun by Allies.

Probably no other aircraft in history has been developed in so many quite different forms for so many purposes — except, perhaps, for the Mosquito. Flown long before World War II as a civil prototype, after a frantic design process led by two temporarily hired Americans well-versed in modern stressed-skin construction, the first 88s were transformed into the much heavier, slower and more capacious A-1 bombers which were just entering service as World War II began. The formidable bomb load and generally good performance were offset by inadequate defensive armament, and in the A-4 the span was increased, the bomb load and gun power substantially augmented and a basis laid for fantastically diverse further development.

In 1940 to 1943 about 2000 Ju 88 bombers were built each year, nearly all A-5 or A-4 versions. After splitting off completely new branches which led to the Ju 188 and 388, bomber development was directed to the steamlined S series of much higher performance, it having become accepted that the traditional *Luftwaffe* species of bomber was doomed if intercepted, no matter how many extra guns and crew it might be lumbered with. Indeed even the bomb and fuel loads were cut in most S sub-types, though the S-2 had fuel in the original bomb bay and large bulged bomb stowage (which defeated the objective of reducing drag). Final bomber versions included the P series of big-gun anti-armour and close-support machines, the Nbwe with flamethrowers and recoilless rocket projectors, and a large family of Mistel composite-aircraft combinations.

Dornier Do 217

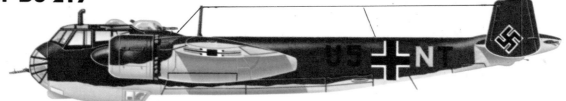

▲ Dornier Do 217E-2/R19

Dornier Do 217E-2, K-2, M-1, J-2/N-2, P-1

Type: (E, K, M) four-seat bomber; (J, N) three-seat night fighter; (P) four-seat high-altitude reconnaissance aircraft.

Engines: (E-2, J-2) two 1580 hp BMW 801A or 801M 18-cylinder two-row radials, (K-2) two 1700 hp BMW 801D, (M-1, N-2) two 1750 hp Daimler-Benz DB 603A 12-cylinder inverted-vee liquid-cooled, (P-1) two 1860 hp DB 603B supercharged by DB 605T in the fuselage.

Dimensions: span 62 ft 4 in (19 m), (K-2) 81 ft 4½ in (24·8 m), (P-1) 80 ft 4 in (24·4 m); length 56 ft 9¼ in (17·3 m), (E-2 with early dive brakes) 60 ft 10½ in (18·5 m), (K-2 and M-1) 55 ft 9 in (17 m), (J and N) 58 ft 9 in (17·9 m), (P) 58 ft 11 in (17·95 m); height 16 ft 5 in (5 m) (all versions same within 2 in).

Weights: empty (E-2) 19,522 lb (8850 kg), (M-1) 19,985 lb (9000 kg), (K-2, J and N) all about 21,000 lb (9450 kg), (P) about 23,000 lb (10,350 kg); loaded (E-2) 33,070 lb (15,000 kg), (K-2, M-1) 36,817 lb (16,570 kg), (J and N) 30,203 lb (13,590 kg), (P) 35,200 lb (15,840 kg).

Performance: maximum speed (E-2) 320 mph (515 kph), (K-2) 333 mph (533 kph), (M-1) 348 mph (557 kph), (J and N) about 311 mph (498 kph), (P) 488 mph (781 kph); service ceiling (E-2) 24,610 ft (7500 m), (K-2) 29,530 ft (9000 m), (M-1) 24,140 ft (7358 m), (J and N) 27,560 ft (8400 m), (P) 53,000 ft (16,154 m); range with full bomb load, about 1300 miles (2100 km) for all versions.

Armament: (E-2) one fixed 15 mm MG 151/15 in nose, one 13 mm MG 131 in dorsal turret, one MG 131 manually aimed at lower rear, and three 7·92 mm MG 15 manually aimed in nose and beam windows; maximum bomb load 8818 lb (4000 kg), including 3307 lb (1500 kg) external; (K-2) defensive armament similar to E-2, plus battery of four 7·92 mm MG 81 fixed rearward-firing in tail and optional pair fixed rearward-firing in nacelles (all sighted and fired by pilot), and offensive load of two FX 1400 radio controlled glide bombs and/or (K-3 version) two Hs 293 air-to-surface rocket guided missiles; (M-1) as E-2 except MG 15s replaced by larger number of MG 81; (J-2 and N-2) typically four 20 mm MG FF cannon and four 7·92 mm MG 17 in nose plus Mg 131 for lower rear defence (N-2 often had later guns such as MG 151/20 in nose and MG 151/20 or MK 108 30 mm in Schrage Musik upward-firing installation); (P) three pairs of MG 81 for defence, and two 1102 lb (496 kg) bombs on underwing racks.

History: first flight (Do 217V1) August 1938; (pre-production Do 217A-0) October or November 1939; first delivery of E series, late 1940; termination of production, late 1943.

Superficially a scaled-up Do 215, powered at first by the same DB 601 engines, the 217 was actually considerably larger and totally different in detail design. Much of Dornier's efforts in 1938—40 were devoted to finding more powerful engines and improving the flying qualities, and when the BMW 801 radial was available the 217 really got into its stride and carried a much heavier bomb load than any other *Luftwaffe* bomber of the time. Early E models, used from late 1940, had no dorsal turret and featured a very long extension of the rear fuselage which opened into an unusual dive brake. This was soon abandoned, but the 217 blossomed out into a prolific family which soon included the 217J night fighter, often produced by converting E-type bombers, and the N which was likewise produced by converting the liquid-cooled M. Several series carried large air-to-surface missiles steered by radio command from a special crew station in the bomber. Long-span K-2s of III/KG 100 scored many successes with their formidable missiles in the Mediterranean, their biggest bag being the Italian capital ship *Roma* as she steamed to the Allies after Italy's capitulation. The pressurised high-altitude P series had fantastic performance that would have put them out of reach of any Allied fighters had they been put into service in time. From 1943, Dornier devoted more effort to the technically very difficult Do 317, which never went into service.

Henschel Hs 123

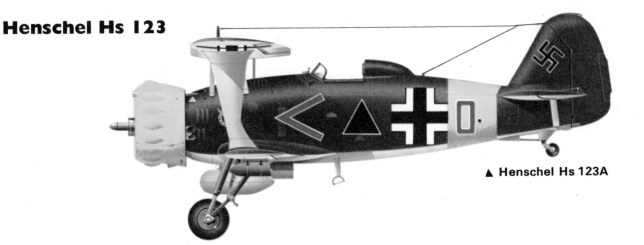

▲ Henschel Hs 123A

Henschel Hs 123A-1

Type: single-seat dive bomber and close-support aircraft.
Engine: one 880 hp BMW 132 Dc nine-cylinder radial.
Dimensions: span 34 ft 5½ in (10·5 m); length 27 ft 4 in (8·3 m); height 10 ft 6½ in (3·2 m).
Weights: empty 3316 lb (1504 kg); loaded 4888 lb (2217 kg).
Performance: maximum speed 214 mph (345 kph); initial climb 2950 ft (900 m)/min; service ceiling 29,530 ft (9000 m); range 530 miles (850 km).
Armament: two 7·92 mm Rheinmetall MG 17 machine guns ahead of pilot; underwing racks for four 110 lb (50 kg) bombs, or clusters of anti-personnel bombs or two 20 mm MG FF cannon.
History: first flight, spring 1935 (public display given May 8); first delivery (Spain) December 1936; final delivery, October 1938.

Though representing a class of aircraft generally considered obsolete by the start of World War II, this trim little biplane was kept very hard at work until 1942, achieving results which in retrospect seem almost unbelievable. The prototype needed extensive modification to produce the A-1 production version, which was tested in the Spanish Civil War. Contrary to the staff college theories then adhered to by the newly formed *Luftwaffe*, the Henschels were able to give close support to ground troops of a most real and immediate kind, strafing and bombing with great accuracy despite the lack of any radio link or even an established system of operation. Eventually the *Luftwaffe* realised that the concept of a close-support aircraft was valid, and a few Henschels were allowed to operate in this role, but all the effort and money was put into the Ju 87, and the Hs 123 was phased out of production before World War II. Yet in the Polish campaign these aircraft proved unbelievably useful, having the ability to make pinpoint attacks with guns and bombs and, by virtue of careful setting of the propeller speed, to make a demoralising noise. Moreover, it established an extraordinary reputation for returning to base even after direct hits by AA shells. As a result, though the whole force was incessantly threatened with disbandment or replacement by later types, the Hs 123 close-support unit II (Schlacht)/LG2 was sent intact to the Balkans in April 1941 and thence to Russia. Here the quite old biplanes fought around the clock, proving far better adapted to the conditions than more modern types and continuing in front-line operations until, by the end of 1944, there were no more left.

Junkers Ju 87 'Stuka'

▲ Junkers Ju 87D-1

(see pages 140/141 for cutaway drawing of Ju 87D-3)

Junkers Ju 87B and D

Type: two-seat dive bomber and ground attack aircraft.
Engine: (Ju 87B-1) one 1100 hp Junkers Jumo 211Da 12-cylinder inverted-vee liquid-cooled; (Ju 87D-1, D-5) 1300 hp Jumo 211J.
Dimensions: span (Ju 87B-1, D-1) 45 ft 3¼ in (13·8 m), (D-5) 50 ft 0½ in (15·25 m); length 36 ft 5 in (11·1 m); height 12 ft 9 in (3·9 m).
Weights: empty (B-1, D-1) about 6080 lb (2750 kg); loaded (B-1) 9371 lb (4250 kg), (D-1) 12,600 lb (5720 kg), (D-5) 14,500 lb (6585 kg).
Performance: maximum speed (B-1) 242 mph (390 kph), (D-1) 255 mph (408 kph), (D-5) 250 mph (402 kph); service ceiling (B-1) 26,250 ft (8000 m), (D-1, D-5) 24,000 ft (7320 m); range with maximum bomb load (B-1) 373 miles (600 km), (D-1, D-5) 620 miles (1000 km).
Armament: (Ju 87B-1) two 7·92 mm Rheinmetall MG 17 machine guns in wings, one 7·92 mm MG 15 manually aimed in rear cockpit, one 1102 lb (500 kg) bomb on centreline and four 110 lb (50 kg) on wing racks; (D-1, D-5) two MG 17 in wings, twin 7·92 mm MG 81 machine guns manually aimed in rear cockpit, one bomb of 3968 lb (1800 kg) on centreline; (D-7) two 20 mm MG 151/20 cannon in wings; (Ju 87G-1) two 37 mm BK (Flak 18, or Flak 36) cannon in under-wing pods; (D-4) two underwing WB81 weapon containers each housing six MG 81 guns.
History: first flight (Ju 87V1) late 1935; (pre-production Ju 87A-0) November 1936; (Ju 87B-1) August 1938; (Ju 87D-1) 1940; termination of production 1944.

Until at least 1942 the Ju 87 'Stuka' enjoyed a reputation that struck terror into those on the ground beneath it. First flown with a British R-R Kestrel engine and twin fins in 1935, it entered production in 1937 as the Ju 87A with large trousered landing gear and full equipment for dive bombing, including a heavy bomb crutch that swung the missile well clear of the fuselage before release. The spatted Ju 87B was the first aircraft in production with the Jumo 211 engine, almost twice as powerful as the Jumo 210 of the Ju 87A, and it had an automatic device (almost an autopilot) to ensure proper pull-out from the very steep dive, as well as red lines at 60°, 75° and 80° painted on the pilot's side window. Experience in Spain had shown that pilots could black-out and lose control in the pull-out. Later a whole formation of Ju 87Bs in Spain was late pulling out over misty ground and many hit the ground. In Poland and the Low Countries the Ju 87 was terribly effective, and it repeated its success in Greece, Crete and parts of the Russian front. But in the Battle of Britain its casualty rate was such that it was soon withdrawn, thereafter to attack ships and troops in areas where the Axis still had some air superiority. In 1942–45 its main work was close support on the Russian front, attacking armour with big guns and even being used as a transport and glider tug. Total production, all by Junkers, is believed to have been 5709.

Junkers Ju 87D-3

1 Spinner
2 Pitch change mechanism housing
3 Blade hub
4 Junkers VS 11 constant-speed airscrew
5 Anti-vibration engine mounting attachments
6 Oil filler point and marker
7 Auxiliary oil tank (5·9 Imp. gal./26,8 l capacity)
8 Junkers Jumo 211J-1 12-cylinder inverted-vee liquid cooled engine
9 Magnesium alloy forged engine mount
10 Coolant (Glysantin-water) header tank
11 Ejector exhaust stubs
12 Fuel injection unit housing
13 Induction air cooler
14 Armoured radiator
15 Inertia starter cranking point
16 Ball joint bulkhead fixing (lower)
17 Tubular steel mount support strut

18 Ventral armour (8 mm)
19 Main oil tank (9·9 Imp gal. (45 l capacity)
20 Oil filling point
21 Transverse support frame
22 Rudder pedals
23 Control column
24 Heating point
25 Auxiliary air intake
26 Ball joint bulkhead fixing (upper)
27 Bulkhead
28 Oil tank (6·8 Imp. gal./31 l capacity)
29 Oil filler point and marker (Intava 100)
30 Fuel filler cap

31 Self-sealing starboard outer fuel tank (33 Imp. gal./150 l capacity)
32 Underwing bombs with *Dienartstab* percussion rods
33 Pitot head
34 Spherical oxygen bottles
35 Wing skinning
36 Starboard navigation light
37 Aileron mass balance
38 'Double wing' aileron and flap (starboard outer)
39 Aileron hinge
40 Corrugated wing rib station
41 Reinforced armoured windscreen
42 Reflector sight
43 Padded crash bar
44 Signal flare tube
45 Braced fuselage mainframe
46 Front spar/fuselage attachment point

47 Pilot's seat (reinforced with 4-mm side and 8-mm rear armour)
48 Inter-cockpit bulkhead
49 Sliding canopy handgrip
50 External side armour
51 Pilot's back armour (8 mm)
52 Headrest
53 Aft-sliding cockpit canopy (shown part open)
54 Radio mast cut-out
55 Anti-crash hoop (magnesium casting)
56 Radio mast
57 Radio equipment (FuGe 16) compartment
58 Additional (internal) side armour
59 Canopy track
60 Handhold/footrests
61 Braced fuselage mainframe
62 Rear spar/fuselage attachment point
63 Radio-operator/gunner's seat (folding)

64 Floor armour (5 mm)
65 Armoured bulkhead (8 mm)
66 Ammunition magazine racks
67 Additional (external) side armour with cut-out for hand grip
68 Internal side and head armour
69 Sliding canopy section (shown part open)
70 Ring-and-bead gunsights
71 Twin 7·9-mm Mauser MG 81Z machine gun on GSL-K 81 mount
72 Canopy track fairing
73 Peil G IV D/F equipment
74 Circular plexiglass access panel
75 Back-to-back L-section stringers (fuselage horizontal break)
76 First-aid stowage
77 Z-section fuselage frames
78 Radio aerial
79 Faired elevator mass balance
80 Starboard elevator
81 Tailplane structure

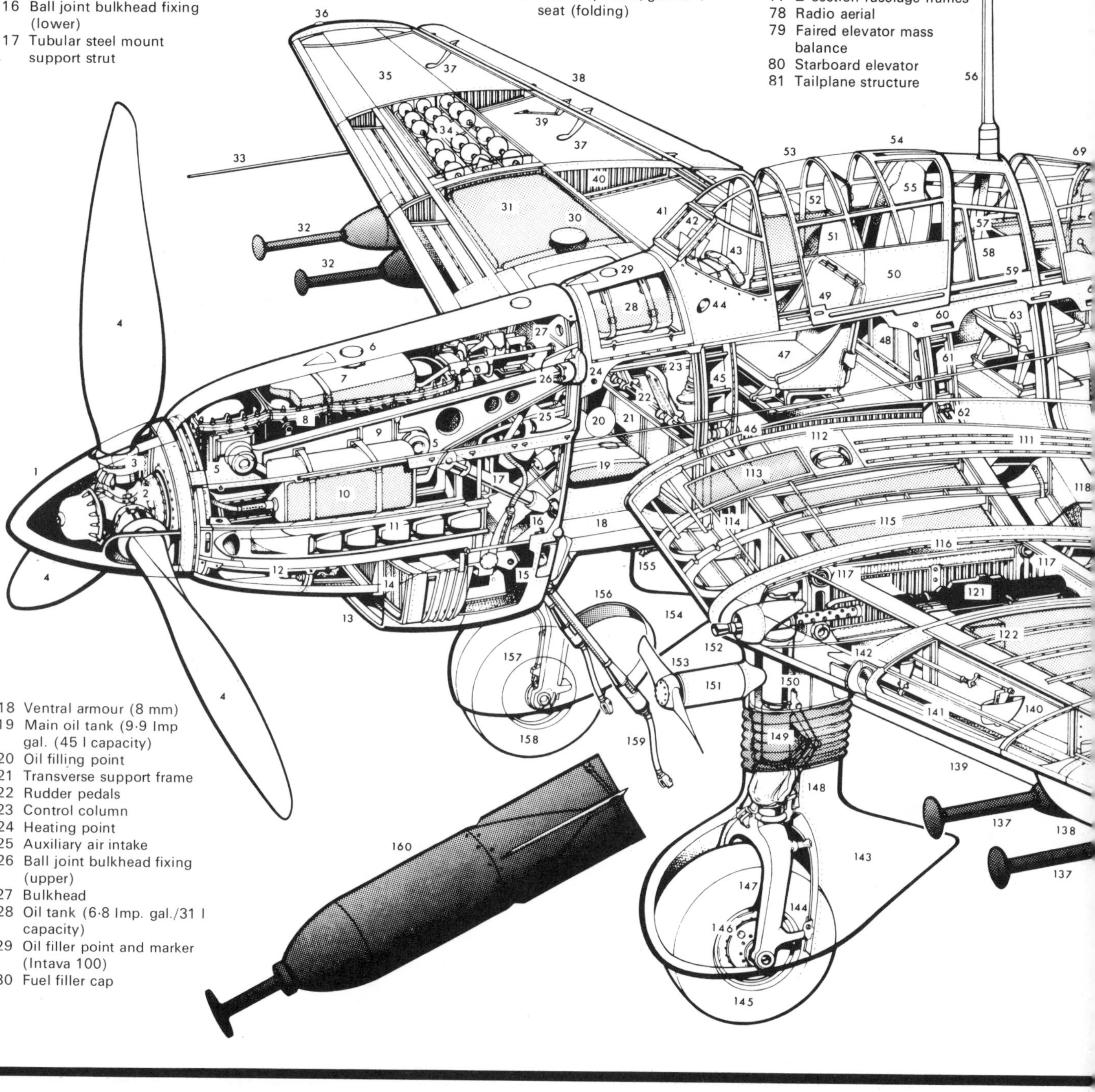

82 Tailplane brace/spar attachment point
83 Tailplane bracing strut
84 Fuselage skinning
85 Control runs
86 Tailfin attachment fairing
87 Tailfin structure
88 Rudder horn balance
89 Rudder
90 Rudder trim tab controls
91 Rudder trim tab
92 Rudder control linkage
93 Rudder post
94 Rear navigation light
95 Elevator tab
96 Port elevator
97 Faired elevator mass balance

98 Tailplane front spar
99 Control pulley circular access panels
100 Rudder lower hinge fairing
101 Tailplane bracing strut
102 Emergency tailskid
103 Tailwheel
104 Tailwheel leg
105 Jacking point
106 Fuselage stringers
107 Master compass
108 Crew entry step (port and starboard)
109 Entry step support (with control run cut-outs)

117 Ball-and-socket wing attachment points
118 Armoured coolant radiator (port and starboard)
119 Inboard flap structure
120 Flap hinge
121 Rheinmetall-Borsig MG 17 machine gun of 7,92-mm calibre (port and starboard)

137 Dienartstab percussion rod attachments
138 ETC 50/VIII fairing
139 Air brake (extended)
140 Air brake activating mechanism
141 Air brake (retracted)
142 Landing lamp
143 Wheel spat
144 Fork/spat attachment
145 Port mainwheel

110 Wing root fairing
111 Non-slip walkway (aft section external metal strakes)
112 Fuel filler point
113 Non-slip walkway (forward section composite surface)
114 Leading-edge structure
115 Self-sealing port inner wing fuel tank (52·8 Imp. gal./240 l capacity)
116 Wing-joint external cover strip

122 Ammunition tank (1,000 rounds capacity) inboard of rib
123 Port outer self-sealing fuel tank (33 Imp. gal/150 l capacity)
124 Corrugated wing rib
125 ETC bomb rack support bar
126 ETC bomb rack underwing fairing
127 Port outboard flap
128 Port aileron
129 Aileron mass balance
130 Rear spar
131 Wing rib
132 Port navigation light
133 Front spar
134 Wing leading edge
135 Underwing bomb load (two 110-lb/50-kg bombs) on multi-purpose carrier
136 Bomb shackles

146 Brake reservoir filler point
147 Cantilever fork
148 Leather shroud
149 Oleo-pneumatic shock absorber
150 Mainwheel leg
151 Siren fairing
152 Barrel of MG 17 machine gun
153 Wind-driven siren
154 Starboard wheel spat
155 PVC ventral bomb rack
156 Bomb cradle
157 Starboard wheel fork
158 Starboard mainwheel
159 Bomb release trapese
160 551-lb (250-kg) bomb with *Dienartstab* attachment

Focke-Wulf Fw 189 Uhu (Owl)

▲ Focke-Wulk Fw 189A-1

Focke-Wulf Fw 189A-2

Type: three-seat reconnaissance and close support aircraft.
Engines: two 465 hp Argus As 410A-1 12-cylinder inverted-vee air-cooled.
Dimensions: span 60 ft 4½ in (18·4 m); length 39 ft 4½ in (12 m); height 10 ft 2 in (3·1 m).
Weights: empty 5930 lb (2690 kg); loaded 8708 lb (3950 kg).
Performance: maximum speed 217 mph (350 kph); climb to 13,120 ft (4000 m) in 8 min 20 sec; service ceiling 23,950 ft (7300 m); range 416 miles (670 km).
Armament: one 7·92 mm MG 17 machine gun in each wing root, twin 7·92 mm MG 81 manually aimed in dorsal position and (usually) twin MG 81 in rear cone with limited field of fire; underwing racks for four 110 lb (50 kg) bombs.
History: first flight (Fw 189V1) July 1938; first delivery (pre-production Fw 189A-0) September 1940; final delivery August 1944.

Today the diversity of aircraft layout makes us forget how odd this aircraft seemed. It looked strange to the customer also, but after outstandingly successful flight trials the 189 was grudgingly bought in quantity as a standard reconnaissance aircraft. Though it flew in numbers well before the war – no two prototypes being alike – it was unknown by the Allies until it was disclosed in 1941 as 'the Flying Eye' of the German armies. On the Eastern front it performed beyond all expectation, for it retained its superb handling (which made it far from a sitting duck to fighters) and also showed great toughness of structure and more than once returned to base with one tail shot off or removed by Soviet ramming attack. Attempts to produce special attack versions with small heavily armoured nacelles were not so successful, but 10 Fw 189B trainers were built with conventional nacelle having side-by-side dual controls in a normal cockpit, with an observer above the trailing edge. The Fw 189A-3 was another

dual-control version having the normal 'glasshouse'. Eventually the sole source became French factories with assembly at Bordeaux-Merignac, which halted as Allied armies approached. There were many different versions and several developments with more powerful engines, but the basic A-1, A-2 (better armament) and A-3 were the only types built in numbers, the total of these versions being 846.

Junkers Ju 188 and 388

▲ Junkers Ju 188D-2

Junkers Ju 188A, D and E

Type: five-seat bomber (D-2, reconnaissance aircraft).
Engines: (Ju 188A) two 1776 hp Junkers Jumo 213A 12-cylinder inverted-vee liquid-cooled; (Ju 188D) same as A; (Ju 188E) two 1700 hp BMW 801G-2 18-cylinder two-row radials.
Dimensions: span 72 ft 2 in (22 m); length 49 ft 1 in (14·96 m); height 16 ft 1 in (4·9 m).
Weights: empty (188E-1) 21,825 lb (9900 kg); loaded (188A and D) 33,730 lb (15,300 kg); (188E-1) 31,967 lb (14,500 kg).
Performance: maximum speed (188A) 325 mph (520 kph) at 20,500 ft (6250 m), (188D) 350 mph (560 kph) at 27,000 ft (8235 m), (188E) 315 mph (494 kph) at 19,685 ft (6000 m); service ceiling (188A) 33,000 ft (10,060 m), (188D) 36,090 ft (11,000 m), (188E) 31,170 ft (9500 m); range with 3300 lb (1500 kg) bomb load (188A and E) 1550 miles (2480 km).
Armament: (A, D-1 and E-1) one 20 mm MG 151/20 cannon in nose, one MG 151/20 in dorsal turret, one 13 mm MG 131 manually aimed at rear dorsal position

and one MG 131 or twin 7·92 mm MG 81 manually aimed at rear ventral position; 6614 lb (3000 kg) bombs internally or two 2200 lb (1000 kg) torpedoes under inner wings.
History: first flight (Ju 88B-0) early 1940; (Ju 88V27) September 1941; (Ju 188V1) December 1941; (Ju 188E-1) March 1942.

In 1939 Junkers had the Jumo 213 engine in advanced development and, to go with it, the aircraft side of the company prepared an improved Ju 88 with a larger yet more streamlined crew compartment and more efficient pointed wings and large squarish tail. After protracted development this went into production as the Ju 188E-1, fitted with BMW 801s because the powerful Jumo was still not ready. The plant at Bernburg delivered 120 E-1s, and a few radar-equipped turretless E-2s and reconnaissance F versions before, in mid-1943, finally getting into production with the A-1 version. Leipzig/Mockau built the A-2 with flame-

damped exhaust for night operations, and the A-3 torpedo bomber. The Ds were fast reconnaissance aircraft, and the Ju 188S was a family of high-speed machines, for various duties, capable of up to 435 mph (696 kph). Numerous other versions, some with a remotely controlled twin-MG 131 tail turret, led to the even faster and higher-flying Ju 388 family of night fighters, reconnaissance and bomber aircraft. Altogether about 1100 Ju 188 and about 120 388s were delivered, and at the war's end the much larger and markedly different Ju 288 had been shelved, while the Ju 488, a much enlarged four-engined 388, was about to fly at Toulouse. All these aircraft, and the even greater number of stillborn projects, were evidence of the increasingly urgent need to make up for the absence of properly conceived new designs by wringing the utmost development out of the obsolescent types with which the *Luftwaffe* started the war.

Arado Ar 196

▲ Arado Ar 196A-3

Arado Ar 196A-3

Type: two-seat maritime reconnaissance aircraft.
Engine: 960 hp BMW 132K nine-cylinder radial.
Dimensions: spar 40 ft 8 in (12·4 m); length 36 ft 1 in (11 m); height 14 ft 4½ in (4·4 m).
Weights: empty 6580 lb (2990 kg); loaded 8223 lb (3730 kg).
Performance: maximum speed 193 mph (310 kph) at 13,120 ft (4000 m); initial climb 980 ft (300 m)/min; service ceiling 23,000 ft (7020 m); range 670 miles (1070 km) at 158 mph (253 kph).
Armament: two MG FF 20 mm cannon in wings outboard of propeller disc, one MG 17 7·92 mm in top decking and twin MG 17 on pivoted mounting aimed by observer. Rack under each wing for 110 lb (50 kg) bomb.
History: first flight (196V1) May 1938; first operational service August 1, 1939.

One of the very few float seaplanes to be used in

World War II outside the Pacific area, the Ar 196 was designed as a replacement of the He 60 biplane on the catapults of all the German Navy's capital ships. Its duties were thus primarily reconnaissance and shadowing of surface vessels, but in comparison with such Allied types as the Curtiss Seagull and Fairey Seafox it had a much higher performance and eventually was given formidable armament. Four prototypes powered by the 880 hp BMW 132 Dc engine (derived in Germany from the Pratt & Whitney Hornet) were flown in 1938, two with twin floats and the others with a large central float. The following year 26 Ar 196A-1s were built, entering service in August aboard *Scharnhorst*, *Gneisenau*, the pocket battleships and at shore bases on the North Sea. In 1940 the Ar 196A-3 entered service and this type made up the bulk of the 401 aircraft built. Though quite outclassed by the best fighters, the A-3 was a versatile multi-role aircraft which actually spent most of the war operating on sea

patrols from coastal bases, mainly on the Bay of Biscay and islands in the Mediterranean. Batches were built by Vichy-France at Saint Nazaire and, in a slightly modified A-5 form, by Fokker at Amsterdam in 1943–44. About 50 served with co-belligerent Balkan air forces in the Adriatic and Black Sea. The type was never developed as an effective anti-submarine search and strike machine, despite its obvious potential.

Focke-Wulf Fw 190

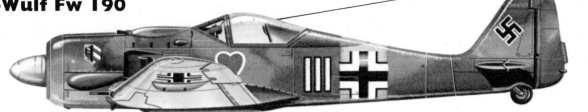

Focke-Wulf Fw 190D-9, F-8, Ta 152H-1 and Fw 190A-8

▲ Focke-Wulf Fw 190F-8   (see pages 144/145 for cutaway drawing)

Type: single-seat fighter bomber.
Engine: (A-8, F-8) one 1700 hp (2100 hp emergency boost) BMW 801Dg 18-cylinder two row radial; (D-9) one 1776 hp (2240 hp emergency boost) Junkers Jumo 213A-1 12-cylinder inverted-vee liquid-cooled; (Ta 152H-1) one 1880 hp (2250 hp) Jumo 213E-1.
Dimensions: span 34 ft 5½ in (10·49 m), (Ta 152H-1) 47 ft 6¾ in (14·5 m); length (A-8, F-8) 29 ft (8·84 m), (D-9) 33 ft 5¼ in (10·2 m), (Ta 152H-1) 35 ft 5½ in (10·8 m); height 13 ft (3·96 m), (D-9) 11 ft 0¼ in (3·35 m), (Ta 152H-1) 11 ft 8 in (3·55 m).
Weights: empty (A-8, F-8) 7055 lb (3200 kg), (D-9) 7720 lb (3500 kg); (Ta 152H-1) 7940 lb (3600 kg); loaded (A-8, F-8) 10,800 lb (4900 kg), (D-9) 10,670 lb (4840 kg), (Ta 152H-1) 12,125 lb (5500 kg).
Performance: maximum speed (with boost) (A-8, F-8) 408 mph (653 kph), (D-9) 440 mph (704 kph), (Ta 152H-1) 472 mph (755 kph); initial climb (A-8, F-8) 2350 ft (720 m)/min, (D-9, Ta 152) about 3300 ft (1000 m)/min; service ceiling (A-8, F-8) 37,400 ft (11,410 m), (D-9) 32,810 ft (10,000 m), (Ta 152H-1) 49,215 ft (15,000 m); range on internal fuel (A-8, F-8 and D-9) about 560 miles (900 km), (Ta 152H-1, 745 miles (1200 km).
Armament: (A-8, F-8) two 13 mm MG 131 above engine, two 20 mm MG 151/20 in wing roots and two

MG 151/20 or 30 mm MK 108 in outer wings; (D-9) as above, or without outer MG 151/20s, with provision for 30 mm MK 108 firing through propeller hub; (Ta 152H-1) one 30 mm MK 108 and two inboard MG 151/20 (sometimes outboard MG 151/20s as well); bomb load (A-8, D-9) one 1100 lb (500 kg) on centreline; (F-8) one 3968 lb (1800 kg) on centreline; (Ta 152H-1) none normally carried.
History: first flight (Fw 190V1) June 1, 1939, (production Fw 190A-1) September 1940, (Fw 190D) late 1942.

Though flown well before World War II this trim little fighter was unknown to the Allies, and caused a nasty surprise when first met over France in early 1941. Indeed, it was so far superior to the bigger and more sluggish Spitfire V that for the first time the RAF felt not only outnumbered but beaten technically. In June 1942 an Fw 109A-3 landed by mistake in England, and the 'Focke-Wulf' was discovered to be even better than expected. It was faster than any Allied fighter in service, had far heavier armament (at that time the standard was two 7·92 mm MG 17s over the engine, two of the previously unknown Mauser cannon inboard and two 20 mm MG FF outboard), was immensely strong, had excellent power of manoeuvre and good pilot view. It was also an extremely small target, much lighter than any Allied

fighter and had a stable wide-track landing gear (unlike the Bf 109). Altogether it gave Allied pilots and designers an inferiority complex. Though it never supplanted the 109, it was subsequently made in a profusion of different versions by many factories.
The A series included many fighter and fighter bomber versions, some having not only the increasingly heavy internal armament but also two or four 20 mm cannon or two 30 mm in underwing fairings. Most had an emergency power boost system, using MW 50 (methanol/water) or GM-1 (nitrous oxide) injection, or both. Some were two-seaters, and a few had autopilots for bad weather and night interceptions. The F series were close-support attack aircraft, some having the Panzerblitz array of R4M rockets for tank-busting (also lethal against heavy bombers). The G was another important series of multi-role fighter/dive bombers, but by 1943 the main effort was devoted to what the RAF called the 'long-nosed 190', the 190D. This was once more the fastest fighter in the sky, and late in 1943 it was redesignated Ta 152 in honour of the director of Focke-Wulf's design team, Prof Kurt Tank. The early 152C series were outstandingly formidable, but the long-span H sacrificed guns for speed and height. Tank himself 'walked away' from a flight of P-51D Mustangs which 'bounced' him on a test flight; but only 10 of the H sub-type had flown when the war ended.

Focke Wulf Fw 190A-8

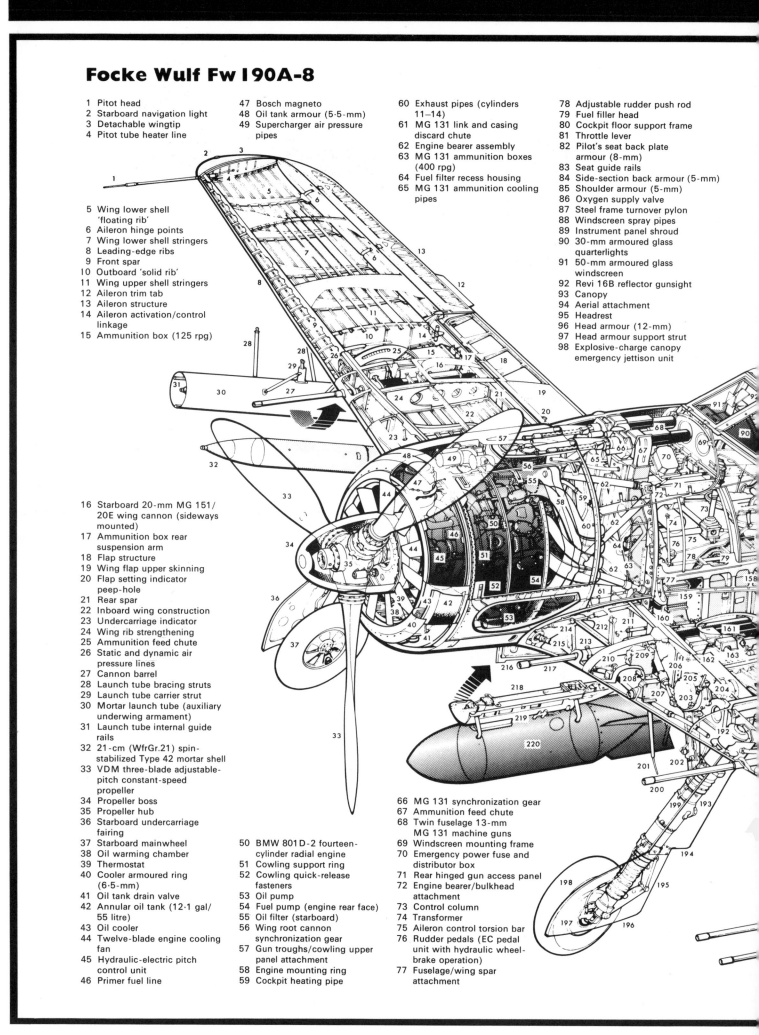

1 Pitot head
2 Starboard navigation light
3 Detachable wingtip
4 Pitot tube heater line
5 Wing lower shell 'floating rib'
6 Aileron hinge points
7 Wing lower shell stringers
8 Leading-edge ribs
9 Front spar
10 Outboard 'solid rib'
11 Wing upper shell stringers
12 Aileron trim tab
13 Aileron structure
14 Aileron activation/control linkage
15 Ammunition box (125 rpg)
16 Starboard 20-mm MG 151/20E wing cannon (sideways mounted)
17 Ammunition box rear suspension arm
18 Flap structure
19 Wing flap upper skinning
20 Flap setting indicator peep-hole
21 Rear spar
22 Inboard wing construction
23 Undercarriage indicator
24 Wing rib strengthening
25 Ammunition feed chute
26 Static and dynamic air pressure lines
27 Cannon barrel
28 Launch tube bracing struts
29 Launch tube carrier strut
30 Mortar launch tube (auxiliary underwing armament)
31 Launch tube internal guide rails
32 21-cm (WfrGr.21) spin-stabilized Type 42 mortar shell
33 VDM three-blade adjustable-pitch constant-speed propeller
34 Propeller boss
35 Propeller hub
36 Starboard undercarriage fairing
37 Starboard mainwheel
38 Oil warming chamber
39 Thermostat
40 Cooler armoured ring (6·5-mm)
41 Oil tank drain valve
42 Annular oil tank (12·1 gal/55 litre)
43 Oil cooler
44 Twelve-blade engine cooling fan
45 Hydraulic-electric pitch control unit
46 Primer fuel line

47 Bosch magneto
48 Oil tank armour (5·5-mm)
49 Supercharger air pressure pipes
50 BMW 801D-2 fourteen-cylinder radial engine
51 Cowling support ring
52 Cowling quick-release fasteners
53 Oil pump
54 Fuel pump (engine rear face)
55 Oil filter (starboard)
56 Wing root cannon synchronization gear
57 Gun troughs/cowling upper panel attachment
58 Engine mounting ring
59 Cockpit heating pipe

60 Exhaust pipes (cylinders 11–14)
61 MG 131 link and casing discard chute
62 Engine bearer assembly
63 MG 131 ammunition boxes (400 rpg)
64 Fuel filter recess housing
65 MG 131 ammunition cooling pipes
66 MG 131 synchronization gear
67 Ammunition feed chute
68 Twin fuselage 13-mm MG 131 machine guns
69 Windscreen mounting frame
70 Emergency power fuse and distributor box
71 Rear hinged gun access panel
72 Engine bearer/bulkhead attachment
73 Control column
74 Transformer
75 Aileron control torsion bar
76 Rudder pedals (EC pedal unit with hydraulic wheel-brake operation)
77 Fuselage/wing spar attachment

78 Adjustable rudder push rod
79 Fuel filler head
80 Cockpit floor support frame
81 Throttle lever
82 Pilot's seat back plate armour (8-mm)
83 Seat guide rails
84 Side-section back armour (5-mm)
85 Shoulder armour (5-mm)
86 Oxygen supply valve
87 Steel frame turnover pylon
88 Windscreen spray pipes
89 Instrument panel shroud
90 30-mm armoured glass quarterlights
91 50-mm armoured glass windscreen
92 Revi 16B reflector gunsight
93 Canopy
94 Aerial attachment
95 Headrest
96 Head armour (12-mm)
97 Head armour support strut
98 Explosive-charge canopy emergency jettison unit

99 Canopy channel slide
100 Auxiliary tank: fuel (25·3 gal/115 litre) or GM-1 (18·7 gal/85 litre)
101 FuG 16ZY transmitter-receiver unit
102 Handhold cover
103 Primer fuel filler cap
104 Autopilot steering unit (PKS 12)
105 FuG 16ZY power transformer
106 Entry step cover plate
107 Two tri-spherical oxygen bottles (starboard fuselage wall)
108 Auxiliary fuel tank filler point
109 FuG 25a transponder unit
110 Autopilot position integration unit
111 FuG 16ZY homer bearing converter

112 Elevator control cables
113 Rudder control DUZ-flexible rods
114 Fabric panel (Bulkhead 12)
115 Rudder differential unit
116 Aerial lead-in
117 Rear fuselage lift tube
118 Triangular stress frame
119 Tailplane trim unit
120 Tailplane attachment fitting
121 Tailwheel retraction guide tube
122 Retraction cable lower pulley
123 Starboard tailplane
124 Aerial
125 Starboard elevator
126 Elevator trim tab

138 Elevator trim tab
139 Port elevator structure
140 Tailplane construction
141 Semi-retracting tailwheel
142 Forked wheel housing
143 Drag yoke
144 Tailwheel shock strut
145 Tailwheel locking linkage
146 Elevator actuation lever linkage
147 Angled frame spar

165 Rear spar
166 Spar construction
167 Flap position indicator scale and peep-hole
168 Flap actuating electric motor
169 Port 20-mm MG 151/20E wing cannon (sideways mounted)
170 Aileron transverse linkage
171 Ammunition box (125 rpg)
172 Ammunition box rear suspension arm
173 Aileron control linkage
174 Aileron control unit
175 Aileron trim tab
176 Port aileron structure
177 Port navigation light
178 Outboard wing stringers
179 Detachable wingtip
180 A-8/R1 variant underwing gun pack (in place of outboard wing cannon)
181 Link and casing discard chute
182 Twin unsynchronized 20-mm MG 151/20E cannon
183 Light metal fairing (gondola)
184 Ammunition feed chutes
185 Ammunition boxes (125 rpg)
186 Carrier frame restraining cord
187 Ammunition box rear suspension arms
188 Leading-edge skinning
189 Ammunition feed chute
190 Ammunition warming pipe

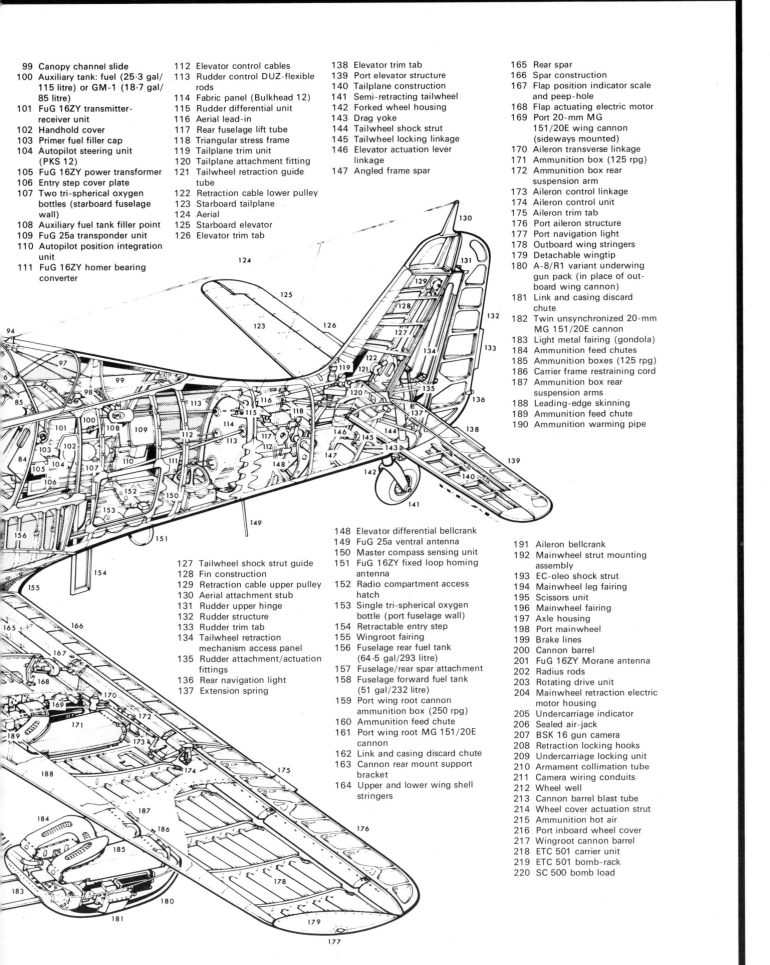

127 Tailwheel shock strut guide
128 Fin construction
129 Retraction cable upper pulley
130 Aerial attachment stub
131 Rudder upper hinge
132 Rudder structure
133 Rudder trim tab
134 Tailwheel retraction mechanism access panel
135 Rudder attachment/actuation fittings
136 Rear navigation light
137 Extension spring

148 Elevator differential bellcrank
149 FuG 25a ventral antenna
150 Master compass sensing unit
151 FuG 16ZY fixed loop homing antenna
152 Radio compartment access hatch
153 Single tri-spherical oxygen bottle (port fuselage wall)
154 Retractable entry step
155 Wingroot fairing
156 Fuselage rear fuel tank (64·5 gal/293 litre)
157 Fuselage/rear spar attachment
158 Fuselage forward fuel tank (51 gal/232 litre)
159 Port wing root cannon ammunition box (250 rpg)
160 Ammunition feed chute
161 Port wing root MG 151/20E cannon
162 Link and casing discard chute
163 Cannon rear mount support bracket
164 Upper and lower wing shell stringers

191 Aileron bellcrank
192 Mainwheel strut mounting assembly
193 EC-oleo shock strut
194 Mainwheel leg fairing
195 Scissors unit
196 Mainwheel fairing
197 Axle housing
198 Port mainwheel
199 Brake lines
200 Cannon barrel
201 FuG 16ZY Morane antenna
202 Radius rods
203 Rotating drive unit
204 Mainwheel retraction electric motor housing
205 Undercarriage indicator
206 Sealed air-jack
207 BSK 16 gun camera
208 Retraction locking hooks
209 Undercarriage locking unit
210 Armament collimation tube
211 Camera wiring conduits
212 Wheel well
213 Cannon barrel blast tube
214 Wheel cover actuation strut
215 Ammunition hot air
216 Port inboard wheel cover
217 Wingroot cannon barrel
218 ETC 501 carrier unit
219 ETC 501 bomb-rack
220 SC 500 bomb load

Arado Ar 234 Blitz

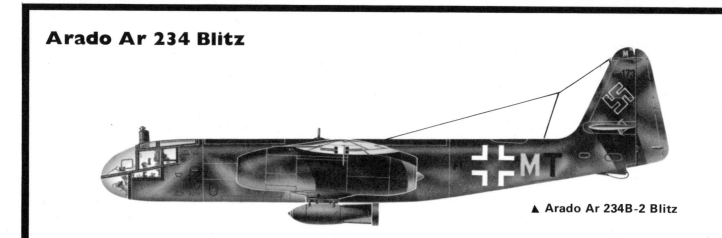

▲ Arado Ar 234B-2 Blitz

Arado Ar 234B

Type: single-seat reconnaissance bomber.
Engines: two 1980 lb (900 kg) thrust Junkers Jumo 004B axial turbojets.
Dimensions: span 46 ft 3½ in (14·2 m); length 41 ft 5½ in (12·65 m); height 14 ft 1¼ in (4·3 m).
Weights: empty 11,464 lb (5200 kg); loaded 18,541 lb (8410 kg); maximum with rocket takeoff boost 21,715 lb (9850 kg).
Performance: maximum speed (clean) 461 mph (742 kph); service ceiling 32,800 ft (10,000 m); range (clean) 1013 miles (1630 km), (with 3300 lb bomb load) 684 miles (1100 km).
Armament: two fixed MG 151 20 mm cannon in rear fuselage, firing to rear and sighted by periscope; various combinations of bombs slung under fuselage and/or engines to maximum of 3300 lb (1500 kg).
History: first flight (Ar 234V1) June 15, 1943, (Ar 234V9 with landing gear) March 1944, (Ar 234B0 pre-production) June 8, 1944; operational delivery September 1944.

As the first jet reconnaissance bomber, the Ar 234 marked the most successful fruit of Germany's remarkably bold introduction of high-performance turbojet aircraft in 1944. Its design was begun under Walter Blume in 1941, after long studies in 1940 of an official specification for a jet-propelled reconnaissance aircraft with a range of 1340 miles. The design was neat and simple, with two of the new axial engines slung under a high wing, and the single occupant in a pressurised cockpit forming the entire nose. But to achieve the required fuel capacity no wheels were fitted. When it flew on June 15, 1943 the first 234 took off from a three-wheel trolley and landed on retractable skids. After extensive trials with eight prototypes the ninth flew with conventional landing gear, leading through 20 pre-production models to the operational 234B-1, with ejection seat, autopilot and drop tanks under the engines. Main production centred on the 234B-2, made in many sub-variants, most of them able to carry a heavy bomb load. Service over the British Isles with the B-1 began in September 1944, followed by a growing force of B-2s which supported the Battle of the Bulge in the winter 1944–45. In March 1945, B-2s of III/KG76 repeatedly attacked the vital Remagen bridge across the Rhine with 2205 lb (1000 kg) bombs, causing its collapse. Though handicapped by fuel shortage these uninterceptable aircraft played a significant role on all European fronts in the closing months of the war, 210 being handed over excluding the many prototypes and later versions with four engines and an uncompleted example with a crescent-shaped wing.

Heinkel He 162

▲ Heinkel He 162A-2 'Volksjäger'

Heinkel He 162A-2

Type: single-seat interceptor.
Engine: one 1760 lb (800 kg) thrust BMW 003E-1 or E-2 Orkan single-shaft turbojet.
Dimensions: span 23 ft 7¾ in (7·2 m); length 29 ft 8½ in (9 m); height 6 ft 6½ in (2·6 m).
Weights: empty 4796 lb (2180 kg); loaded 5940 lb (2695 kg).
Performance: maximum speed 490 mph (784 kph) at sea level, 522 mph (835 kph) at 19,700 ft (6000 m); initial climb 4200 ft (1280 m)/min; service ceiling 39,500 ft (12,040 m); range at full throttle 434 miles (695 km) at altitude.
Armament: early versions, two 30 mm Rheinmetall MK 108 cannon with 50 rounds each; later production, two 20 mm Mauser MG 151/20 with 120 rounds each.
History: first flight December 6, 1944; first delivery January 1945.

Popularly called *Volksjaeger* (People's Fighter), this incredible aircraft left behind so many conflicting impressions it is hard to believe the whole programme was started and finished in little more than six months. To appreciate the almost impossible nature of the programme, Germany was being pounded to rubble by fleets of Allied bombers that darkened the sky, and the aircraft industry and the *Luftwaffe*'s fuel supplies were inexorably running down to a stop. Experienced aircrew had nearly all been killed, materials were in very short supply, and time had to be measured not in months but in days. So on September 8, 1944 the RLM issued a specification calling for a '750 kph jet fighter to be regarded as a piece of consumer goods and to be ready by January 1, 1945'. Huge numbers of workers were organised to build it even before it was designed, and Hitler Youth were hastily trained in primary gliders before being strapped into the new jet. Heinkel, which had built the world's first turbojet aircraft (He 178, flown August 27, 1939) and the first jet fighter, (He 280 twin-jet, flown on its jet engines April 2, 1941) won a hasty competition with a tiny wooden machine with its engine perched on top and blasting between twin fins. Drawings were ready on October 30, 1944. The prototype flew in 37 days and plans were made for production to rise rapidly to 4000 per month. Despite extreme difficulties, 300 of various sub-types had been completed by VE-day, with 800 more on the assembly lines. I/JG1 was operational at Leck, though without fuel. Despite many bad characteristics the 162 was a fighter of futuristic kind, created in quantity far quicker than modern aircraft are even drawn on paper.

Messerschmitt Me 262

▲ Messerschmitt Me 262A-2a

Messerschmitt Me 262A-1a
Schwalbe (Swallow), Me 262A-2
Sturmvogel/(Stormbird), Me 262B-1a

Type: (A-1a) single-seat fighter, (A-2a) single-seat bomber, (262B-1a) two-seat night fighter.
Engines: two 1980 lb (900 kg) thrust Junkers Jumo 004B single-shaft axial turbojets.
Dimensions: span 40 ft 11½ in (12·5 m); length 34 ft 9½ in (10·6 m), (262B-1a, excluding radar aerials) 38 ft 9 in (11·8 m); height 12 ft 7 in (3·8 m).
Weights: empty (A-1a, A-2a) 8820 lb (4000 kg), (B-1a) 9700 lb (4400 kg); loaded (A-1a, A-2a) 15,500 lb (7045 kg), (B-1a) 14,110 lb (6400 kg).
Performance: maximum speed (A-1a) 540 mph (870 kph), (A-2a, laden) 470 mph (755 kph), (B-1a) 497 mph (800 kph); initial climb (all) about 3940 ft (1200 m)/min; service ceiling 37,565 ft (11,500 m); range on internal fuel, at altitude, about 650 miles (1050 km).
Armament: (A-1a) four 30 mm MK 108 cannon, two with 100 rounds each, two with 80; (A-1a/U1) two 30 mm MK 103, two MK 108 and two 20 mm MG 151/20; (A-1b) as A-1a plus 24 spin-stabilised R4/M 50 mm rockets; (B-1a) as A-1a; (B-2a) as A-1a plus two inclined MK 108 behind cockpit in Schräge

Musik installation; (D) SG 500 Jagdfaust with 12 rifled mortar barrels inclined in nose; (E) 50 mm MK 114 gun or 48 R4/m rockets; bomb load of two 1100 lb (500 kg) bombs carried by A-2a.
History: first flight (262V1 on Jumo 210 piston engine) April 4, 1941; (262V3 on two Jumo 004A-0 turbojets) July 18, 1942; (Me 262A-1a) June 7, 1944; first delivery (A-0 to Rechlin) May 1944; first experimental combat unit (EK 262) June 30. 1944; first regular squadron (8/ZG26) September 1944.

In the Me 262 the German aircraft industry created a potentially war-winning aircraft which could have restored to the *Luftwaffe* command of the skies over Germany. Compared with Allied fighters of its day, including the RAF Meteor I, which entered service at the same time, it was much faster and packed a much heavier punch. Radar-equipped night fighter versions and sub-types designed to stand off from large bomber formations and blast them out of the sky were also developments against which the Allies had no answer. Yet for years the whole programme was held

back by official disinterest, and by the personal insistence of Hitler that the world-beating jet should be used only as a bomber!
It was in the autumn of 1938 that Messerschmitt was asked to study the design of a jet fighter, and the resulting Me 262 was remarkably unerring. First flown on a piston engine in the nose, it then flew on its twin turbojets and finally: in July 1943, the fifth development aircraft flew with a nosewheel. Despite numerous snags, production aircraft were being delivered in July 1944, and the rate of production was many times that of the British Meteor. On the other hand the German axial engines were unreliable and casualties due to engine failure, fires or break-up were heavy. The MK 108 gun was also prone to jam, and the landing gear to collapse. Yet the 262 was a beautiful machine to handle, and, while Allied jets either never reached squadrons or never engaged enemy aircraft, the 100 or so Me 262s that flew on operations and had fuel available destroyed far more than 100 Allied bombers and fighters. Even more remarkably, by VE-day total deliveries of this formidable aircraft reached 1433.

Messerschmitt Me 163 Komet (Comet)

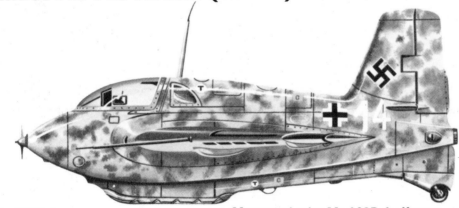

Messerschmitt Me 163B-1

▲ Messerschmitt Me 163B-1a Komet

Type: single-seat interceptor.
Engine: one 3750 lb (1700 kg) thrust Walter HWK 509A-2 bi-propellant rocket burning concentrated hydrogen peroxide (T-stoff) and hydrazine/methanol (C-stoff).
Dimensions: span 30 ft 7 in (9·3 m); length 18 ft 8 in (5·69 m); height 9 ft (2·74 m).
Weights: empty 4191 lb (1905 kg); loaded 9042 lb (4110 kg).
Performance: maximum speed 596 mph (960 kph) at 32,800 ft (10,000 m); initial climb 16,400 ft (5000 m)/min; service ceiling 54,000 ft (16,500 m); range depended greatly on flight profile but under 100 km (62 miles); endurance 2½ min from top of climb or eight min total.
Armament: two 30mm MK 108 cannon each with 60 rounds.
History: first flight (Me 163V1) spring 1941 as glider, August 1941 under power; (Me 163B) August

1943; first operational unit (I/JG400) May 1944.

Of all aircraft engaged in World War II the Me 163 was the most radical and, indeed, futuristic. The concept of the short-endurance local-defence interceptor powered by a rocket engine was certainly valid and might have been more of a thorn in the Allies' side than it was. Even the dramatically unconventional form of the Me 163, with no horizontal tail and an incredibly short fuselage, did not lead to great difficulty; in fact, the production fighter was widely held to have the best and safest flight characteristics of any aircraft in the *Luftwaffe*. But the swift strides into uncharted technology were bold in the extreme. It was partly to save weight and drag that the tailless configuration was adopted, and partly because the moving spirit behind the project was at first Dr Alex Lippisch, who liked tailless designs. Choice of two rocket propellants that reacted violently when they came into contact solved

the problem of ignition in the combustion chamber but added an extremely large element of danger. Moreover, the 163 had no landing gear, taking off from a jettisoned trolley and landing on a sprung skid, and the landing impact often sloshed residual propellants together causing a violent explosion. Many aircraft were lost this way, and the original test pilot, glider champion Heini Dittmar, was badly injured when the skid failed to extend. Nevertheless by 1944 these bat-like specks were swooping on US bomber formations with devastating effect. Numerous improved versions were flying at VE day, but only 370 Komets had seen service and these had suffered very high attrition through accidents.

Junkers Ju 88G-I

1 Starboard navigation light
2 Wingtip profile
3 FuG 227 Flensburg radar array
4 Starboard aileron
5 Aileron control lines
6 Starboard flaps
7 Flap-fairing strip
8 Wing ribs
9 Starboard outer fuel tank (91 Imp. Gal.)
10 Fuel filler cap
11 Leading-edge structure
12 Annular exhaust slot
13 Cylinder head fairings
14 Adjustable nacelle nose ring
15 Twelve-blade cooling fan
16 Propeller boss
17 Three-blade variable-pitch VS 111 propeller
18 Leading-edge radar array
19 Lichtenstein SN-2 radar array
20 Solid nose
21 Bulkhead
22 Gyro compass
23 Instrument panel

24 Armoured-glass windscreen sections
25 Folding seat
26 Control column
27 Rudder pedal/brake cylinder
28 Control lines
29 Pilot's seat
30 Sliding window section
31 Headrest
32 Jettisonable canopy roof section
33 Gun restraint
34 WOP/gunner's seat
35 13-mm MG 131
36 Radio equipment
37 Ammunition box (500 round)
38 Lichtenstein SN-2 indicator box
39 FuG 227 Flensburg indicator box
40 Control linkage
41 Bulkhead
42 Armoured gun mounting
43 Aerial post/traverse check
44 Fuel filler cap
45 Whip serial
46 Forward fuselage fuel tank (105 Imp. Gal.)

47 Fuselage horizontal construction joint
48 Bulkhead
49 Fuel filler cap
50 Aft fuselage fuel tank (230 Imp. Gal.)
51 Access hatch
52 Bulkhead
53 Control linkage access plate
54 Fuselage stringers
55 Upper longeron
56 Maintenance walkway
57 Control linkage
58 Fuselage horizontal construction joint
59 'Z'-section fuselage frames
60 Dinghy stowage
61 Fuel vent pipe
62 Master compass
63 Spherical oxygen bottles
64 Accumulator
65 Tailplane centre-section carry-through
66 Starboard tailplane
67 Elevator balance
68 Aerial
69 Starboard elevator
70 Elevator tab
71 Tailfin front spar/fuselage attachment
72 Tailfin structure
73 Rudder actuator

74 Rudder post
75 Rudder mass balance
76 Rudder upper hinge
77 Rudder tab (upper section)
78 Inspection/maintenance handhold
79 Rudder structure
80 Tailfin rear spar/fuselage attachment
81 Rudder tab (lower section)
82 Rear navigation light
83 Elevator tab
84 Port elevator
85 Elevator balance
86 Elevator tab actuator
87 Heated leading-edge
88 Tail bumper/fuel vent outlet
89 Tailwheel doors
90 Tailwheel retraction mechanism
91 Shock-absorber leg
92 Mudguard
93 Tailwheel
94 Access hatch
95 Fixed antenna
96 D/F loop
97 Lower longeron
98 Nacelle/flap fairing
99 Port flap
100 Wing centre/outer section attachment point
101 Aileron controls

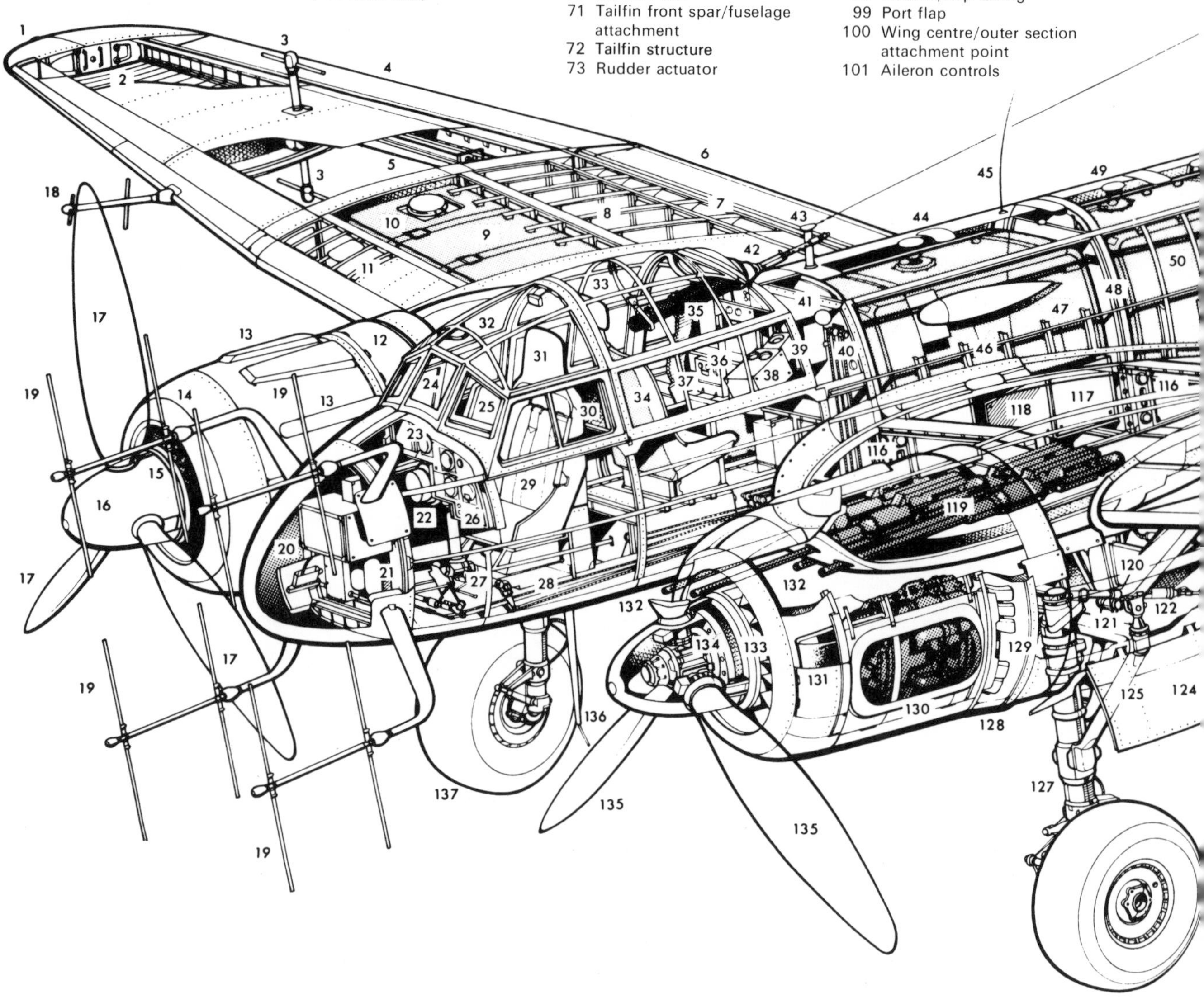

102 Aileron tab (port only)
103 Aileron hinges
104 Rear spar
105 Port aileron
106 Port navigation light
107 FuG 101a radio altimeter antennae
108 Wing structure
109 Leading-edge radar array
110 Front spar
111 Pitot head
112 Landing lamp
113 Mainwheel well rear bulkhead
114 Port outer fuel tank location (91 Imp. Gal.)
115 Ventral gun pack (offset to port)

116 Ball and socket fuselage/ wing attachment points
117 Port inner fuel tank location (93·4 Imp. Gal.)
118 Ammunition boxes (200 rpg)
119 Four MG 151 cannon
120 Mainwheel leg retraction yoke
121 Leg pivot member
122 Mainwheel door actuating jack
123 Mainwheel door (rear section)

124 Mainwheel door (front section)
125 Leg support strut
126 Port mainwheel
127 Mainwheel leg

128 Annular exhaust slot
129 Exhaust stubs (internal)
130 BMW 801D engine (partially deleted for clarity)
131 Annular oil tank
132 Cannon muzzles (5 deg. downward angle)
133 Twelve-blade cooling fan
134 Propeller mechanism
135 Three-blade variable-pitch VS 111 propeller
136 FuG 16ZY antenna
137 Starboard mainwheel

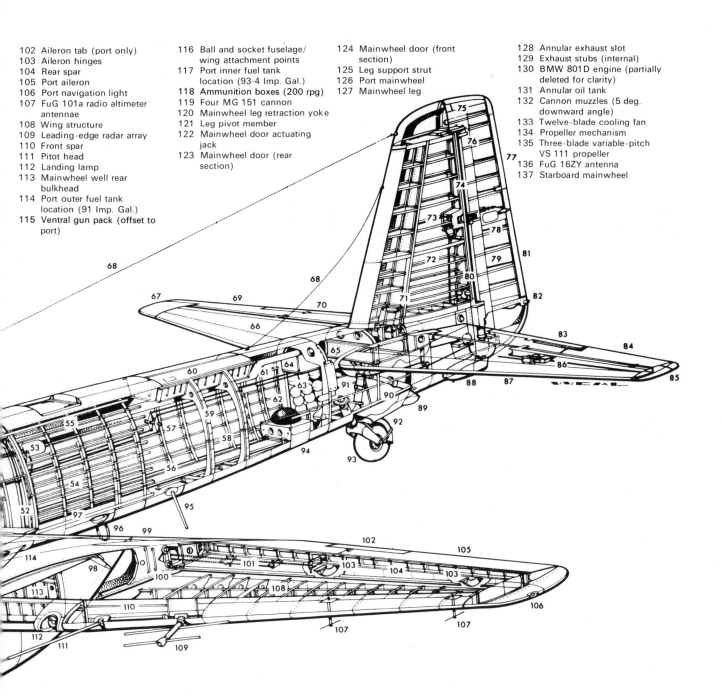

Fighters of Hitler's Aces

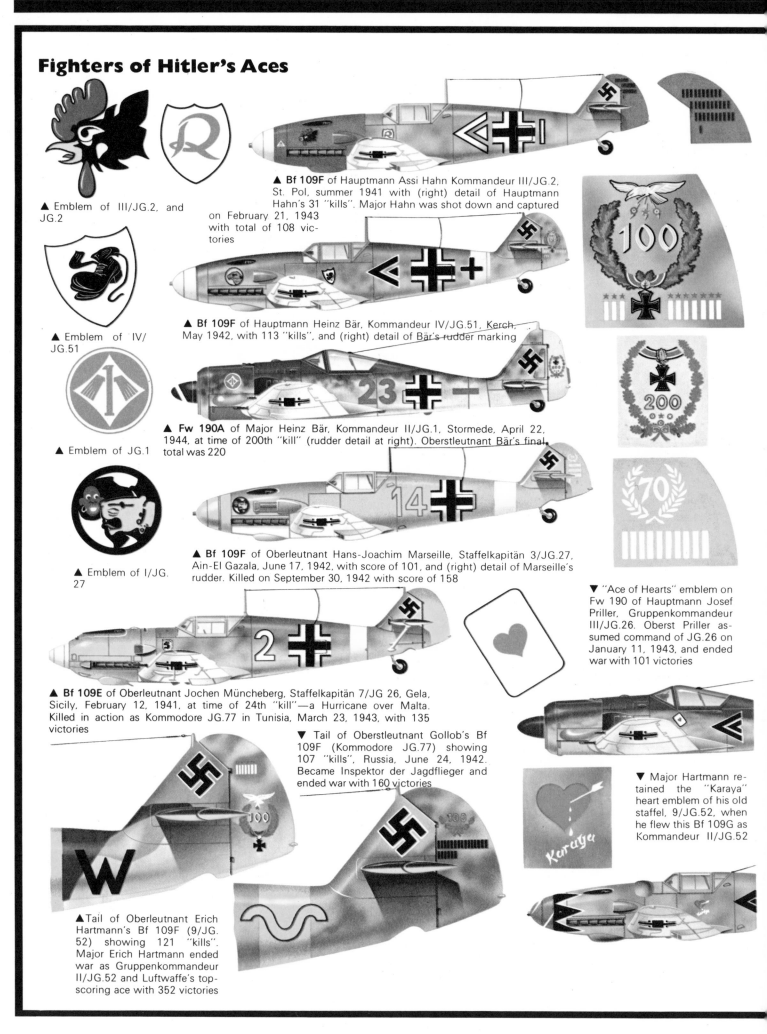

▲ Emblem of III/JG.2, and JG.2

▲ Emblem of IV/JG.51

▲ Emblem of JG.1

▲ Emblem of I/JG.27

▲ Bf 109F of Hauptmann Assi Hahn Kommandeur III/JG.2, St. Pol, summer 1941 with (right) detail of Hauptmann Hahn's 31 "kills". Major Hahn was shot down and captured on February 21, 1943 with total of 108 victories

▲ Bf 109F of Hauptmann Heinz Bär, Kommandeur IV/JG.51, Kerch, May 1942, with 113 "kills", and (right) detail of Bär's rudder marking

▲ Fw 190A of Major Heinz Bär, Kommandeur II/JG.1, Stormede, April 22, 1944, at time of 200th "kill" (rudder detail at right). Oberstleutnant Bär's final total was 220

▲ Bf 109F of Oberleutnant Hans-Joachim Marseille, Staffelkapitän 3/JG.27, Ain-El Gazala, June 17, 1942, with score of 101, and (right) detail of Marseille's rudder. Killed on September 30, 1942 with score of 158

▼ "Ace of Hearts" emblem on Fw 190 of Hauptmann Josef Priller, Gruppenkommandeur III/JG.26. Oberst Priller assumed command of JG.26 on January 11, 1943, and ended war with 101 victories

▲ Bf 109E of Oberleutnant Jochen Müncheberg, Staffelkapitän 7/JG 26, Gela, Sicily, February 12, 1941, at time of 24th "kill"—a Hurricane over Malta. Killed in action as Kommodore JG.77 in Tunisia, March 23, 1943, with 135 victories

▼ Tail of Oberstleutnant Gollob's Bf 109F (Kommodore JG.77) showing 107 "kills", Russia, June 24, 1942. Became Inspektor der Jagdflieger and ended war with 160 victories

▼ Major Hartmann retained the "Karaya" heart emblem of his old staffel, 9/JG.52, when he flew this Bf 109G as Kommandeur II/JG.52

▲Tail of Oberleutnant Erich Hartmann's Bf 109F (9/JG. 52) showing 121 "kills". Major Erich Hartmann ended war as Gruppenkommandeur II/JG.52 and Luftwaffe's top-scoring ace with 352 victories

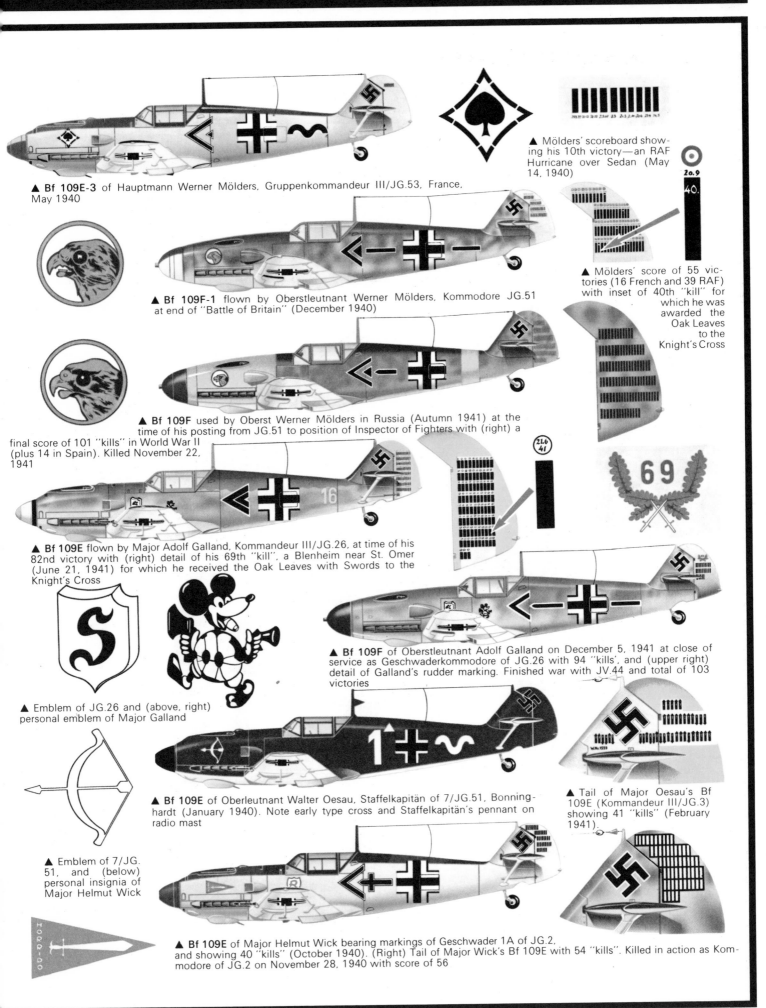

▲ Bf 109E-3 of Hauptmann Werner Mölders, Gruppenkommandeur III/JG.53, France, May 1940

▲ Mölders' scoreboard showing his 10th victory—an RAF Hurricane over Sedan (May 14, 1940)

▲ Mölders' score of 55 victories (16 French and 39 RAF) with inset of 40th "kill" for which he was awarded the Oak Leaves to the Knight's Cross

▲ Bf 109F-1 flown by Oberstleutnant Werner Mölders, Kommodore JG.51 at end of "Battle of Britain" (December 1940)

▲ Bf 109F used by Oberst Werner Mölders in Russia (Autumn 1941) at the time of his posting from JG.51 to position of Inspector of Fighters with (right) a final score of 101 "kills" in World War II (plus 14 in Spain). Killed November 22, 1941

▲ Bf 109E flown by Major Adolf Galland, Kommandeur III/JG.26, at time of his 82nd victory with (right) detail of his 69th "kill", a Blenheim near St. Omer (June 21, 1941) for which he received the Oak Leaves with Swords to the Knight's Cross

▲ Emblem of JG.26 and (above, right) personal emblem of Major Galland

▲ Bf 109F of Oberstleutnant Adolf Galland on December 5, 1941 at close of service as Geschwaderkommodore of JG.26 with 94 "kills", and (upper right) detail of Galland's rudder marking. Finished war with JV.44 and total of 103 victories

▲ Bf 109E of Oberleutnant Walter Oesau, Staffelkapitän of 7/JG.51, Bonninghardt (January 1940). Note early type cross and Staffelkapitän's pennant on radio mast

▲ Tail of Major Oesau's Bf 109E (Kommandeur III/JG.3) showing 41 "kills" (February 1941).

▲ Emblem of 7/JG. 51, and (below) personal insignia of Major Helmut Wick

▲ Bf 109E of Major Helmut Wick bearing markings of Geschwader 1A of JG.2, and showing 40 "kills" (October 1940). (Right) Tail of Major Wick's Bf 109E with 54 "kills". Killed in action as Kommodore of JG.2 on November 28, 1940 with score of 56

Messerschmitt Bf 109G-14/U4

1 Starboard navigation light
2 Starboard wingtip
3 Fixed trim tab
4 Starboard Frise-type aileron
5 Flush-riveted stressed wing-skinning
6 Handley Page leading-edge automatic slot
7 Slot control linkage
8 Slot equalizer rod
9 Aileron control linkage
10 Fabric-covered flap section
11 Wheel fairing
12 Port fuselage machine-gun ammunition-feed fairing
13 Port Rheinmetall Borsig 13-mm MG 131 machine gun
14 Engine accessories
15 Starboard machine-gun trough
16 Daimler Benz DB 605AM twelve-cylinder inverted-vee liquid-cooled engine
17 Detachable cowling panel
18 Oil filler access
19 Oil tank
20 Propeller pitch-change mechanism

21 VDM electrically-operated constant-speed propeller
22 Spinner
23 Engine-mounted cannon muzzle
24 Blast tube
25 Propeller hub
26 Spinner back plate
27 Auxiliary cooling intakes
28 Coolant header tank
29 Anti-vibration rubber engine-mounting pads

39 Oil cooler outlet flap
40 Wing root fillet
41 Wing/fuselage fairing
42 Firewall/bulkhead
43 Supercharger air intake
44 Supercharger assembly
45 20-mm cannon magazine drum
46 13-mm machine-gun ammunition feed
47 Engine bearer upper attachment
48 Ammunition feed fairing
49 13-mm Rheinmetall Borsig MG 131 machine gun breeches

66 90-mm armourglass wind-screen
67 'Galland'-type clear-vision hinged canopy
68 Framed armourglass head/back panel
69 Canopy contoured frame
70 Canopy hinges (starboard)
71 Canopy release catch
72 Pilot's bucket-type seat (8-mm back armour)
73 Underfloor contoured fuel tank (88 Imp. gal./400 litres of 87 octane B4)
74 Fuselage frame
75 Circular access panel
76 Tail trimming cable conduit
77 Wireless leads
78 MW 50 (methanol water) tank (25 Imp. gal/114 litres capacity)
79 Handhold
80 Fuselage decking
81 Aerial mast

30 Elektron forged engine bearer
31 Engine bearer support strut attachment
32 Plug leads
33 Exhaust manifold fairing strip
34 Ejector exhausts
35 Cowling fasteners
36 Oil cooler
37 Oil cooler intake
38 Starboard mainwheel

50 Instrument panel
51 20-mm Mauser MG 151/20 cannon breech
52 Heelrests
53 Rudder pedals
54 Undercarriage emergency retraction cables
55 Fuselage frame
56 Wing/fuselage fairing
57 Undercarriage emergency retraction handwheel (outboard)
58 Tail trim handwheel (inboard)
59 Seat harness
60 Throttle lever
61 Control column
62 Cockpit ventilation inlet
63 Revi 16B reflector gunsight (folding)
64 Armoured windshield frame
65 Anti-glare gunsight screen

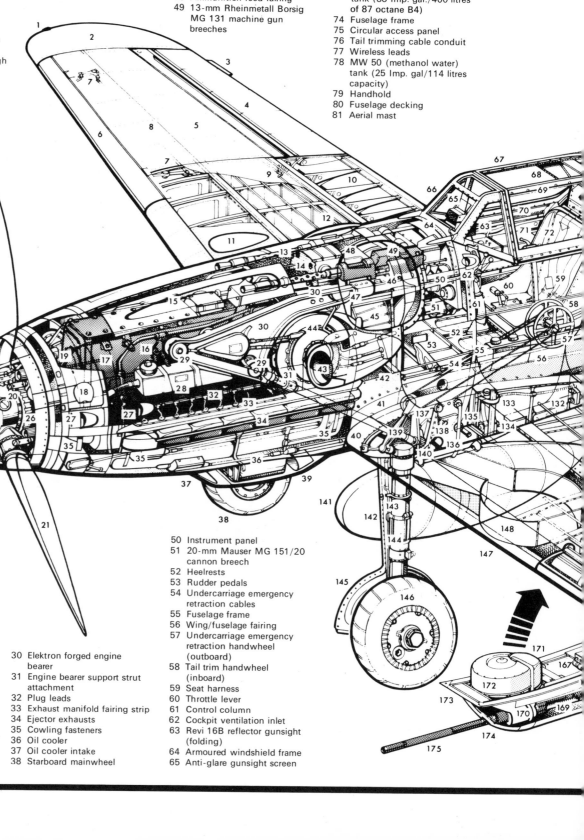

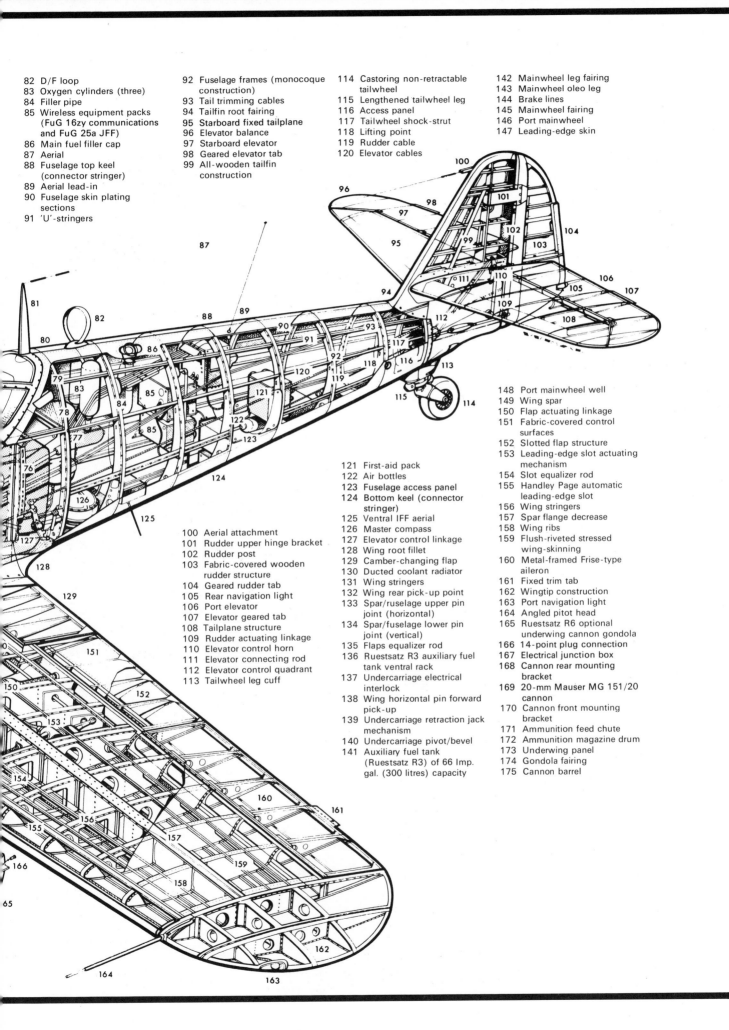

82 D/F loop
83 Oxygen cylinders (three)
84 Filler pipe
85 Wireless equipment packs (FuG 16zy communications and FuG 25a JFF)
86 Main fuel filler cap
87 Aerial
88 Fuselage top keel (connector stringer)
89 Aerial lead-in
90 Fuselage skin plating sections
91 'U'-stringers

92 Fuselage frames (monocoque construction)
93 Tail trimming cables
94 Tailfin root fairing
95 Starboard fixed tailplane
96 Elevator balance
97 Starboard elevator
98 Geared elevator tab
99 All-wooden tailfin construction

114 Castoring non-retractable tailwheel
115 Lengthened tailwheel leg
116 Access panel
117 Tailwheel shock-strut
118 Lifting point
119 Rudder cable
120 Elevator cables

142 Mainwheel leg fairing
143 Mainwheel oleo leg
144 Brake lines
145 Mainwheel fairing
146 Port mainwheel
147 Leading-edge skin

100 Aerial attachment
101 Rudder upper hinge bracket
102 Rudder post
103 Fabric-covered wooden rudder structure
104 Geared rudder tab
105 Rear navigation light
106 Port elevator
107 Elevator geared tab
108 Tailplane structure
109 Rudder actuating linkage
110 Elevator control horn
111 Elevator connecting rod
112 Elevator control quadrant
113 Tailwheel leg cuff

121 First-aid pack
122 Air bottles
123 Fuselage access panel
124 Bottom keel (connector stringer)
125 Ventral IFF aerial
126 Master compass
127 Elevator control linkage
128 Wing root fillet
129 Camber-changing flap
130 Ducted coolant radiator
131 Wing stringers
132 Wing rear pick-up point
133 Spar/ruselage upper pin joint (horizontal)
134 Spar/fuselage lower pin joint (vertical)
135 Flaps equalizer rod
136 Ruestsatz R3 auxiliary fuel tank ventral rack
137 Undercarriage electrical interlock
138 Wing horizontal pin forward pick-up
139 Undercarriage retraction jack mechanism
140 Undercarriage pivot/bevel
141 Auxiliary fuel tank (Ruestsatz R3) of 66 Imp. gal. (300 litres) capacity

148 Port mainwheel well
149 Wing spar
150 Flap actuating linkage
151 Fabric-covered control surfaces
152 Slotted flap structure
153 Leading-edge slot actuating mechanism
154 Slot equalizer rod
155 Handley Page automatic leading-edge slot
156 Wing stringers
157 Spar flange decrease
158 Wing ribs
159 Flush-riveted stressed wing-skinning
160 Metal-framed Frise-type aileron
161 Fixed trim tab
162 Wingtip construction
163 Port navigation light
164 Angled pitot head
165 Ruestsatz R6 optional underwing cannon gondola
166 14-point plug connection
167 Electrical junction box
168 Cannon rear mounting bracket
169 20-mm Mauser MG 151/20 cannon
170 Cannon front mounting bracket
171 Ammunition feed chute
172 Ammunition magazine drum
173 Underwing panel
174 Gondola fairing
175 Cannon barrel

that Milch saw as 'a matter of life and death'.
It was 'as though war had not broken out'.
When he took over from Udet, however, the
situation improved; better organisation, new
techniques, higher priorities, energetic leadership and sheer necessity ensured that in
20 months from November 1941 aircraft
production increased by 270 percent from
12,401 planes to 15,409 in 1942, 24,807 in
1943 and 40,593 in 1944. By this date it was
not the loss of aircraft that was proving
dangerous, but the loss of aircrew—some
20 percent per month (a total of 29,830
killed, wounded, and missing out of 96,917
for the whole war in that year alone). The
lack of well-trained pilots goes a long way to
explain the *Luftwaffe*'s weakness in the sky
in the last year.

But even more important was the *Luftwaffe*'s failure to deal with the Allied strategic
air offensive. 'It is from this that all else
comes', Milch believed. Not only did it
cause a drain on pilots but it also robbed the
Luftwaffe of the very wherewithal by which
it operated—fuel. It had been possible to
cope with the crisis caused by the onslaught
upon the aircraft industry in February 1944;

Defence of the Reich

production of the desired 2000 single seater
fighters was reached by June. But not so with
the onslaught which caused the *Luftwaffe* by
September to be receiving only 1/5 of its
minimum fuel requirements. However many
planes might be available, they were now
largely useless. The *Luftwaffe* was defeated
by the strategic bombing against which it
had evolved no fully effective defence.

The inadequacy of the *Luftwaffe* to meet
this threat was exemplified by a conversation
in March 1942. To Milch's demand for 3600
fighters, at least, per month, Jeschonnek
replied, 'I do not know what I should do
with more than 360'. While production did
in fact rise from 700 in February 1943 to a
climax of 3375 in September 1944, the
tactical operations of the *Luftwaffe* swallowed
them up—the vital defence of the *Reich* was
left ill-equipped until the end. The numbers of day-fighters rose from 120 in March
1943 to 473 in February 1944, declining to
281 in May—these few against the overwhelming odds of the Allies.

Defeat in defence of the *Reich* was, however, no foregone conclusion. The night-
fighter arm, which reached a strength of some
700 planes, inflicted such losses upon the
RAF (12 percent in the Nuremberg raid of
March 1944) that the night-offensive was
suspended. But this victory had come too
late. In the failure to stop the far more important USAAF daylight raids lay the key to
the whole situation. When they had operated
without fighter protection, the American
bombers experienced crippling losses—as
high as 26 percent on October 14, 1943,
raid upon Schweinfurt. At this point the
Luftwaffe was victorious. Victory was not to
last, for the Mustang fighter gave to the
USAAF the escort which permitted it to
carry on. Heavily outnumbered, the *Luftwaffe* pilots put up a brave show; the events
of early 1944 indicated that, had they had

Above: The *Luftwaffe* had a very
important role to play in the supply
of ground troops from the air but it
was never strong enough to do so
effectively. In North Africa, when the
situation became critical and
Rommel was in danger of being cut
off, his supply line came to depend
considerably on the Ju52.

Right: Luftwaffe searchlights of a
Flak battalion in a *Wehrmacht*
parade through Berlin, in 1939. In the
early phases of the war, the mobility
of these searchlights was of prime
importance for the fundamental
reason that their numbers were
relatively small.

Left: The 88mm Flak during a night
air-raid around the city of Hamburg.
These guns were organised into
large batteries which 'boxed' certain
areas of the sky with rapid and
intense fire. Despite them, Allied
air-raids on Germany became
increasingly effective during the
course of the war.

Right: The Battle of Britain – the
disposition of the opposing air
forces. The principle targets of the
Luftwaffe are shown clearly here.
They changed from the RAF airfields
in the first half of the battle to the
major cities and towns in the
second. It was this switch that
ruined the *Luftwaffe*'s chances.

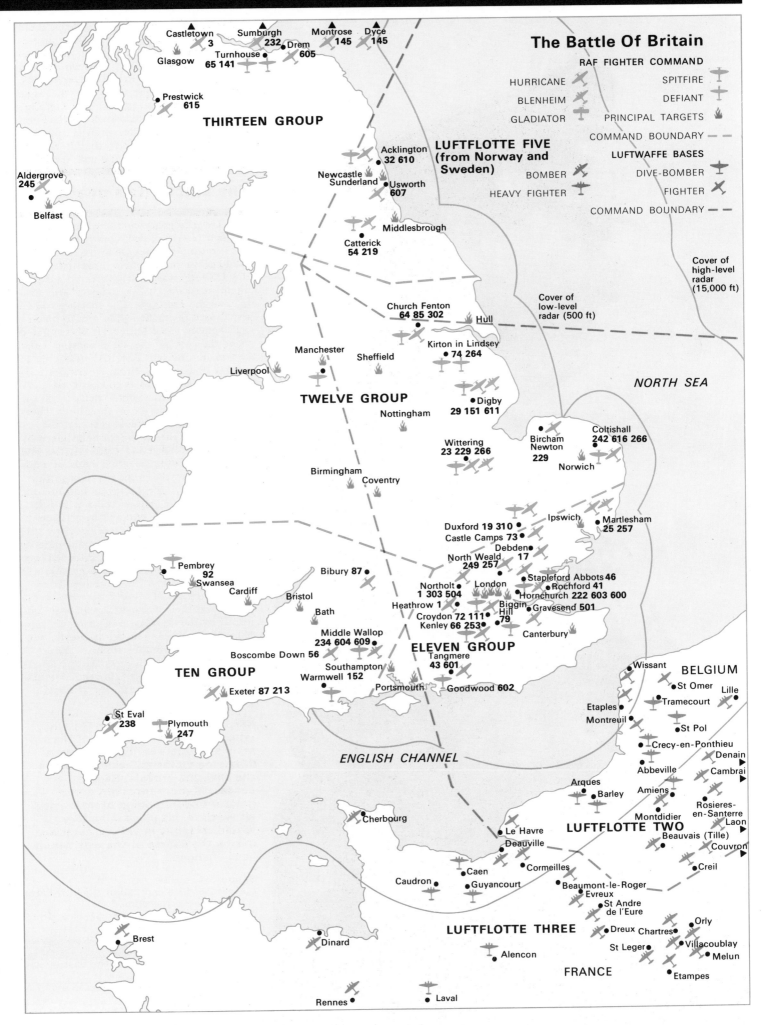

The Battle Of Britain

RAF FIGHTER COMMAND

HURRICANE   SPITFIRE

BLENHEIM   DEFIANT

GLADIATOR   PRINCIPAL TARGETS

COMMAND BOUNDARY – –

LUFTWAFFE BASES

BOMBER   DIVE-BOMBER

HEAVY FIGHTER   FIGHTER

COMMAND BOUNDARY – –

Castletown **3**

Sumburgh **232**

Montrose **145**

Dyce **145**

Drem **605**

Turnhouse

Glasgow **65 141**

Prestwick **615**

THIRTEEN GROUP

Aldergrove **245**

Belfast

Acklington **32 610**

Newcastle
Sunderland

Usworth **607**

**LUFTFLOTTE FIVE
(from Norway and
Sweden)**

Middlesbrough

Catterick **54 219**

Cover of
high-level
radar
(15,000 ft)

Church Fenton **64 85 302**

Hull

Cover of
low-level
radar (500 ft)

Manchester

Sheffield

Kirton in Lindsey **74 264**

Liverpool

TWELVE GROUP

Digby **29 151 611**

Nottingham

NORTH SEA

Wittering **23 229 266**

Bircham
Newton **229**

Coltishall **242 616 266**

Norwich

Birmingham

Coventry

Ipswich

Martlesham **25 257**

Duxford **19 310**

Castle Camps **73**

Debden **17**

North Weald **249 257**

Pembrey **92**

Swansea

Cardiff

Bibury **87**

Bristol

Bath

Northolt **1 303 504**

London

Stapleford Abbots **46**

Rochford **41**

Hornchurch **222 603 600**

Heathrow **1**

Biggin
Hill **79**

Gravesend **501**

Croydon **72 111**

Kenley **66 253**

Canterbury

Middle Wallop **234 604 609**

ELEVEN GROUP

Boscombe Down **56**

Tangmere **43 601**

Southampton

Warmwell **152**

Portsmouth

Goodwood **602**

TEN GROUP

Exeter **87 213**

St Eval **238**

Plymouth **247**

ENGLISH CHANNEL

Wissant

BELGIUM

St Omer

Lille

Etaples

Tramecourt

Montreuil

St Pol

Crecy-en-Ponthieu

Denain

Abbeville

Cambrai

Arques

Barley

Amiens

Rosieres-
en-Santerre

Montdidier

Laon

Cherbourg

Le Havre

Deauville

Beauvais (Tille)

Couvron

Caen

Cormeilles

Creil

Caudron

Guyancourt

Beaumont-le-Roger

Evreux

St Andre
de l'Eure

LUFTFLOTTE TWO

Brest

Dinard

Dreux

Chartres

Orly

Villacoublay

St Leger

Melun

Alencon

LUFTFLOTTE THREE

FRANCE

Rennes

Laval

Etampes

155

the necessary numbers of planes, defeat could have been avoided. Despite fighter protection the bombers continued to suffer not insubstantial losses. But German fighters took a heavy toll. The Berlin raid on March 6 saw 80 fighters shot down for the same number of American planes. The *Luftwaffe* simply could not sustain such losses. From this point on the Allies enjoyed complete air-mastery over the *Reich*; the US fighters left their protective rôle and took the offen-

The Luftwaffe's death

sive. Defence policy continued to be inadequate; a reserve of 800 fighters was thrown away in the Ardennes Offensive rather than used against the bombers. From May 1944 the USAAF was entirely free to turn its attention on the vital oil industry—the final blow to the *Luftwaffe*. The shortage of fuel also caused the night-fighter arm to become considerably less effective. (It also suffered from the loss of the early-warning radar system in France.) The RAF was able to resume its bombing. From November 1944 on, the *Luftwaffe* was as good as dead.

The saga of the fighter defence of the *Reich* is a sad one. From the outset it was plagued by the indifference of the *Luftwaffe*'s leaders, who ignored the warnings given by Milch, Kammhuber and others. By the time of the devastating bombing raids of mid-1943, which served as the red-light to Goering and others, the *Luftwaffe* had lost the initiative. The fight was still not hopeless, however, as Milch outlined in a report to Goering in June 1943: 'To achieve any success . . . the fighter forces must out-number the enemy by four to one . . . Provided they receive new reinforcements, the prospects of the day-fighter can be viewed with complete assurance.' They did not receive the planes and their defeat in the air was confirmed by the destruction of their fuel supplies. Hitler simply refused to transfer adequate numbers from the fronts to the *Reich* or to acknowledge, until too late, the defensive rôle of the *Luftwaffe*. Thus the continuation of its prime, tactical, task ensured the *Luftwaffe*'s death.

Reichsmarschall **Hermann Goering, whose *Luftwaffe* was one of the main architects behind so many *Blitzkrieg* victories, acknowledging the cheering crowds. Had he possessed more foresight and a greater understanding of strategic air warfare, his place in history would certainly now be greater and maybe the course of the war would have changed.**

Suggested reading
David Irving: **Rise and Fall of the Luftwaffe** (Weidenfeld & Nicholson, 1973)
William Green: **Warplanes of the Third Reich** (Macdonald, 1970)
Caius Bekker: **The Luftwaffe War Diaries** (Macdonald, 1966)
Adolf Galland: **The First and the Last** (Methuen, 1955)
Alfred Price: **Instruments of Darkness** (Ian Allen, 1968)
J. Killen: **The Luftwaffe** (Muller, 1967)

Die Kriegs—marine—
the neglected service

The *Tirpitz* fires her guns in anger.

Dr Paul Kennedy

The German navy was by far the weakest of the three armed services throughout World War II. It consistently had to face heavy enemy odds, an experience which was, for a long time, unknown to the army and the *Luftwaffe*. In addition, Germany's geographical position made it difficult for her to seek to gain command of the sea from the homeland itself. Yet, although the Navy's chances of success against superior Allied seapower were never great, the service was much more daring and aggressive than it had been in the 1914-18 war and many individual successes were achieved. The *Graf Spee* terrorised Allied shipping lanes before it was caught at the River Plate; the *Bismarck* achieved an epic first cruise; the 'Channel Dash' saw German capital ships impudently sailing through waters which had been regarded as British since the seventeenth century.

However, for many reasons, the German surface fleet swiftly gave way in importance to the U-boats. In 1942 and 1943 the long, hard struggle known as the 'Battle of the Atlantic' reached its climax but even the U-boats could not keep up with improved Allied counter measures. 'Too little, too late' might have been the Navy's epitaph as well as the *Luftwaffe*'s.

Above: The *Kriegsmarine* had the means to defeat Britain by submarine warfare.
Below: A German sailor dressed in 'blues' with boatswain's pipe.

Left: Admiral Doenitz succeeded Raeder as Navy chief. It was Doenitz who understood the importance of submarines.

Right: German capital ships at sea during fleet manoeuvres, 1938. From the deck of the *Graf Spee* can be seen the *Admiral Scheer* followed by the *Gneisenau*.

Die Kriegs-marine—
the neglected service

Die Kriegsmarine

The Navy – what need have we of that? I cannot conceive of a European war which will hang in the balance because of a few ships.

Adolf Hitler 1936

With enough U-boats we can and will finish off the British Isles. What the army and the air-force has failed to do is possible for us, for we can strangle them, starve them into submission, just as their blockade did to us in 1918. But we must have more submarines and better submarines. They can be given to us, but will they be?

attr. Karl Doenitz 1941

On November 21, 1918, one of the most important and unprecedented events in the history of sea power took place when the German High Seas Fleet steamed into the Firth of Forth and voluntarily surrendered to the Royal Navy. Restricted throughout World War I to the North Sea and Baltic by Germany's unfavourable geographical position, unable to match the superior strength of the British fleet, hampered by a divided command structure and internal dissensions, and always overshadowed by the army, the German surface navy had never been able to carry out the rôle envisaged for it by its creator, Admiral von Tirpitz. Now, to fulfil one of the demands of the armistice settlement, it was being forced to give itself up without a fight to its old enemy. Although Germany had built up its fleet to be the second largest in the world, it appeared that it was abandoning any further claim to be a sea power.

Exactly seven months later, however, on June 21, 1919, that same High Seas Fleet scuttled itself without the permission of its British captors in the anchorage of Scapa Flow. By this action Admiral von Reuter and his crews had not only prevented the victorious Allies from laying hands upon first-class German warships, but they had also redeemed the honour of the navy and provided a symbol of resistance for the rest of the service. Out of the watery consummation at Scapa Flow there would arise, Phoenix-like, a restored German fleet at

Pocket battleships

some future date. Certainly, none of the naval leaders in the post-1919 years, Trotha, Behncke, Zenker and the rest, ever believed that the humiliating surrender meant anything other than a temporary defeat or that the navy's size would always remain the 'treaty fleet' of eight old, pre-Dreadnought battleships and some smaller vessels. As early as 1921 the first tentative steps were taken to revive operational planning; as one officer put it, even if they had no fighting navy, 'at least we must prepare ourselves *theoretically* for war'. Like the rest of the German nation during the 1920s and early 1930s, the navy's attitude was essentially a revanchist and expansionist one, hidden only by a thin crust of deference to the Versailles settlement and to Weimar democracy. Only in the decision of 1928 to begin building the

Deutschland-class of so-called 'pocket-battle-ships' (*Panzerschiffe*) was there any sign given to the outside world of this feeling in the navy: for such vessels, with their high speed and long cruising range, were clearly designed for commerce-raiding on the high seas and not for the restricted waters of the Baltic. It symbolised the ambitious ideas of such naval writers as Vice-Admiral Wolfgang Wegener, who argued that only by breaking out to the Atlantic trade-routes through the occupation of Scandinavia and Iceland could Germany overcome her unfavourable geographical position and thus defeat Great Britain in a future war. Nevertheless, the German navy was still very small when Adolf Hitler came to power in 1933.

In the years following 1928 the service was commanded by Admiral Erich Raeder,

An alliance with London

who had made his name as Hipper's Chief of Staff in the battle-cruiser actions of World War I and who had also written the German official naval history of the overseas surface raiders. A cautious, stable and systematic officer, Raeder was not the sort of person to take dramatic decisions or to urge the swift build-up of the fleet in order to fight Britain and France; Wegener's ideas were acknowledged by the Commander-in-Chief but the latter preferred to concentrate his energies upon the slow but steady warship construction programme and upon improving the organisation of the navy. Besides, no great change could take place in German naval policy without the backing of the *Fuehrer*.

Hitler's attitude towards the navy depended largely upon his attitude towards Britain. At the back of his mind, he had always planned that Germany should become a great *world* power in the future; but he also firmly believed that it would be possible to achieve an alliance with London during the early stages of Germany's recovery, provided that he gave assurances that Berlin would not re-assume the pre-

Right: The *Reich*'s ships were kept active till the very end of the war against Russia. Here, the cruiser *Prinz Eugen* is in action at the Battle of Gdynia in the Baltic. This took place early in 1945 when submarine warfare had already become the dominant weapon.

Above: Nowhere was the expansion of Germany's war economy more dramatically illustrated than in the launching of a great ship. Here, the *Prinz Eugen,* 1938.

Left: Hitler leaving the yacht *Aviso Grille* after having made an inspection of his fleet at Kiel in 1938.

1914 policy of naval and colonial expansion. After 1935 or so, however, Hitler's doubts about the likelihood and desirability of an English alliance increased in reaction to what he considered to be the obstructionism of the British government. This latter development now forced him to compress his step-by-step programme of expansion and to contemplate a war with the sea-powers by the mid-1940s. Thus the Czech crisis of 1938 gave the impetus to his decision to permit the navy's famous 'Plan Z'—the construction of an enormous surface fleet for trans-Atlantic warfare—even though the greater part of Germany's rearmament measures still had to be devoted to the army and the *Luftwaffe* in order to implement his more immediate aims on land. No-one could doubt that, with a future fleet of 13 battleships, four aircraft-carriers, 33 cruisers and 250 U-boats, all of modern design, Germany would be in a position by 1944 to challenge

British superiority

Britain, and possibly the United States, for mastery of the high seas.

As it happened, however, war between Germany and the western Allies came five years too early even for Hitler's compressed programme, since the *Fuehrer* had never believed that Britain and France would go to war over Poland in 1939 and was amazed when they did so. As events were soon to show, Germany was strong enough on land and in the air to gain easy victories in the first nine months of the war—but the conflict had broken out far too soon for Raeder, just as it had done for Tirpitz in 1914. In addition, Germany laboured under the same crucial geographical disadvantage as it had done in the previous war: its overseas shipping, and the ability of its fleet to reach the Atlantic, were both at the mercy of Britain, which lay athwart the two exits from the North Sea. So long as this strategical inferiority remained, Germany's naval effort was bound to suffer; only by turning Britain's flank, or by achieving numerical superiority, could the disadvantage be overcome.

The second of the alternatives, numerical

Above: The battleship *Tirpitz* on one of her rare sorties in Norwegian waters, accompanied by her escort ships. The greatest danger faced by these expeditions of Germany's capital ships was that of air observation by the RAF.

Right: The *Scharnhorst* docked at Kiel before the war. It is Sunday and a service is held astern.

Far right: Captain's inspection on board a destroyer in 1942.

superiority, was quite out of the question in 1939. At the outbreak of war the German fleet consisted of the battlecruisers *Scharnhorst* and *Gneisenau*, fine, fast vessels, each with nine 11-inch guns, but probably still too weak to engage in a toe-to-toe fight with 15-inch gunned British capital ships; the 'pocket-battleships' *Deutschland*, *Lützow* and *Graf Spee*, brilliantly-designed long-range raiders but once again no match for a battleship; the heavy cruisers *Admiral Hipper* and *Blücher*; six light cruisers; 34 destroyers and torpedo-boats; and 57 submarines. Against this the

Overwhelming odds

British could deploy 15 battleships and battlecruisers, six aircraft-carriers, 59 cruisers, hundreds of escort vessels and 38 submarines, while the French navy consisted of seven battleships and battlecruisers, two aircraft-carriers, 19 cruisers and a large number of destroyers and submarines. Admittedly, many of the British vessels were old and slow, and the Allies had to station squadrons in various parts of the globe for the defence of their extra-European trade and other interests. Yet the odds were overwhelmingly tilted against the German navy,

Above: German warships leaving their base in a Norwegian fiord during the early war years. Photographed from the deck of the *Tirpitz,* this picture shows the *Admiral Hipper,* followed by the *Admiral Scheer* and destroyers.

Left: The *Gneisenau* together with an attending cruiser in action against *HMS Glorious* in June 1940.

and Raeder recognised on the first day of the war that it would now be futile to pursue the 'Plan-Z' building programme. Apart from the two *Bismarck*-class battleships and the heavy cruiser *Prinz Eugen*, work on all other large vessels, including the aircraft-carrier *Graf Zeppelin*, was suspended.

Because the German surface navy was in no position to challenge its enemies for command of the sea, the early part of the war was—like the land campaign—a 'Phoney War', broken only by the occasional sortie of a German raider. The *Deutschland* cruised without much success in North Atlantic waters in the first two months of the war, and the *Scharnhorst* and *Gneisenau* overwhelmed the British auxiliary cruiser *Rawalpindi* in late November but failed to destroy the convoy it was escorting.

Only with the cruise of the pocket-battleship *Graf Spee*, commanded by Captain Hans Langsdorff, was Raeder's strategy of disrupting Allied naval communications and tying down far larger enemy forces put to real effect. Langsdorff was able to steam around the Indian and South Atlantic oceans unhampered for the first three months of the

Left: German sailors marching through an Italian port, illustrating the close cooperation between the *Kriegsmarine* and the Italian navy in the Mediterranean.

Right: Raiders in the English Channel. This photograph, which was taken from the *Prinz Eugen*, shows the *Gneisenau* and, in the distance, the *Scharnhorst* during their dash down the Channel in February, 1942.

Below: The end of the *Graf Spee*, scuttled in 1939 in the neutral waters of the Plate estuary off Montevideo for fear that she might fall into British hands. The first disaster for the *Kriegsmarine*.

war, but in December 1939 he was brought to action by the British cruisers *Exeter*, *Ajax* and *Achilles* in the famous 'Battle of the River Plate'. Although the superior 11-inch shells of the *Graf Spee* damaged the *Exeter* so severely that the latter had to retire from the battle, the German vessel was also hit repeatedly, causing Langsdorff to enter the neutral port of Montevideo to secure repairs. Four days later, fearing that his ship would be overwhelmed by fresh British forces, he

Few powerful raiders

had her scuttled in the Plate estuary. By this action, he had not only relieved the Royal Navy of an immediate threat to Allied shipping routes but he had also obscured the important diversionary effects of the commerce-raiding strategy. For example, in October 1939 the British Admiralty had had to direct nine battleships and battlecruisers, five aircraft-carriers and many smaller warships to the protection of trade against the depredations of the *Graf Spee* and *Deutschland*. Yet, because Germany possessed so few powerful raiders, and because Hitler feared the loss of further 'big ships', this strategy was never fully exploited.

In the spring and early summer of 1940, however, the strategical handicap under which Germany was operating was removed by the lightning attacks upon Denmark, Norway, the Netherlands, Belgium and France. Within two months of the beginning of these thrusts to the north and to the west, the Germans had broken free from Britain's grip upon the North Sea and had achieved Admiral Wegener's old dream—access to the Atlantic. From the deep fiords of Norway, from the well-developed ports of Britanny, German warships could now steam directly out to the high seas. Moreover, in knocking France out of the war the *Wehrmacht* had effected an enormous shift in the naval balance of power; indeed, the British were so alarmed that the French navy would become, not neutral, but actually hostile, that they ruthlessly sought to eliminate it by their attacks upon it in Oran and Dakar in July 1940. To crown it all, Mussolini, with the jackal's sense of timing, now entered the war, thereby forcing the British Admiralty to divert more warships to the Mediterranean theatre.

Yet, despite the defection of France and the entry of Italy, the surface units of the

Sunk by her own escorts

German navy were still inferior to the forces which the Royal Navy retained in North Atlantic waters. Furthermore, the occupation of Norway had not been achieved without heavy losses to Raeder's miniscule fleet. The heavy cruiser *Blücher* had been sunk by Norwegian defence forces off Oslo; the light cruiser *Karlsruhe* was damaged by a British submarine and eventually had to be sunk by her own escorts; her sister-ship, the *Königsberg*, achieved distinction by being the first major warship to be sunk by enemy aircraft; ten destroyers were wiped out in the Narvik

fiord battles; and many other warships, including the *Scharnhorst*, *Gneisenau*, *Lützow* (formerly the *Deutschland*) and *Hipper* were damaged. By the summer of 1940, when Hitler and his advisors were discussing the prospects for an invasion of England, there was virtually no German surface navy at all. But thanks to the failure of the *Luftwaffe* to achieve aerial superiority over the RAF, this embarrassing fact was of little relevance.

All this meant that, although Germany was now placed in a strategical position more favourable for naval warfare than at any other time in her history, she simply lacked the strength to fight her enemy in a full fleet battle. Thus the history of the surface war was to remain one of occasional sorties by major warships, which disturbed the Allied trade routes and caused alarm in London but nevertheless did not represent a persistent and determined challenge to the Royal Navy's predominance. Looking at the broader strategical pattern of the war, one might conclude that the most important rôle of the German fleet had been to pin down in home waters so many major warships of the Royal Navy which were desperately needed elsewhere, in the Mediterranean and especially in the Far East. This does not mean, however, that the various cruises of German vessels lacked interest and excitement, or that they could be regarded by the British as mere 'pin-pricks'. The story of the *Bismarck* in particular was to show how dangerous a

The secret raiders

sortie by Raeder's ships could be.

Along with the German strategy to interrupt Allied trade through the cruises of their large, conventional warships went plans to use their 'secret raiders' for the same purpose. These vessels were designed so as to look like normal merchantmen, but they concealed behind their innocent exterior a set of guns, torpedo-tubes and other offensive equipment. Their task was not to engage Allied warships—they were not powerful enough for that—but to attack individual merchantmen on the high seas, thereby spreading alarm and upsetting Allied commerce. Well before the outbreak of war the German Naval Staff had made preparations for these raiders—and the larger warships— to be refuelled and rearmed by supply ships at a series of secret oceanic meeting-places, and by early 1940 the first of the disguised vessels had broken out. Most of them headed for the South Atlantic and Indian oceans, where they could prey upon shipping with less risk of being engaged by hostile warships. Individual vessels, such as the *Atlantis* and the *Pinguin*, achieved great successes in capturing or sinking enemy merchantmen; the *Thor* actually sank one and disabled two other British auxiliary cruisers; and the *Kormoran* sank the Australian cruiser *Sydney* although its own crew was also forced to abandon ship. In fact, these raiders sank a total of 133 ships of 829,644 tons, almost twice the tonnage sunk by the conventional warship raiders.

Nevertheless, their strategical importance was not all that great, if only because they preyed upon individual ships and not convoys, and because they represented no threat to Britain's command of the sea. Moreover, they enjoyed their greatest spell of success in the period 1940–1941, when the Royal Navy was hardest pressed. With the growth of Allied air and sea power, and with fewer secret raiders sent out from Germany, this campaign began to peter out. Several of them managed to return home, but the rest were sought out and overwhelmed one by one: the *Atlantis* by the cruiser *Devonshire*, the *Python* by the cruiser *Dorsetshire*, the *Kormoran* by the cruiser *Sydney*, the *Pinguin* by the cruiser *Cornwall*, the *Komet* by British destroyers. With the improvement in aerial reconnaissance and ship identification procedures, and with the tightening of the British blockade in European waters, the end of this type of commerce-raiding was in sight. By late 1943 only the raider *Michel* was at sea, and she was sunk soon after by an

Battle of the Atlantic

American submarine in the Pacific.

The first of the voyages after the fall of France undertaken by a major warship was that of the *Admiral Scheer*, which broke through the Denmark Strait into the North Atlantic in November 1940 and overwhelmed five merchantmen of a British convoy and its escorting auxiliary cruiser *Jervis Bay*. The German warship then proceeded to undertake the longest and most successful cruise of all, returning home only in late March 1941. The superb cruising qualities of these diesel-engined pocket battleships were merely emphasised once again by the two less noteworthy sorties of the turbine-driven heavy cruiser *Hipper* at the same time.

Meanwhile, in January 1941 the *Scharnhorst* and *Gneisenau* had been sent into the Atlantic, the first German capital ships to do so in wartime. In terms of sinkings, their achievement was not great, if only because they had the habit of encountering convoys which were being escorted by 15-inch gunned British battleships. Nevertheless, they disrupted the crucial Atlantic convoy system, took enemy attention from the *Scheer* and *Hipper*, and heightened the feeling on both sides that the surface 'Battle of the Atlantic' was reaching its peak. For, waiting in the wings was the new battleship *Bismarck*, boasting a massive armoured protection, long range and high speed, a displacement of 53,000 tons, and eight 15-inch guns. If this mammoth warship, more formidable than any single British capital ship, was to be joined by the *Scharnhorst*, *Gneisenau*, *Scheer*, *Hipper* and the new heavy cruiser *Prinz Eugen*, the British would be hard pressed to maintain their command of the sea; or, at least, they could only do so by abandoning the Mediterranean to their foes, which

Grand Admiral Doenitz, Commander of the submarine arm, planning the dispositions and attacks of his wolf packs. He was later to become Commander-in-Chief of the Navy and, upon the death of Hitler, titular head of the German *Reich*.

would accomplish another of Hitler and Raeder's aims.

Yet such a combination could not be assembled. The *Scharnhorst* and *Gneisenau* needed repairs in Brest, the *Scheer* and *Hipper* were undergoing refits; and the pressure was upon the navy to take decisive action. On May 21, 1941, therefore, the *Bismarck* and *Prinz Eugen*, under the overall command of Admiral Guenther Luetjens, refuelled in a Bergen fiord before setting off into the Atlantic via the Denmark Strait. Despite the stormy and foggy weather, they were picked up by radar-equipped British cruisers, which alerted the Home Fleet and led its nearest heavy force, the old battle-cruiser *Hood* and brand-new battleship *Prince of Wales*, towards the German raiders. The encounter which followed is one of the most famous in the annals of naval history. Casting aside the advantage of his superior fire-power, the British Admiral Holland approached the German squadron obliquely, firing with only the front turrets and exposing his ships to the careful, steady salvoes of the well-trained German gunners. Within five minutes of the opening of the battle, the *Hood* blew up, the victim of enemy shells plunging vertically through her weakly-armoured deck. No more serious blow was made by German warships to the Royal Navy during the whole of World War II than this swift sinking of 'the mighty *Hood*'.

At this point Luetjens made what in retrospect was clearly his greatest mistake: instead of returning to Norwegian waters, and perhaps even polishing off the damaged

The epic Bismarck chase

and retreating *Prince of Wales* on the way, he elected to carry on with his original plan to disrupt the Atlantic convoys. Had he retraced his route, he might have been able to take out again as well the *Bismarck*'s new sister-ship, the *Tirpitz*, within a few months. Instead, he plunged ahead, despite the fact that he was still being shadowed by British cruisers, that other heavy units of the Royal Navy would be directed towards him, and that two shells from the *Prince of Wales* had damaged the *Bismarck*, affecting its speed and fuel reserves. On the next day, Luetjens released the *Prinz Eugen* for independent raiding and turned the *Bismarck* towards the French port of St Nazaire, the only one outside Germany in which he could obtain repairs. This decision brought him even closer into the Royal Navy's net, as the shadowing by cruisers and attack by ancient Swordfish torpedo planes from the carrier *Victorious* indicated.

Then followed a series of mistakes on both sides which served only to increase the tension and to make the story of the *Bismarck* 'chase' such an epic. On the night of May 24/25, the German ship escaped the radar net of the shadowing British cruiser; yet, unaware of this, Luetjens sent a long radio message to Raeder on the following day, which gave away his position once again. Even so, faulty calculations by the British Admiralty sent all the Royal Navy's warships rushing northwards towards the

Above: The *Prinz Eugen* being steered by manpower, by means of two rudders from destroyers, after being crippled aft by a torpedo from planes of the RAF Coastal Command.

Above right: The *Bismarck* in action against *HMS Hood,* May, 1941. Photograph taken from the *Prinz Eugen.*

Right: Training on a light flak gun on board the *Prinz Eugen,* while she is harboured at Brest.

Above: The numbers of daily tasks that had to be done at sea were always considerable. Here a company of sailors clean out the barrels of a cruiser's guns, ready for the next action.

Right: The *Bismarck,* once again firing at *HMS Hood,* this time at night. The *Hood* was blown up off Greenland. The visual effects of naval gunfire in the dark could be quite dramatic, as shown.

Above: Painting the hull of a battle-cruiser in Kiel harbour, 1938. This was an arduous but important task, preventing the premature ageing of the ship's superstructure by corrosion.

Iceland-Faeroes passage just when they were only 100 miles from the *Bismarck*, which was then able to steam undisturbed towards St Nazaire! By the time this error had been discovered and contact had again been made with the German battleship by a Catalina flying-boat, many of the British vessels were short of fuel and nearly all were many miles behind her: only the Gibraltar-based 'Force Z' centred on the carrier *Ark Royal*, had the chance to intercept. Yet the carrier's Swordfish planes made a false torpedo attack, upon the cruiser *Sheffield*, which at least revealed the faultiness of the magnetic

At sea I am a coward

detectors and allowed these to be changed before the second aerial assault, this time upon the *Bismarck* itself. With the final torpedo of all, a fatal hit was made which jammed the battleships' rudders. Thereafter, the *Bismarck* could only circle hopelessly, fight off destroyer attacks and await the arrival of superior British forces. At 1040 on May 27, 1941, she was scuttled by her own crew after she had been blasted for hours by gun and torpedo fire.

The sinking of the *Hood* had given the German navy its greatest victory; that of the *Bismarck* its greatest defeat, and not just in terms of one fine ship and its crew. For the loss of Germany's great battleship also symbolised a turning-point for the entire surface navy, which henceforward ceased to contend North Atlantic waters. The decision was Hitler's alone, and greatly resented by Raeder; the latter, however, was never able to influence the Fuehrer very much. In part, this was due to Hitler's own character and background, which had little connection with the sea. Like the Kaiser before him, Hitler feared to lose his big ships: 'On land, I am a hero; at sea, I am a coward', he once told Raeder. The U-boats, he felt, could interrupt Allied commerce just as well as battleships, with no risk to Germany's prestige from the sinking of a major vessel. Furthermore, with Hitler concentrating more and more of his attention upon the campaigns in Russia, with the army and the

Luftwaffe striving to increase their own influence at the expense of the navy's—the assignment of control of all land-based aircraft to Goering in early 1942, and the cutting of the navy's oil quotas are examples here—Raeder was less and less important in the formulation of what one may term German 'grand strategy'.

On the other hand, the future of capital ships had clearly been called into question by new technological developments in any case. The existence of long-range reconnaissance aircraft, which had reported the *Bismarck*'s departure from Bergen and spotted her in mid-Atlantic; of radar devices, which had allowed the British cruisers to shadow for so long; and of aircraft-carriers, which could reach out to cripple or even sink an opposing naval force, not 20, but 200 miles away: all this signalled the end of the heavy-gunned capital ship, and the battles in Pacific waters only confirmed it. Even when the German battleships were in harbour, they were in constant danger from Bomber Command's raids. For all these reasons, then, it was decided to pull back to German and Norwegian bases the *Scharnhorst, Gnei-*

The Channel dash

senau and *Prinz Eugen*, which were resting at Brest. Yet the so-called 'Channel Dash' of February 11–13, 1942, which gave Hitler a great propaganda victory by revealing that German warships could burst through the Straits of Dover without the British being able to prevent them, was nevertheless a strategic retreat. The Royal Navy could now abandon its battleship escort of important Atlantic convoys and deploy those vessels elsewhere, for example.

After the spring of 1942, therefore, the German surface fleet was restricted to operations in one area only, apart from the Baltic—the waters off Norway, where more and more of the heavy units were stationed to deter an Allied invasion. However, the first sortie made led to the ignominious encounter of the *Lützow*, *Hipper* and six destroyers with a far weaker British force, which was escorting an Arctic convoy in late December 1942. The news of this failure, coming as it did in the midst of the battle for Stalingrad, confirmed all of Hitler's old prejudices against the surface navy—and this despite the fact that the *Fuehrer* himself had been chiefly responsible for the orders which so restricted the German warships. In January 1943 he ordered the scrapping of all major vessels and the transfer of their armaments to strengthen Norway's land defences, which in turn provoked Raeder to hand in his resignation. No doubt the latter's constant criticism of the 'Barbarossa' operation, which had after all been the chief reason why Hitler had reduced the navy's priority in armament procurement and production in 1940, played a role in the Grand Admiral's dismissal. His successor, Admiral Karl Doenitz, was—symbolically enough—head of the German U-boat arm: we will examine his role in that arena shortly. Doenitz was soon able to achieve a far better relationship with Hitler and to rescue the big ships from their fate;

Above: German torpedo boats in action on a sweep in the North Sea. These vessels proved useful in the English Channel and the North Sea, releasing the larger fleet destroyers for work in the Arctic and Bay of Biscay.

yet they never fully recovered their place in German naval strategy. Their main task, in Hitler's eyes, was to augment Norway's defences against invasion; their main achievement, so far as the Allies were concerned, was to pose a constant threat to the Arctic convoys and to tie up major fleet units in home waters. Hence the many attempts, by midget-submarines, by carrier aircraft and by heavy bombers, to put the chief danger, the battleship *Tirpitz*, out of action; hence, too, the attack upon St Nazaire, which possessed the only dry-dock in France which could house the ship.

In December 1943 the last great surface action of the war took place in European waters when the battlecruiser *Scharnhorst*, seeking to disrupt an Arctic convoy, was itself surprised by superior forces. Aircraft played no part in this battle but the improved British radar allowed the battleship *Duke of York* to pick out its weaker opponent in the darkness and to blast it to pieces. This left the *Tirpitz* as the only active unit, which stimulated the British into more and more attacks upon the lone battleship throughout 1944. Eventually, on November 12 of that year, Lancaster bombers managed to drop several 12,000-lb bombs through her decks, causing her to topple over and sink in

Above: The face of a U-boat commander. It was these men who increasingly dominated sea warfare and in whose hands lay the fate of the merchant shipping upon which Great Britain was so dependent throughout the war. Churchill believed the U-boat threat to be his greatest peril.

Right: A German heavy cruiser of the *Hipper* class silhouetted against the setting sun in a Norwegian fiord. Life in the *Kriegsmarine*, however, was not all picturesque scenery, especially in the cramped conditions aboard ship. It was harder and more unpleasant than that experienced by other *Wehrmacht* forces.

Tromsö Fiord. Virtually all the other large warships were now serving as stationary gun-platforms or training-vessels by this time, and coming under increasing attack from the Allied strategic bombing campaign. The *Gneisenau* had already been paid off following bomb damage in 1942, and the *Lützow*, *Scheer* and *Hipper* suffered a similar fate in 1945. Only the *Prinz Eugen* of the larger German warships survived intact to the end. If the story of the German surface fleet in World War II is one of disappointments, unfulfilled hopes and eventual rejection by its own national leader, the same cannot be said for the U-boat arm. Here, too, there was a precedent in World War I, where the High Seas Fleet had been inactive for most of that conflcit whereas the German submarines nearly brought Britain to her knees in 1917. Even during the *Weimar* period the navy had secretly kept up its interest in submarines, and under Hitler the service was openly built up. At first the U-boats were small, short-range vessels and even at the outbreak of war only 22 were ocean-going, but more important than this was the aggressive tradition of the submarine branch, the ease with which these boats could be constructed compared with, say, a battleship, Germany's technological strength and the leadership of Doenitz. The latter, who had two years of experience with submarines in World War I, carefully guarded his service in the early years of its growth and established an important place for it in Hitler's mind. This was partly because of the

Doenitz and the U-boats

Fuehrer's distrust of the large surface ships and his wish for quick successes, which he believed the U-boats could give him; and partly because Doenitz attracted him more than the formal and distant Raeder. When Doenitz became Commander-in-Chief of the navy in January 1943, for example, he quickly saw the importance of being frequently with the *Fuehrer* if he was to ward off the machinations of Goering and to ensure that sea power was accorded a proper place in German strategy. And finally, of course, there was the undeniable fact that the U-boats *were* achieving many successes and often seemed close to bringing the commerce of the Allies across the Atlantic to a halt.

With the outbreak of war the U-boat arm received an unexpected boost, since it was clearly in a position to expand more rapidly than the surface navy, whose building programme was drastically curtailed. Immediately, the submarine construction rate was raised from 20 to 30 boats a month, most of them being the medium-size VII C type of 770 tons. Even so, it would be difficult for

the U-boats to have a great influence upon the early stages of the war, not only because of the small number of vessels ready for sea and the inevitable problems of hasty expansion, but also because Doenitz and his crews had to learn from experience what developments had occurred in the Royal Navy's anti-submarine tactics in the inter-war years.

From the very beginning of the war, the British revealed that they were going to take the U-boat menace seriously, even though

Battle for the convoys

they were too confident about their ability to detect submarines. Although there were to be many exceptions, they hoped to gather Allied ships into convoys and to escort them across the sea. The problems facing the British Admiralty here were enormous, for they had to provide cover for literally thousands of merchantmen with quite inadequate escort forces; and, as the U-boats increased the range of their operations, this protection had to be extended from the coastal and Atlantic convoys to ones in more distant waters. Furthermore, although the

U-boats were the usual—and by far the most lethal—enemy to Allied shipping, attacks from German aircraft or even surface vessels had also to be provided against.

Thus the overall characteristics of the struggle to control the sea-lanes, especially the broad Atlantic highway across which the food, raw materials and armaments for Britain's war effort had to be brought, were relatively simple. It was a long, hard, drawn-out battle, with success to be measured not in some lightning campaign but in the monthly tables of Allied merchant vessels and German submarines sunk in innumerable small engagements; it was a battle fought chiefly around the convoys, everything depending upon whether the U-boats could overwhelm the escorting forces and sink sufficient ships to bring Britain to her knees; and it was, therefore, a war not just of two opposing navies but of two opposing technologies. Could the Asdic, the underwater detecting device, pick up the U-boats before they surfaced, and would the newer radar sets be available to allow the Allies to 'see' at night?; would the panoply of escorts be able to fight off a whole 'wolf-pack' of U-boats?; would the Germans' use of long-range bombers to spot and attack convoys be successfully

The early U-boat arm – a parade at Kiel in 1935 at which four submarines, just off the production line, were inaugurated into the *Kriegsmarine*. Numbers grew rapidly later in the war, when their importance was realised.

countered by Allied fighters and anti-submarine patrols by Coastal Command?; would the new 'schnorkel' device permit the U-boats to attack with impunity?; finally, would the Allies, and especially the Americans, be able to replace the merchant shipping as swiftly as it was being sunk?

The early stages of the U-boat war were naturally low-keyed, as both sides struggled to change their organisation from a peacetime to a wartime basis. The smaller submarines were employed in laying mines around British harbours, an activity which not only led to many sinkings but also to the diversion of British escort vessels to mine clearance duties. The larger U-boats, for their part, achieved fame not so much by the extent of their sinkings but by a few individual successes. In September 1939 the U-29 sank

The Royal Oak is sunk

the aircraft-carrier *Courageous*, and in mid-October the U-47 under Lieutenant-Commander Guenther Prien daringly penetrated the defences of the main British naval base at Scapa Flow and sank the battleship *Royal Oak*, a deed which gave an immense boost to

the submarine service. Yet the sinking of the liner *Athenia* in the previous month revealed that the old problems of keeping to the international conventions on submarine warfare and of maintaining good relations with neutral states were still to be overcome. However, Raeder was soon able to persuade a more cautious Hitler to agree to unrestricted U-boat warfare around Britain, a decision aided by the arming of British merchantmen and by the American neutrality proclamations. By 1940 the campaign was one with 'no holds barred' on either side.

By the end of 1939 114 Allied merchantmen totalling 420,000 tons had been sunk by U-boats, a figure which the British and French merchant marines could clearly take in their stride; after all, the British merchant marine totalled over 21 million tons. Moreover, in March 1940 a shortage of raw materials and Hitler's desire to increase land armaments led to the reduction in the submarine construction, the first of many alterations which would occur as a result of external forces. Finally, all available U-boats were diverted from commercial warfare to the Norwegian campaign, where they experienced many frustrating torpedo failures. Yet, when the smoke had cleared from Hitler's

Blitzkrieg campaigns, the U-boat arm discovered to its joy that the strategical picture had been amazingly transformed: for the use of French and, to a lesser extent, Norwegian bases for the submarines and the long-range 'Condor' aircraft meant that the

Protection of commerce

campaign against British shipping could now reach much further into the Atlantic—to 25° West, whereas the British at this time could usually only provide escorts up to about 15° West. In June 1940, the first month of this changed situation, Allied ship losses to U-boats were 58 vessels of 284,000 tons and in October they reached 63 vessels of 350,000 tons, figures which provoked the British Admiralty to divert many more warships from anti-invasion duties into commerce protection.

Despite these successes, the U-boats were still not achieving what had been hoped from them. This was partly due to their small numbers (in February 1941 the total of ocean-going U-boats was as low as 21); partly to their diversion into the Mediterranean, to operate against British warships there; and partly to the rough weather of the oncoming winter months. In addition, the British were now launching more and more corvettes, ubiquitous escort vessels which were smaller (and therefore far cheaper) than destroyers; and they were also aided by the increasingly 'un-neutral' acts of the United States in 1940 and 1941, especially the transfer to the Royal Navy of 50 old destroyers and the provision of anti-submarine protection to all shipping in an ever-extending western hemisphere 'security zone'. The Canadians, too, were providing increased naval aerial protection for the important convoys which sailed from Halifax.

Of all these factors, the first was recognised by Doenitz as being the key one. He had earlier estimated that he would require 300 U-boats to cut the British convoy system across the globe, yet at times he had an operational strength of only a tenth of that figure. His plans, to use the submarines in packs and to launch attacks from the surface of the sea, where the Asdic device could not function, were always restricted by the lack of adequate forces: only when Speer assumed responsibility for U-boat production did the situation change. In the twelve months December 1940—November 1941 and the

Submarine climax

U-boats sank 1,726,000 tons of Allied merchant vessels in the North Atlantic alone, but it was noticeable that about two-thirds of these had *not* been in convoy and that German aircraft were causing even greater damage—at least until the British introduced the new escort carriers to deal with that particular menace. These figures suggested that Germany was failing to achieve its main aim, that of disrupting the Allied convoys, and that more attention would have to be paid to that problem.

The real climax of the U-boat campaign

came in the years 1942 and 1943, for obvious reasons. By then, both sides had appreciated the nature and importance of the struggle and were throwing all their resources into it; by then, too, it was apparent that only the U-boat arm of the German navy could influence the outcome of the maritime war; and finally, everyone realised that, with the German attack upon Russia now held, the defeat of Hitler's *Reich* was inevitable provided that the massive flow of goods and men from the USA could proceed uninterrupted across the Atlantic. With the American entry into the war at the end of 1941, the German need to cut the sea-routes had greatly increased.

The early months of 1942 were memorable ones for the U-boats, not so much in the North Atlantic, but along the American seaboard, where there were few convoys or other forms of protection for merchant shipping: nearly 500,000 tons of shipping, much of it consisting of oil tankers, was sunk by the end of March, and the figures only began to drop when the US Navy instituted countermeasures in the early summer months. By that time however, the German submarine production plan was taking effect and Doenitz was deploying almost 150 boats all over the globe, with many sinkings being achieved

Underwater warfare demanded a number of highly specialised skills, each of which was only aquired by men of above-average intelligence and physical endurance. *Right:* Sailors undergoing escape training.

The *Reich* war flag – shown in every ocean by the U-boat arm, feared by merchantmen of all the Allied nations, the symbol of Germany's power carried to the farthest limits.

in the Caribbean and South Atlantic. And in the most vital area of all, the North Atlantic, he now had sufficient of the larger U-boats to form them into strong 'wolf-packs' and to send them against the convoys in the region known as the 'air gap'—those 600 or so miles in mid-ocean for which aerial support could be provided neither from Canada, Iceland nor the United Kingdom. In the last six months

7,790,000 tons are sunk

of 1942, sinkings by U-boats rose rapidly, so that by the end of the year submarines had sunk 1160 merchantmen of 6,266,000 tons, whilst sinkings by other services raised this to 1664 ships of 7,790,000 tons. Even the immense Allied shipbuilding efforts could not keep pace with these figures, and Britain's stocks of food, oil and other raw materials were very low indeed. More worrying still was the fact that many vessels were being lost in convoy and that more and more U-boats were being made ready for the fray. Not surprisingly, Allied leaders meeting at Casablanca in January 1943 considered that

Above: U-boats tied up in open harbour, 1936. This was to prove impossible during the war and massive concrete pens were built to guard against RAF bombing.

Below: A returning U-boat commander, as he is greeted at the dockside. Submariners were among the foremost heroes of Germany at war and their exploits were much publicised.

these developments were seriously affecting all their other plans. A drastic counter-offensive was imperative.

After a certain 'lull' in the stormy winter months, the U-boat offensive was resumed in full earnest, 108 merchant ships of 627,000 tons being sunk in March 1943 alone. Many of these casualties occurred when a 'pack' of 38 U-boats tore into two Allied convoys in the mid-Atlantic air gap. However, the battle then took a sudden and decisive turn: the counter-attack planned by the new British Commander-in-Chief, Western Approaches, Admiral Sir Max Horton, had begun. Support groups, each usually consisting of an escort carrier and fast frigates and destroyers, ranged around the convoys, picking off the U-boats as they moved in to attack; very-long-range Liberator bombers closed the air gap and prevented the wolfpacks from coordinating their assaults in advance; improved radar, depth-charges and other devices increased the Allies' chances of both spotting and sinking their enemy; and Coastal Command's patrols in the Bay of Biscay with aircraft equipped with improved radar and 'Leigh Light' searchlights took a

Revolutionary schnorkel

very heavy toll of returning and out-going U-boats. Between March and November 1943 204 U-boats were sunk, with great depletions in the ranks of the skilled submariners, so that as early as May of that year Doenitz was forced to recall his fleets from the North Atlantic until new measures against the improved Allied detection and sinking devices could be devised.

The new measures Doenitz had in mind were the revolutionary 'schnorkel'— type submarines, which allowed the boats to charge their batteries at periscope depth; other types—such as the XXI and the 'Walter' hydrogen peroxide/diesel type—which were faster and much more efficient than the existing U-boats; new radar devices; and the accoustically-guided torpedo. However, all of these developments had suffered from the decision to concentrate upon the production of standard types, upon the increasing lack of raw materials in German industry and upon the prior claims of other services. Pulling back the U-boats from the North Atlantic could hardly be a short-term measure, therefore, yet whenever a fresh attempt was made to rupture the convoy system further losses were suffered: in the first three months of 1944 only three merchant ships were sunk in the North Atlantic, yet 36 U-boats did not return to base. And the signs were that convoy defences were stiffening up in other areas also. At this, Doenitz cancelled all further operations against convoys until the newer submarines were ready, and many U-boats were diverted instead to anti-invasion work.

By the time of the D-Day landings, many of the boats had been fitted with 'schnorkel' devices; but, although this reduced their losses, the Allied command of the sea and air was so firm that the sinkings by German submarines were kept to a minimum. With the seizure of Brittany, the U-boats were

Above: U-boats setting out on route for the shipping lanes around Britain, in 1941. It was in doggedly pursuing this strategy of stranglehold on Britain's supplies that Germany came nearest to defeating her enemy.

deprived of many of their best ports and had instead to be based upon Norway. Moreover, the strategic bombing campaign—and in particular the minelaying in the Baltic—was disrupting U-boat trials and training, thus throwing Doenitz's planned counter-offensive ever more behind schedule. All this explains why, although the submarine fleet reached its peak strength, of 463 boats, only in March of 1945, it was unable to influence the closing stages of the war. Just as the newer types, which were far harder to detect and which travelled much faster under water, were setting out to challenge the Allied command of the sea once again, Germany itself was being overrun by the armies of her enemies.

If Doenitz's 'last fling' had failed, there

The greatest threat

is no doubt that the U-boat threat had been the greatest ever posed to the western Allies. They had sunk 14,300,000 tons of merchant shipping, 6,840,000 tons of it in the North Atlantic, and they had also disposed of 175 Allied warships—in all cases, the majority being British. They themselves lost 785 of the 1162 U-boats built and commissioned during the war, and once again it

Above: A U-boat resupplying in the protection of a submarine pen on the Atlantic coast in 1944. It was from such secure bases that the U-boats went singly or in twos and threes, later to meet up at predetermined rendezvous with other submarines in order to form a hunting pack to destroy Allied convoys.

Right: Dive! A submarine commander shutting the entry hatch into the conning tower as a U-boat prepares to dive. Emergency dives were a common feature of submarine warfare in the days of Allied supremacy. Seconds could make all the difference between life and death from a U-boat killer.

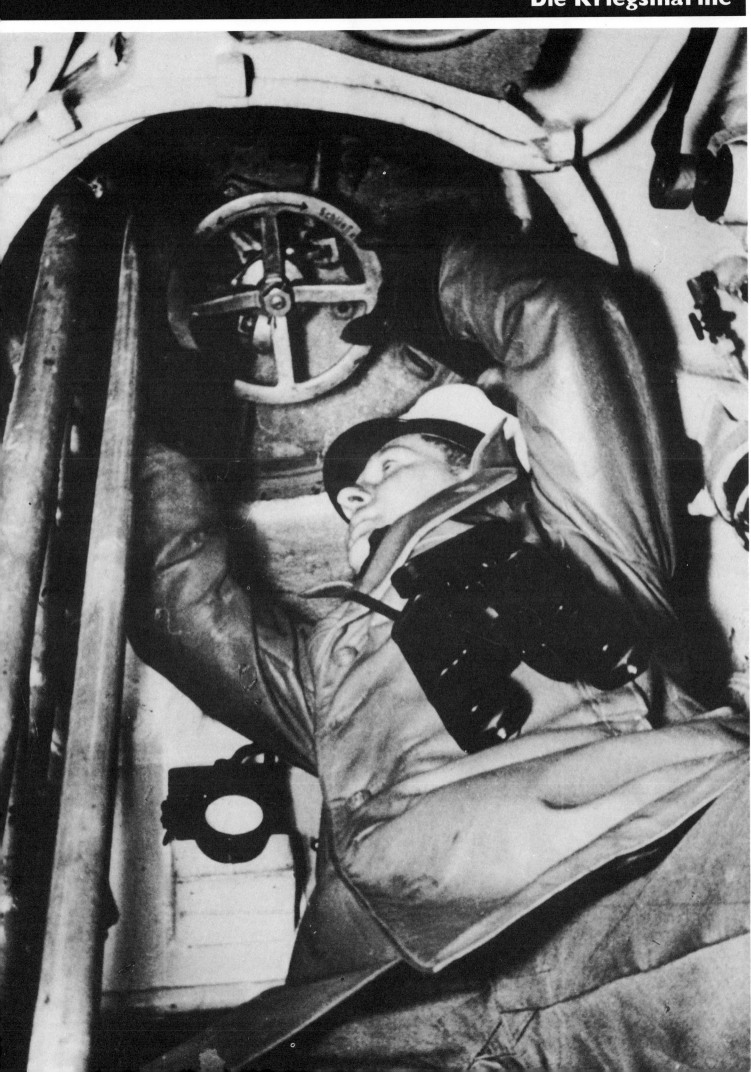

Scharnhorst

Class: name ship of her class of battle cruisers or light battleships.
Displacement: 31,850 tons standard, 38,900 tons full load.
Dimensions: length 771 ft (234 m) oa; beam 98½ ft (30 m); draught (8·2 m).
Machinery: 3-shaft Brown-Boveri geared turbines, 160,000 shp; 12 Wagner boilers. Speed: 31½ knots.
Guns: nine 11-inch (3 x 3), twelve 5·9-inch (6 x 2), fourteen 4·1-inch AA (7 x 2), sixteen 37-mm AA, ten (later 38) 20-mm AA.
Torpedo Tubes: six 21-inch.
Aircraft: four floatplanes.
Protection: 12–13-inch (305–330 mm) belt, 12-inch (305 mm) turrets, 4-in (101 mm) decks.
Fuel/Radius: 6300 tons oil/10,000 miles (16,000 kilometres) at 17 knots.
Complement: 1800 officers and men.

History: launched October 3, 1936 and commissioned 1939; took part in operations in the Atlantic 1939–1940, during which she sank the armed merchant cruiser *HMS Rawalpindi* south-east of Iceland. During the Norwegian Campaign she helped to sink the aircraft carrier *Glorious* and destroyers *Ardent* and *Acasta*. She cruised in the Atlantic once more in 1941 and with *Gneisenau* sank 115,000 tons of Allied shipping. On her return to Brest she was subjected to constant bombing and finally in February 1942 she and *Gneisenau*, with *Prinz Eugen*, broke out and escaped in daylight through the English Channel. After repairs to mine damage she was sent to Norway and took part in a bombardment of Spitzbergen with *Tirpitz*. She was sunk on December 26, 1943, by the Home Fleet in the Battle of North Cape. by gunfire from the battleship *Duke of York* and destroyers' torpedoes.

Like other German ships, her tonnage was considerably understated to comply with international treaties. She was built with heavy protection, but the armament was relatively light as the 11-inch mountings for three projected 'pocket battleships' had already been ordered. She and her sister were not particularly good seaboats and suffered from spray interference in bad weather. As completed she had a straight stem, but at the beginning of the war an 'Atlantic' clipper stem was fitted in an attempt to improve sea-keeping.

Gneisenau

Gneisenau

Class: *Scharnhorst* Class battlecruiser or light battleship.
Displacement: 31,850 tons standard, 38,900 tons full load.
Dimensions: length 771 ft (234 m) oa; beam 98½ ft (30 m); draught 27 ft (8·2 m).
Machinery: 3-shaft Brown-Boveri geared turbines, 160,000 shp; 12 Wagner boilers. Speed: 32 knots.
Guns: nine 11-inch (3 x 3), twelve 5·9-inch (6 x 2), fourteen 4·1-inch AA (7 x 2), sixteen 37-mm AA (8 x 2).
Torpedo Tubes: six 21-inch (2 x 3).
Aircraft: four floatplanes.
Protection: 12—13-inch (305—330 mm) belt, 12-inch (305 mm) turrets, 4-inch (101 mm) decks.
Fuel/Radius: 6300 tons oil/10,000 miles (16,000 kilometres) at 17 knots.
Complement: 1800 officers and men.

History: launched December 8, 1936 and commissioned in 1939; operated with the *Scharnhorst* in the Atlantic in 1939—40, Norwegian Campaign April—June 1940, and then in the Atlantic in 1941. With her sister she was always regarded as one of the 'lucky twins', but after the passage through the Channel in February 1942 her luck deserted her. She was damaged by a bombing raid on Kiel on the night of February 26/27, 1942, and was then towed to Gdynia and decommissioned there in July 1942. Work began on a total reconstruction which involved lengthening the hull and replacing the 11-inch guns with twin 15-inch but the work was stopped in 1943 for lack of materials and labour. She was finally scuttled as a blockship at Gdynia on March 28, 1945, and the wreck was finally broken up under Russian supervision in September 1951.

Unlike the *Scharnhorst* she was completed with the 'Atlantic' or clipper bow and capped funnel, but could always be distinguished by having her mainmast stepped against the funnel. In 1942 she had 14 additional 20-mm AA guns in three quadruple and two single mountings.

Admiral Hipper

Class: name-ship of her class of heavy cruisers.
Displacement: 13,900 tons standard, 18,600 tons full load.
Dimensions: length 675¾ ft (206 m) beam 70 ft (21·3 m); draught 19 ft (5·8 m).
Machinery: 3-shaft Blohm & Voss geared turbines, 132,000 shp; 12 Lamont boilers. Speed: 32 knots.
Guns: eight 8-inch (4 x 2), twelve 4·1-inch AA (6 x 2), twelve 37-mm AA (6 x 2), four 20-mm AA (4 x 1).
Torpedo Tubes: twelve 21-inch (4 x 3).
Aircraft: three floatplanes.
Protection: 3-inch (76 mm) belt, 4-inch (101 mm) turrets, 1¼—2½-inch (32—63 mm) deck.
Fuel/Radius: 4250 tons oil/6800 (10,880 kilometres) miles at 20 knots.
Complement: 1600 officers and men.

History: launched February 6, 1937 and completed 1939. She took part in North Sea operations in 1939—40 and at the outset of the Norwegian Campaign she was damaged by ramming by the British destroyer *Glowworm*. Between June 1940 and February 1941 she sank 12 ships in the Atlantic, and was then transferred to Norway. With the *Lützow* she failed to destroy a Russia-bound convoy and was then driven off by destroyers in the Battle of the Barents Sea. She ended her days in the Baltic and was scuttled at Kiel after being damaged by bombs early in 1945.
Like the Italians and Japanese, German cruiser designers found that they could not incorporate all the qualities of high speed, gunpower and armour within the internationally agreed limit of 10,000 tons. Yet, despite an increase of nearly 40 per cent the *Admiral Hipper* Class were not good

value for the money lavished on them. The enormous horsepower yielded no higher speed than foreign cruisers with much less power, and the endurance was too low for extended cruising. The *Hipper* suffered from chronic machinery trouble, largely due to the exaggerated emphasis on high-pressure steam. The armour was heavy but was concentrated on a thin waterline belt and the turrets, leaving the machinery vulnerable.

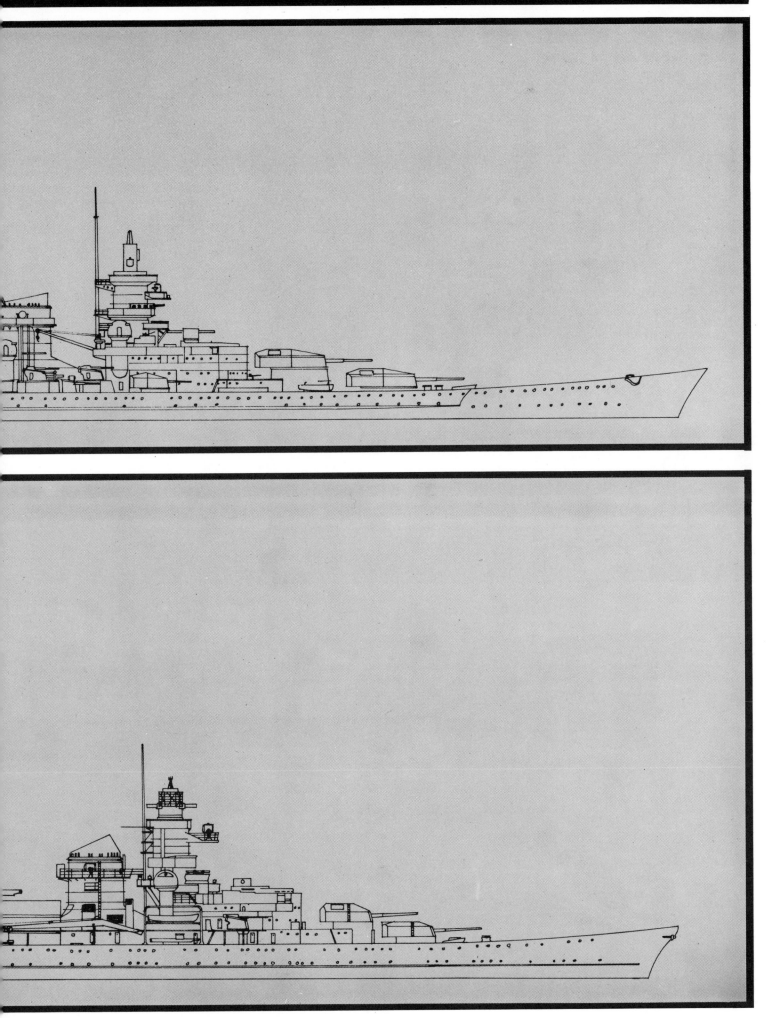

Admiral Graf Spee

Class: modified *Deutschland* Class armoured cruiser or 'pocket battleship'.
Displacement: 12,100 tons standard, 16,200 tons full load.
Dimensions: length 609 ft (186 m) oa; beam 70 ft (21·3 m); draught 21½ ft (6·5 m).
Machinery: 2-shaft MAN diesels, 54,000 bhp. Speed: 26 knots.
Guns: six 11-inch (2 x 3), eight 5·9-inch (5 x 1), six 4·1-inch AA (3 x 2), eight 37-mm AA, ten 20-mm AA.
Torpedo Tubes: eight 21-inch (2 x 4).
Aircraft: one floatplane.
Protection: 4-inch (101 mm) belt, 2–5½-inch (51–140 mm) turrets, 1½–2-inch (38–51 mm) decks.
Fuel/Radius: 2436 tons oil/8900 miles (14.240 kilometres) at 20 knots.
Complement: 1150 officers and men.

History: launched June 30, 1934 and commissioned in 1936 as Fleet Flagship; served on Non-intervention Patrol during Spanish Civil War 1936–37 and represented German Navy at Coronation Naval Review in May 1937. She was sent into Atlantic on August 21, 1939, to avoid the British blockade, and from September to December sank nine ships totalling 50,000 tons. She was damaged in the Battle of the River Plate on December 13, 1939, and took refuge in Montevideo. On December 17, she was scuttled off Montevideo.
Built to evade the restrictions of the Versailles Treaty, which aimed at allowing the German Navy to build only coast defence ships, the three 'pocket battleships' were as much a political gesture as anything. Although their tonnage was falsified and their endurance quoted as almost double what it really was, they were ingenious ships, the first large vessels with diesel propulsion. Much feared when they were built, the defeat of the *Graf Spee* showed that they were not capital ships, but merely overgunned cruisers.

100 60 30 10   180 160 140 100

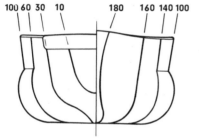

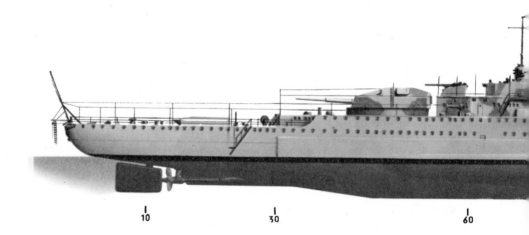

10   30   60

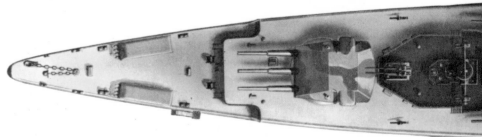

100   140   160   180

5 10   25   50   75   100
FEET

© Profile Publications Limited

Prinz Eugen

Class: modified *Admiral Hipper* Class heavy cruiser.

Displacement: 14,800 tons standard, 19,800 tons full load.

Dimensions: length 689 ft (210 m) oa; beam 71½ ft (21·7 m); draught 19 ft (5·8 m).

Machinery: 3-shaft Brown-Boveri geared turbines, 132,000 shp; 12 Lamont boilers. Speed: 32 knots.

Guns: eight 8-inch (4 x 2), twelve 4·1-inch AA (6 x 2), twelve 37-mm AA (6 x 2), eight 20-mm AA (2 x 4).

Torpedo Tubes: twelve 21-inch (4 x 3).

Aircraft: three floatplanes.

Fuel/Radius: 4250 tons oil/6800 miles (10,880 kilometres) at 20 knots.

Complement: 1600 officers and men.

History: launched August 22, 1938 and completed 1940; she sailed on May 21, 1941, with *Bismarck* on 'Operation Rheinuebung', the sortie into the Atlantic. On May 24 she took part in the Battle of the Denmark Strait, and one of her hits possibly caused the fatal fire in *HMS Hood.* On orders from Admiral Luetjens she broke away and reached Brest safely, but did not leave until February 1942, when she escaped through the Channel with *Scharnhorst* and *Gneisenau* in 'Operation Cerberus'.

She served on training duties in the Baltic in 1944, and while covering the withdrawal of ground forces in the East she damaged the light cruiser *Leipzig* badly in collision. She surrendered at Copenhagen in May 1945 and was allocated to the U.S.A. She was severely damaged in the 1946 nuclear tests at Bikini, and was finally sunk on November 15, 1947 at Kwajalein.

Tirpitz

Class: *Bismarck* Class battleship.

Displacement: 42,900 tons standard, 52,600 tons full load.

Dimensions: length 822¾ ft (250·5 m) oa; beam 118¼ ft (36 m); draught 29½ ft (8·8 m).

Machinery: 3-shaft Brown-Boveri geared turbines, 138,000 shp; 12 Wagner boilers. Speed: 29 knots.

Guns: eight 15-inch (4 x 2), twelve 5·9-inch (6 x 2), sixteen 4·1-inch AA (8 x 2), sixteen 37-mm AA (8 x 2), fifty-eight 20-mm AA (4 x 4, 16 x 2, 10 x 1)

Torpedo Tubes: eight 21-inch (2 x 4).

Aircraft: six floatplanes.

Protection: 12·6-inch (317 mm) belt, 7–14-inch (178–355 mm) turrets, 4½-inch (114 mm) decks.

Fuel/Radius: 8780 tons oil/9000 miles (14,400 kilometres) at 19 knots.

Complement: 2530 officers and men. .

History: launched April 1, 1939 but not completed until 1941. She sailed for Norway in January 1942, to become the main threat to Allied convoys to North Russia. In July 1942 fears that she was at sea led to the dispersal and destruction of convoy PQ.17, and thereafter she was the target of repeated attacks by aircraft and from submarines. She was damaged by midget submarines (X-Craft) in Kaa Fiord in September 1943; in April 1944 she was damaged by British carrier aircraft, and again in August. In September, Lancaster bombers damaged her, and when she moved to Tromso to act as a stationary coast defence battery she was finally sunk by 12,000 lb (5400 kg) bombs and capsized The *Tirpitz* owed her long immunity as much to nature as to any design-features, for the Norwegian fiords effectively prevented aircraft from mounting conventional attacks. On the few occasions she was hit she proved quite vulnerable to damage, and on one occasion a 750 lb (337 kg) bomb went through to her keel but failed to explode. Post-war examination of the hull proved that her underwater protection relied mainly on her colossal beam, and that she lacked the sophisticated protection systems of contemporary British and

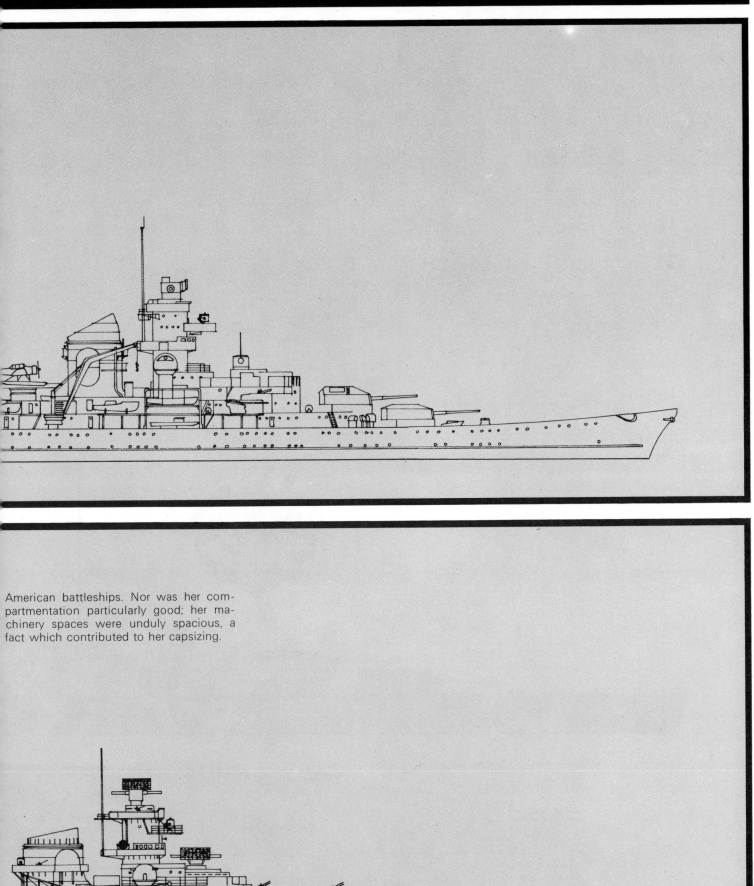

American battleships. Nor was her compartmentation particularly good; her machinery spaces were unduly spacious, a fact which contributed to her capsizing.

Bismarck

Class: name-ship of her class of battleships.

Displacement: 41,700 tons standard, 50,900 tons full load.

Dimensions: length: 822¾ ft (250·5 m) oa; beam 118¼ ft (36 m); draught 28½ ft (8·7 m).

Machinery: 3-shaft Brown-Boveri geared turbines, 138,000 shp; twelve Wagner boilers. Speed: 29 knots.

Guns: eight 15-inch (4 x 2), twelve 5·9-inch (6 x 2), sixteen 4·1-inch AA (8 x 2), sixteen 37-mm AA (8 x 2), thirty-six 20-mm AA (4 x 4, 6 x 2, 8 x 1).

Torpedo Tubes: none.

Aircraft: two floatplanes.

Protection: 12·6-inch (317 mm) belt, 7–14-inch (178–355 mm) turrets, 4½-inch (114 mm) decks.

Fuel/Radius: 7900 tons oil/8100 miles (12,960 kilometres) at 19 knots.

Complement: 2200 officers and men.

History: launched February 14, 1939 and completed late in 1940. After working up in the Baltic to the end of April 1941 she sailed with *Prinz Eugen* on May 21 to raid in the Atlantic, and engaged the *Prince of Wales* and *Hood* in the Denmark Straits on May 24. Despite the fact that some of their shells failed to explode she or *Prinz Eugen* started an ammunition fire in *HMS Hood*, which caused her to blow up, and they then inflicted damage on the *Prince of Wales*. She was then damaged by torpedoes in two attacks by British carrier aircraft, which jammed her rudders. She was brought to action by the battleships *King George V* and *Rodney* on May 27, and after being badly damaged by gunfire was finally torpedoed by the cruiser *Dorsetshire*.

The *Bismarck* was a strange mixture of old and new. Her disposition of anti-aircraft guns with six directors was unmatched for its day, yet she retained the antiquated idea of separate low-angle and high-angle gun batteries. Although widely believed to have an advanced and massive system of armour protection, it was little different from *Scharnhorst*'s in thickness and showed no improvement over her model, the 1915 battleship *Baden*. In that respect she did not incorporate the latest ideas on armour disposition, and in her last fight it was only half an hour before she was silenced. Her machinery was very large and powerful, and yet her sea speed was only half a knot faster than her smaller and heavier armoured opponent *HMS King George V*.

Lützow

Lützow

Class: armoured cruiser or 'pocket battleship', re-rated as a heavy cruiser.
Displacement: 11,700 tons standard, 15,900 tons full load.
Dimensions: length 616¾ ft (188 m) oa; beam 68 ft (21 m); draught 19 ft (5·8 m).
Machinery: 2-shaft MAN diesels (eight 9-cyl. motors), 54,000 bhp.
Speed: 26 knots.
Guns: six 11-inch (2 x 3), eight 5·9-inch (8 x 1), six 4·1-inch AA (3 x 2), eight 37-mm AA (4 x 2), twenty-two 20-mm (1 x 4, 18 x 1).
Torpedo Tubes: eight 21-inch (2 x 4).
Aircraft: two floatplanes.
Protection: 3¼-inch (83 mm) belt, 5½-inch (139 mm) turrets, 1¼–3-inch (32–76 mm) decks.
Fuel/Radius: 2784 tons oil/10,000 miles (16,000 kilometres) at 20 knots.
Complement: 1150 officers and men.

History: launched May 19, 1931 as the *Deutschland* and completed in 1933; served as a seagoing training ship until the Spanish Civil War, when she joined the Non-Intervention Patrol. During this period she was bombed by Spanish Government aircraft.

On August 24, 1939, she was sent into the Atlantic to evade the British blockade but returned in November after sinking only two ships. She was renamed *Lützow* in February 1940, as Hitler did not wish a ship bearing the name *Deutschland* to be sunk(!)—it is also possible that the German Navy wanted to revive a famous Jutland name. After service in Norway in 1940 she remained in northern waters, and in December 1942 she and the *Hipper* suffered an ignominious defeat at the hands of British destroyers in the Battle of the Barents Sea. It was this action which

caused Hitler to threaten the scrapping of the entire surface fleet and led to the resignation of Admiral Raeder.

The *Lützow* went to the Baltic for training duties in 1944 but was used to support the withdrawal in the East until bombed at Swinemuende in April 1945; she was scuttled in May 1945. By 1944 she had been considerably altered, with a funnel cap and a quadruple 20-mm 'flak vierling' AA mounting on her forward turret. At the end of 1944 she had single 40-mm Bofors like the *Admiral Scheer*.

Admiral Scheer

Class: *Admiral Graf Spee* Class armoured cruiser, re-rated as a heavy cruiser.
Displacement: 12,100 tons standard, 16,200 tons full load.
Dimensions: length: 616¾ ft (188 m) oa; beam 71¼ ft (21·7 m); draught 19 ft (5·8 m).
Machinery: 2-shaft MAN 9-cyl. diesels (four motors per shaft), 54,000 bhp.
Speed: 26 knots.
Guns: six 11-inch (2 x 3), eight 5·9-inch (8 x 1), six 4·1-inch AA (3 x 2), twenty 37-mm AA (10 x 2).
Torpedo Tubes: eight 21-inch (2 x 4).
Aircraft: two floatplanes.
Protection: 4-inch (101 mm) belt, 5-inch (127 mm) turrets, 1½–2-inch (38–51 mm) decks.
Fuel/Radius: 2523 tons oil/9100 miles (14,560 kilometres) at 20 knots.
Complement: about 1150 officers and men.

History: launched April 1, 1933 and completed 1934. She served on the Non-Intervention Patrol in the Spanish Civil War from 1936 to 1937, but when war broke out in 1939 she remained in home waters, and underwent a major refit in 1940. In October 1940 she began a cruise in the South Atlantic and the Indian Ocean, in which she sank 17 ships before returning in March 1941. In 1942 she went to Norway but the following year she withdrew to the Baltic for training. She was sunk in Kiel by RAF bombs on April 9, 1945, and the wreck was later buried under rubble when the basin was filled in after the War.

The *Admiral Scheer*'s appearance changed radically. In 1940 her original tower bridge, similar to that in the *Graf Spee*, was replaced by a lighter foremast of tubular type similar to that in the *Lützow*. Radar

aerials were added to the forward and after fire controls, and the funnel was capped. Later the mixed battery of close-range anti-aircraft guns was replaced by a uniform outfit of 10 twin 37-mm guns, but in 1945 these were replaced by 10 single 40-mm Bofors guns.

U.107

Class: Type IXB U-boat.
Displacement: 1051 tons surfaced/ 1178 tons submerged.
Dimensions: length 251 ft (76·5 m) oa; beam 22¼ ft (6·7 m); draught 15½ ft (4·7 m).
Machinery: surfaced, 2-shaft MAN 9-cyl. diesels, 4400 bhp; submerged, 2-shaft SSW electric motors, 1000 shp. Speed: 18¼/7¼ knots.
Torpedo Tubes: four bow and two stern 21-inch (22 torpedoes carried).
Guns: one 4·1-inch, one 37-mm AA, one 20-mm AA.
Fuel/Radius: surfaced, 166 tons oil/ 8700 miles (13,920 kilometres) at 10 knots. Submerged, none/64 miles (102 kilometres) at 4 knots.
Complement: 48 officers and men.

History: launched July 2, 1940 and completed in October that year, under Lieutnant Hessler. In 14 patrols she sank 38 ships totalling 217,700 tons, and shared the credit for sinking a further three ships. She operated out of Lorient, and ranged as far as Freetown in West Africa on her patrols. In August 1944 she was scheduled for transfer to Norway as Allied forces were overrunning France, but while on passage on August 18 she was sunk with all hands by a Sunderland flying boat south-west of Belle Isle.

The Type IX series of U-boats were developed from the prototype IA ocean-going design, which was itself an expansion of a successful World War I design. Although regarded by the U-boat Arm as too large and clumsy for the Atlantic, the 14 IXB boats sank by themselves an aggregate of 1·4 million gross tons of shipping, or 10 per cent of the entire total sunk by U-boats from 1939 to 1945, a far better performance than any other class. Furthermore U.107 holds the record of 14 ships sunk on one patrol, and ranked the fifth highest scoring U-boat. The advantage of the Type IX series was their better habitability and high torpedo capacity, which enabled them to stay at sea longer than the 750-ton Type VII boats.

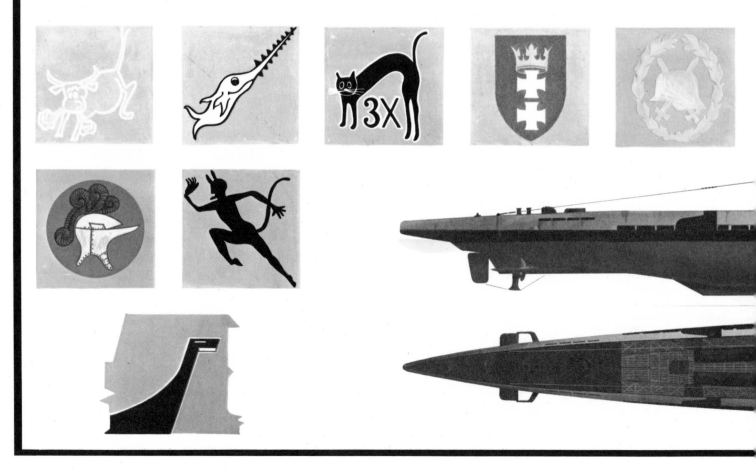

Above: Life in a U-boat was often hard. Here, submariners brave the bitter cold of the Icelandic Sea. Note that the gun is frozen solid.

the sea. The U-boats proved to be a far more serious peril but even they were always too few in number to achieve a real dislocation of the convoy routes. As far as Hitler and the German High Command was concerned, World War II was primarily a land affair; and the navy did not even take second place, for Goering was always able to secure priority

Such very heavy odds

for the claims of the *Luftwaffe*. Raeder, and even Doenitz after him, always had to struggle to make Hitler realise what was at stake—and what success they obtained in this respect was all too often temporary.

Even if the German Navy had been accorded a higher priority in defence allocations, however, it is debatable whether the final result would have been much different. The plain fact was that, in taking on Britain, Russia and especially the United States, Germany had bitten off more than she could chew: even by 1942 its armaments expenditure was down to 25 percent of that of the Allies. The superiority of the Anglo-American surface fleets, and even more the radar devices, improved depth charges, long-range anti-submarine aircraft, escort carriers, and the flocks of corvettes, frigates and destroyers which contributed to the defeat of the U-boat were the outward sign of this ever-increasing industrial and technological dominance. When examined in this light, the final question might well be, not 'Why did the German navy fail?', but rather, 'How did it achieve so much against such heavy odds?'.

Above: A U-boat firing a last shot at a sinking Allied merchantman, late in 1941. Often a torpedo attack would prove insufficient to sink the ship quickly. In such a circumstance, the U-boat would surface and finish off the enemy vessel with the gun that was carried on the deck of all submarines. This proved to be a more economical way of completing the attack than firing the more valuable and numerically limited torpedoes. Occasionally a wounded submarine, forced to surface, would have only this gun with which to defend itself against an enemy destroyer – or even an airplane that had found the U-boat out. But the gun was insufficiently powerful to put up much resistance and a surfaced U-boat was generally a doomed one.

had been British forces involved on the great majority of occasions. The entire campaign had been a lengthy, relentless fight to the death, for upon its outcome lay so much else. Churchill put it best when he wrote: 'Battles might be won or lost, territories might be gained or quitted, but dominating all our power to carry on the war, or even to keep ourselves alive, lay our mastery of the ocean routes . . . The only thing that ever really frightened me during the war was the U-boat peril.'

Although the campaigns of the German surface fleet and of the U-boats during World War II appear so different in character, the reasons for the eventual failure of both are the same. To a large extent, it was a case of 'too little, too late'. The war had begun at least five years too soon for Raeder's 'Plan Z' and as a consequence his few big ships were never able to do more than to disturb temporarily the British command of

Suggested reading
Sir Basil Liddell Hart: **History of the Second World War** (Cassell's, London, 1970)
F. Ruge: **Sea Warfare 1939–1945: A German Viewpoint** (Cassell's, London, 1957)
D. Macintyre: **The Naval War against Hitler** (Batsford, London, 1971)
S. W. Roskill: **The War at Sea**, 3 vols. (HMSO, London, 1954–1961)
S. W. Roskill: **The Navy at War 1939–1945** (Collins, London, 1960)
J. Creswell: **Sea Warfare 1939–1945: A Short History** (Longmans, London, 1950)
E. P. Von der Porten: **The German Navy in World War Two** (Arthur Barker Ltd., London, 1970)

Science and Technology—
brilliance and confusion

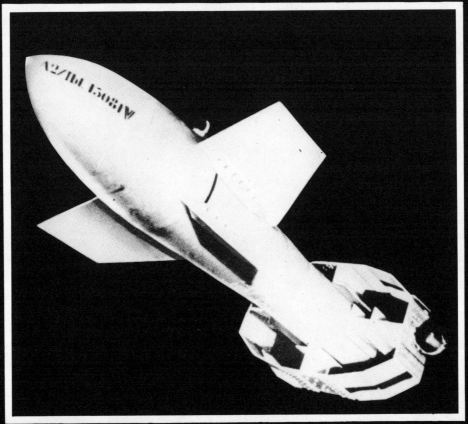

Fritz X anti-ship missile.

Matthew Cooper

The application of modern science and technology to the military machine revolutionised warfare and international relations. It gave to weaponry a destructive power of immense and terrifying proportions and shifted the emphasis away from the numbers and quality of men in favour of the numbers and quality of machines. It ensured that the scientist and technologist had an influence upon the conduct of war second only to that of ministers and generals.

It was only with the advent of World War II that the experiences of the Great War, the advanced technology of the Industrial Revolution and the continuing investigations of modern science were fully combined and, in theory at least, were exploited to the full. In this development the Third *Reich* played a significant part and its achievements in the field of rocketry and, to a lesser extent, in aircraft and underwater warfare bore important influence on post-war developments. Germany's researchers revealed an inventiveness not surpassed by those on the Allied side and it was fortunate for Hitler's opponents that the German political machine failed to appreciate their importance – or the war might have ended differently.

Above: The giant Wuerzburg radar. Germany failed to develop potential in the field.
Below: The *Hochdruckspumpe,* the V-3, designed to force shells out at speed.

Left: Bernard Rust, who proved to be an ineffectual Minister of Science, failing to make the most of his Ministry.

Right: A V-1 'doodlebug' which is being towed into its concrete bunker at a secret launching site in Northern France.

Science and Technology— brilliance and confusion

Science and Technology

▌Science can look after itself. It is a process which generates its own movement, success breeding upon success, advance upon advance. We National Socialists have only to ensure that it is not polluted by bad blood and therefore by false and destructive ideas. We have achieved that ▌ and the results speak for themselves.

Adolf Hitler 1939

▌We in the Third Reich set great store by technological achievement. We should elevate those who pursue it to the status of heroes, for it is largely through ▌ them that we shall win this present war.

Josef Goebbels 1943

The Third *Reich* has too often been portrayed as a ruthlessly efficient centralised state, in which all effort during the years 1939–1945 was geared towards the requirements of total war. Reality, however, was somewhat different. The actual course of events proved not that totalitarian nations are necessarily best equipped to deal with the problems of modern war, but quite the opposite. One of the best examples lies in the scientific and research field, for here it was the Democracies who achieved the indispensable co-ordination between requirement and research, between political direction and science, and not Germany. In contrast, her programme was characterised by chaos rather than by determined organisation. Her lack of any central planning which could co-ordinate the various centres of technological effort was to ensure that the Germans, despite their many achievements, ultimately failed to produce any war-winning weapon.

During the war there were three main groups of research, each completely independent of the other. Firstly there were the *Wehrmacht* establishments, divided upon service lines; the *Heereswaffenamt* (Army Weapons Office); *Marinewaffenamt*, and the Air Ministry *Technischesamt* (Technical Office—which were responsible for the development, testing and procuring of weapons, and the translating of the requirements of the armed forces into technical specifications for industry. The idea was sound, but

A lack of harmony

only in the case of the Army did it work well. For the *Luftwaffe*, with its fatal preoccupation with its tactical rôle and the failures of its planners, the arrangement left much to be desired, and the relationship between Air Ministry and industry too often lacked harmony and understanding—as exemplified by the personal enmity between Field-Marshal Milch, the deputy head of the *Luftwaffe* and sometime head of the technical office, and Willi Messerschmidt, the renowned aircraft designer and manufacturer. Rivalries between the services impeded any proper exchange of information, as did the obsessive desire for secrecy.

Any idea of forming a central office of the *Wehrmacht* High Command to co-ordinate all research effort was opposed not only by the individual services, but also by industry,

owing to the fear that direct interference would hamper its freedom of action and development—a view held by Hitler who reversed his decision to set up such an institution on the same day as it was made.

Secondly, there was the very important private sector of industrial research conducted by such companies as Heinkel, Messerschmidt, Krupp, I.G. Farben, Zeiss and Siemens. These firms undertook work for themselves in order to present to the *Wehrmacht* armaments which had already been tried and tested. The Navy, especially, relied on research undertaken by private enterprise. But again there was no interchange of information, this time owing to the restrictions and competition of private enterprise. Also the very existence of the large and expensively equipped private enterprise re-

Little mental agility

search centres had the effect of discouraging the *Wehrmacht* from setting up its own establishments.

Thirdly, there were the University research centres and the thirty or so institutes of the Kaiser Wilhelm *Gesellschaft*, which were all linked to the *Reich* Research Council, a body with a grand title but little power of direction. Once again there was no worthwhile liaison with the other groups. Finally, some mention must be made of the smaller research bodies such as those under the auspices of the Ministry of Posts (which did valuable work, among other areas, in the nuclear field and also succeeded in 'unscrambling' supposedly secret telephone conversations, including WSC-FDR conversations after 1942, according to General Gehlen).

The Germans had not learnt from their unhappy experience in World War I that centralisation and direction of research was vital. Just as there was no central agency, nor was there a single scientific adviser to Hitler; the *Reich* Minister for Science, Education and Public Affairs, Dr Bernard Rust, never even attempted this rôle. Rust was a weak

Right: Fritz Todt, *Reich* Minister for Armaments and Production, in a *Luftwaffe* general's uniform with soldiers and civilians at one of the army's research centres in 1942. His efforts to harmonise research came to little, as did those of his successor, Speer.

Above: National Socialist flirtation with inventors. Goebbels at a Nuremberg Rally with designers Heinkel, Messerschmidt, Porsche and Minister Todt.

Left: Himmler, Special Commissioner for the V-2 rocket programme, with Doernberger on a visit to Peenemuende.

leader of little mental agility, whose attitude towards scientists was indicated soon after his appointment when he declared the 'scientists are charlatans, devoid of original ideas'. According to a contemporary joke, a Rust was 'the standard unit of measurement for the minimum time elapsing between the passing of a decree and its cancellation'. In many ways he typifies the Third *Reich*'s curiously ambivalant attitude towards scientists and researchers. On the one hand relatively high salaries were paid to researchers, and the traditional German respect for practical attainment still proved valuable. But on the other there was the anti-intellectualism of the National Socialists which manifested itself in a general disregard for scientists and their views among the nation's leaders. When war broke out Rust made little effort to ensure that scientific and technical personnel were directed to jobs in which they could be of most use to the

Antisocial elements

national effort, and later on some 10,000 had to be released from the *Wehrmacht* in order to use their skills according to their ability.

This unfortunate inefficiency in the organisation of research was not peculiar to Germany—the Allies suffered too. But this lamentable situation was further compounded by the special factors to which science in the Third *Reich* was alone subjected. Foremost among these was the policy carried out by the National Socialists towards the Jews and other 'antisocial' elements. Although the numbers of Jews expelled or imprisoned during the Thirties constituted a relatively small proportion of Germany's scientists (at most 12 percent), the repercussions were particularly grave. Rust once addressed himself to a leading mathematician and asked, 'Is it really true, Professor, that your Institute suffered much from the departure of the Jews and their friends?', to which the reply was, 'Suffered? No, it hasn't suffered, Herr Minister, it just doesn't exist any more.' Not only were the Jews themselves rejected, but so was their work. Certain methods of physics were branded 'Jewish physics', and the Germans who espoused

Above: The picture which typifies much of what was wrong with the *Reich*'s scientific and research efforts. An aircraftman fits a bomb onto the Me262 jet fighter – the result of Hitler's uninformed interference with this plane.

Right: A photograph taken from the air by an Allied plane shows a V-2 experimental launch pad at Peenemuende, in 1944. Rockets and their transporters are arrowed.

them as 'White Jews'; while in the search for the atomic bomb Germany laboured under the disadvantage of not only losing Einstein (he had left for the United States at the beginning of the persecution) but also losing his valuable theory of relativity—since it had been declared invalid by the National Socialist theorists.

As a corollary to this, there was a small but growing and influential number of German scientists who, realising the intellectual and moral enormity of Hitler's *Reich*, sought to retain their positions but at the same time undertake no work which would significantly help the war effort.

Two other factors must also be considered when evaluating the success or otherwise of Germany's research. First was the Third *Reich*'s isolation from the world of international research, especially during the war, and the consequent loss of all the advantages that the exchange of scientific knowledge between friendly nations brings. Niels Bohr, the eminent Danish physicist, was the most important of many scientists who refused to work with the Germans and who gave their very considerable services to the Allies (who also had the benefit of the many exiled German Jew researchers). The second factor was the strong but mistaken belief of Germany's rulers that the war would be a short one and that costly scientific research, especially if long-term, would be of little or no benefit and

therefore would not justify any great effort spent on it. As a result the necessary determination for expensive and long-term research was not forthcoming until too late.

But despite such disadvantages the scientists and technicians of the Third *Reich* were able to undertake a range of research projects unrivalled by the Allies. Their expertise and imagination was particularly impressive. For example, the use of air as a weapon was something that particularly interested German scientists. A 'wind cannon' was developed which fired a 'bolt of air under great pressure from a weapon standing some 30 ft high with a sloping barrel 50 ft long. During tests it was shown that the cannon could smash a board one inch thick over a

Left: Guderian, Inspector of Armoured Troops, being shown the development of a new anti-tank shell at one of the army's test ranges in Prussia. Ballistic and explosives research formed an important part of Germany's scientific effort and made a positive contribution to the war machine.

range of 200 yds. Intended as an anti-aircraft gun, the prototype proved unsuccessful. Also developed was a 'hurricane cannon' which attempted to produce artifical vortices in the air which would cause the destruction of enemy aircraft by throwing them out of co-ordination. Success of a kind was at last achieved, but the weapon was never used operationally. Thirdly, air pressure was used in the 'sound cannon'—two large parabolic reflectors of different size which were attached on to the front of a combustion tube fed with an oxy-methane mixture. This projected a beam of intensive sound energy which would, it was thought, kill a man within a minute under a distance of 60 yds and severly incapacitate him at up to 300 yds. Tests were instituted but the project did not develop.

Pressure was also the prime idea behind the development of the *Hochdruckpumpe*, the high pressure pump gun which was intended to bombard such distant and important targets as London, Antwerp and Luxemburg. It was no less than 150 ft long and fired an 8 ft projectile by means of successively firing a number of charges which were contained in paired lateral projections along the tube. By such means the missile was ejected at a speed of 4800 ft per second—sufficient to carry it 85 miles. However, allied air activity and the faults innate in the construction of the gun (usually one of the component sections would explode during firing) ensured that this weapon was of no practical use to the German war effort.

Much intensive work was carried out upon guns and ballistics. An arrow projectile—a shell stabilised not as was usual by its spin but by special lateral fins—was a significant development used against the Russians (it was considered too secret to be used against the western Allies). Hollow explosive charges, shell clusters and the use of concrete as a shell housing were other developments.

Contrary to popular belief, the Germans were as far advanced in radar technology at the beginning of the war as the British. In 1938 they had invented the 'Freya' radar set, a mobile piece of equipment operating on the decimetre wave which could determine distance but not height. Far better was the 'Wuerzburg' radar, which came into production at the beginning of the war. It used an ultra-short wave length of 53 cm and could achieve excellent results, reading the location, course and altitude of aircraft with very great accuracy up to a distance of 25 miles. With its range of up to 90 miles the 'Freya' served as the early warning radar, while the 'Wuerzburg' gave the precision necessary for anti-aircraft guns and interceptors. In an Allied field the Germans did well with the 'X apparatus', a radio-direction beam invention which brought bombers directly over their targets at night, and which

signalled the moment to release bombs. It was not effectively jammed until 1941. The 'Lichtenstein' was an airborne radar for use with night fighters, and was used operationally for the first time on August 9, 1941. However, it could have been in use as early as the spring of 1940, when it was first required, had it not been rejected earlier by the *Luft-*

Limited brain-power

waffe authorities. As it was, it was not until mid-1942 that the set's difficulties were finally overcome.

Up to 1942, then, the electronic warfare of the German Air Force was as advanced as the British, it's greatest failing lying not with the quality of the equipment but with the system of use (co-ordination between radar, central control, and aircraft was not developed until late 1942). But by this time it was apparent that the Germans were lagging behind considerably. Goering gave the reason: 'I have long been aware of the fact that there is nothing the British do not have. Whatever equipment we have, the enemy can jam it without so much as a by your leave. . . Gentlemen, It's not manpower you have too little of, it's brain power in your brain boxes to make the inventions we need.' This, however, was only part of the story, for lack of official interest and direction contributed in the main to the unfortunate state of affairs which manifested itself so dramatically in 1943. At that time, during the Battle of Hamburg, the RAF dropped thousands upon thousands of strips of silver paper

An Me110G-4 night fighter with the Lichtenstein radar in its nose. Such aids were of considerable importance and had the *Luftwaffe* developed them earlier the war in the air would have been even tougher for the bombers.

which resulted in paralysing the radar system. Known as 'Window', the Germans had been aware of its effect since mid-1942, but had failed to seek a counter-measure due to official lethargy.

This short-sightedness had also been responsible for the rejection in 1938 of Dr Esau's research in the field of radar. He had

Amateur radio banned

then found the 4.4 mm wave, but this was only later developed into the 'Heidelberg' radar set towards the end of 1944—far too late. This was a considerable improvement upon the 'Giant Wuerzburg' then in service (a 40 mile range), and reached as far as 240 miles. In other words, the *Luftwaffe* could

have had a radar which was able to detect the take-off of Allied bombers in Norfolk early in the war. The realisation by the High Command that the war in the air over Germany would be won by such inventions came too late, although the six new radar systems developed between July and December 1943 is evidence of the drive that was initiated. But even then, German research was severely behind that of the Allies, due in no small way to the fact that before the war amateur radio enthusiasts had been banned, the authorities thereby cutting off thousands of small inventors. In the end Germans were forced to copy captured Allied equipment—for example the so-called '*Rotterdamgeraet*' for use in detecting submarines.

In the field of marine development, research was almost automatically confined to the

submarine, since this was the only area where Germany, after 1940, could hope to defeat Great Britain. The U-boats of 1939 were in many respects similar to those that had been in operation in 1918, for although their range had been increased, their under-

Danger from aircraft

water speed and limited capacity to move below the surface were much the same (only some six knots for a few hours at a time). Owing to lack of oxygen underwater, a U-boat had to run its engines by means of electric power and therefore had continually to surface to recharge its batteries (during which time it would be powered by its diesel engines). This made the U-boat a diving boat rather than an underwater vessel and consequently this not only limited its operations but also ensured that it was extremely vulnerable to air detection which had reached dangerous proportions by 1942. German research was to solve this problem with supreme success, but too late.

The only improvement which saw operational service was the schnorkel. It was an old concept, being essentially an air pipe which could be extended like a periscope above the surface of the sea in order to supply the U-boat and its engines with the necessary oxygen. But the end of 1943 all German submarines had been fitted with the schnorkel. However, while it considerably reduced the danger from aircraft, it did not eliminate it, and, just as important, it did nothing to increase the U-boats' underwater speed.

Of far greater importance was the development of an entirely new, indeed revolutionary, engine designed by Professor Walter. The first experiments took place in 1940. A closed circuit turbine was substituted for the diesel-electric combination, and the oxygen source was switched from the surface air to the decomposition, induced by a catalyst, of hydrogen peroxide in the fuel Ingolin. Thus Walter's invention, coupled with a redesigned hull, enabled the new Type XVII U-boats to operate at high speeds totally submerged for long periods. In July 1943 the approval for construction of the Type XVII was given, and the first four were supplied at the end of 1944. During trials they reached an underwater speed of 21 knots. An improved, larger version was immediately embarked upon but never completed. In July 1943 the approval for the construction of the

Vulnerable shipyards

Type XXI was also given. This was regarded as a stop-gap until the Walter submarine could be brought into service; it had a conventional engine with increased battery capacity and capable of an underwater speed of 17.5 knots. 120 were completed but, like the Type XVII, they were not to see action. One interesting feature in the production of these U-boats was the brilliant way in which the German technologists overcame all the manufacturing difficulties posed by congested and vulnerable shipyards. The various parts of the submarines were built in inland factories, transported to the coast and there assembled quickly. Thus, whereas the old types of U-boats had taken eleven and a half months in drydock to build, prefabrication meant that the new types took only two months.

But, despite the submarine revolution which had taken place in the Third *Reich*, the new developments came too late to exert any influence upon the war. As Speer recalls: 'At the time, Doenitz and I often asked ourselves why we had not begun building the new type of U-boat earlier. For no technical innovations were employed; the engineering principles had been known for years. The

Ultimate war winner

new boats, so the experts assured us, would have revolutionised submarine warfare.' So they would have. Had the Third *Reich*'s leaders placed more emphasis upon marine warfare earlier, research might well have meant the introduction in sufficient numbers of these new U-boats which, in turn, would have ensured for Germany the all-vital supremacy of the Atlantic.

Before Hitler's aquisition of power Germany had the great advantage of having the cradle of nuclear science within its borders—at the University of Goettingen. It took the National Socialists only a few weeks in the Spring of 1933 to destroy this ancient foundation as a centre of research. The University was never to recover from the expulsion or forced resignation, mentioned earlier, of numbers of 'politically unreliable' and Jewish professors and scholars. Nor, indeed, was German nuclear physics.

The German nuclear research and the search for the ultimate war winner—the atomic bomb reveals the folly of allowing scientists to determine their own aims and progress during wartime. It is clear that the ultimate Allied supremacy in this field was no foregone conclusion. Indeed it was a German, Dr Otto Hahn, who in 1938 found that if uranium atoms were bombarded with neutrons, atomic energy would result. But with the exception of one man, Professor von Ardenne, the men involved in research did not envisage the possibility of an atomic

The construction and development of new U-boats was a triumph for the *Reich*'s research. Unfortunately for the *Kriegsmarine*, the revolution in submarine design came too late to have any effect upon the sea war.
Construction time was greatly reduced during the war despite the difficulties and delays caused by Allied bombing.
***Right:* Two submarines at different stages of construction, the nearest showing its torpedo tubes clearly.**
***Centre:* A vessel nears completion.**
***Far right:* Finishing touches to the lethal load that the submarines carried around the world to the destruction of Allied shipping.**
***Top right:* Piling up stores to load on to a submarine. U-boats were often away from home for long periods of time.**

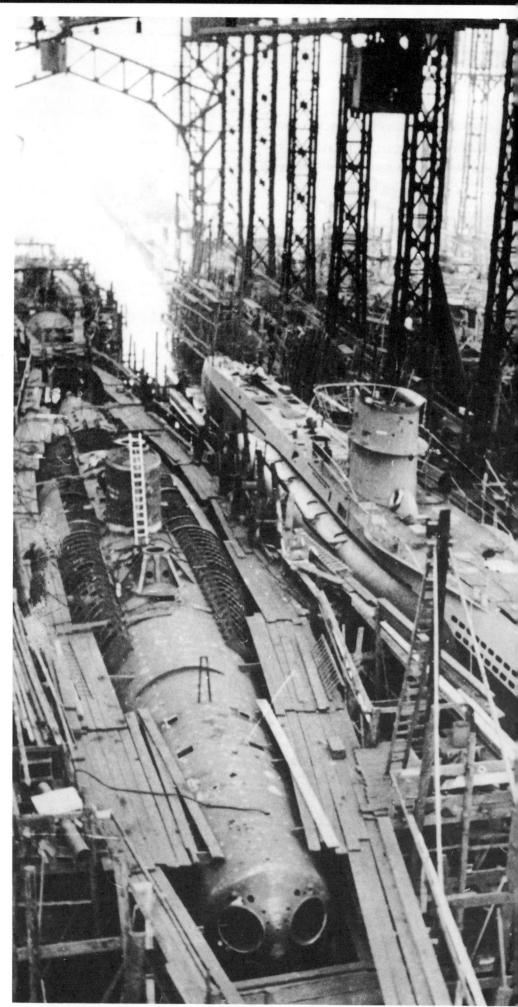

Left: Professor Werner Heisenberg, the reluctant director of Germany's atomic bomb effort.

Right: The industrial process indispensable to Germany's atomic bomb development – the hydro-electric works of Rjukan in occupied Norway, which produced the heavy water necessary for experiments with uranium. Part of the works was blown up by Norwegian saboteurs in British uniform, flown in by the RAF.

Below: V-2s ready for launching, October 1944. They had a mobile launching pad and therefore could evade Allied aerial detection to some extent.

bomb during the war and therefore failed to fire their political masters with the necessary enthusiasm for its development.

Von Ardenne, who worked in the *Reichspost* laboratory, had his ideas dismissed as those of a dilettante by men such as von Weizsacker, a leading physicist. Another, Werner Heisenberg, the head of the Kaiser Wilhelm Institute atomic research laboratory, while he envisaged that an atomic bomb would be 'about as big as a pineapple',

The Jewish physics

nevertheless succeeded in impressing upon Speer and others the virtual impossibility of producing such a weapon in Germany. Heisenberg, who was never a Nazi, has claimed that he exaggerated the problems in order to discourage the authorities from trying to acquire the bomb. Speer was put off by the modest demands for money and material made by Heisenberg which had led him to believe that the atom bomb development would have no significance in the war effort. Others such as Esau, the first Plenipotentiary to Goering for Nuclear Physics and titular head of the atomic energy project, even went so far as to attempt to prevent any idea of the possibility of manufacturing such a bomb from leaking out, fearful that they might be ordered to make one and suffer unpleasant consequences in the event of failure. Also, as an Allied report suggested in 1945: 'German science is not without guile, and took advantage of the lack of understanding of science by those in authority to engage in interesting scientific research, under the guise of war work, that could not possibly help the war effort'. The characters of the scientists, too, could serve against purposeful development of the A-bomb; Esau, for example, had little drive, and Gerlach, his successor, even less, both being stolid workers with little vision.

Another disadvantage for the development of the German A-bomb was the dominance of theory over practice which caused a divorce between the physicists and the engineering industry and denied the Germans any significant material achievements in the nuclear field. Heisenberg and his men preferred to build up a solid theoretical basis rather than progress through trial and error, and therefore there was no immediate urgency to get the uranium pile 'critical'—an indispensable step in the progress towards a bomb.

German nuclear research, then, was left almost entirely in the hands of the scientists. Owing to the contributions of men such as Einstein, Hitler referred to nuclear physics as 'Jewish physics', and this attitude coloured the whole approach towards development. While the Allies put a prodigious effort into the project, the German leadership, believing the war would be over before any results were produced, failed to give it anything like the resources it needed. There was no effective central agency, no purposeful direction and no proper organisation. While the Germans were ahead in some respects before 1942, the complete failure of their scientists to gain recognition and support from the

government meant that little further progress was achieved. Perhaps Germany never had the necessary economic resources to produce such a revolutionary weapon, and certainly the purely practical mistake which caused the German physicists to use heavy water instead of graphite as a 'breaking substance' in the reactor, ensured that failure would be definite.

Of all the end-products of the Third *Reich*'s research, it is the rockets which not only have fired the imagination of all who have read about them, but also, and far more important, have served as the basis of a vast post-war development—a development which has taken man to the moon. In the field of rocketry, wartime Germany was supreme. But there was no guarantee that this, too, would not suffer the usual debilities inherent in the *Reich*'s research—the initial paucity of interest and resources, the lack of central direction and the abundant variety of projects which resulted in the dissipation of effort.

In the early 1930's rocket research had been undertaken by such pioneers as Oberth and Winkler, and had interested the Army to a point where they placed Captain (later Major-General) Dr Walter Dornberger in charge of secret weapons' development. He was assisted by Dr Werner von Braun, the man who more than any other was responsible for Germany's lead in this field (he also supervised the post war US rocket pro-

Rocket development

gramme). In 1933 the A1 was developed (the forerunner of the V2), followed by the A2 in 1934, which flew to a height of 6500 ft and the A3 in 1937 (a large rocket standing 21 ft tall, weighing 16,500 pounds and powered by a liquid fuel LOX/ethanol motor).

However Dornberger was given only limited resources for this highly experimental and expensive work. By 1939 his staff consisted of only some 300 men, and the High Command proved reluctant to allocate scarce raw materials to a project which might well not be operational until after the war was over. The *Luftwaffe*, too, was suspicious of the Army's rocketry and gave no help. After the Battle of Britain the programme was given a higher priority—one leading contemporary expert reckoned that in the early war years perhaps one third of all German scientists worked upon the rocket development in some way (fuel, navigation, tele-communications etc)—but this still was not enough. It was only after the successful firing of the A4 rocket on October 3, 1942, that the situation changed—though somewhat late. With a rocket reaching a range of nearly 120 miles and an altitude of some 50 miles, the attitude of Germany's leadership altered considerably. Now, with a war-winning weapon within his grasp, Hitler gave the project the backing it should have had from the start. Money and equipment was injected into the programme, and the rocket centre at Peenemuende was enlarged (its ultimate cost was £50 million), eventually housing over 2000 scientists. A committee was even instituted to co-ordinate develop-

Above top: A V-1 finds its target, as it falls down in central London. This photograph was taken from the Law Courts in the Strand.

Above: A production line of V-1s deep underground. This gave protection from Allied bombing. These centres were built largely by slave labour brought in from the occupied territories. Such labour made a major contribution to the German war effort.

Right above and below: An experimental V-2 fails in launching during early trials at Peenemuende in January, 1943. Such failings were a common experience. Sometimes they resulted in loss of life; certainly they caused serious delays in the programme.

Far right: The prototype of the A46, forerunner of the A9, shortly before launching, January 1945.

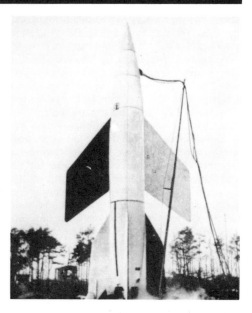

ment on the rocket (in fact it became something of a hindrance, headed as it was by an expert not in rocketry but in locomotives!). But even with all this it took a further nine months from the first successful firing for the project to be given top priority in the German armaments programme. Ominously the A4 was designated *Vergeltungswaffe 2*— V2—(Vengeance Weapon).

The V2 project survived the RAF attacks on Peenemuende in August 1943 and while further development work was carried out in Upper Austria, an underground production line was set up in the Harz mountains. This

V-1 and V-2 rivalry

meant that the programme was set back by a number of months and time was of the essence for Hitler's Germany. The V2 which was ready for operational firing by mid-1944 was a considerable improvement on the first A4. It was capable of a range of over 200 miles carrying a load of 1650 pounds of high explosive. Standing 46 ft tall it weighed over $12\frac{1}{2}$ tons at launch (nine tons of which was fuel). Manufacturing time was cut down from 19,000 man hours in 1943 to only 4000 in 1945 (each V2 contained over 30,000 parts).

The other major German rocket weapon was the Fi103 (designated V1), the *Luftwaffe*'s flying bomb. Launched by catapult, the V1 was powered by a petrol-fuel pulse-jet motor which was extremely simple in design and manufacture. The V1 was in essence a small pilotless aircraft 27 ft long weighing 2 tons and carrying 1870 lbs of high explosive in its nose. After launch it reached a height of between 1000 and 7000 ft and proceeded at a cruising speed of 400 mph over a maximum range of 180 miles (later extended to 250 miles). Distance and direction were predetermined by means of a propellor mechanism which, once it had completed a specific number of revolutions, would cut the engine thus causing the V1 to dive steeply towards its target.

In many ways the V1 and V2 were rivals. Both performed much the same function in considerably different ways. The V1 was both simple and cheap to make, taking only about 280 man hours to manufacture. It cost between 1500 and 10,000 marks as against the 75,000 of the V2 and took but a part of the 200,000 skilled workers and the 1000 tons of aluminium a month of the larger rocket. Their warheads were both around a ton in weight. The V1 however had several disadvantages. Its launching pads were easily destroyed by enemy air action, whereas the V2 was mobile; its relatively slow speed and height allowed it to be shot down or even trapped by barrage balloons, whereas the V2 was supersonic and neither seen nor heard until its impact (the V1, however, did tie down a significant proportion of Britain's air defences); Lastly, the V1 was not only inaccurate, but also it could not be depended upon to detonate—neither, as it turned out, could the V2.

There was inevitably much rivalry between the Army and the *Luftwaffe*, each service championing its own weapon to the exclusion of the other—the Army especially was reluctant to abandon or even to economise its seven-year old rocket programme. Faced with a difficult choice between the two, the High Command decided upon a middle course by continuing with both weapons, concentrating on neither.

The first Fi103 flight took place in December 1942, and in the middle of 1943 the weapon was placed in full production. Owing to an inability to fulfil the schedule, combined with Allied bombing of the launching areas, the *Luftwaffe* opened its V1 offensive on June 13, 1944, six months later than planned. A total of 105,000 were directed at England, most of them at London, but only one fifth of them ever reached their

The Vengeance campaign

targets; 2419 fell on London and 30 on Portsmouth, while 3957 were shot down. About 1600 of these V1s were launched from modified He111 bombers. The casualties caused were 6184 dead and 17,981 were injured. Aimed against Antwerp the V1 proved itself to be even less reliable—of the 5000 fired only 211 ever exploded upon the city.

The V2 offensive opened on September 6, 1944; two were fired at Paris, but both failed in flight. On September 8 the attack on England began, but the Army's much-vaunted secret weapon proved to be no better than the *Luftwaffe*'s. Of the 4000 odd V2s fired, less than 1500 ever reached the country, causing 2500 deaths. Another 2050 came down over Brussels, Antwerp and Liége. The rocket's weaknesses soon became only too apparent. Its design still had many faults—faults which could on occasions cause it to explode on the launch pad or in descent, or which might send it violently off course. Its payload, also, was far too small, while its speed on impact (over 3500 mph) caused it to dig itself into the ground before exploding; and it thus expended most of its force upon making a deep hole.

The rocket offensive was not a serious threat to the British war effort as a whole, owing to the weaknesses of the weapons and the late timing of its advent. However the

nature of the V campaign was particularly unpleasant for the inhabitants of the South of England and did cause the government to draw up plans for the evacuation of London (something not done even during the Blitz). This is an indication of the potential that lay in Hitler's rockets.

Other rocket developments abounded,

Anti-aircraft potential

illustrating both German ingenuity and the diffusion of effort which marked the *Reich*'s research. This was in no small measure due to the keen conflict of interest between the Army and the *Luftwaffe*, and it resulted not only in a lack of co-operation in research but also in a series of policies which took no account of Germany's real and pressing military needs. By 1943 it had become painfully apparent that what the *Reich* needed was not terror weapons but an effective anti-aircraft system—which could be provided by rockets (a new 'secret' weapon to smash the hard-won Allied air supremacy). But the Army concentrated on the former to the detriment of the latter—the *Luftwaffe*'s requirement. Thus even as late as January 1945 there were 2210 scientists and engineers working on the never completed A4-B and A9/A10, (considerably heavier versions of the V2), while only 335 were members of the C2 'Waterfall' and 'Typhoon' anti-aircraft programmes. Advocating the development of 'Waterfall' in mid-1943 a leading German authority wrote: '. . . every expert, every worker, and every man-hour devoted to the speeding of this programme will yield results proportionately far more effective for winning the war than the same resources invested in any other programme. Delaying such a programme can mean the difference between victory and defeat'. After the war Speer wrote: 'To this day I think that this rocket ('Waterfall'), in conjunction with jet fighters, would have beaten back the Western Allies air offensive. . . Instead gigantic effort and expense went into developing and manufacturing long-range rockets which proved to be, when they were at last ready for use . . . an almost total failure. Our most expensive project was also our most foolish one.'

The 'terror weapons' programme concentrated primarily upon two extensions of the A4. One was the A4-B, a winged version of the A4 which was designed to glide to its target after the engine had cut out, thus significantly increasing its range. This had reached test-flight stage by January 1945. The other was the impressive A9/A10 which had resulted from the A4-B tests. It was designed to enable Germany to bombard the USA. (This was a requirement which had previously led to the 'Laffarenz Project'—a special container with three V2's which would be towed across the Atlantic by a Type XXI U-boat to within range of the American seaboard. There the containers would be brought into an upright position, the rockets fuelled from the submarine and fired.)

Work was being concentrated upon this rocket towards the end of 1944, but the war ended before it reached prototype stage. It

was to have a range of some 3000 miles, and consisted of two stages—the A10 booster rocket and the A9 second stage (this being a streamlined, winged version of the A4) and as such it would have been almost twice the size of the V2. The A10 booster would take the rocket 110 miles up into the stratosphere where it would separate and descend to the earth by means of special parachutes, and there be recovered and used again. The A9 would continue up to an altitude of some 217 miles, and then descend to 28 miles. There the air would be dense enough for the wing controls to operate, and the rocket would glide down onto its target—hopefully somewhere in the USA.

The *Rheinbote* (Rhine Messenger), manufactured by Rheinmetall, was the only other ground-to-ground rocket to be used operationally. It was a four-stage missile, the first two of which separated six miles after launch, the others remaining with the warhead. Powered by solid fuel, it had a range of 136 miles. It was an accurate rocket whose chief weakness lay in its extremely light warhead—only 88 pounds. At least 220 were successfully fired at Antwerp but little damage resulted.

There were several ground-to-air rockets

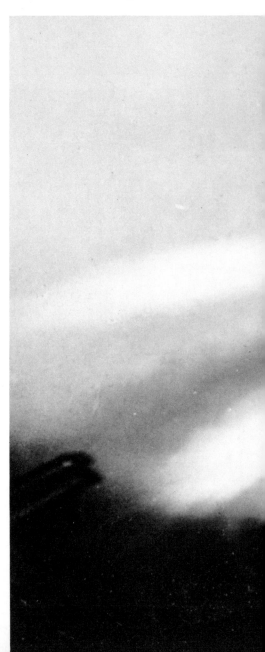

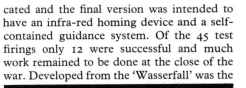
but none were used operationally. The *Feuerlilie* F25 was first flown in 1943 but cancelled the following year. It was six feet tall and flew at subsonic speeds for three miles. Its successor, the F55, was 16 ft tall, flew faster than the speed of sound, and had a range of roughly six miles. It consisted of two stages, one powered by solid—and the other by liquid-fuel. First tested in mid-1944, the war came to an end before much more could be accomplished. The '*Hecht*'—an 8 ft tall 'flying bomb' type of anti-aircraft missile which was launched from a ramp—was only developed to the prototype stage.

The '*Enzian*' was a highly powerful missile based on the Me163 Komet aircraft—an unmanned version made of plastic wood and powered by 4 booster rockets. Its warhead was 660 pounds of high explosive fired by a

The Rhine daughter

proximity fuse. Sixty were completed but none saw service. Likewise the Hs117 '*Schmetterling*' was based upon another operational weapon—the Hs293 glider bomb. The design was unwisely rejected in 1941 and resurrected in 1943—too late to iron out

all its teething troubles before the war ended. It had a range of 33,000 ft, a warhead of 50 pounds and was guided to its target by means of a radio transmitter which fed impulses to its servo-controlled fins. Had this weapon been used it would have proved itself effective against the high-flying Allied bomber formations.

The '*Rheintochter*' (Rhine daughter) R1 was a missile designed to be used with two radars (known as the Rheinland system), one of which traced the aircraft while the other guided the rocket to the target. The R1 was in two stages, the booster separating over a mile up and the main rocket continuing to 20,000 ft. It was 20 ft tall and carried a 250 pound warhead. Eighty were fired and the rocket had all the appearance of becoming a successful and much needed weapon. But promising though the project was it had not reached completion by May 1945. There were also an R2 and an R3.

Lastly the C2 '*Wasserfall*' (Waterfall) must be considered. Its design was based upon the A4, but its physical appearance was shorter and slimmer with four stub wings above its middle. It stood 26 ft tall, possessed an effective range of 17 miles and carried a warhead of 675 pounds. It was highly sophisti-

cated and the final version was intended to have an infra-red homing device and a self-contained guidance system. Of the 45 test firings only 12 were successful and much work remained to be done at the close of the war. Developed from the '*Wasserfall*' was the

Sinking of the Roma

'*Taifun*' (Typhoon) barrage rocket. It was only six ft tall and, having no guidance system, was designed merely to keep the Allied bombers at bay. It, too, only reached the development stage.

There were also several rockets designed to be fired from aircraft. The BV143 and BV246 were anti-ship missiles which were intended to be dropped from aircraft to within 10 ft of the surface of the sea and then fly, wavehopping to their targets, guided by a number of differing homing devices. The 143 was 20 ft long and had a range of 10 miles, while the 246 was only 11 ft long with a slightly greater range. However good the idea might have been on paper it did not work out well in practice, and the project was scrapped. The SD1400 '*Fritz X*' was a similar weapon. There were several versions, all radio-controlled, 15 ft long, and carrying a 3300 pound warhead. The aimer situated in the aircraft could direct the '*Fritz*' by means of a joy-stick control and a bright tracking flare situated in the missile's tail. It was not a particularly efficient weapon but it did achieve the famous sinking of the battleship *Roma*. Its successor was the X4, a 6⅔ ft long missile guided by pulses sent along a wire unspooled from the wing tip (there was a similar weapon intended for land use, the X7). Also a number of glide bombs were designed by Henschel. The Hs293, the world's first guided missile, was in many ways a miniature aircraft, 12 ft long, carrying a 1100 pound warhead. It was radio controlled and relied on its rocket motor and its gliding capabilities to reach the target. It was used mainly against lightly-armed ships and

Left: Take-off of the rocket '*Enzian*', in June 1944.
Below: The Waterfall rocket, launched from Peenemuende in autumn 1944. It was with such anti-aircraft rockets that the *Reich*'s air defence could have proved invulnerable.

In the struggle to make the most of
their scientific developments, the
Germans even made use of their
U-boats as rocket platforms.
Above: A sea-to-surface rocket
launched from a submerged IX C
Class U-boat.

Right: Crew members placing
rockets in their launching frames
before firing. Designed for
concentrated bombardment, rockets
used in this manner were not the
success that the *Reich* had hoped
they might prove.

Above: The Me163 rocket-powered
plane, one of the few unconventional
designs which actually flew and saw
action. It did not, however, do well
in combat to the relief of the Allies.

Right: The Adder, a man-guided
rocket designed to blast the Allied
bombers out of the sky. None of
these rockets were used and
many deaths resulted from tests.

Above: An underground assembly plant for the He162, the 'People's Fighter'. A unique development in research, it took just three months for conception, design and first flight.

merchantmen, and in this rôle was relatively successful. The Hs294 was designed to shed its wings at the end of its journey and continue as an acoustic-homing torpedo to its target. Other Henschel projects were begun but never completed.

Germany's researchers also utilised rocket propulsion in their aircraft designs. Most notable was the Messerschmidt 163 'Komet', which was an audacious concept and incorporated some remarkable design innovations. It was a short, stubby, delta-shaped plane powered by a liquid-fuelled rocket motor at its rear. Upon take-off its undercarriage

A manned rocket bomb

dropped off to allow the proper aerodynamic forces to come into play around its structure and landing was done on skids. The Me163 flew well, reached a top speed of 593 mph, and could climb at over 10,000 ft per minute. The first test flight took place in May 1941 and the first production Me163 entered the *Luftwaffe* three years later. But despite its promise, the aircraft did not do well in combat. This was owing to a combination of its high speed and poor armament. By the end only 279 'Komets' had been produced, manufacture ending in February 1945.

An improved design resulted in the Me263. Although it never reached test flight stage it was a plane of evident good qualities. Its projected maximum speed was 620 mph, and its rate of climb was 49,000 ft in only three minutes.

Lastly, there also existed the Bachem 8-349 A1 'Natter' (Adder), a novel answer to the problem posed by the Allied bombers. It was a rocket powered aeroplane of the simplest and cheapest design which was launched vertically and which was heavily armed with rockets. It was to be sent right into the Allied bomber formations at a maximum speed of some 500 mph and, after having shot down as many aircraft as possible, the pilot would bale out. He and the *Natter* would then be recovered. Work began in late 1944, but none were ever used against the Allies, and the only manned test flight ended in complete failure.

Just as in rocketry, Germany led the world in jet aircraft research. But the saga of the development of the Reich's jets has been considered by historians as one of the great 'might-have-beens' of the war, as a lost opportunity which sealed the fate of the *Luftwaffe* and gave to the Allies undisputed mastery of the skies over Germany. For many it is the 'cause célèbre' of faulty planning, official apathy and downright ignorance adversely affecting promising research. But was this so?

Certainly at the beginning, Germany's leaders failed to grasp the immense significance of the jet engine. It was indeed a German, Professor Ernst Heinkel, who was the first man to take steps to overcome the limitations of the conventional driven aircraft. On August 27, 1939 his He178, the world's first jet aircraft, took to the air and eight weeks later, in front of senior *Luft-*

Research into jets

waffe personnel, it reached a speed of 510 mph. But this failed to impress the officials, included amongst whom was General Udet, the influential chief of aircraft procurement and supply. He remained sceptical of the military value of this revolutionary development till his suicide in November 1941. Thus no official support was given to jet research in these vital early years, and Heinkel was left to continue research on his own. To his credit he did so undaunted, and in April 1941 his He280 twin engine jet prototype flew for the first time.

By the spring of 1942, Heinkel believed that the He280, which had a maximum speed of 497 mph , was ready for series production, but the *Luftwaffe* High Command did not agree. Further tests continued and, fitted with two Jumo 004's, the He280 reached 509 mph. But in March 1943 Heinkel was ordered to discontinue work on the plane, the *Luftwaffe* having decided to concentrate on the Me262. It has been argued that this was a lost opportunity for an early introduction of a jet aircraft into service. However in many ways, especially in range, the He280 was inferior to the Me262, and production delay would have ensued from its turbo-jets.

At his own expense and initiative, Professor Willy Messerschmidt began research into his Me262 at the end of 1938, and it was not until March 1940 that the *Luftwaffe* gave him a development contract for three prototypes. On June 18, 1942, the plane made its first jet powered flight, and successful tests continued until well into the next year. But still the *Luftwaffe* High Command failed to grasp the full implications of the weapon. Even Udet's successor, Erhard Milch displayed little enthusiasm at first, and even as late as October 1942 the *Luftwaffe* considered preparations for series production of the plane to be premature.

However in mid-1943 the situation changed. Firstly the General of the Fighter Arm, Adolf Galland, flew the Me262 and pronounced it a 'tremendous stroke of fortune for us', then Hermann Göring saw, and was impressed by the jet and finally, in June, it was decided to release the plane for series

production 'because of its superior speed as well as its many other qualities'. Even then, the *Luftwaffe* envisaged the production of only 60 a month from May 1944. This, however, was optimistic, and a certain amount of continued official apathy and scepticism resulted in the following response from the head of the Fighter Staff, Otto Saur: '. . . we deserve to be soundly reproached. . . We simply assumed that we would have a goodly number of machines available for rigorous testing by January or February; we assumed that we would produce at least 30-40 during March, 60 per month by May, and soon thereafter 75-80 per month. It is now June and we do not have one single machine [in operational service]. We have only ourselves to blame—we were incapable of finding the necessary resources, incapable of concentrating our efforts, and incapable of approaching the problem with the energy and determination warranted by its vital importance.'

All this is true. There was indeed bad planning (as exemplified by Hitler's misguided order that the Me262 be developed as a jet bomber and not as a jet fighter) and inexcusable apathy, but these factors did not in fact delay the jet's introduction. Even if Hitler himself had been at the production line in order to speed the project along, the Me262 would not have been ready any sooner than it was. For of all the components which went to make up the plane, none were more important than the jet engines. Work on these (the Junkers 044 turbine) had begun in late 1939 and was continued until June 1944 when they were put into series production. Tests and modifications to such a revolutionary engine must of necessity take a long time, and the Jumo 004 was no exception. Even by mid 1944 it was still considered insufficiently developed, and certainly it was not until then that the engine was advanced enough to go onto the production line. Because of this, it is the consensus of opinion of all those who worked on the project that the Me262 was introduced into service as soon as was practicable. Therefore any amount of enthusiasm on the part of Germany's leaders could not have materially affected the outcome. The Me262 was simply too late.

However, German research had managed to produce the first jet aircraft to see combat, and thus claims a unique position in aviation history. The Me262 itself was a good aircraft. Its maximum speed was 540 mph which far exceeded that of contemporary conventional aircraft, as did its weight of fire. It was a tragedy for the *Luftwaffe* that only 200 Me262's (out of 2000 produced) ever fired their guns in anger.

Another remarkable development was the Heinkel 162, the Peoples' Fighter (*Volksjaeger*), which was conceived, designed and flown within three months—surely the shortest time ever for any plane. The order for a simple and cheaply produced yet effective jet fighter was given to Heinkel in September 1944; in December the first prototype was flown successfully and in February 1945 the He162 was in series production. A monthly output of 2000 machines was aimed at. There were to be no half-

measures here.

The configuration of the He162 was remarkably similar to that of the V1 flying bomb. Its back-mounted turbo-jet, while it made for ease of production, caused the plane to be somewhat unstable around its longitudinal axis and therefore in need of careful handling by the pilot. Its maximum speed was 562 mph.

Whatever potential the He162 might have had as a 'miracle plane' flown by legions of

Too late to see action

semi-trained Hitler Youth pilots (as such it would have probably been suicidal) which would have sweep the Allies from the skies of Germany (Goering's original idea), it was too late to see action. Only 120 had been accepted by the *Luftwaffe* by the end of the war.

The only other jet propelled plane to enter into service was the Arado 234 'Blitz', the first operational jet bomber. Work on the planes began in late 1940, the first prototype was flown in June 1943, and the first Ar234 entered into service a little over a year later. It proved itself to be a fairly handy aircraft, but only 210 were ever completed. Powered by two Jumo 004 engines, its maximum speed was 461 mph and it could carry a 3300 lb bomb load. The Ar234's most noted action was the bombing of the Remagen bridge.

Other plans for jet aircraft abounded. Perhaps the most ambitious was the Junkers 287, which was designed to possess higher speeds than any Allied fighter interceptor. A radically new design was the end-result, for the Ju287-VI had swept-forward wings built into a He177A airframe, and was powered by four Jumo 004 engines, two under the wings and two either side and below the cockpit. The prototype reached a maximum speed of 404 mph. More impressive was the designer's estimated figures for the projected V3 version, which, powered by six turbojets, would reach a top speed of 537 mph.

The *Blohm und Voss* P202 was a projected jet powered by two Jumo 004s which had wings which swivelled on the centre line of the fuselage over an angle of 35°. The left wing would lead in the configuration during high speed flight. Another, the Messerschmidt P1102 project, was a swing-wing bomber powered by three turbo-jets. The Junkers EF09 was a jet vertical takeoff fighter, as was the Focke-Wulf *Triebfluegel* which was to have multi-directional jets. Such was the inventiveness of the Third *Reich*'s researchers.

Suggested reading
Robert Jungk: **Brighter than a Thousand Suns** (Gollanz & Hart Davies, 1958)
David Irving: **The Mare's Nest** (William Kimber, 1965)
R. Lusar: **German Secret Weapons of the Second World War** (Spearman, 1963)
L. Simon: **German Research in World War II** (Chapman & Hall, 1959)
Brian Ford: **German Secret Weapons: Blueprint for Mars** (Ballantine, 1969)
David Irving: **The Virus House** (William Kimber, 1967)

Nazi Political Warfare— persuasion and subversion

Vlassov reviews German-uniformed Russians.

Professor Donald Watt

The political warfare waged by Nazi Germany, like everything else in the 12 years of Adolf Hitler's personal rule, was an imperfect amalgam of practices. Hitler dominated this field as all others but his behaviour suggests that, despite his belief in the effectiveness of British propaganda in destroying German morale in World War I, he regarded the employment of political warfare methods as a substitute for military force, to be used only when adequate force was not available.

Of the main branches of political warfare, propaganda, subversion, clandestine intelligence gathering and sabotage ('dirty tricks'), Hitler understood the first, practised the second (though the 'Fifth Column' was very largely fantasy), was not particularly interested in the third (though the SS were) and employed the last only on a tactical level. As a practitioner of political warfare, he had an uncanny sense of timing and for the kind of approach to which his opponents were most vulnerable; but he was a clumsy executant. The greatest failure of Nazi political warfare was in the Soviet Union, where racial contempt and extermination by Germans made the arousal of Russian anti-Soviet feeling almost impossible.

Above: Walter Schellenberg, energetic head of the Foreign Intelligence Service.
Below: Hitler with the Croatian puppet leader, Dr Pavelic, in 1942.

Left: A poster recruiting Belgians for the *Waffen* SS. Efforts were made to form 'foreign' legions.

Right: Volunteers for the Spanish Blue Legion on train for the Russian front. This unit rendered valuable service and provided excellent propaganda material.

WALLONIE
Viens à nous!
SS Division blindée - WALLONIE

Nazi Political Warfare — persuasion and subversion

Nazi Political Warfare

> *War has two aspects – the military and the political. Both are indispensable to each other, and this is a lesson which our opponents have failed to grasp. While the armed forces tear at the fabric of the enemy, political warfare eats away at his heart, mind and soul . . . . . Political warfare must aim at the total corruption of the body politic.*

> *It is foolish to enter upon a war without first having taken steps to ensure that the enemy's political machine, his will to resist, is seriously undermined. It must be rendered inoperative by continuous attacks upon it by all means – propaganda, force, and so-called diplomacy.*

Adolf Hitler 1938 & 1941

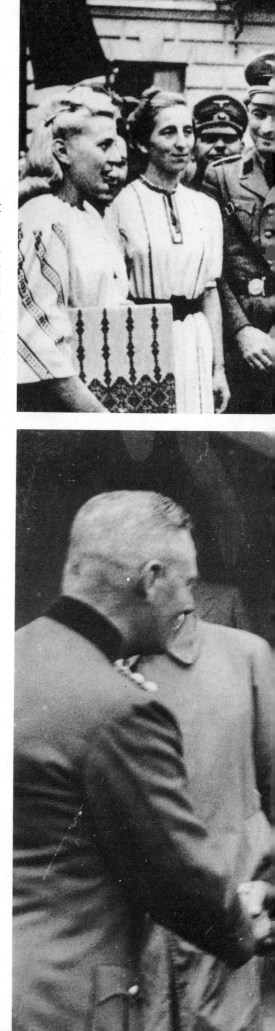

Political warfare (or psychological warfare in American parlance) is a term coined during World War II for direct assault by non-military means on the morale of the enemy. Its main weapons are sabotage, subversion and propaganda of different kinds. It employs non-military means in the sense that large formations of army, navy or air force personnel are not involved. It does not however exclude commando raids, irregular warfare, support of guerrilla or partisan bands, the fomentation of discontent, mutiny or rebellion among the forces or civilian population of the enemy and his allies. It can be used in time of peace as well as in time of war. It can aim at a *coup d'état* which will overturn an inimical government as much as at a rebellion or civil war. It was an essential part of the technique by which Hitler acquired Austria and the Sudetenland in 1938, occupied Prague and the Memelland in 1939 and fomented conflict with Poland over the Free City of Danzig, just as it was a part of his military victory over Poland and his conquest of Norway, Denmark, the Netherlands, Belgium, France and Jugoslavia. He does not appear to have used it against Greece and only to a limited extent against Britain in 1940-41, and then unsuccessfully in the Middle East. He used it against the United States and the Soviet Union, with very limited success in the first case, while in the second he refused to avail himself of the real weapons at his disposal despite the

Clandestine subsidies

urging of his military advisers; he did use it however as part of the means by which he secured the support of Finnish, Baltic, Slovak, Romanian, Hungarian, Italian and Spanish forces on the Eastern Front.

From this it will be clear that an account of Hitler's use of political warfare must be to some extent an account of the entire German effort in World War II and its antecedents, something we have altogether too little space for here. What is needed however is a little more analysis of the nature of Nazi political warfare, some account of its particular institutions and weapons and an estimate of the reasons for its success or failure.

When Hitler came to power on January 30, 1933, he inherited a military machine that had accustomed itself to the idea of political warfare from World War I, and had devel-

oped a number of the necessary institutions. A considerable effort had gone into subversive work against Germany's enemies during World War I, especially against Czarist Russia and the British Empire in the Middle East and in Ireland. German clandestine subsidies had encouraged the subject nationalities of the Russian empire from Finland and the Baltic republics through Poland and the Cossacks of the Ukraine to the Georgians of the Caucasus. A German mission had been active among the tribes of Iran attempting to turn them against the British-owned oil wells of Abadan. Contacts had been made with the tribes of Afghanistan and the Ottoman Empire had been encouraged in its attempts to raise a Holy War against Britain and France. When the first

Espionage intelligence

Russian revolution came in March 1917 Germany had smuggled Lenin and his closest followers from their exile in Switzerland to St Petersburg and German money had kept the Bolshevik cause going in its blackest moments in the summer of that year. Germany had backed Sir Roger Casement in his attempts to raise an army among the Irish prisoners of war and a German submarine had ferried him to Ireland.

In propaganda and the acquisition of clandestine information however the Germans had been a long way second to Britain. British propaganda was credited with a large part of the responsibility for the American entry into the war and with the collapse of morale on the home front in the Austro-Hungarian and German empires. And Germany was a long way second to Britain in the effective use of espionage and intelligence gathering generally.

The vast bulk of this political warfare had been carried out by the German foreign ministry and by the appropriate sections of the army and navy. After the collapse of Germany and the concurrent collapse of the Ukrainian and Don Cossack states in the face of the Red Army, the only parts of this clandestine warfare apparatus that were kept

Right: Hitler introducing Chamberlain to General Keitel, in 1938. During the pre-war years Hitler, in his own words, was 'able to run rings around the foreigners'.

Above: Heads of the Nazi Police and Secret Service meet – Heinrich Muller, Gestapo Chief, with Reinhard Heydrich, Head of the *Reich* Security Service.

The Nazi Governor of Poland meets Ukrainian women.

in being were the military intelligence contacts with the Ukrainian and Cossack exiles, and the similar contacts established during the war with Flemish nationalists in Belgium and with Bretons in France. At the same time the terms of the Treaty of Versailles opened a whole new area of clandestine activity in its creation of large German and other discontented minorities throughout eastern Europe. German minorities existed in Eupen-Malmédy in Belgium, in the Italian South Tyrol, in northern and central Yugoslavia, in the now Romanian province of Transylvania, in the Czech Sudeten provinces, in Polish Silesia and the Corridor, in the League of Nations territories of the Saar and Danzig, in Lithuanian Memel, in South African South West Africa and in Danish Schleswig. In all these territories strong nationalist economic pressures were to develop to bear down and destroy the economic institutions of these German minorities, to break the cohesion of the German communities and to force their members off the land. In the mid 1920s therefore, the Foreign Ministry developed an undercover financial network to pump German money into these agencies and keep them alive and flourishing.

During the 1920s also the various German intelligence agencies were rationalised and combined. As Hitler was taking power this process was just ending. Official propaganda was concentrated in the hands of the press and political archive sections of the Foreign

Overpage: 'You have the key to the camps, French workers, liberate the prisoners by working in Germany.' An exhortation to Frenchmen to work for the Nazis, which, it was alleged, would ensure the freedom of prisoners of war from the camps. This was a bogus promise. What releases there were, were made on other grounds. Posters were used, like any propaganda, as much to undermine the confidence of the enemy as to gain what advantages the Nazis could from the resources of the enemy – such as manpower.

Ministry, whence a ceaseless campaign was waged against the War Guilt clauses of Versailles. Here too the work of a number of private 'grey propaganda' agencies, such as the *Wirtschaftspolitische Gesellschaft* (Economic Political Association) was co-ordinated. Clandestine intelligence gathering and the machinery for subversion and sabotage was concentrated in the *Abwehr*, a joint military naval intelligence service under the Ministry of Defence. Interception and cryptography was concentrated in a new agency, the *Forschungsamt* (Research Office), which, in order to keep it out of the hands of the extreme Nazis, was attached to Goering's staff in the newly created German air ministry.

To this existing machinery Hitler brought five new elements: first, personal charismatic leadership to replace impersonal patriotism as a centre for nationalist sentiment; second, an enormously strong belief in the importance of propaganda; third, contact with a network of extreme German nationalists and Nazis among the German minorities abroad; fourth, an equally strong pull on right wing anti-Bolshevist and anti-semitic movements, especially in the non-Catholic or ex-Catholic areas of Europe, coupled with a special appeal to those extreme nationalist movements who also thought of themselves as 'Aryan'; fifth,

SS propaganda activities

a contempt for officialdom and a method of government that encouraged the proliferation of differing and rival agencies of a party character, which he used or threw to one side according to their own effectiveness in particular cases.

This last element is the explanation for the difficulty one has in always elucidating what the main line in German propaganda or political warfare was at any one time. Thus in 1933 propaganda abroad was officially taken away from the Foreign Ministry and put into the hands of Goebbels' newly founded Ministry of Propaganda. In practice however the organisation of measures to win support abroad for Germany, the distribution of propaganda materials, the use of money to secure outlets for German views and so on continued in most cases to be organised by the German embassies abroad, to some of which, though by no means all, attachés sent from the Ministry of Propaganda were attached, while in others the critical figure was the press attaché reporting to the press department of the Foreign Ministry. As the SS strength grew, so it began to intervene in propaganda activities abroad, while under von Ribbentrop, who became Foreign

Top: Rauter, Security Chief in the Netherlands, reviewing his men. They were responsible for the suppression of opposition and for political warfare.

Right: Mussolini and rescuers after Skorzeny's rescue of the Italian in 1944.

Minister in 1938, a very large part of the responsibility for propaganda abroad was officially recovered by the Foreign Ministry.

In much the same way the conduct of subversive activities against specific governments became disputed between a number of different agencies. Where support was given to local Nazi or crypto-Nazi parties, it might be given from the German Embassy, as was, for example, the clandestine financing of Konrad Henlein's Sudeten German party in Czechoslovakia. It could be given through various Nazi party organisations of which the *Auslandsorganisation* (Foreign Organisation) of the Nazi Party was the official body. It could be placed in the hands of some *ad hoc* representative of Hitler's own staff, as the

The Secret Service

organisation and control of pressure on the Austrian government was placed in the hands, firstly of Theo Habicht as Gauleiter for Austria, and later of Wilhelm Keppler. It could be assumed by the SS whose *Volksdeutsche Mittelstelle* (Liaison Office for German Minorities abroad) was charged with the fomentation of trouble in the rump of Czechoslovakia after Munich. It might remain in the hands of the Army High Command or the *Abwehr* as, for example, the recruitment of 'free Russian forces' after 1941 was lodged with the Army while relations with Flemish or Breton nationalists remained with the *Abwehr*.

The outbreak of World War II complicated matters still further by multiplying the number of intelligence agencies. Ribbentrop's Foreign Ministry, the separate German armed services, the SS and even the Post Office (which succeeded in 'unscrambling' Churchill's coded transatlantic telephone conversations with President Roosevelt and giving advance warning of Italy's capitulation to the Allies) all entered the decipherment and interception business. The position of the *Abwehr* was challenged and its rôle finally taken over in most respects by the *Sicherheitsdienst* (the Security Service) of the SS, metamorphosed as it were under Himmler into the *Reichssicherheitshauptamt* (the Reich Security Main Office). Walther Schellenberg was the driving force in this enterprise, once he had made his reputation by kidnapping the heads of the British Secret Service in the Netherlands across the Dutch frontier at Venlo in November 1939.

Theoretically the various Nazi organisations had entirely separate rôles. The *Aussenpolitisches Amt der NSDAP* (the Foreign

Overpage: A poster attempting to recruit *Waffen* SS volunteers in the fight against Jewish-dominated England. This provides a good example of the Nazi attempt to coordinate its subject nations in the continuing struggle of the Fatherland. These attempts met with little success, however, due in no small way to their repressive policies. In Russia, too, the reality of repression countered Nazi attempts to win-over the population.

Policy Office of the Nazi Party) advised on and conducted party foreign policy, and relations between the party and foreign political figures. Its head was Alfred Rosenberg, the Baltic German, who was regarded as the party's main philosopher. The *Auslandsorganisation* (AO) controlled, organised and supervised all Nazi party organisation among German citizens abroad, with branches from San Francisco to Shanghai. Relations with German minorities abroad were the responsibility of the *Verein des Deutschtums im Ausland* (Union for Germans Abroad) until its supercession by the *Volksdeutsche Mittelstelle* in 1937. Advice on foreign policy and a part in negotiation with

Sabotage attacks

foreign statesmen conducted by the office of the Fuehrer and of his deputy was conducted by Joachim von Ribbentrop and his *Dienstelle von Ribbentrop* (Office Ribbentrop) up to 1938 and his appointment as Foreign Minister.

In practice, of course, where a particular office succeeded in taking an initiative successfully, there it tended to stick irrespective of any theoretical disqualification; distinctions between the party, the offices of the party leader and his deputy and the official organs of the state became difficult to maintain when the party was the state, its leader the Chancellor and head of state. Thus it was Rosenberg who acted as the intermediary between Hitler and Vidkun Quisling, the Norwegian leader whose treasonable actions played so large a part in the occupation of Norway. It was von Ribbentrop who negotiated the Anglo-German Naval Agreement and the anti-Comintern pact with Japan; the original Axis agreements with Italy were the reply of the Foreign Ministry. Relations with General Franco, leader of the insurgent Spanish nationalist military and subsequently *El Caudillo*, were conducted in part through the AO, the head of whose branch in Spanish Morocco intervened at the opening of the Spanish Civil War to secure German arms and aircraft for Franco's forces and partly through Admiral Canares, head of the *Abwehr*, whose Spanish political connections dated back to the 1914-18 war.

Political warfare and subversion played a large part in Hitler's successful expansion of power before 1939. In the case of Austria, the initial phase which culminated in the abortive coup of July 1934 in which a group of Austrian Nazis attempted to seize power in Vienna and assassinated the Austrian Chancellor, Engelbert Dolfuss, was led by Theo Habicht, appointed *Gauleiter* (Provincial Leader) of Austria in 1933. He organised violent radio propaganda attacks by the German radio in Munich against the Austrian government. He incited members of the Austrian Nazi party to sabotage attacks, mainly with bombs, against offices of the Austrian provincial governments and the principal Austrian political party. He organised an Austrian stormtroop legion among those who sought refuge in Germany once the Austrian police had got on to their terrorist activities. He certainly had a hand

in the coup. With its failure his rôle came to an end. A press truce and a Gentlemen's Agreement between Germany and Austria were signed in 1936.

The second phase which was to end with the annexation of Austria under threat of invasion in March 1938 involved pressure on the new Austrian Chancellor to take into his government representatives of the so-called neutral opposition, that is ultra right wing Austrian political figures who lacked any overt Nazi connections but were in fact last-ditch supporters of an Austrian union with Germany and Hitler. The strategy involved keeping the Austrian Nazis under strict discipline and control, the job given to Hitler's personal representative, Wilhelm Keppler. It was the discovery by the Austrian police that the Austrian Nazis resentment of Keppler's control had led to their drafting plans for another coup which led to the series of events which ended in the replacement of Schusnigg by the crypto-Nazi Seyss-Inquart, under extreme military threats from Berlin, the inviting in of German troops and Hitler's proclamation of Austria's annexation to Germany.

The course of pressure on Czechoslovakia which resulted in the Munich conference of September 1938 was much more carefully organised at first. Henlein was ordered to advance demands for autonomy for the Sudeten German minority in Czechoslovakia that would be too severe for the Czech government to concede. In his initial planning Hitler saw Henlein's rôle as the creation of a dispute which he, Hitler, could utilize to provide an occasion which, together with a carefully organised incident (the assassination of the German minister in Prague was discussed), would provide an excuse for the conquest of all Czechoslovakia in a sudden all out military attack. In the event, his

Sell-out at Munich

handling of the situation was inept, his own propaganda assaults on the Czech government so violent that, driven by the imperative desire to avoid war, the British premier, Neville Chamberlain, aided and abetted by Mussolini, compelled the Czechs to cede the Sudetenland to him at the Munich conference. His desire for war was thwarted and he was forced to organise a second political campaign against the Czechoslovak state by inciting the Slovak and Ruthene separatists and the German minority. As an exercise in political warfare it was ineptly handled, and Hitler was forced, as against Austria, to substitute open military threat for clandestine political warfare. Under threat the Czech president was forced to invite the Fuehrer to make the Czech provinces a German protectorate, and the Slovak leaders forced to ask for independence under German leadership. The unhappy Ruthenes were abandoned to the mercies of Hungary who

Right: **The occupation of Austria and the politicians behind it. Goering talks to Seyss Inquart, the former Austrian Minister of the Interior, on this occasion wearing SS uniform.**

annexed the Ruthene areas after a day of independence.

Against Poland the campaign was more carefully orchestrated. Hitler made serious and lengthy efforts to persuade the Polish government to meet his desires in the matter of Danzig and the Polish Corridor, ignoring a prolonged and savage campaign against the German minority in western Poland. When Polish intransigence thwarted his hope of negotiation, pressure began through the newspapers of the German country areas bordering on Poland who were for the first time freed of censorship to write of Polish persecution of the German minority. Thereafter Hitler employed three means of pressure. Trouble was incited among the German minority in Poland by agents of Himmler's SD. The government of the Free City of

Making a fake attack

Danzig, which was completely Nazi, were incited into a conflict with Poland over the Polish customs inspectors in Danzig. And as the final stage in the preparations for attack on Poland an SD unit faked a 'Polish' attack on the German radio station at Gleiwitz, complete with corpses (of concentration camp inmates) in Polish uniform. This was intended to provide the occasion for the German assault on Poland, originally timed for four o'clock in the morning on August 26, 1939. Hitler countermanded his orders for the attack too late to prevent the 'incident' from being staged. In the meantime Hitler's own speeches and the German press raged over Polish 'atrocities' against the German minority in Poland and the German Foreign Ministry produced a White Book of diplomatic correspondence, much of it faked, on these atrocities to follow with the declaration

Left: **Soldiers from a propaganda company showing foreign journalists a faked Polish atrocity. Like the attack on the Gleiwitz radio station, such fakes often used the bodies of concentration camp victims.**

of war.

In the German assault on Poland itself *Abwehr* units played their part ahead of the main German forces in sabotage and guerrilla activities, some in civilian clothes, some in Polish uniforms. One unit acted on August 25, before the countermanding orders could be issued, occupying the Jablonka pass in Southern Poland and holding out for some days against the Polish frontier troops. Others acted to prevent Polish 'scorched earth' measures being applied in Polish Silesia's industrial and mining areas. One unit organised among the German minority even captured the town of Kattowitz from the Poles before the regular German troops arrived.

The conquest of Poland was followed by a new intrusion by the German Foreign Ministry into the field of political warfare. In this case the action was led by a special section formed in the archive department of the Foreign Ministry. This had first intervened as a force in German propaganda against the War Guilt clauses of the Treaty of Versailles in the 1920s, pioneering the selective publication of diplomatic documents with the enormous series, *Die internationale Politik der Europaeische Maechte*, and allowing selected foreign historians known to be sympathetically disposed to Germany access to files from which material casting doubt on the German case had, unbeknownst to them, been carefully removed. It now developed a unit under Dr Fritz Berber, head of the once independent German Institute for Foreign Policy, to screen the captured archives of the Czechoslovak and Polish governments and to publish white books showing or purporting to show the war guilt of the conquered and the support they enjoyed from allegedly neutral governments such as that of the United States. Their activities were later extended to Belgian, Norwegian and French archives. Their two most successful publications were the so-called second *Polish White Book* which threw allegations against Roosevelt and his diplomatists and the *Secret Archives of the French General Staff* which published material on French military schemes to bomb Russian oil fields from bases in Turkey. Other damaging material on Czech subsidies of British and French journalists passed

The Nazi's Trojan Horse

largely unnoticed in the later years of the war.

The German military conquest of Poland, Norway and the Netherlands gave rise to an enormous mythology about the German 'fifth column', a phrase dating from a remark allegedly made by the Spanish nationalist general Mola in the early days of the Spanish Civil War. He had, he was alleged to have said, four columns marching on Madrid, held by Spanish Republican forces. But the real assault would be opened by the fifth column which, so he was alleged to have continued, was already in Madrid, spies, saboteurs, defeatists, a Trojan Horse already within the city's walls. The phrase was made enormous use of by Spanish left-wing

Republican propaganda to justify counter-measures against alleged pro-Franco sympathisers. In the circumstances of 1940, with the sudden overwhelming collapse of all western Europe, save only Britain, the overwhelming power and universal presence of the Nazi fifth column, spies, saboteurs, sympathisers, special operations troops caught the public imagination with contagious collective hysteria. The typical fifth columnist was pictured either as a German agent planted years before Hitler came to power or as a parachutist disguised as a civilian, usually as a nun. The British interned all enemy aliens above the age of 16, the overwhelming majority of them being Jewish refugees from

Tentacles of conspiracy

Nazism, and rounded up those who had supported the various British Nazi and Fascist organisations. The Americans panicked themselves with the chimaera of a Nazi conspiracy spreading its tentacles like an octopus from the Niagara border to Patagonia.

The facts were rather different. Despite the Norwegian Major Quisling's role in inciting Hitler's attention towards Norway, no Norwegian traitors took any part in the German attack on Norway. Some *Abwehr* units in disguise operated in central Norway, perhaps 100 in all. No fifth column played any part in the German conquest of the Netherlands, though in the initial assault on the Dutch frontier, *Abwehr* units in Dutch uniform in some cases had limited success in seizing bridges over strategic water barriers. Parachutists played a more important rôle, but in German uniform, not in disguise. The dropping of dummy parachutists in German uniform was practised both in the Netherlands and in Belgium to add to the demoralisation of the opposing forces and to distract them into searching the rear areas rather than making ready to meet the main German assault. The usual rôle was played by small numbers of *Abwehr* units. In the case of Britain, the United States and Latin America there was no fifth column whatever. The British had eliminated or taken over the entire German espionage network in Britain. In America the pro-Nazi movements were minute and the Nazi '*Bund*' movement organised among German citizens was a total failure. The *Abwehr* were under orders

Vidkun Quisling, on the left, the Norwegian Nazi collaborator, standing next to an SS representative of Himmler on the occasion of the march-past of the first Norwegian volunteer *Waffen* SS unit in October 1941. Outside of Germany, National Socialism was never strong, although collaboration with the Germans was often more extensive than some have since cared to admit. Quisling was probably the most notorious of all the collaborators and his name became associated with collaboration to the extent that it became common to talk in terms of 'a Quisling'.

Above: French recruits entering the barracks of the French Legion. As the banner states, the Legion was dedicated to fighting Bolshevism, the factor that was meant to unite many nationalities. The ideals of recruits were often suspect.

Right: French volunteers back from the Eastern front, marching through Paris in 1943. The bemedalled N.C.O. fought for Germany for two years.

to refrain from sabotage in America until after America's entry into the war.

In the German attack on Jugoslavia, fifth column and political warfare measures were more effective. The main target of the German political warfare campaign was the Croats, long opposed to Serbian domination of the state. They failed to support the leading political figure in Croatia, Dr Matchek, who instead of fomenting rebellion called on Croatian reservists to obey orders for mobilisation. But Veesenmayer of the Foreign Ministry encouraged the Croat extremist,

Field Security Police

Pavelic, to proclaim an independent Croatia as soon as the German attack started. Some Croatian units refused to fight. Others even attacked Yugoslav army command posts. German minority members played an active military rôle as in Poland. *Abwehr* units seized crucial positions, bridges and airfields.

At this point it is worth pausing to see how the German political warfare machine had developed during the first two years of warfare. At the tactical level this was governed very much by the development of Himmler's empire, *Reichssicherheitshauptamt*, *Sicherheitsdienst* and SS, by the side of the Army High Command with its *Abwehr*, field security police, radio interception and field radio propaganda units. As an intelligence

Above: Lord Haw Haw, who regularly gave broadcasts from Berlin to the British people. Most laughed at his talks but some were disturbed by them. He was hanged after the war for treason against the Crown.

Left: Dutch SS on parade. Recruits to the SS came from a surprising number of nations overrun by the Germans.

gathering organisation *outside* German occupied territory, the *Abwehr* was only intermittently competent. As an organisation of special operations, its special unit the *Lehrregiment* Brandenburg had a long list of successes. Even here it was about to be challenged by the SS leader, Otto Skorzeny, the man who was to lead the rescue of Mussolini. At the field radio propaganda

Bogus broadcasts

level the Army High Command had scored notable success with the radio campaign against French troops during the Phoney War period, broadcasting in French from stations just across the border. These certainly played a part in the progressive collapse of French army morale even before the German *Blitzkreig* started. The 'black' radio stations, which pretended to be organs of resistance groups within the enemy like the 'New British Broadcasting Company' or the bogus Russian Leninist station run by the German ex-Communists, Thaelmann, Kaspar and Albrecht, came under the Ministry

of Propaganda and had only limited success.

At the strategic level control of political warfare was disputed between the Ministry of Propaganda, the *RHSA*, the Foreign Ministry and the Army High Command. Goebbels retained control over his Ministry, over the media of press, radio and film to the bitter end. The carefully orchestrated attacks of the German press, the foreign language radio broadcasts of, for example, William Joyce, 'Lord Haw Haw', and the Americans, Kaltenbach and Chandler, the superb exploitation of the discovery of the bodies of the Polish officers, murdered at Katyn, which destroyed relations between Russia and the Polish exile government in London, were all Goebbels' work. The Foreign Ministry was responsible for the not altogether ineffective encouragement of isolationism in the United States in 1940 and the employment of George Sylvester Viereck, who played so effective a part in encouraging the activities of the

The biggest challenge

America First Committee. Substantial funds were placed at his disposal.

The Foreign Ministry was equally responsible for the whole mobilisation of right-wing European political leadership behind Hitler's banner in the crusade against 'Bolshevism', the anti-Comintern Pact. They used this treaty organisation, which, since its original signature between Germany and Japan and Italy's accession in November 1937, had been moribund even before the signature of the Nazi-Soviet non-aggression pact of August 1939, as the agency first for binding Hitler's European allies to Germany and then for recruiting their armies to fight alongside the *Wehrmacht* against Russia. Between November 1940 and March 1941 Hungary, Romania, Slovakia and Bulgaria were forced to adhere to the anti-Comintern pact and it was the agreement of the Regent, Prince Paul, of Jugoslavia to follow their example which provoked the overthrow of his government and the seizure of power by the young King Peter in March 1941. When Hitler's forces invaded Russia in June 1941 they were accompanied by Romanians, Hungarians and Slovaks, together with divisions from Spain and Italy and volunteers from Vichy France, from Belgian and Dutch Fascists. The SS in pursuit of the same ideal recruited from Scandinavia, the Netherlands, and from the inhabitants of the independent Baltic republics annexed by the Soviet Union in 1940, Latvians, Estonians and Lithuanians as well as from Bosnia, Albania and the Ukrainian minority in Galicia.

The invasion of Russia presented Germany's political warfare experts with their biggest challenge. It is fair to say that they failed it entirely for all the reasons that made the

Cossacks in German uniform, resting on the Eastern front in 1943. Such units hated their former Soviet masters and provided excellent fighters for the Nazis. Their fate at the end of the war was to be death at the hands of the Russians.

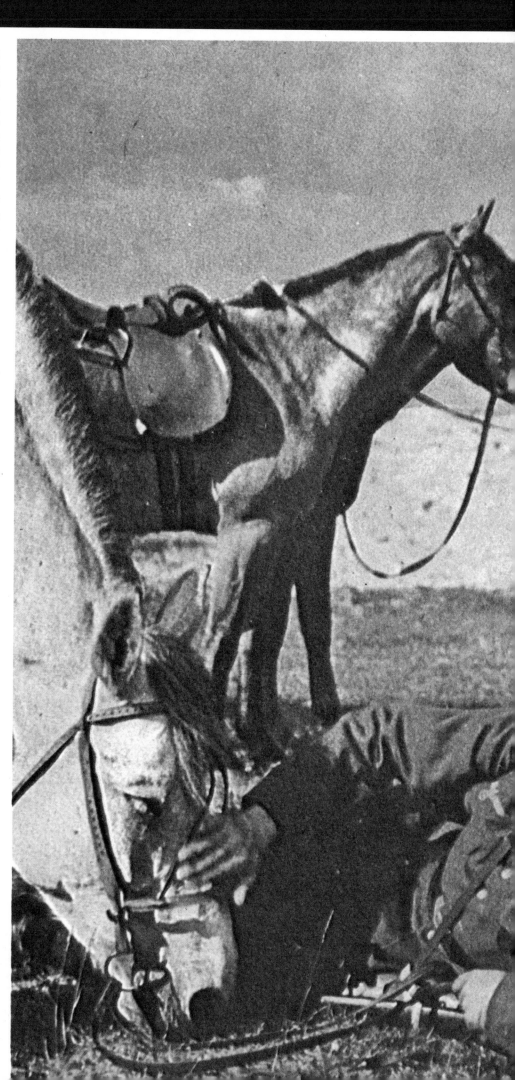

Nazi German war machine so incompetent a military force at the level of high strategy and so obstinate and difficult an enemy on the ground. Political warfare in Russia was governed overall by Hitler. This gave it from the beginning two major weaknesses. Hitler was determined (indeed it was an article of faith with him) to create a German Empire in the East. All who lived there whether Russian, Ukrainians, Cossacks, Georgians, Adzhars, Armenians, Kazaks, Kalmucks, Kughiz, Svanetians, Azerbajanis, Tadjiks, Tartars, Turkestanis, Uzbecks, Ingush, Ossetes, Karachai, Chechens, Balkar-Kamarden or Daghestanis were Slavs in his eyes, fit only to be serfs and bondmen to the new master-race. 'Only the German may bear arms', he declared.

Hitler's second weakness was that political warfare of the kind he had practised between 1935 and 1939-40 was in his eyes a substitute for real force, only to be used when real

Mass surrenders

force was lacking. In 1941-42, he felt more than strong enough to destroy Soviet Russia. It was only after the defeats at Stalingrad and Kursk marked the end of his chances (if not his hopes) of conquering Russia that he began to yield to the urgings of those who wanted to recruit allies for Germany either among Russia's satellite peoples or among Russian anti-Stalinists themselves. Russia was to be stripped of every educated man and every trained official. The courts were to be left behind. It was a war of extermination. Thus ran his address to his generals on March 30, 1941.

The opening phases of the German attack on Russia were greeted by mass surrenders of Soviet troops on a scale which led one eyewitness to call it the second Russian revolution. Between July and December 1941 nearly four million Soviet soldiers surrendered. By the end of the war more than five and a half million prisoners had been taken on the eastern front. Nearly four million of those died in German captivity, the majority of starvation and typhus within six months of their initial capture in the campaigns of 1941. Of the remainder some 80,000 donned some kind of German uniform, rendering themselves liable in 1945 to forced repatriation to the Soviet Labour camps if nothing more, and for many their fate was indeed a lot worse.

Political warfare in Russia was the responsibility of several conflicting agencies. In theory everything in occupied Russia came under Alfred Rosenberg's *Ostministerium* (Ministry of the East) save for the war areas which were under the High Command of the Army, propaganda (disputed between Ribbentrop's Foreign Ministry and Goebbel's Propaganda Ministry), economics which came into dispute between Goering and Sauckel (the plenipotentiary for labour recruitment), and political purges (the SS). In practice Ribbentrop's Foreign Ministry was soon excluded and Goebbel's energies occupied by propaganda *per se* rather than by political warfare in Russia. The real contest lay between Rosenberg, the SS and the High Command of the Army.

All three found themselves faced with the same pair of dilemmas. To do anything they had to fight the policy of extermination and exploitation practised by the SD special commandoes, Sauckel's forced Labour Recruitment measures and the RHSA's treatment of Soviet prisoners of war even after their removal for forced labour purposes to Germany in 1942. To make any positive move they had to decide whether to back the Russians who were still the most numerous and to go hard headed for a Free Russia movement, a kind of Rapallo in exile, or to back the satellite races against Russian nationalism. The two policies were largely exclusive. The Germans tried both.

Support for the subject nationalities came from the beginning from Rosenberg and the *Ostministerium* encouraged as German forces approached the Caucasus and the Caspian by the Foreign Ministry's hopes of enlisting Turkish interest in the Turkic tribes of the Trans-Caspian. For most of 1942 a similar policy was followed by the Army Command which raised batallions of Moslem volunteers originally to be used on sabotage special duties under the *Abwehr* as early as October 1941. In April 1942 so called national legions were raised. In July Army Group B advancing through the area of the Don Cossacks found Cossack units deserting wholesale, and survivors of the Cossack anti-Soviet republic of 1917-18 emerging from hiding to join them. In the rear of Army Group A a self governing Cossack district was set up and a limited autonomy promised. When the German army began its headlong retreat from these areas, after the Stalingrad débâcle, they were accompanied by over 70,000 Cossack fighting men. Rather similar accidents brought thousands of Kuban Cossacks, Kalmucks and mountaineers from the Caucasus

Partisan warfare

back with the German retreat from the Caucasus, 220,000 in all. To these had to be added a further 35,000 from the Crimean Tatars.

While this was going on the German armed forces in central and nothern Russia had been steadily recruiting Russian prisoners of war and deserters as military auxiliaries, drivers, orderlies, stretcher bearers, labourers, interpreters etc. In November 1941 there may have been as many as 200,000 of these. In December 1941, when large scale Partisan warfare began behind the German lines in White Russia, the rear area commanders recruited battalions of these auxiliaries into an anti-partisan militia. The first so-called Russian People's Army was set up under a turncoat Soviet official in a self-governing county near Briansk in 1941. This emboldened the Central Army Group to propose in October 1941 that Smolensk be made the self governing capital of the German occupied area and the centre of recruitment for anti-Soviet forces but Hitler quashed the idea.

The policy which was to lead eventually to the creation of the Russian Freedom Army under General Vlassov began in the *Wehrmacht* propaganda section and had to be fought against Hitler's opposition all the way. Vlassov himself was one of the six Soviet army commanders under Marshal Zhukov defending Moscow in the winter of 1941–42. He fell into German hands as the result of the failure of an attack designed to relieve Leningrad in January 1942, Vlassov having been sent by Stalin to act as deputy to the general commanding the whole Leningrad front and as supervisor of the attack. The attack failed as Vlassov had prophesied, the army making it was cut off by the Germans and Vlassov preferred to stay with his troops which held out until June 1942 rather than return to face Stalin's wrath. He fell into German hands after hiding in disguise for a fortnight and almost immediately proposed a Russian liberation movement, threatening that it would have to lean on Britain and America if Germany would not back it.

The subsequent history of the Vlassov movement is tragic and bloody. Vlassov did not achieve his full aims until November 1944, five months after D Day. Many of the volunteer units had by then been sent to man the coastal fortifications of France against the British and Americans. Indeed the first prisoners of war from those units were already being handed over to Soviet control that very month. Others, including the Cossacks were used in Jugoslavia and Italy where a Kalmuck unit found itself fighting a unit of American-born Japanese, surely the oddest

of the war's many grim ironies. By this date the SS had embraced the idea of a Russian Freedom Army, something Himmler had previously denounced, though the military SS had recruited SS Divisions from the minorities for anti-partisan warfare, especially among the Ukranians. In April 1944, impressed by the success Army-inspired Russian Freedom propaganda was having even then in provoking desertions from the Red Army, Himmler adopted for his own the idea of a pan-European anti-Bolshevik crusade. By September 1944, now in command of the Russian Reserve Army, Himmler was persuaded to meet Vlassov, to authorise the setting up of an all-Russian free government and the combining of all the various free Russian units, plus the various other non-Russian batallions, brigades etc. into a Russian liberation army to consist originally of two divisions. A grand committee for the liberation of the Peoples of Russia was set up in Prague in November 1944. Two divisions were slowly raised, some 50,000 in all from the 800,000 Russian citizens in German uniform. Their only effective action was the part they played in combination with the Czech resistance in 'liberating' Prague from the retreating German troops, a last vain desperate attempt to work their passage back into the good graces of the western allies whom, bemused by Goebbel's propaganda, they believed to be on the verge of war against

their Soviet allies. Like the Turcomen and Cossack troops who had retained their separate existence and all the other Soviet citizens found under German control, whether soldiers, prisoners of war, slave labourers or concentration camp inmates, they were duly handed back to Soviet custody, and in the case of the leaders, Vlassov himself included, to execution. Only those who had fought in the Ukranian SS division escaped repatriation by persuading their British captors that they were Poles.

The failure of German political warfare in Russia to break the hold Stalin maintained on Soviet loyalties, even that Stalin who had terrorised the peasantry of western Russia in the collectivisation programme of the early 1930s and broken the Army leadership in the purges, is always held to be the most flagrant example of the stupidity and wickedness shown in Hitler's management of Germany's war effort. But his propagandists had very little success with their anti-Bolshevik campaign for a European crusade against Bolshevism in Europe. Germany's war aims, as Hitler propounded them, and as Himmler, Speer, Sauckel, Goering and others put them into practice, rested too clearly on the dehumanisation and exploitation of all non-Germans and gave the lie too clearly to the propaganda of Goebbels and the pan-European dreams of the SS theorists. One cannot reasonably expect the alliance and loyalty of those whom one's minions are all too clearly treating as subject peoples. It is the measure of the effectiveness of German political warfare, divided, contradictory, racialist, incompetent as it was, and of the fears aroused by the Stalinist system that so many thousands of ordinary men and women preferred to serve Nazism against Soviet Russia even under the looming shadow of defeat. In the end however Nazi political warfare failed because Germany's armies were defeated. Political warfare can aid the victorious; but it is very rare for it to turn defeat into victory.

Alfred Rosenburg, Minister for the Occupied Eastern Territories, with his deputy, Dr Alfred Meyer.

Suggested reading

Robert Cecil: **The Myth of the Master Race, Alfred Rosenberg and Nazi Ideology** (London, Batsford, 1972)

L. de Jong: **The German Fifth Column in the Second World War**

Gerald Reitlinger: **The House Built on Sand. The Conflicts of German Policy in Russia 1939–1945** (London, Weidenfeld, 1960)

Norman Rich: **Hitler's War Aims, Vol. I Ideology and the Course of Expansion, Vol. II The Establishment of the New Order** (New York, Norton, 1974)

Paul Seabury: **The Wilhelmstrasse. A study of German Diplomacy under the Nazi Regime** (Berkeley, University of California Press, 1954)

D. C. Watts: **Personalities and Policies. Studies in the Formulation of British Foreign Policy in the 20th Century** (London, Longmans Green, 1965, esp. Essay 5, 'Influence from without: German influence on British opinion 1933–1938 and the efforts to counter it'.)

Hitler–
the supreme War Lord

Adolf Hitler plans his campaigns.

Dr William Carr

Had it not been for the horror and brutality of Nazi
rule revealed in all its ghastly detail in the post-war
trials at Nuremberg, Hitler would long ago have taken
his place alongside the other great war leaders of the
mid-twentieth century. It was the horrific extermination
of European Jewry and the – often exaggerated – stories
of his irrational fanaticism and blind rages which made
him appear the exception – an unreal demoniacal figure.
In fact Hitler rose to power in an age of 'great men'
– Roosevelt, Churchill, Stalin, Mussolini – and had much
in common with them. They were all men of stature, charismatic leaders who towered above their fellow men.
In military matters even his bitterest critics among
the German generals grudgingly recognised Hitler's expertise. Certainly Hitler
can claim at least some of
the credit for leading the
German armies from one
spectacular victory to another in a manner unrivalled
since the days of Napoleon.
Yet he also led his armies
to the greatest defeat in
their history at Stalingrad.
Was this his mistake alone?
Or were his advisers also
to blame? Or does the answer lie more in the formidable coalition of major
powers that were gathered
after 1942 for the utter destruction of Nazi tyranny?

Above: Hitler outside Warsaw,
September 1939, viewing *Luftwaffe*
raids on the city.
Below: Visiting troops on the
Western front, 1940, with von
Rundstedt.

Left: Hitler victorious, at the victory
parade after the successful invasion
of Poland.

Right: Hitler studying the map during
the 1942 summer campaign in Russia.
On his right is General Jodl, the
Wehrmacht Chief of Staff.

Hitler—
the supreme
War Lord

I follow in the footsteps of Frederick. He, with Prussia, was Great; I, with Germany, am invincible. There is continual speculation as to where I get my ability as a war leader. It is said, and correctly, that I was only a corporal in the last war. My strength, however, lies in the fact that I have Germany's interests at heart. I know what is good for her people – I sense it. If a general tells me to move an Army here, or there, I know in my own mind what is right. Events have proved that.

Adolf Hitler 1942

Until fairly recently it was fashionable to dismiss Hitler as a mere dilettante in military affairs, the opinionated corporal of the 1914–18 War quite out of his depth as a supreme commander, and a carpet-biting maniac to boot who pulled Germany down to total defeat through his insanely irrational conduct of the war. This unfavourable verdict owed a great deal to the memoirs of certain German generals who rushed into print after the war eager to blame the deceased *Fuehrer* for all that had gone wrong after 1942 whilst claiming full credit on behalf of the army for the earlier successes.

With the return of much captured material to German archives a more accurate and historically credible picture of Hitler the war leader is at last beginning to emerge. It is clear that he did possess at least some of the qualities one expects to find in a supreme commander. Far from being an incorrigible ignoramus, he was in reality exceptionally well informed about and passionately interested in military matters. He had, for example, an astonishing knowledge of weaponry—which he constantly paraded to impress his audience; and he took a lively interest in the development of new weapons —it was Hitler who appreciated the potential significance of armoured and motorised units and pressed for their expansion at a time when most generals were still highly sceptical of *Blitzkrieg* tactics. When war came he soon displayed an exceptional grasp of military strategy and a keen eye for opera-

Celebrated intuition

tional possibilities which greatly impressed even those generals who were hostile to the Nazis and contemptuous of the 'Bohemian corporal'. At his daily military conferences Hitler did not rant and rave all the time as is often supposed. On the contrary; he normally displayed a thorough acquaintance with the immediate tactical situation and argued cogently and persuasively most of the time. Only when all else failed did he fall back on his celebrated 'intuition' and bring further discussion to an abrupt end. Nor can it be denied that he showed remarkable devotion to duty and dogged perseverance in the conduct of the war, a side of his personality too often obscured by the familiar picture of the indolent coffee-house Bohemian who shied away from regular work.

On the other hand, when the tide turned against Germany after 1942 Hitler's weaknesses as a war leader were quickly revealed. The stubborn streak in his character grew more pronounced as he insisted more and more on 'National Socialist fanaticism' as the answer to a deteriorating strategic situation. Permission to retreat in the face of superior enemy forces was not ordinarily granted by a supreme commander who insisted vehemently and with monotonous regularity that will power could and must close the yawning credibility gap between Germany's imperialist ambitions and the capacity of her armed forces to realise these. An elastic defence system was rendered utterly impossible because Hitler saw defeatism and cowardice in every attempt to withdraw to new positions. Towards the end of the war he

Emphasis on armour

became neurotically suspicious of his closest military advisers sensing that they did not share his 'National Socialist' resolve to fight on until 'five minutes after midnight'. Though his quarrels with generals and staff officers have been somewhat exaggerated in the past—one must remember that his reaction varied considerably depending on the individual—there is no doubt that after the July Plot of 1944 Hitler's relations with his advisers were extremely strained—not that it mattered much to the course of the war by then.

After the crucial changes in army command in February 1938 Hitler began at last to exert decisive influence over military strategy. At his insistence stronger emphasis was laid on the build-up of armoured and motorised divisions. During the Munich Crisis he was deeply involved in the detailed preparations for the attack on Czechoslovakia. In the spring of 1939 it was Hitler who took the initiative in ordering plans to be drawn up for the attack on Poland. And on the very eve of war Hitler personally addressed the commanding generals at the Berghof on the ob-

Right: Hitler with his staff in the *Fuehrer* Headquarters, 1939. From left to right, front row: Dietrich, press chief, Keitel, head of *Wehrmacht* High Command, Hitler, Jodl, Bormann, Hitler's pilot Below and Hoffman, Hitler's offical photographer.

jectives of the Polish campaign. But once Germany was at war in September 1939, though Hitler visited the front line daily, he did not interfere in the conduct of operations.

If the generals inferred from this that Hitler would recede gracefully into the background and allow them to determine the grand strategy of the war as Hindenburg and Ludendorff had done before them, they were very quickly disillusioned. On October 9 Hitler ordered plans to be drawn up for an attack on France and the Low Countries in November. The generals were profoundly shocked. They had been perfectly content to remain on the defensive in the west until the 'phoney war' petered out—for they supposed that Britain and France would soon acquiesce in the *fait accompli* and allow Germany to remain master of Eastern Europe. Hitler would have none of it. As *Fuehrer* he claimed the right to determine politico-military strategy. Logically this was an inevitable extension of the totalitarian principle to the military sphere. But in a more profound sense it signified Hitler's resolve to set out on a revolutionary grand strategy which called for the defeat of the west and war against Russia to achieve the imperialist ambitions he had nurtured since the mid-1920s.

In fact the attack in the west did not take place in the autumn of 1939 for several reasons. The generals argued against a new campaign before the army had recovered from the Polish war. Weather reports were adverse. And, finally, a staff officer carrying campaign plans crash-landed in Belgium making postponement of the operation mandatory. Quite certainly Hitler's mounting frustration in the winter of 1939–40 deepened his instinctive dislike of the socially exclusive officer corps and fed his suspicions that behind their technical objections lay a lack of confidence in his judgement and an un-martial desire to avoid further military engagements.

For Germany one good thing came out of the

Time to reconsider

dark winter months: time to reconsider the plan of attack. Drafted hastily and without conviction in October by General Franz Halder, chief of the general staff, the original plan was to attack through Belgium, roll back the Anglo-French armies and secure bases for an air and sea attack on Britain. With time on their hands the high command, army command and Hitler all started to criticise this unimaginative repetition of the Schlieffen Plan of pre-World-War-I days certain to lead to the same kind of slogging match between equally-balanced armies in Northern France. The alternative strategy, the so-called 'Scythe Cut' operation, which led to the most spectacular German

Above: Hitler with his entourage in occupied Paris. On his right is Speer, who gave him a commentary on the architecture of the capital.

Left: Reichsmarschall Hermann Goering, greeting Hitler on his birthday, April 20, 1941.

Overpage: A propaganda poster which declares that 'Adolf Hitler is Victory'. The German people, together with many of their military leaders, believed this until well on into the war. The poster neatly sums up the total domination that Hitler had over the policies of the war.

victory since Sedan, owed at least something to Hitler's nose for tactical possibilities. He sensed, instinctively perhaps, that the Halder Plan would not do. While he was searching around for an alternative, Lieutenant General Erich von Manstein, the brilliant young chief of staff of army group A, managed to catch the *Fuehrer*'s ear with a new plan. The gist of it was to lure the Anglo-French armies into Belgium and Holland by a feint attack in the north and make the main thrust through the wooded Ardennes and across the Meuse towards the Channel ports. Hitler was attracted by the element of surprise and audacity not to say risk in the new plan and finally ordered its adoption.

Before the attack in the west took place Hitler's attention was diverted to Scandinavia. Since the beginning of the war Admiral Erich Raeder, commander-in-chief of the navy, had tried to interest Hitler in the acquisition of Norwegian bases from which to attack the British fleet. This was in effect part of a wider anti-British strategy advocated by naval command since the days of *Tirpitz* and supported by the foreign office. In place of Hitler's anti-French, anti-Russian and pro-British strategy Raeder and Ribbentrop took Germany back to the early years of the century when William II had tried (in vain) to unite the whole of Europe against Britain. At first Hitler showed little interest. Then in January 1940, frustrated by delays in the west and itching for action, he authorised plans for an attack. This would probably have been delayed had it not been for strong—and well founded—rumours that an Anglo-French force was ready to embark for Norway in an attempt to assist the Finns

Operation Yellow

in their last desperate struggle against Russia. Recognising the potential threat to vital Swedish ore supplies on which the German steel industry was still heavily dependent, Hitler decided to attack. On April 9 just 24 hours before British destroyers commenced to mine Norwegian waters, Hitler invaded Denmark and Norway. By the end of the month, after initial setbacks in Norway, both countries were firmly in German hands.

On May 10 'Plan Yellow', the offensive in the west, commenced with Hitler supervising the campaign from a field headquarters at Munstereifel. Everything went according to plan. Von Bock's attack in the north drew the Anglo-French armies into the Low Countries while von Rundstedt's armour, thrusting through the Ardennes forest, had crossed the Meuse by May 14. On May 15 the Dutch armies surrendered. So swift was the advance that Hitler could not believe his good fortune. Fearing a counter-attack from the French armies in the south— a not unreasonable anxiety—he ordered Rundstedt's armour to halt on May 16 until

Hitler talking to wounded servicemen in 1942. His concern for his troops varied from a sentimentality, shown here, to an utter callousness which saw them as no more than numbers on a piece of paper.

the infantry caught up. However, a young corps commander and fervent advocate of dynamic *Blitzkrieg* tactics, General Heinz Guderian, pressed ahead under cover of 'forward reconnaissance' and in defiance of Hitler's orders. On May 20 Guderian had reached Abbeville dragging the German army after him. Thanks to his initiative the

The Master of Europe

risky gamble had succeeded and Hitler quickly ordered the advance to continue.

Four days later a new crisis arose this time with more serious long-term consequences for Germany. The British had been driven back to the coast and German armour was poised for a last victorious thrust when the cautious Rundstedt suddenly halted the advance on May 24 with Hitler's approval. The *Fuehrer* together with Jodl and Keitel believed that Rundstedt was right not to risk his tanks in the unfavourable Flanders terrain when they would be needed to deal with the 65 French divisions still in the field. Goering's intervention was another factor. Anxious to have the honour of finishing off the British, he probably persuaded Hitler

that it was politically wiser to let the *Luftwaffe* have the credit for this rather than Bock and Rundstedt. The 48-hour delay before Hitler ordered the advance to continue on May 26 turned out disastrously for Goering. Bad weather grounded his aircraft and when they did take to the air the British Spitfires proved a match for the Messerschmidt 109s. Meanwhile the British had re-organised their perimeter defences and were able to evacuate 200,000 British and 130,000 French and Belgian troops from Dunkirk. On June 5, the day that port fell, a major German offensive was launched along the Somme. Twelve days later the French sued for an armistice which was signed on May 22 at Compiègne in the railway carriage where the Germans signed their armistice 22 years previously.

Germany was now indisputable master of Europe and the *Fuehrer* was accorded a hero's welcome on his return to Berlin. His reputation stood at its height—the sycophantic Keitel dubbed him the 'greatest commander of all time'. Characteristically, Hitler claimed all the credit for the spectacular victory; without his flair 'Scythe Cut' would not have been adopted and without his drive the campaign would never have been launched. Henceforth he was persuaded that

the infallibility of which he had been long convinced in the political realm extended to military strategy as well. And by and large his generals swallowed their reservations and followed him eagerly—as long as he was winning.

By comparison the 'miracle of Dunkirk' was very small beer. Everyone in Berlin assumed that Britain would accept the inevitable and surrender gracefully. Significantly, Hitler's thoughts were already turning to the acquisition of Lebensraum in the east. For a time he toyed with the possibility of launching a *Blitzkrieg* in the east in the autumn of 1940. In the end he decided reluctantly but rightly that insufficient time remained that year to conquer Russia and postponed the operation until the spring of 1941.

The provisional decision to attack Russia made it all the more essential to eliminate Britain from the war quickly and so nip in the bud any danger of a two-front war situation developing. Thus after Britain's peremptory rejection, on July 22, of Hitler's recent peace offer, the Fuehrer decided, reluctantly perhaps, to attempt an invasion of Britain in the early autumn.

From the start there were grave doubts on the German side about the feasibility of this risky amphibious operation. The army doubted the capacity of the navy to provide adequate cover against the powerful British fleet. And naval command, conscious of severe losses during the Norwegian campaign, shared these doubts. Only Goering remained confident that he could dominate the skies over Britain and so fulfil the essential pre-condition for an invasion.

On August 13, 'Eagle Day', Goering's *Luftwaffe* commenced a major offensive striking at British airfields and radar installations and sought to destroy the RAF in air battles. Whether the attacks would have succeeded had they been pressed home relentlessly it is impossible to say. Whatever chance there might have been of victory—and it was probably slim—was thrown away when Goering suddenly switched the *Luftwaffe* to the bombing of London on September 7 probably in retaliation for an Allied air attack on Berlin. The climax of the Battle of Britain came on September 15, a date long to be remembered in British history, when 60 German aircraft—representing half the total bomber force over London that day—were shot down at the cost of 26 British fighters. By the end of the month Hitler had postponed

'Operation Sealion' until the spring; British sea and air power was obviously unbroken and turbulent weather was in the offing. This was, in fact, the end of the entire enterprise. Looking back at this critical stage in the war it does not seem that any special blame

Franco rebuffs Hitler

attaches to Hitler either for the failure to attack Britain earlier in the summer when Fighter Command was desperately weak or for the failure of the *Luftwaffe* to achieve air mastery over the island. Hitler's advisers shared at least as much of the responsibility for these mistakes.

What then could be done to drive Britain out of the war? For a time Hitler toyed with the peripheral strategy advocated by the navy, the essence of which was to undermine Britain by striking at sensitive points such as Gibraltar and Suez on her lines of communications with her empire. However, this strategy proved no more successful partly because Hitler did not pursue it with his customary ruthlessness and partly because the pawns did not behave as expected. Thus, when General Franco, much impressed by Britain's continued resistance, finally refused to bring Spain into the war Hitler swallowed the rebuff and made no attempt to seize Gibraltar—the key to the Western Mediterranean. By the end of 1940 his plans were upset by the Italians retreating in disorder in North Africa and in deep trouble in Greece which they had attacked in October much to Hitler's annoyance. To help them German troops under General Erwin Rommel were sent to Libya early in 1941. They succeeded, temporarily, in redressing the balance and pushed the British back to the Egyptian borders. But lasting victory was denied the Germans basically because Hitler, unlike Churchill, failed to grasp the importance of the Mediterranean theatre of war. No serious attempt was made to seize Malta—the key to the Eastern Mediterranean. Nor did Hitler concentrate all his efforts on driving the British right out of the Middle East, as Raeder's staff constantly urged him to. Had he done so the Anglo-American landings in Italy in 1943 would scarcely have been possible. All Hitler achieved by committing men and materials to North African campaigns was the dissipation of his own forces. This failure undoubtedly represents a major strategic error on Hitler's part.

Eastward expansion

Long before Rommel's troops landed in Africa Hitler had decided to give absolute priority to eastward expansion. In November 1940 Molotov made it brutally plain during vital conversations in Berlin that the Soviet Union intended in future to concentrate on the Balkans and had no interest whatsoever in diversionary schemes in the Middle East to destroy the British Empire. Any lingering hope Ribbentrop may have had of including Moscow in a vast anti-British front stretching from Madrid to Tokyo was dead. The stiffening Russian attitude and evidence that their

armies were being modernised probably convinced Hitler that the attack on Russia must go ahead even though Britain remained undefeated. Nor did he leave out of his calculations the strong possibility that the Americans would enter the war by 1942. Time was again running out for Germany as Hitler saw it; either she took steps to control the whole of Europe to the Urals while the military balance was in her favour, or she would one day be destroyed by Russia and America combining against her. The risks of waiting appeared infinitely greater than the risk of attacking in the east before the war in the west was over. He even persuaded himself that war in the east was the key to all his problems; Britain, deprived of her last potential ally in Europe, would have to surrender because once Russia was defeated the Americans would face a much greater threat in the Pacific from Japan and would be unable to come to Britain's assistance. If Britain still did not give in then Raeder's plan for a drive through the Middle East toward India might well be adopted. On December 18 Hitler finally decided to attack Russia in the spring of 1941.

The attack was not launched in the spring because of Balkan complications. Continuing Italian difficulties in Greece plus the British occupation of Crete made it imperative for Germany to intervene and remove this growing threat to her flank. Hitler was also anxious to bring Yugoslavia completely within the Axis sphere of influence to safeguard raw material supplies and to prevent Yugoslavian airfields being used to bomb the vital Romanian oil fields. Early in April the last of the successful *Blitzkriege* was launched against Greece and Yugoslavia. By the end of the month both countries were completely crushed; Italy had been rescued from her

Kick in the door

folly; Crete was in German hands; and Germany's flank was secured for Operation Barbarossa.

It is easy enough to blame Hitler for the fatal mistake of attacking Russia. As Germany had no reasonable grounds for expecting a Russian attack, Hitler obviously bears massive responsibility for this act of aggression. Yet in the initial stages his generals were as confident as Hitler that the Russian armies could be easily defeated. No-one appreciated the colossal scale of the logistical problems to be faced in the interior of Russia. And as little information was available about the Russian armies, their strength was grossly underestimated. It was deceptively easy to believe that the Fuehrer was right as always when he told Jodl that 'they had only to kick in the door and the whole rotten structure will come crashing down'.

On June 22 three armies led respectively by von Leeb in the north, von Bock in the centre and von Rundstedt in the south, 3,000,000 men in all, swept deep into the heart of Russia on a thousand-mile front carrying all before them; hundreds of thousands of prisoners were taken and in many areas the Germans were hailed as liberators. But attempts to envelope and annihilate the

Russian armies first at Bialystok-Minsk and then at Smolensk failed; the simple fact was that the German infantry, being largely unmechanised, was unable to move quickly enough over rain-soaked tracks and could not seal off the escape route of the encircled Russians in time. These failures convinced army command that priority must be given to an assault on Moscow where it was supposed that the Russians would concentrate their forces in defence of the capital city thereby offering the Germans one last chance of annihilating the Russians before the onset of winter. To their dismay Hitler refused to modify the original plan. Full of contempt for the 'fossilised and out-of-date theories' of his general staff, he insisted that Moscow could wait. More important on economic and political grounds was the capture of Leningrad; this would cut the Russians off from the Baltic, protect German imports of Swedish ore and enable contact to be made

Irrational optimism

with the Finns. Similarly in the south the wheat of the Ukraine and the oil of the Caucasus remained essential objectives for Germany's economic survival. After weeks of argument Hitler finally overruled army command on August 21. Bock was ordered to halt the advance on Moscow and Guderian's armour was switched from the central to the southern front to help Rundstedt wipe out the Russian armies in the Kiev region.

It is by no means certain that Hitler was wrong to have his own way. Although Leningrad was not taken, the Kiev encirclement was a great success; 665,000 prisoners were taken; Rundstedt occupied the Ukraine and most of the Crimea; and the road to Moscow was open. Hitler now agreed to attack the city. But he insisted that the drive on Leningrad continue and even ordered Rundstedt to advance to the Caucasus simultaneously—an early example of Hitler's irrational optimism which led to a fatal dispersal of German effort at a crucial moment when Russian resistance around Moscow was hardening. Early in October Bock's offensive netted 600,000 prisoners and brought him within 40 miles of Moscow. Then a series of misfortunes intervened. In mid-October rain and fantastic mud slowed down the advance. Snow was now falling and the cold spell caught the Germans without winter equipment. On December 1 Bock attacked Moscow; next day a reconnaissance battalion from von Kluge's Fourth Army was within sight of the Kremlin but had to withdraw hastily. By December 5 Bock was halted all round the perimeter of Moscow and unable to take the city. Twenty-four hours later at twelve minutes past five on the morning of December 6 General Zhukov hurled one hundred divisions at the German positions and the *Blitzkrieg* era came to an abrupt end.

The Germans faced an unprecedentedly grave situation. If Hitler's constant interference had brought the Germans to this plight—and the arguments are by no means all on one side—it cannot be denied that he was equal to the occasion. If he ever had a 'finest hour' this was it. On December 19,

Hitler and Goering in 1941. By this stage in the war, the *Reichsmarschall's* influence was on the wane. It was his showing in the Battle of Britain, a less than impressive effort, that largely brought about this decline in favour.

after dismissing a number of generals including Bock and Guderian, Hitler took over as commander-in-chief from Brauchitsch and declared his intention of training the army in a 'National Socialist way'. That way

Hitler's misconduct

was to order the troops to stand fast at all costs. A wise and courageous decision as it turned out for under the hammer blows of Zhukov's offensive a retreat could easily have become a rout as happened to Napoleon's Grand Army a century before. By March the Russian offensive had ground to a halt.

That does not alter the fact that by the spring of 1942 Germany had lost in Russia 200,000 men killed and 700,000 wounded and that an enemy confidently assumed to be at death's door was still very much alive. Furthermore on December 11, 1941, Hitler added a formidable enemy to the list when he declared war on the United States following the Japanese attack on Pearl Harbor. No doubt American intervention was inevitable sooner or later, and Hitler cannot really be blamed for supporting his Tripartite Pact partner. The fundamental error had been his encouragement of Japanese aggression in the Pacific area in the first place when he should have been persuading Japan to join him in the attack on Russia. As a direct result of that blunder Stalin had been able to switch troops from the Far East to the European front at a critical stage in the war. Looked at in retrospect it is clear that once America, Russia and Britain were banded together against Germany controlling between them vast resources in manpower and materials then Hitler had in effect lost the war. Even when Germany mobilised her economy for total war in 1943-4 there was still virtually no hope of victory trapped as she was in a two-front war. All the same, defeat would not have ended in the utter catastrophe of 1945 had it not been for Hitler's misconduct of the war.

Reference has been made already to Hitler's failure to recognise the importance of the Mediterranean theatre of war. Hence Rommel's new offensive in the summer of 1942 which took him to within 65 miles of Alexandria could not then alter the course of the war. Meanwhile in Russia a new offensive was launched in July on the southern front with the aim of securing the oil of the Caucasus. Elated by early successes, Hitler promptly changed the plan of campaign and attempted to take both Stalingrad and the Caucasus simultaneously, an undertaking quite beyond the capacity of his forces. Already the northern flank of the Sixth Army stretching along the Don from Voronezh to Stalingrad was dangerously overextended and held by unreliable satellite troops, so desperate was

Germany's manpower shortage. Attempts to draw Hitler's attention to the mounting danger of a Russian counter-attack likely to cut off von Kleist's forces in the Caucasus only produced great outbursts of rage from the Fuehrer, who stubbornly insisted that the Russians were 'finished'.

Worse followed. Having persuaded himself that the capture of Stalingrad, the 'Mecca of communism', would have enormous prestige value, he recklessly committed the Sixth Army to a war of attrition in this sector. When the inevitable Russian counter-attack came on November 19, 1942, 20 divisions were trapped at Stalingrad. Turning a deaf ear to all entreaties that he abandon an untenable position, he ordered the Sixth Army to stand fast. No doubt he was influenced to some

extent by news of the Egyptian situation; General Montgomery was driving Rommel out of Egypt while in the latter's rear an Anglo-American force had landed in Algeria. Once again Hitler was let down by Goering who boasted that he could supply the beleagured Germans in Stalingrad indefinitely

Few would ever return

but was unable to do so owing to atrocious weather conditions and shortage of aircraft. In the end, on January 31, von Paulus surrendered. 108,000 men were taken prisoner, few of them ever returning to Germany. For this disaster Hitler's stubborn refusal to face the facts was wholly to blame. It would have

been a still greater disaster had not General Kurt Zeitzler, Hitler's new chief of staff, persuaded him to allow the withdrawal of the Caucasus forces before they, too, were cut off. The Stalingrad catastrophe was the beginning of the end for Germany. In May the Axis forces in North Africa including 125,000 Germans finally surrendered. On July 5 the last German offensive in Russia ('Operation Citadel') was launched on the Kursk salient. Within days Hitler's extravagant hopes of decisive victory were dashed and from now on the Germans were forced back slowly but surely towards their own frontiers. On July 10 Anglo-American forces landed in Sicily. True, when they landed in Italy on September 3 Hitler was still able to hold two-thirds of the country, largely because of the dilatory tactics of the invaders. For some months the Anglo-Americans were pinned down in Central Italy by 25 German divisions sorely needed elsewhere. By the summer of 1943 the allies were getting the upper hand in the Battle of the Atlantic, Hitler's 'first line of defence in the west', while in the air Allied bombers pounded remorselessly at German cities. Despite all the portents of disaster, Hitler's determination to fight on 'until the clock strikes thirteen' never wavered. Now a sick man sustained by massive drug injections, he simply ignored the brutal facts, withdrawing more and more into an inner sanctuary where will power and fanaticism bridged the yawning chasm between dream and reality. Where Mussolini—and Goebbels too—would have tried to disengage in the east to cut down the odds, Hitler rejected Soviet peace feelers out of hand in the summer of 1943 and adhered tenaciously to a path certain to end in disaster.

Even so he never quite lost hope that victory might still be won by some miraculous turn of events, just as his hero Frederick the Great had been rescued in his hour of need. Thus he welcomed the long-awaited Allied landing in Europe, confident that the invaders would suffer a crushing defeat as at Dieppe in 1942. Then at last Germany's fortunes would change. The 59 divisions tied up in the west would be switched eastwards bringing the Russians to their knees; new-type submarines would force the Allies once more onto the defensive in the Atlantic; and flying bombs and rockets raining down on British cities would break the nerve of the civilian population.

With a flash of the old intuition Hitler pre-

dicted, correctly, a landing in Normandy and strengthened that sector—but not sufficiently to tip the balance against an invader. That apart, he committed many grave errors during the fighting in the west. He interfered in the conduct of individual battles generally exerting a degree of control from a distant headquarters incompatible with military efficiency and initiative. And as always he refused to withdraw his forces—to the line of the Seine—when it was abundantly clear that the landings had succeeded. The inevitable happened when the Americans broke out of their bridgehead; part of the German forces was trapped first in the Mortain-Falaise pocket and later at the Seine crossing; the operations cost Germany 500,000 men and most of their equipment. As for the much-vaunted war-winning V1s and V2s, they came too late in the day. The launching sites were systematically bombed and eventually overrun by Allied forces before too much damage was caused.

Only the Allied failure to sweep into defenceless Germany in the late summer of 1944 saved Hitler. This afforded him a breathing space much like that enjoyed by Imperial Germany in the winter of 1917/18 when the eastern front collapsed and Ludendorff was able to launch one last offensive in the west.

By this time Hitler was well aware that the war could not be won. What he hoped to do at this late stage was exploit signs of disagreement in the grand coalition. If he could convince the western powers that Germany still had a sting in her tail might they not be ready to make peace with him and even join with him in a crusade against bolshevism? Such

fantastic optimism is a shattering revelation of the extent to which he was out of touch with reality. Yet what alternative had he? Army command agreed that an offensive in the west was tactically correct however risky the undertaking. The only difference of opinion was about objectives. The over-

Hitler foresees the end

ambitious *Fuehrer* dreamt of splitting the Anglo-American forces and seizing Antwerp whereas his more sober advisers thought they would be lucky to take Liége. Hitler had his way in the end. But without air power and with only 32 divisions at his disposal he had no hope of reaching Antwerp and could certainly not have stayed there had he, by a miracle, got there. As usual, tight control of tactics worked out in great detail at Hitler's headquarters impeded the commanders in the field. Only because of fierce German resistance plus good leadership and favourable terrain did the Germans escape encirclement.

The Ardennes failure represented Germany's last throw. When the Russians launched their last great offensive in March 1945 they smashed through the German lines—stabilised by the end of 1944—because Germany was without reserves. Not that she could have avoided defeat; for by this time her economy was in total disarray. But the line might possibly have been held further east with reserves—that is the real indictment of the Ardennes offensive.

Hitler who had so often exhorted his troops to stand fast deserted his own post in April 1945 by putting a bullet through his head in the Berlin bunker. Characteristically he continued to the very end to blame his 'cowardly' generals for letting him down. Obviously his personal responsibility for plunging Germany into a struggle she could not win is a great one. Yet others through miscalculation had done that before him. What Hitler lacked was the greatness of character and breadth of vision which would have led him to break off a hopeless struggle against impossible odds in the interest of the nation's survival. In other words the real indictment of Hitler the war leader is that for all his talk he did not really believe that Germany mattered more than he did and so was prepared to sacrifice the German people needlessly on the altar of his own ambitions.

Hitler after the July 1944 bomb plot attempt, looking haggard and depressed.

Suggested reading
H. Clark: **Barbarossa** (London, 1965)
B. H. Liddell Hart: **History of the Second World War** (London, 1970)
P. Schramm: **Hitler the man and the military leader** (London, 1972)
W. L. Shirer: **The rise and fall of the Third Reich** (London, 1960)
J. Strawson: **Hitler as military commander** (London, 1971)
C. Wilmot: **The struggle for Europe** (London, 1952)

Index

Page numbers in italic type indicate illustrations.
Page numbers which are in bold type indicate text and illustrations on that page.

Picture Credits

The publishers wish to thank the following photographers and organisations
who have supplied photographs for this book.
Photographs have been credited by page number. Where more than one
photograph appears on the page, references are made in order of columns
across the page and then from top to bottom.
Some references have, for reasons of space, been abbreviated as follows:
   Bapty & Co Ltd, London : **Bapty**
   Blitz Publications, London : **Blitz**
   Deutsches Museum, Munich : **D.M.**
   Imperial War Museum, London : **IWM**
   Private Collection : **PC**
   Suddeutsch Verlag GmbH, Munich : **Sudd**
   Ullstein GmbH, Berlin : **Ullstein**

13: Sudd. **14:** Sudd/Sudd/PC. **15:** JG Moore Collection. **16:** Sudd/Sudd.
18: Sudd. **19:** Sudd/Time-Life, London. **20:** Sudd/Sudd/Sudd. **22:** Bapty-
Signal/Blitz-Signal. **23:** Sudd/Sudd/Time-Life. **24:** Sudd/Sudd/Sudd. **26:**
IWM/Sudd. **29:** Sudd. **30:** PC/PC/PC. **31:** JG Moore Collection. **32:** PC/
Sudd. **33:** PC. **34:** IWM. **36:** Sudd/PC. **38:** IWM. **40:** PC. **41:** Sudd. **42:**
Sudd. **44:** Sudd. **46:** Sudd/Sudd/Sudd. **48:** Sudd. **49:** PC. **50:** Bapty-
Signal/Sudd/Sudd. **51:** Bapty-Signal. **52:** Sudd/Sudd. **53:** PC. **54:** IWM.
56: Sudd/Sudd/PC. **58:** IWM. **60:** PC/Sudd. **62:** Bapty-Signal. **63:** Blitz-
Signal. **65:** IWM. **66:** Sudd/Sudd/Sudd. **67:** Bapty-Signal. **68:** Sudd. **69:**
Sudd/Sudd/Sudd. **72:** Sudd/Sudd. **76:** Sudd. **80:** IWM/Sudd/PC. **81:** PC.
84: Sudd/Sudd/PC/Sudd. **85:** PC. **92:** Sudd/Sudd. **93:** IWM. **94:** Blitz-
Signal/Bapty-Die Wehrmacht. **97:** Sudd. **98:** Sudd/Sudd/PC. **99:** Sudd.
100: Sudd/Sudd. **101:** PC. **102:** Sudd. **104:** Sudd/PC/Sudd. **105:** Sudd/
Sudd. **106:** Sudd. **108:** Sudd/Sudd. **109:** PC. **110:** Bapty-Fligende Front/
Bapty-Fligende Front/Blitz-Signal. **111:** Bapty-Balkenkreutz. **112:** Sudd/
Sudd. **113:** Sudd. **114:** Sudd/Bapty-Fligende Front. **115:** Robert Hunt
Library, London. **116:** PC/PC. **117:** PC/PC. **118:** IWM/Blitz-Signal/IWM.
119: PC. **120:** PC/IWM/PC/IWM. **121:** IWM. **122:** Bapty-Fligende Front.
124: Sudd/PC/Sudd/Sudd. **125:** PC. **126:** Bapty-Fligende Front. **128:** PC/
IWM/PC/Sudd. **129:** PC. **130:** Bapty. **154:** Bapty-Fligende Front/PC/Sudd.
156: Sudd. **157:** IWM. **158:** PC/PC/Blitz-Signal. **159:** Sudd. **160:** Sudd/
IWM. **161:** Sudd. **162:** Bapty-Signal/PC. **163:** Blitz-Signal/IWM/US Navy,
Washington. **164:** PC/IWM/IWM. **166:** Bapty-Signal. **168:** IWM/PC/IWM/
IWM/IWM. **169:** PC. **170:** Bapty-Signal/PC. **171:** Bapty-Signal. **172:** Sudd.
174: Blitz-Signal. **175:** Blitz-Signal/Blitz-Signal/Sudd. **176:** Ullstein/Ullstein.
177: Ullstein. **179:** PC. **183:** IWM. **187:** US Navy. **191:** IWM. **192:** Ullstein/
Ullstein. **193:** PC. **194:** PC/PC/PC. **195:** PC. **196:** PC/PC/PC. **198:** PC/PC.
199: PC. **200:** IWM. **202:** Ullstein. **203:** Blitz-Signal. **204:** PC/D.M./Sudd.
206: IWM/PC/D.M./D.M./PC. **208:** D.M. **209:** PC. **210:** D.M./IWM/D.M./
PC. **211:** PC. **213:** PC. **214:** PC/PC/Sudd. **215:** Blitz-Signal. **216:** PC/Sudd.
217: PC. **218:** IWM. **220:** PC/PC. **222:** IWM. **224:** PC/PC. **226:** Sudd. **228:**
Sudd/Sudd/PC. **229:** PC. **230:** Bapty-Signal. **232:** Sudd. **233:** Sudd. **234:**
Sudd/Sudd/Sudd. **235:** Bapty-Signal. **236:** Sudd/Sudd. **237:** Sudd. **238:**
IWM. **240:** Sudd. **243:** Bapty-Signal. **244:** PC. **Front Cover:** Bibliothek
Nattionale, Paris-Signal. **Front end paper:** Bapty-Signal. **Back end paper:**
Sudd.